The Early Economic Writings of Alfred Marshall, 1867–1890

Volume 2

Alfred Marshall about 1892

The Early Economic Writings of Alfred Marshall, 1867–1890

Edited and Introduced by

J. K. Whitaker

Professor of Economics
University of Virginia

Volume 2

THE FREE PRESS
A Division of Macmillan Publishing Co., Inc.
NEW YORK

The Free Press
A Division of Macmillan Publishing Co., Inc.
866 Third Avenue, New York, N.Y. 10022

First published 1975 by The Macmillan Press Ltd.

Library of Congress Catalog Card Number: 74-29102

Printed in Great Britain

printing number
1   2   3   4   5   6   7   8   9   10

Contents

Titles given by Marshall himself are in quotation marks

Introduction

This Volume continues the printing of a selection of Marshall's early writings. Part III reproduces the surviving portions of a manuscript on international trade composed by Marshall in the mid 1870s. The two pairs of chapters from it that Sidgwick had printed for private circulation in 1879 are restored here to their original setting. Part IV reproduces various miscellaneous notes on economic theory including some significant contributions as well as many fragments of historical or illustrative interest. Finally, Part V reproduces four pieces on wider issues. Appendixes describe the editing of the manuscripts and account for unexplained editorial changes shown in the text.

Editorial commentary is kept to a minimum, an extended introduction having been given in Part I, printed in Volume 1 (which also includes as Part II Marshall's earliest essays on economic theory). Full details will be found in the Contents, which are given in full for both Volumes on pp. v–ix of Volume 1, where also a list of brief titles for citations appears on pp. xvii–xviii.

In each Volume, Parts are divided into Sections, such as Section IV.3, and often Sections into Items, such as Item IV.3.2. Cross references are given in such terms when possible, so that 'above' will refer to Volume 1 for references to Parts I and II. But page references to Volume 1 are expressly indicated.

PART III

'The Theory of Foreign Trade and other Portions of Economic Science Bearing on the Principle of Laissez Faire'

III 'The Theory of Foreign Trade and Other Portions of Economic Science Bearing on the Principle of Laissez Faire'

III.1 General Introduction

During the years 1873–7, Marshall laboured over the composition of a volume dealing with problems of international trade. The history of the project and its abandonment was briefly discussed in Section I.4 above. Marshall gave further information about it in a letter written to E.R.A. Seligman in April 1900.[1]

> In about 1873 I decided that my first book would be on International Trade, with reference to Protection, etc. on the analytical and realistic sides; but not on the historical. So I began to write, and in 1875 visited [the] U.S.A., chiefly in order to study enlightened Protectionism on the spot.
>
> The work was in two parts. The first was to be addressed to the general reader; the second, in smaller type, to academic students exclusively. The second part began with an introductory chapter on my favourite theme – The One in the Many, the Many in the One; and showed how with modifications in detail the pure theory of Foreign Trade was applicable to many industrial and other problems.

[1] Printed in J. Dorfman, 'The Seligman Correspondence', *Political Science Quarterly*, Vol 56 (Sept 1941) pp. 408–10.

Then came three chapters on the pure theory of Foreign Trade; and then two on Domestic Trade. These were introduced for the purpose of leading up to 'Consumers Rent', which I wanted to apply in an economic measure of the *indirect* effects of customs duties, whether 'Protective' or not.

By June 1877, I had nearly finished a first draft of Part I, and of all of Part II except that last chapter, which I found very troublesome (and which I am quite sure now I shall never write). My work was then broken off by an advertisement of the Principalship of University College, Bristol; and by my being drawn into writing a hollow Economics of Industry, in which truth was economized for the benefit of feeble minds.

Then I became seriously ill; and in '78 or '79, Sidgwick asked me to lend him the MSS. Later on he asked my leave to print some chapters for private use in the economic discussion society at Cambridge. I consented. He chose Ch. II, III, V, and VI. I did not know for some time afterwards which he had chosen, and of course the crude draft was printed verbatim without corrections even of the most obvious flaws. This explains (i) their general crudity, (ii) the absence of explanation of their drift, (iii) the want of any reference to the *real* conditions of foreign trade; they were given – very badly – in Part I, (iv) the fact that Domestic Trade is treated *after* Foreign Trade ....

As to the MSS. I withdraw entirely Case II of the Foreign Trade and my whole treatment will be different from that in these papers. Chapter I of Part II explained away a good deal of the succeeding chapters; i.e., explained that they belonged to the economic toy shop rather than practical work shop.

Substantial portions of the manuscript have survived, and these, together with the four chapters printed at Sidgwick's expense, allow the detailed plan of the book to be determined. It was as follows, the title being that given on a manuscript title page.[2]

---

[2] This title differs slightly from the one given in the first edition of the *Principles*: 'In 1875–7 I nearly completed a draft of a treatise on *The Theory of Foreign Trade, with some allied problems relating to the doctrine of Laissez Faire*'. See *Principles II*, p. 38.

The Theory of Foreign Trade (*and other Portions of Economic Science Bearing on the Principle of Laissez Faire*)
Part I

Part II

Chapters IV–VII of Part I are reproduced in Sections III.2–4 below (Ch. VII being incomplete). Chapters I–IV of Part II are reproduced in Section III.5 below, under the heading, *The Pure Theory of Foreign Trade*, which Sidgwick gave when printing Chapters II and III. (Chapters I and IV are not quite complete.) Chapters V and VI of Part II are reproduced in

Section III.6 below, under the heading, *The Pure Theory of Domestic Values*, given when Sidgwick printed them.[3]

The first three chapters of Part I have entirely disappeared. Portions were probably incorporated in Marshall's subsequent writings, especially Book III, Ch. III, of the *Economics of Industry*, Book I, Ch. II, of *Industry and Trade*, and Book III of *Money Credit and Commerce*. But no direct descent can be traced. The last chapter of Part II appears never to have been written, the only reference to it being in the letter to Seligman just quoted, while the contents of the Appendixes may only be surmised.[4]

Even the completed chapters were not quite finished, references, for example often being left incomplete. But the draft was sufficiently polished for a clean manuscript to be carefully copied, probably in 1876, the year of the latest reference.[5] This copy was probably sent to Macmillan and Co. in the spring of 1877, and also read by some of Marshall's colleagues in Cambridge.[6]

The editing of the manuscript has been complicated by omissions – especially of quotations and references – and various other imperfections, and also by the presence of frequent alterations and additions of undetermined later date. Many of these are simple rewordings, involving no change of sense. In such cases the original version has been restored, to attain greater stylistic uniformity and authenticity, but in a few cases the revision has been accepted as distinctly clearer.

---

[3] There are indications that Chapters VI and VII of Part I had been interchanged in an earlier draft, and that Chapters V and VI of Part II had once formed a separate Part III.

[4] The evidence on the contents of the missing portions is derived as follows. *Part I*; for Ch. I – see Ch. IV § 13, Ch. V § 1 and Ch. VI §§ 2, 3, 11, 12; for Ch. II – see Ch. VI § 2; for Ch. III – see Ch. IV §§ 4, 12. *Part II*; for Ch. VII – see letter to Seligman just quoted; for Appendixes – see *Pure Theory of Foreign Trade* Ch. I § 2, Ch. II § 1 and *Pure Theory of Domestic Values* Ch. I § 5, Ch. II § 2.

[5] Chapter IV, Part I, quotes from Bagehot's 'Postulates of English Political Economy', which was published in the spring of 1876. The statistics of the surviving portions of the manuscript are as follows. *Part I*: Ch. IV 41 folios; Ch. V 63 folios; Ch. VI 53 folios. *Part II*: Ch. I 31 folios; Ch. IV 24 folios. There are also several loose pages, including the title page and a complete set of international trade diagrams, and over fifty pages of fragments and rough notes relating to Part I, Ch. VII. There are indications that the copy was not made by Marshall, though the handwriting is very like his.

[6] See Section I.4, above, and *Memorials*, p. 26n.4.

Those additions and alterations which involve a change in sense are indicated in footnotes, with the text reporting the original. A few essential commas have been added, but no attempt has been made to standardise or modernise Marshall's rather haphazard punctuation and capitalisation of terms. Editorial additions or changes are indicated by the usual square brackets, but a few slight changes, such as the addition of commas, have been made silently.

The Sidgwick chapters have been reproduced unchanged from the printed version.[7] But no attempt has been made to preserve pagination, and misprints and errors have been corrected and references amplified. Further details are indicated in the Introductions to Sections III.5 and 6 below.

Marshall's unfinished book is often flawed and imperfect, and Sidgwick's eye was keen when he selected its four finest chapters.[8] But the remaining chapters contain many interesting passages and are also of value for the further light they throw upon Marshall's ambitions and development at a critical early stage of his career as an economist. References to points of detail will be found in the introductions to the separate chapters, which follow.

III.2 'Foreign Trade in its Bearing on Industrial and Social Progress'

III.2.1 *Introduction*

The continuous stream of argument which runs through the two chapters reproduced in this Section – Chapters IV and V of Part I of Marshall's book – is meandering. This, and the frequent digressions, make it difficult to comprehend the chapters as a whole, even after several readings. Marshall's marginal summaries, reproduced at the end of this introduction,

---

[7] A. Marshall, *The Pure Theory of Foreign Trade. The Pure Theory of Domestic Values*, Series of Reprints of Scarce Tracts in Economic and Political Science, No. 1 (London School of Economics and Political Science, London, third impression 1949). The 1949 impression, used here, was re-edited by G. S. Dorrance who listed in his editorial commentary some, but by no means all, of the mistakes and misprints.

[8] In his last years, Marshall went over some of his surviving manuscripts. Looking over Chs. IV–VI of Part I he wrote 'There seems to be nothing of use in this bundle: much of it is crude. 14. 12. 21. Written apparently about 1873.' Of course, the chapters could not have been published then as a contribution to knowledge, but now they have attained historical interest and their crudity may be excused.

help so far as they go, but are incomplete. It therefore seems desirable to construct an analytical table of contents. As § 2 of Ch. IV indicates, Marshall's discussion falls into four main parts, and headings relating to these are also included in the following table, but are not inserted in the text, on the ground that they would give a false interruption of continuity. Quotation marks indicate the parts of the Table which are direct quotations.

Analytical Table of Contents: Part I, Chs. IV, V

Chapter IV   '*Foreign Trade in its Bearing on Industrial and Social Progress*'

§ 1   Foreign trade increases the intercourse of nations.
§ 2   The influence of foreign trade on industrial and social progress falls under four heads.

First head   'the influence exerted on individual industries in a country by the competition of the corresponding industries in other countries.'

§ 3   Foreign competition constrains the freedom of action of an individual industry, inhibiting some potentially-beneficial changes as well as some trade conspiracies.
§ 4   The constraints imposed by foreign competition on the collective action of all a country's industries are frequently exaggerated: example of compulsory reduction of child labour.

Second head   'the influence exerted on capital and labour generally in a country by the opportunities which foreign trade develops for their migration to other countries.'

§ 5   The migration of capital and labour is slow and may be affected in opposite ways by the immediate and the remote effects of some change, such as a reduction in work hours (see § 8).
§ 6   The migration of capital unaccompanied by its owner.
§ 7   This migration depends on the foreign rate of interest, not the rate of profit: the difference between the two depends upon the supply of skilled managers in the foreign country.

§ 8   The beneficial effects of an increase in wages on the efficiency of labour; the changing habits of the English working classes; high wages do not necessarily lead to the sustained export of capital.

§ 9   The development of the money market, and the issuing of government and railway bonds, aid the temporary migration of capital.

§ 10   The migration of capital accompanied by its owner.

§ 11   The migration of the working classes.

§ 12   Differences between countries in the real reward to labour.

§ 13   The principle of comparative advantage, rather than that of absolute advantage, applies even if labour and capital migrate freely, providing that land is scarce.

Chapter V   '*Foreign Trade in its Bearing on Industrial and Social Progress (Continued)*'

§ 1   Introductory.

Third head   'the influence which foreign trade exerts on the steadiness of the employment of the industries of a country.'

§ 2   The evils of fluctuations in incomes.

§ 3   The solution of Lassalle.

§ 4   Difficulty of the inductive study of the effects of foreign trade on economic fluctuations.

Subheading under third head   The relationships between economic fluctuations, foreign trade and England's economic development over the last 100 years.

§ 5   General approach to the question.

§ 6   The separation of employers and employed; the localisation of industry.

§ 7   The increased use of fixed capital.

§ 8   The development of the money and capital markets.

§ 9   The separation of producers and consumers.

§ 10   The widening of markets and the improvement of communications.

§ 11   The ineffectiveness of direct inductive methods in this case.

§ 12   General conclusion as to the beneficial effect of foreign trade in England's past and future economic development: probably, but not necessarily, applicable to other countries.

Fourth head 'the influence which foreign trade exerts on the rate of growth of particular industries in a country, causing certain classes of occupations to predominate over others, and thereby modifying the causes which will determine the material and moral well-being of the country in the future.'

§ 13   An industry may exert beneficial social and indirect economic influences.
§ 14   Individual interests might not encourage the growth of such industries without aid.
§ 15   English economists have not stressed this sufficiently.
§ 16   Difficulties of securing a skilled work force in a nascent industry.
§ 17   International trade may hurt the working classes temporarily, because the locking up of fixed capital in ships etc. reduces the circulating capital in the country.
§ 18   Considerations of national defence.

The ambitiousness of Marshall's undertaking in these brief chapters almost guarantees that they will prove sketchy and frequently unpersuasive. Nevertheless, there are many attractive passages. Particular interest attaches to the following.

(i) The attempt at a general analysis of the role played by foreign trade in England's industrial development (Ch. V, §§ 4–12, which surely should have been expanded into a separate chapter). Marshall effectively demonstrates the inadequacy of 'those who base broad inferences on narrow tables of statistics',[1] but the grounds on which he rests his own conclusions are also unconvincing.

(ii) The statement of Marshall's views on 'the economy of high wages' (spread through Ch. IV, §§ 3, 5, 8, 11, 12). This is probably his clearest pronouncement on a theme which runs through much of his early writing.[2]

---

[1] From the marginal summary for Ch. V, § 11, reproduced immediately below.
[2] See, however, *Economics of Industry*, Book II, Ch. VII, § 2, Ch. XI, § 4; and Book III, Ch. III, §§ 4, 5.

(iii) The discussion of Lassalle's proposals (Ch. V, §§ 13, 14). Of all the earlier socialists, Marshall seems to have found Lassalle the most persuasive and claimed to have once read almost all Lassalle's writings.[3]

(iv) The striking discussion of the foundations of the infant-industry argument (Ch. V, §§ 13, 14), which looks forward to the later chapter on American protectionism.[4]

Attention should also be drawn to the clear acceptance of a wages-fund approach (Ch. V, § 17). It is only in discussing the 'wages of superintendence' (Ch. IV, § 7) that any hint of the distribution theory of the *Economics of Industry* emerges. This fact leads to an interesting conjecture about the evolution of the theory.[5]

Marshall added marginal summaries to large portions of the manuscript of Chapters IV and V. These summaries are sufficiently complete to be of interest and read as follows:

Chapter IV

§ 1   Foreign trade has played a prominent part in political history; and has been an important factor of progress.

§ 2   Enumeration of the chief topics of this and the following chapter.

§ 3   The influence which foreign trade competition exerts on the conditions of capital and labour in individual industries: controlling their action with regard to wages, prices and hours of labour; thus preventing some injurious or some beneficial improvements.

§ 4   The influence of foreign trade competition on the conditions of capital and labour generally. This insofar as it is direct is unimportant. For instance it exerts no direct influence on the amount of leisure which a country can afford to its workers generally. An influence in this direction

---

[3] In a letter of 12 Feb 1906 to H. S. Foxwell; Marshall Library, Marshall 3:49. This was probably at an early stage of Marshall's studies, although hardly before 1868 when he went to Dresden to improve his German. Marshall's copies of F. Lassalle, *Das Systeme der Erworbenen Rechte* (2 volumes; Brodhaus, Leipzig, 1861) and of Lassalle's later pamphlet exchange with Schulze-Delitzsch are retained in the Marshall Library. Also see *Memorials*, p. 334 (written in 1907): 'it was my desire to know what was practicable in social reform by State and other agencies which led me to read Adam Smith and Mill, Marx and Lassalle, forty years ago'.

[4] See Section III.4, below.

[5] See Vol 1, pp. 47–8, above.

is indeed exerted by foreign competition, but not by foreign trade competition.

§ 5   But the effect of foreign trade in promoting the emigration of capital requires careful consideration. This migration is in general a slow process.

§ 6   The migration of capital unaccompanied by its owner involves difficulties. Capital is more ready to engage in the foreign carrying trade than to migrate to foreign countries.

§ 7   In this inquiry we are concerned with the current rate not of profits but of interest. In this connection too little importance has been attached to the character and mental qualities which further industrial progress; and to a free scope for the talents of the working classes.

§ 8   Thus a rise in wages does not necessarily cause the emigration of capital. A rise in labourers' wages increases on the average their unselfish more than their selfish expenditure. Recapitulation.

§ 9   Temporary investments of capital in foreign countries are facilitated by foreign trade.

§ 10   The migration of capital accompanied by its owners is not governed in the main by economic causes and is of slight but of increasing importance.

§ 11   The migration of the working classes is promoted by the energising influences of some new countries.

Chapter V

§ 1   The relation of this chapter to the system of Protection to native industries.

§ 2   The evils which arise from economic fluctuations are partly dependent on perverted ambition; but may not on that account be ignored. A small uncertainty may be a healthy stimulant, but not a great uncertainty. Even the working man may be prompted by an interruption of his work to a beneficial change, particularly in a new country. But frequent interruptions cause serious moral and economic injury.

§ 3   In a system of free competition the interests of the individual in relation to the steadiness of industry do not always coincide with the collective interests of society. This has been noticed by Socialists. Their earlier speculations not directly instructive for practical purposes. But Lassalle proposed to make use of all the practical knowledge of modern times, and to improve the condition of the working man, chiefly by abolishing commercial risk through the agency of the State. His work not thorough, but suggestive. The affinity between Socialism and some form of Protectionism.

§ 4 The influence of foreign trade on the steadiness of industry cannot be determined by the direct method [or] inductive method. For firstly there are scarcely any trustworthy materials for a history of the steadiness of employment. Though perhaps trade guilds may soon commence to supply them. Secondly, the influence of foreign trade in the matter cannot be separated from other influences. For economic causes do not produce their full effects at once: therefore the method of 'concomitant variations' is inapplicable. And if we compare the average results of two long periods, the conditions of the problem are not the same in both, as may be made clearly manifest by an examination of the particular case of the changes which have affected the steadiness of employment in England during the last hundred years.

§ 5 The general character of these changes. Proposed method of procedure.

§ 6 These changes considered more in detail. Production on a large scale has contributed to the decay of the system of yearly hirings, which conduced to steadiness of employment. A social discord arising from increasing free competition in the Labour market: but this perhaps transitional. The localisation of industry. Foreign trade is to be in great part credited with whatever effects arise from the localisation of industry, from the system of production on a large scale, and from the use of expensive machinery.

§ 7 Expensive machinery affords an inducement to steady work, but tends to augment fluctuations of prices. Examination of this last point in detail. Trade combinations explicit or tacit tend to keep prices from falling low. Foreign trade weakens the form of such combination.

§ 8   The efficiency and the delicacy of the English Money Market. The influence of those who work chiefly on borrowed capital.

§ 9   The producer cannot easily gauge the consumers' wants, which may vary rapidly. The demand for the building and other materials required for commercial undertakings is liable to extreme fluctuations.

§ 10   England's exceptional need of wide markets in which she may purchase corn. The steadying influence of wide markets generally, depends largely upon the ease with which information is transmitted. The disturbing influences arising from the distance between producer and consumer have probably nearly reached their maximum; but the steadying influence arising from a widening of markets is capable of unlimited increase.

§ 11   This analysis shows how the effects of various causes are intermingled, so as to be incapable of being separated by the direct application of Statistics. But this difficulty occasions no misgivings to those who base broad inferences on narrow tables of statistics, particularly some American Protectionists.

§ 12   But this analysis also assists the reader to weigh against each other the influences which foreign trade exerts to disturb and to steady industry. The latter certainly preponderant in England now. Conclusions of this nature obtained for one country may probably hold for others; but not necessarily.

§ 13   The influence which foreign trade exerts on the variety [and] relative magnitude of a country's industries. Conditions under which the immediate interests of individuals may fail to induce them to set on foot new industries which are capable of thriving ultimately.

III.2.2   *Text of Part I, Chapter IV:*
'*Foreign Trade in its Bearing on Industrial and Social Progress*'

§ 1   Commerce is known in political history as the cause of some treaties and of many battles. Commerce has frequently raised between nations a rivalry that has culminated in hatred:

but it has worked without ceasing to give nations that knowledge of each other, which alone can afford a solid basis for friendship.

The habits of thought and feeling which are the outcome of a nation's experiences, the resultant of a nation's industry, develop new life when brought into contact with those of other nations. We have been told how English plants and animals have proved themselves superior in strength and resources to those of corresponding species in countries that have had but little communication with others. For the English species are the survivors of a long conflict that has been waged in England between domestic and imported species. Some of the domestic species have succumbed, and others have combined with the foreigners, and have given birth to new varieties abler and more plastic than their parents. So those nations have made most progress, which have had the largest opportunities for absorbing the best qualities of other nations, and for assimilating their most fertile thoughts: those nations have, in general, progressed most rapidly whose trade has afforded them the widest intercourse with other nations. On this subject much has been written; and much more has to be written from the standpoints which have been attained by science during the present generation.

§ 2   Passing to questions concerning the influence which foreign trade exerts on the industrial and social progress of a civilised country at the present time, we may arrange the most important of them under four heads, according as they relate to : —

(i) the influence exerted on individual industries in a country by the competition of the corresponding industries in other countries,

(ii) the influence exerted on capital and labour generally in a country by the opportunities which foreign trade develops for their migration to other countries,

(iii) the influence which foreign trade exerts on the steadiness of the employment of the industries of a country,

(iv) the influence which foreign trade exerts on the rate of growth of particular industries in a country, causing certain classes of occupations to predominante over others, and thereby modifying the causes which will determine the material and moral well-being of the country in the future.

These divisions will be investigated in order, special reference being had to England as a representative of an old country; and to America as a representative of a new. This investigation and particularly the latter portion of it will prepare the way for the discussion in a later chapter[1] of some of the subtler portions of the doctrine of Protection to native industries to which British economists generally have not paid sufficient attention.

§ 3   Foreign competition imposes limits on the freedom with which separate action can be taken by individual industries in a country. Although the changes that have come over most of the leading English trades have exhibited on the whole, a close correspondence with one another: each trade has found the occasion for each step at its own time and has taken each step in its own mode. Some of these steps have been such as to cause, for the time, at least, an increase in price of the commodities produced by the trade in question relatively to other commodities. Movements that have this immediate effect are liable to be cut short, if the trade is closely run by rival producers in other countries. Thus on the one hand foreign competition frequently prevents or renders harmless the wrongful attempts of trade conspiracies on the part of employers or of employed against the public welfare: and on the other hand it crushes some healthy efforts. On the one hand resistance to the introduction of machinery is readily set aside when the workers can be shown that, in consequence of foreign competition, the resistance will cause an immediate diminution in the demand for their labour. On the other hand when in foreign countries rival workers are willing for low wages to keep machinery at work during long hours, an increase of wages or a diminution of the hours of labour in a trade may be thereby rendered unattainable, even in cases in which such a movement would in the long run be beneficial to the country. This influence of foreign competition is not indeed different in nature from that of the home competition which would be occasioned by a large influx of newcomers into the trade;

---

[1] [Part I, Ch. 7 (see Section III.4 below).]

but it is sharper in its action. Such an influx cannot in general be prevented for any great length of time in a trade in which the wages are abnormally high. By this I mean a trade in which the wages are considerably higher than in other trades of the same order; i.e. in other industries which have similar advantages and disadvantages (account being taken of the hours of work), which require natural qualities equally rare and artificial habits equally difficult.[2] But wages may cease to be abnormally high not only if they are lowered, but also if there is a rise in the average standard of efficiency in the trade: i.e., in the qualities which are habitually demanded of those who are employed in it. The influx of newcomers into a trade must in England, (though not in America), in general be slow: and, in the absence of foreign competition, wages may remain abnormally high, sufficiently long to effect, provided certain conditions be present, a rise in the average standard of efficiency. If this be effected, a movement, which commenced by causing a particular trade to gain at the expense of the general body of consumers, will have terminated in an arrangement which is every way innocuous, which is beneficial directly to workers in the trade, and indirectly to the rest of society. To some extent then for evil but to a great extent for good, foreign competition exerts control over the separate action of individual trades.

The influence which foreign trade exerts by this means on the internal economy of a country may, under certain conditions, reach so far as to affect to a considerable extent the general organisation of her industry. Specially subject to this influence will be nations which prefer to regard each change as a development of an old principle. For such nations even when they do adopt a new principle of action do not come upon it, to use a metaphor, at a bound; but rather after the manner of powerful but quiet animals who move without raising from the ground all their feet at once. Such has been the character of England's progress.

§ 4   It is not *prima facie* unreasonable to suppose that foreign competition acting simultaneously on a large number of

---

[2] But compare Part II, Ch. 1 § [4]. [See Section III.5 below; also compare *Economics of Industry*, p. 174.]

trades imposes on their collective action the same direct
restraint which it constantly and obtrusively exerts on the
separate action of any one of them. We have just seen that
through the direct control of the separate action of individual
trades, it does to some extent indirectly control the collective
action of all trades. But popular opinion attributes to it a
power greater and more direct than that which it has. The
nature of the errors which prevail on this subject can be most
conveniently exhibited by the working out in detail a particular problem, the practical applications of which are of
great moment to the present generation. This problem is:
To what extent does foreign commercial competition add to
the severity of the penalties by which any relaxation of the
industrial energies of a country is visited?

Austrians may be heard to complain that the large number of
the holidays which are customary with them, though perhaps
in former times beneficial, produces ruinous results now that
Austrian trade has to compete with that of Protestant countries in which work is more continuous. In England similar
considerations lead many to regard as unattainable the aims
of those who demand that public or private action should be
taken in order to secure, if not to our manhood more leisure
for thought, at least to our childhood and our youth more
leisure for learning.

The rapid progress we are making in the arts of production,
the new skill we each day acquire to make the forces of nature
perform lightly and speedily tasks that had required heavy and
long toil, incline men to think that the nation, if free to choose
its own course, might well afford somewhat more rest from
the labour of production. But it is argued that England is not
free to choose her own course; that any slackening of her
energies would bring about the ruin of a country that is at
once so dependent on foreign trade, and so hemmed round by
foreign competition as England is.

In these positions there are elements of truth. It must be
conceded that just as the maintenance of a given status in
society, in so far as it depends upon wealth at all, requires of
the individual more wealth than it used to; so, because the
place of Austria among nations depends partly upon her
material resources for peace and war, the rapid growth of the

wealth of Protestant countries increases in one direction the evil which is inflicted on her by the slowness of the growth of her wealth. Her industries are grievously oppressed by the taxes required for her army; since she wills that it should be capable of being measured with armies that are supported by the resources of countries whose industry is less intermittent than hers. The ambition of Vienna to be in the front rank of luxury among the cities of the world is a greater burden to the nation than it would be, were not the standard of expenditure set in the Old World and the New by wealth derived from the energy of Anglo-Saxon work. Again, it must be granted that capital will, other things being equal, seek those countries in which it can obtain the highest profits. The rate of profits in England is not sustained by many specially rich gifts of nature: and, if the activity of Englishmen cease to be specially vigorous the extent of England's foreign trade will tell against her indirectly in this; that the connections established by it will offer facilities to her capital for migrating to countries to which nature has been more bountiful. And further it has been conceded that if any particular English industry acting separately relaxes its energies, that industry will be worsted in competition with foreigners.

But let us suppose that the special difficulties which surround the combined action of all English trades can be overcome. Let us suppose, for instance, that the extent to which use was made of the work of children was diminished simultaneously throughout English industries, so as not to alter the relative value of the wares produced by these industries. Turning then to a result of the work of the last chapter[3] we find that, except in so far as the change might lead to the exportation of capital, the income of England – the necessaries, comforts and luxuries which she procures by a year's labour – will not be diminished in a greater ratio than would the income of a country in which the same change occurred but which had no foreign trade: that though the immediate effect of the change might be to cause an alteration of prices and some disturbance of foreign trade, this disturbance will not be injurious to England as a whole; and that so soon as the disturbance is passed, England's

---

[3] [This is one of the few references to the missing Ch. III.]

trade will bear as great a ratio to her resources, and will be conducted on terms at least as advantageous to her as before the change.

§ 5   But foreign trade offers opportunities and incitements to the migration of capital and of labour. Thus it affects indirectly the general relations of capital and labour in a country, and increases the evil effects which a country suffers from any special disadvantage that may accrue to capital or to labour within her boundaries. For this and for other reasons it is necessary to investigate with some care the causes which determine the migration of capital and labour. These causes are more complex than at first sight appears. For except under circumstances almost as abnormal as those of the Irish famine of 1848, this migration is a slow process. Suppose that a particular event – say the passing of a stringent and expensive education law – has as its immediate effect a tendency to drive capital away from the country, but at the same time commences to bring into existence forces which will attract capital to the country. Since the migration of capital is slow, the immediate effects of such an event will not have proceeded far before they commence to be counteracted by its more remote effects. Yet many economists when discussing such cases have taken account only of the immediate effects to the entire neglect of the more remote; and have spoken as though the sole effect of such a law would be to promote the migration of capital.

In examining this question it will be well to consider separately the cases in which the migration of capital is, and those in which it is not accompanied by the migration of those who own the capital. Let us commence with the latter case.

§ 6   A man will not in general invest capital in any commercial undertaking in a foreign country unless he expects to obtain thereby a rate of interest considerably higher than he could derive from a similar undertaking in his own country. The increase in the rate of interest he obtains must be at least sufficient to compensate him for the extra risk, trouble and expense, which the investment occasions to him, over and above those which would be involved by it if he resided in the neighbourhood of the undertaking. He must allow for the fact that he can obtain only imperfect and tardy information about the persons and the circumstances whose movements affect the undertaking and that he cannot rapidly withdraw his capital and apply it to meet any new emergency.

These difficulties appear to be underrated by many economists. But light has been thrown upon them by the mishaps which have occurred to sundry foreign loans during the last few years.[4] It is said that on a mortgage on a real estate which involves to a person acquainted with the circumstances of the place no greater risk than would be covered by an interest of five or six per cent in England, there will be paid from six to eight per cent in New England, from eight to ten per cent in the neighbourhood of large towns in the Mississippi valley, while two per cent a month is frequently paid in extremely remote districts on security which is really good, but with the circumstances of which scarcely anyone is fully acquainted excepting those who are themselves in a position to make profitable use of any capital that may come into their possession.[5] It is said that even in such towns as London and Paris loans to costermongers, which involve very little risk to those who will devote their energies to the business, obtain an interest of five per cent a week, or in some cases five per cent a day. Compound interest being reckoned, five per cent a week is considerably more than a thousand per cent a year, and five per cent a day is more than five thousand million per cent a year.

One effect of these difficulties is seen in the fact that throughout the history of the world the carrying trade has generally been conducted to a large extent by countries whose capital

[4] [The following sentences were inserted at this point in a later revision.] Some light has been thrown on them by the history of certain foreign government and railway loans during the last few years. But the obstacles which impede the safe lending of money to a foreign government or railway are slight as compared with those which hinder a man from forming an estimate of the value of private securities which may be offered to him by individuals resident in distant countries. The statistics of mortgages afford proof of the extent to which capital is prevented from flowing freely to those districts in which private individuals offer high rates of interest for its use.

[5] [The following variant was added at this point. Similar remarks, including the reference to costermongers, are found in the *Economics of Industry*, p. 141, *Principles I*, p. 589.] Capitalists generally are extremely unwilling to undertake much trouble in the supervision of petty loans to people whose affairs are not open to ready inspection. Curious evidence of this is supplied by the fact that even in such towns . . . .

has been large but whose natural resources have not been sufficient to sustain a high rate of interest. Thus for instance Englishmen who engage in the carrying trade, between England and America are not in general separated from their capital to any greater extent than are Americans who engage in the same trade. The great war caused a dearth of capital in America. The thirty-seven thousand miles of railway which were made in America in the ten years that followed the great war opened up, directly and indirectly, opportunities of investment of which Americans could avail themselves with less risk and trouble than Englishmen could. American capitalists preferred the profits of such investments to the profits which they could obtain in the foreign carrying trade, in which they had to compete on equal terms with Englishmen.

It is to these causes chiefly that we must attribute the recent diminution in the amount of shipping owned by Americans. American shipbuilding has been hampered by a heavy customs tariff on iron: moreover the special facilities which America has for building wooden ships have lost much of their importance.

§ 7   The migration of capital, unaccompanied by its owners, is dependent, not upon the rate of profits but upon the rate of interest current in the country to which it migrates. The profits which a capitalist can obtain by the use of his capital in a country are increased by every development of the natural resources of the country; by every advance that is made in the industrial arts, and by every increase in the amount of labour, account being taken of its efficiency, which can be hired by a given expenditure. But these profits exceed the interest which can be obtained for the loan of capital by what economists have called 'the wages of superintendence' i.e., by all that portion of the profits which are retained for themselves by those who conduct business on borrowed capital. Consequently the rate of interest is affected not only by the causes which affect the rate of profits current in a country, but by another in addition. This is the abundance of men who are qualified to compete for the wages of superintendence; whether in the irresponsible control of private enterprises or in the management of public companies. Economists have not laid sufficient stress upon the extent to which the rate of interest which can be offered for the loan of capital in a country depends upon the supply of men capable for this work. Economists have not sufficiently insisted that the extent to which a country is able to attract foreign capital, and to retain her own, depends largely upon the number of her sons who have the sagacity, the energy, the firmness of character and the technical skill that are required for the successful conduct of business. These qualities are partly such as may be acquired by almost any man who has a good general education, and who is advantageously placed: partly they are such as depend on natural genius which, though perhaps more common in some ranks of life than others, is the exclusive property of no one grade of society. Those portions of England and of America which have attracted to themselves the greatest amounts of capital are those which offer the best training in youth and the most open career in manhood to the working classes. Scattered among the vast numbers of these classes there lies latent much practical ability of the highest order. A working man who rises to a post of command brings with him a store of experience which is likely to enable him successfully to develop those inventions and contrivances whereby capital is rendered more efficient.

It may indeed be urged that an invention, in whatever country it be made, rapidly becomes the property of the world. But, since the circumstances of no trade are exactly similar in any two countries, an adaptation of means to ends that is transported from one country to another must in general undergo a process analogous to the translation of a portion of the literature of one country into the language of another. If the merit of a book lies in its form rather than in its substance, the translation can scarcely be effective. And so it will not in general be easy to readjust to the circumstances of another country the improvements in matters of detail, the minor economies which taken together constitute one of the chief factors of success. And with regard to definite inventions that involve substantively new modes of procedure, experience has shown that countries which suffer others to pioneer the way for them, will often get into work each successive improvement just at the time at which it is being abandoned in favour of its

successor in the countries in which mechanical genius has its
home. In competing for the use of foreign capital the latter
class of countries have the same advantage over the former
that the Greek of old had over the barbarian boxer who
guarded ever the place where he had last been struck.

§ 8   It has been said that *ceteris paribus* the greater be the
amount of labour, account being taken of its efficiency, which
can be purchased by a given expenditure in a country, the
greater will be the inducements for foreigners to invest
capital there. It is probable that in every country of the Old
World there are some classes of labourers whose daily wages
are such that an increase of them, if spent in improving the
quantity and quality of their food, would immediately, or at
least in the course of a year, render their labour cheaper to the
capitalist. In western Europe, and particularly in England,
such cases are rapidly becoming rarer. But even where
labourers and their families have a sufficiency of nourishing
food, it is possible for a rise in wages to cause in the course of a
generation so great an increase in the efficiency of labour as to
increase the attractions which are offered to capital.

For a rise in the wages of one generation improves not only
the physical nurture and the school education of the next
generation, but also what is even more important the general
tone of the home influences by which their character is formed :
it is the tone of these influences which determines whether they
are to be fitted to perform those higher classes of work that
require trustworthiness and prompt intelligence and to make a
profitable use of their leisure. If we look at the broad facts of
history we shall, I believe, find that in England at least an
increase in the wages of one generation has thus caused an
increased efficiency in the next generation in every district
except those in which men, women and children have been
subjected to such severe toil as to disincline them for the peaceful pleasures of home. The children of mothers who have been
debased by their work have but little appreciation of any but
sensual pleasures. Many, though by no means all, of such
children, when they grow up, are apt to make such use of any
increase of their wages so as to diminish rather than increase
their own efficiency and the well-being of their households;

so as to increase rather than diminish the expenses of the administration of justice and of the poor law.

It is not generally known that the recent increase in the wages of labour in England has largely increased the proportion of his wages which the husband hands over to the housewife for the expenses of the family.[6] Some of the most trustworthy of the tables in the official Statistical abstracts bear on this point. These tables give an account of the 'principal imported and exciseable commodities retained for home consumption per head of the United Kingdom' for the years 1840–73. I may not lay stress on the rapid growth of the imports of such commodities as bacon, butter and cheese; for the imports of these have increased in a much greater ratio than have the amounts of them produced at home; and consequently in a greater ratio than have the total amounts of them consumed in the United Kingdom. I have therefore selected Tea, Sugar and Currants, which may be classed roughly as family comforts, for comparison with Malt, Spirits and Tobacco, which may be classed roughly as the working man's luxuries. In such a case it is more satisfactory to compare the statistics of small groups of years than of isolated years. Of course some allowance must be made for the diminution in price, owing to a diminution of taxation, of the first group during the interval.[7]

[6] [The following footnote was added at a later time. The reference is to J. E. Cairnes, *Some Leading Principles of Political Economy Newly Expounded* (Macmillan, London, 1874). The discussion of 'Brassey's paradox' – which is 'the rule of uniform cost of labour ... in every country of the civilised world' – is to be found on pp. 282–5, which refer to T. Brassey's *Work and Wages*. On Brassey see Vol 1, p. 80, above.]

Professor Cairnes, *Leading Principles*, p. 285, after making some remarks on Brassey's paradox which show a strange want of insight into the true bearing of Brassey's facts, makes the following unjustifiable statement 'An increase of wages which merely results in an enlarged consumption of beer and spirits is not likely to add much either to the physical powers or to the intelligence and skill of the recipients; and notoriously this is the way in which an increase of wages is, for the most part, taken out in this country'.

[7] [The Table is taken from an earlier draft, in which it was accompanied by a description of the contents. The sources appear to be: *The Statistical Abstract for the United Kingdom in each of the last fifteen years from 1840 to 1854* (reprinted in 1870 'with additions to correspond as nearly as possible with the information contained in the seventeenth number of the abstract for the 15 years from 1855 to 1869': Eyre and Spottiswoode, London, for H.M.S.O., 1870). *The Statistical Abstract ... from 1859 to 1873* (Twenty first Number, Eyre and Spottiswoode, London, for H.M.S.O., 1874). Marshall's copy of the first is retained in the Marshall Library.]

	Average amounts for the years 1840–2	Average amounts for the years 1871–3	Increase during the interval	Ratio of increase to amount at earlier period
Tea *lbs*	1·32	4·01	2·69	2·0 to 1
Sugar (Raw) *lbs*	16·41	42·22	25·81	1·5 to 1
Currants and Raisins *lbs*	1·62	4·47	2·85	1·5 to 1
—	—	—	—	—
Malt *bushels*	1·42	1·88	0·46	0·3 to 1
Spirits British and Foreign } *gallons*	0·9	1·15	0·25	0·3 to 1
Tobacco *lbs*	0·84	1·38	0·54	0·6 to 1

We conclude then that the direct and immediate effects of any change are apt to be over-estimated in comparison with the more remote effects. Changes which are necessary for the improvements of the home and school education of the rising generation, and for fitting them for wholesome pleasures are apt to be opposed in every country on the ground that they would diminish the attractions which the country can offer to capital. But the migration of capital is a slow process: and such changes would, in general, soon largely increase the capacity which the country has for the profitable employment of capital.

§ 9   Mr Bagehot[8] applies the name 'Cosmopolitan Capitalists' to that important class of people, who are in the main devoid of national sentiment; and who wield 'a cosmopolitan loan fund …. which runs everywhere as it is wanted, and as the rate of interest tempts it. A new commodity, one of the greatest growth of recent times, is used to aid these operations. The 'securities' of all well-known countries, their national debts, their railway shares, and so on (a kind of properties peculiar to the last two centuries, and increasing now most rapidly), are dealt in through Europe on every Stock Exchange.

[8] Compare *Fortnightly Review* CXIII, p. 739. [This refers to W. Bagehot, 'The Postulates of English Political Economy: [Part] II', *Fortnightly Review*, N.S. Vol 25 (May 1876) pp. 720–41 (Part I had appeared in February 1876). Both parts are reproduced in W. Bagehot, *Economic Studies*, edited by R. H. Hutton (Longmans Green, London, 1880), where the quotation is on pp. 67–8.]

If the rate of interest rises in any one country the price of such securities falls; foreign countries come in and buy them; they are sent abroad and their purchase-money comes here. Such interest-bearing documents are a sort of national 'notes of hand' which a country puts out when it is poor, and buys back when it is rich.'

The influences thus exerted are in the main temporary and their full discussion belongs more properly to the theory of the money market than to the inquiries on which we are at present engaged. Still it must be remembered that every temporary movement is apt to leave a residual permanent effect. When capital has gone to a foreign country to meet a passing demand, 'friction' so far as it acts at all may tend to help, rather than to hinder, the retention of that capital for permanent investment there.

The rapid movements by which the capital of one country is made to flow in to the relief of the temporary emergencies of another, are in great part effected through the machinery supplied by bills of exchange; which on any sudden rise in the rate of discount in a country are sold in large numbers to foreigners. Again, as has been already noticed,[9] the excess of England's imports over her exports is partly due to the profits on goods sent to America and other new countries which remain wholly or partially in the ownership of Englishmen for several months after they have been landed. In every case in which this is done there is in fact a temporary investment of English capital in the domestic trade of a foreign country. In these and other ways foreign trade with the aid of its machinery of bills of exchange drawn at long dates facilitates temporary migrations of capital; the total effect of which is in the long run of considerable importance.

§ [10] There is not much to be said concerning the migration of capitalists in company with their capital. A high state of civilisation exerts on those who are already wealthy an attraction which is in general superior in force to that exerted by the expectation of obtaining an increased income. Such men do not readily migrate in order to superintend the investment of their capital in a country in which a high rate of profits

---

[9] [This refers to one of the earlier missing chapters.]

is to be obtained, but in which they will be cut off from the social enjoyments to which they have become attached.[10] Much public attention has been directed to a few prominent cases in which English capitalists have set up branch establishments for the manufacture of textile goods on the Continent of Europe, and for that of iron in America. These men have been enabled by various causes to find in foreign countries a good market for their special technical skill and business faculties, as well as for their capital. But it appears that the total amount of capital which has been exported in this way is not of any considerable importance.

Yet the tendency to such migration is unquestionably on the increase. As Mr Bagehot says:[11] 'Young men also now transfer their capital from country to country with a rapidity formerly unknown. In Europe perhaps the Germans are most eminent in so doing. Their better school education, their better-trained habits of learning modern languages, and their readiness to bear the many privations of a residence among foreigners, have gained them a prominence certainly over the English and the French, perhaps above all other nations. But taking the world as a whole, the English have a vast superiority. They have more capital to transfer, and their language is the language of the great commerce everywhere, and tends to become so more and more.... The number of English commercial houses all over the world is immense, and of American very many, and yearly a vast number of young Englishmen are sent out to join them... the emigration of young men with English capital, and to manage English capital, is one of the great instruments of world-wide trade and one of the binding forces of the future.

In this way the same instruments which diffused capital through a nation are gradually diffusing it among nations. And the effect of this will be in the end much to simplify the problems of international trade. But for the present, as is commonly the case with incipient causes whose effect is incomplete, it complicates all it touches.'

---

[10] [The remainder of this paragraph appears to have been added later.]
[11] Loc. cit., p. 740. [See *Economic Studies*, pp. 70–1.]

§[11] Let us next consider the migration of the working classes. This is to a large extent controlled by sentiments and affections. Much has been written with regard to the influence exerted in the matter by family ties and by friendships, by old habits and associations. But insufficient account has been taken of the circumstances which render life in such a country as England uncomfortable to working men who have lived in such a country as the United States. Artisans continually return from America to England, drawn by home affections and the expectation that they may improve rather than injure their economical position. And some of them do find that, account being taken of the hours of work and the steadiness of employment, the wages which they can obtain here are worth as much to them as were those which they could obtain in America. But they can scarcely ever be induced to remain, for they are oppressed and rendered uneasy by the social position which they are constrained to occupy here.[12]

It is a general rule, although there are important objections[13] to it, that when a working man migrates to a new country and obtains in consequence a large increase in his wages, a chief cause of this increase is a change in his own efficiency. If a man's position at home has offered no great scope for enterprising vigour, the opportunities for learning and the stimulus of the energy by which he is surrounded in his new home, are often found to awaken power that had been latent in him so as apparently to change his character. The average of the wages earned in a new country is in general sustained at a high level not so much by the direct effects of her natural resources as by their indirect effects; for they attract a vigorous population, and give rise to social conditions that are favourable to the growth of industrial energy.

§[12] A country of great natural wealth when first opened up may offer enormous returns to capital and labour. It is indeed impossible accurately to compare the comforts and luxuries to be [enjoyed] and the hardships and fatigues to be endured by labourers who work in different countries under

---

[12] [For a more extensive treatment of such questions see Section V.2, below.]

[13] [There is no doubt that 'objections' is the word written, but 'exceptions' was probably intended.]

wholly different conditions. It is for instance impossible to measure against one another the total net advantages which fall to the lot of two labourers who perform a similar task, one amid all the minor comforts and luxuries that are to be cheaply purchased in the neighbourhood of a large town, and the other in the freedom but discomfort of a log hut. No exact estimate can be formed of the amount of exertion under a tropical sun that is equivalent in hardship to the work of a ploughman in a climate propitious to severe and constant work; such as are those of England, New Zealand, and California. We cannot say precisely how much greater are the net advantages that are offered to the labourer in a progressive new country than in an old; but we know that on the whole they are greater. And in particular it is certain as has been already said[14] that among a population almost all of whom are fitted for work which requires intelligence and energy, an abnormally high remuneration will be obtained in employments that demand only patient industry and habits of obedience.

But, subject to these exceptions, recent inductions[15] tend to prove that although there are enormous differences in the average standard of efficiency and consequently in the average wages of labourers in the same occupation in different districts there are few cases in which labour obtains in one country a real reward much superior to that which labour of equal efficiency obtains in another. In the preceding chapter some account was given of the way in which foreign trade competition tends to equalise the money wages of the same task, performed with the same efficiency, in different countries.[16] A closely allied but perhaps more interesting subject of inquiry relates to the causes which tend to equalise the real wages of similar tasks in different countries. In other words an inquiry is needed into the economic and other social forces which tend to effect an equivalence between the necessaries, comforts and luxuries which a labourer can obtain by performing a given task in a given way in one country with those which he can obtain by doing it in another [country]. With

[14] [This must refer again to one of the missing chapters.]

[15] [This possibly refers to Brassey's writings.]

[16] [This argument is probably the one given in Book III, Ch. III, § 6 of the *Economics of Industry*. It is outlined in the next footnote.]

regard to the whole of this question we have as yet but very imperfect data on which to work. But I believe it will be found that one of the chief causes which cooperates with the migration of capital and labour in bringing about such equality as exists, is the influence which a rise in real wages exerts in gradually increasing the supply of efficient workmen.[17]

[§ 13] We have already seen that the benefit which a country derives from foreign trade depends directly upon differences in efficiency between her various industries, and not upon the average efficiency of her industries.[18] It may be well here to examine an illustration of this principle to which a considerable amount of attention has been directed, but the conditions of which have not been duly analysed.

The resources of a new country may be such as to enable her to produce many things with great ease. She will then export some of those things in the production of which she is at the greatest advantage; and among the wares which she imports may be some which she could have produced with less expenditure of capital and labour than was required for their production in the countries from which she buys them. A famous instance in point is the importation of Irish butter into Australia shortly after gold had been discovered there. The capital and labour which produced the butter in Ireland, if it could have been transported without effort to Australia could have produced a larger amount of butter there. But the gold which was produced by a given amount of capital and labour in Australia sufficed for the expenses of purchasing from

---

[17] [The argument of this paragraph remains rather obscure, but is illuminated by the remarkable chapter on 'Local Variations of Value' in the *Economics of Industry* (Book III, Ch. III, especially §§ 4–6). There Marshall distinguishes three forces leading to the equalisation of real task wages (i.e. the payment for performing a given task): (i) migration (ii) induced changes in efficiency, with high initial task wages improving labour efficiency and thus lowering task wages without affecting time wages (iii) the competition between countries in exporting to third markets. The third equalises the money prices of the common exports of two countries, and this equalises between the two countries the money task wages of any occupation producing a jointly-exported commodity. Competition in the labour market of each country then equalises money task wages and money commodity prices even for non-traded commodities. (It is implicitly presumed that rent and interest are about the same in the two countries, so that the argument does not apply to new countries. But even in these, money wages are a good measure of real wages since cheap necessaries are offset by expensive luxuries.)]

[18] See Ch. I § 4. [This refers to the missing Part I, Ch. I.]

Ireland, expenses of transport being included, a greater amount of butter than could have been produced by that amount of capital and labour in Australia. A somewhat similar case is that of the importation of preserved vegetables into some parts of Western America. Farmers who have set themselves to raise wheat or cattle from a vast expanse of rich land are unwilling to be troubled with the petty troubles of a garden; and they frequently have no vegetables excepting those which have been brought to them in tins from inferior soils two thousand miles away. Such a state of things in new countries has not been infrequent but it has in general soon passed away. For a while the returns to capital and labour have been enormous: but they have stimulated immigration, and fostered the growth of native labour. So that, generally speaking, the increase of capital and population has, before many generations have passed transferred a large share of the produce of the soil to private property in the form of rent; and has caused the rate of profits and the rate of real wages to approach nearer to their average level in other countries. It must be repeated that such doctrines as this may not be applied without qualification to the circumstances of countries which have an unhealthy climate. Because the current scale of the wages of superintendence and of labour generally in two countries cannot be fairly compared until account has been taken of the fatigue and other discomforts which the peculiar circumstances of either country attach to the performance of a given task.

Of course the farmer of rich land in any country may raise wheat, and purchase oats which he could have produced with less trouble than was required for producing them on the adjacent poorer land on which they were grown. So the owner of a good vineyard may buy corn from his neighbours on poorer soil. But the economic principle which these facts illustrate has nothing to do with the special theory of foreign trade; they are in no way connected with the difficulties which retard the free migration of capital and labour. The vineyard could supply bountiful crops of corn in lieu of, but not in addition to, its vines. The rich farm could afford heavy crops of oats in lieu of, but not in addition to, its wheat. The returns to the last labour employed are not higher on the rich land than in the poor. The unequal bounty of nature causes inequality in rent, but not any inequalities in profits and wages which could be redressed by the free migration of capital and labour.

What is frequently the case of a single farm or vineyard may be the case of a whole country. Thus Barbados and Guernsey have rich soils, well adapted for the raising of wheat. They are old countries and yet they import wheat; the one in exchange for sugar, the other in exchange for early vegetables and other agricultural produce. But the land in each of them is fully occupied, so that though the total returns which Nature offers to labour are great, a large share of these is the property of the owner of soil. Additional labour applied in them could not win from Nature large additional returns; and there is in them no abnormally high rate of wages or of profits which could be much affected by the levelling action of the free migration of capital and labour. Therefore the case of these islands does not, as has sometimes been supposed, afford any illustration of the special doctrines of foreign trade, or of international values. Their case is similar in every respect to the case of a rich farm whose plough horses are fed by oats brought from neighbouring poorer land. Their case does not afford any exception to the rule laid down at the end of the last section.

With this ends the discussion of the second of the four influences which were enumerated at the commencement of the chapter as the chief of those which foreign trade exerts on the social and industrial progress of a country. The remaining two will be treated in the following chapter.

III.2.3 *Text of Part I, Chapter V :*
'*Foreign Trade in its Bearing on Industrial and Social Progress (Continued)*'

§ 1   It has already been observed[1] that no intelligent student of economic science denies that foreign trade freely carried on has, *prima facie*, a direct tendency to increase the wealth of a country; but that a large number of able economists, in countries other than Great Britain maintain that these direct

---

[1] See Ch. I § 3. [This refers to the missing Ch. I of Part I.]

and beneficial effects are liable to be outweighed by indirect effects which are injurious. Many of the most important of these injurious effects which advocates of 'Protection to Native Industries' ascribe to foreign trade are dependent upon (i) those influences which the foreign trade of a country exerts on the steadiness and constancy of employment of her industries, and (ii) those influences which it exerts on the variety of these industries and the relative magnitude of different groups of them. An investigation of these influences is therefore properly marked off from the matters discussed in the preceding chapter, but, inasmuch as the investigation is of interest also in connection with various social problems it may conveniently be kept apart from the inquiry which will be made in the next chapter as to the principles by which Governments should be guided in taxing foreign trade. I propose then to say something of the nature of the evils which arise from economic fluctuations and then inquire how these are affected by foreign trade.[2]

---

[2] [The following addition was inserted at this point.]

I will commence by quoting from Mr. Carey's writings a few passages illustrative of the charges which he makes against trade to the effect that it causes 'irregularity in the societary movement'. Mr. Carey is the head and representative of an important school of thinkers, and he is never weary of denouncing British economy on the ground that from Ricardo downwards it has given to 'trade' an undue preference over 'commerce'. Unfortunately he is not rigidly consistent in his use of these terms . . . (*). The force of many of his arguments in favour of the plan of Protecting the industries of a country against their foreign rivals would be much diminished if he adhered throughout to [his stated] use of the term. For according to his definition most of the exchanges which are carried on within America belong to trade and not to commerce. We cannot indeed fairly argue that in order to carry out his principles he must necessarily advocate such constitutional changes as would enable the state of Missouri to protect her rising manufactures against the competition of the developed powers of Pennsylvania. But while he never attributes to Foreign trade any advantages that are not properly to be ascribed to it, he is not equally careful to make it clear that the suppression of Foreign trade would not go so far towards removing the greater part of those evils which he contends are occasioned by the substitution of trade for commerce. But among the inexact statements and the loose or irrelevant argument which occupy [a] great part of his lengthy works there lie scattered subtle and suggestive remarks which may reward the patient and cautious reader . . . . [The deletions are of various uncited extracts from Carey (amounting in all to about three manuscript pages). They all appear to come from H. Carey, *Principles of Social Science* (Lippincott, Philadelphia; Trübner, London; 1868; three volumes). Representative of their general drift is the assertion that 'Trade and commerce look . . . always in opposite directions – the one towards frequent and rapid changes of price, and the other towards stability and regularity'. This is quoted by Marshall from Vol II, p. 221 of Carey, while the quotation at the point marked (*) above is from Vol I, p. 210.]

§ 2   The social and economic evils which arise from trade fluctuations and unsteadiness of employment are various and far-reaching. In extreme cases uncertainty with regard to their means of subsistence causes men's lives to be consumed in anxiety. It may be true indeed that much of this anxiety could be avoided by the exertion of a prudent self command. It may be true that when a man is in possession of the necessaries and comforts of life, any further increase of his expenditure does not in general afford a proportionate addition to his happiness. A man in the upper or middle ranks of life who has a fluctuating income incurs distress and inquietude wantonly if he adapts his normal expenditure to the upper instead of to the lower limit of that income. In abandoning the assured and quiet possession of a certain social position for the unstable and perturbed tenure of one somewhat higher, he sacrifices the substance of happiness to obtain its shadow. The evils of his lot may be removed by a firm moderation of extravagant desires more effectively than they can by any possible diminution of trade fluctuations. But although the moralist and the philosophic economist are concerned on many accounts to speculate as to the means whereby such wise moderation may be rendered more common, the practical aims of the present argument require us to deal with human nature as it is. We must assume that men's minds are harassed and that their power of deriving benefit from such means as they possess is diminished by any great uncertainty that affects their incomes.

A small uncertainty may indeed produce good effects that will almost counterbalance its evil effects inasmuch as it may in some ways promote the healthy activity of man's mind, prompting him to inquire into the more remote causes of the changes which affect him, and to discover new arrangements and new courses of action by which he may secure success or ward off disaster. But it is otherwise with a great uncertainty. The constant fear of complete commercial ruin frequently brings a man either to a habit of stolid recklessness which is morally unhealthy, or to a feverish activity which is unhealthy both morally and physically.

But more important still are the evil effects of interruptions of the employment and of the income of the working classes.

It is true that a cessation of a man's accustomed means of obtaining a livelihood invites him to consider whether he may not find better scope and better reward for his energies by changing his occupation or by migrating to another district. In a country which is being rapidly developed, and in which new and important openings for enterprise are continually offering themselves, some benefit may arise from whatever incites the confident ambition of the industrial classes to attempt new undertakings. In such a country as the United States occasional interruptions of work may perhaps on the whole tend to accelerate progress. But a constant recurrence of these interruptions, such as is occasioned there by extremes of climate among other causes, fosters a nervous temperament which is ill adapted not only for many forms of solid happiness, but also for patient work. And in a country in which a man is not likely to utilise periods of enforced idleness in the search for a new field of labour, the economic loss to himself and his country, which the frequent recurrence of such periods involves, is not in general counterbalanced by any economic advantage; while their effects on his character and happiness are of grave and uncompensated injury. If in such periods the provision for a man's household is in jeopardy his mind cannot be in a condition to receive those benefits which he could obtain from well earned leisure in the midst of a sure occupation. Such periods give a man idleness without repose, weariness without the wages and the training which are the reward of work. In trades in which occupation is habitually unsteady, intervals of work, often so intense that it could not be sustained for many days together, are wont to alternate with intervals of debauch and sloth. There is an important lesson in the fact that, if we put aside those trades in which the gentle happiness of home has been rendered impossible through the subjection of women and children to brutalising work, we find that almost every trade in which high wages have been systematically misapplied is one in which employment is fickle and unsteady. And in every trade the chief cause of the bondage of debt to tradesmen and others in which vast numbers of working men spend their lives is due to the instability of their incomes. A member of a powerful trade association may indeed in general be secured by aid of his Union against this bondage.

But none the less will it be found that to the direct and indirect effects of this bondage are to be attributed many of the worst evils that afflict the working classes both in old countries and in new.

§ 3   The great and various evils which arise from every dis-organisation of the industrial system of a country point to sources of conflict between the immediate economic interest of individuals on the one hand, and the economic and higher interests of society taken collectively on the other. It is a noteworthy and suggestive fact that all the various schemes by which socialists have proposed to remove these sources of conflict have proceeded on the assumption that for the well-being of the community it is necessary that the employment of its industries should be settled and seldom broken. The elder communists generally speaking were willing to sacrifice many not only of the luxuries, but also of the comforts and the arts of life, in order to obtain that peaceful content which they supposed to be inherent in Arcadian simplicity of manners. But that socialistic movement, originated by Louis Blanc, and developed by the bold and subtle genius of Lassalle, pro-poses to avail itself of all the resources that are embodied in the complex industries of the modern world.

Lassalle's scheme for the federation of industries[3] claims to make no Utopian demands on the generosity of man; it claims to reward the individual worker according to the efficiency of his work; and to promote that efficiency to the utmost by the use of all those appliances which science has discovered and which the division of labour has rendered practicable. It claims to be able at once to diminish the toil and increase the reward of the worker: partly indeed at the expense of the owner of capital, but mainly through the economies which it proposes to effect by steadying work and removing commercial risk. Lassalle argued that a suspension of work on the part of any branch of industry involves evils both to that branch and to the community in general. He contended that periods of commercial depression, though

---

[3] [The strand which Marshall emphasises here does not seem to have been a prominent one in Lassalle's programme. See, however, p. 147 of the 1899 edition of W. H. Dawson, *German Socialism and Ferdinand Lassalle* (Swan Sonnenschein, London; Scribner, New York; first edition, 1888).]

inevitable under the present system, can yet be avoided. For the reason why in such periods most branches of industry slacken their energies is only that each of them in consequence of its fear to fail of an adequate market for its own wares, refuses to purchase the wares of others; and thus helps to cause the stagnation which it fears.[4] He contends that the State might in general guarantee to each branch of industry an adequate market, since it would thus by sustaining confidence, cause them collectively to supply that market to each other.

Lassalle has not thoroughly treated any of the difficulties which beset his system and many of them he has wholly ignored. But he has rendered one important service to economic thought. He has compelled attention to a flaw in that organisation of labour which is brought about by the free play of the interests of individual producers under the sway of untrammelled competition.

Lassalle has compelled attention to the fact that the individual interest of each may not prompt him to continue his work alone at a time at which the continued work of all together would conduce to the collective interest of all. He has not indeed fairly grappled with the task of proving that the net result of the governmental interference which he proposes would be a benefit. But he has convinced large classes of men that there is a *prima facie* case for inquiring whether there may not be some limitation of individual freedom which a government may rightly impose with the purpose of rendering industry generally more steady and stable.

Lassalle had no bias against foreign trade: but foreign trade would increase the difficulties by which his scheme is surrounded. And indeed during the whole of the present century there has been a subtle, though often a silent sympathy between the school that has required the State to 'protect

---

[4] [The following expanded variant was to be inserted here.]

He observed rightly that the evils of such periods are much aggravated by the fact that in them each branch of industry, afraid that it will not meet with an adequate market for its own wares, refuses to purchase the wares of others; and thus helps to cause the stagnation which it fears. He did not carefully trace the operation of the fundamental causes of such depressions – bad harvests, war, lavish expenditure, rash speculation, the inordinate conversion of circulating capital into fixed. He boldly contended that the State....

native industries', and the more adventurous school which has maintained that the individual should look to the State, or to some smaller community, for guidance and protection in all matters but particularly in the ordering of his daily work. The parallel course of these two schools may indeed be traced throughout history in almost every civilised country. Their earlier work has but little interest save to the student of economic ethology. But from an investigation of the parallel movements of their more recent work the practical economist might obtain considerable aid in inquiries such as the present.

§ 4 It may indeed appear reasonable to suppose that the nature of the influence which foreign trade exerts on the stability and steadiness of a country's industries is capable of being determined by direct observation. But the attempts that have hitherto been made in this direction have been unsatisfactory to the cautious and critical reader. And indeed if we analyse the conditions of the problem that has to be solved, we shall see that the resources of historical and statistical research, proceeding according to the direct inductive method, are as yet wholly inadequate to the task of solving it. Although such an analysis must be long, it will be worth while to attempt it. The matter at issue is of considerable importance in itself; and a careful handling of it will serve to indicate what appears to me to be the right mode of approaching a large group of problems the difficulty of which is in my opinion underrated by many economists, both freetraders and protectionists.[5]

In particular many American economists have the habit of making too extensive a use as it seems to me of arguments hastily built upon a narrow basis of particular historical and statistical facts. A chief reason of this habit is, no doubt, to be found in the fact that they are compelled to adapt their writings in great part to the taste of a class of readers that has considerable practical intelligence, but no thorough training in scientific method. Such readers have, to use their own words, more confidence in facts than in theories. They do not perceive that no conclusion can be based upon a fact until the fact is interpreted, and that in general the process of interpretation

[5] [The next paragraph was originally a footnote but on revision was to be incorporated into the text 'in small print'.]

tacitly assumes certain complex theories. For instance such readers are apt to look with greater suspicion on an argument that a particular cause tends to produce a particular effect if the argument is based upon general reasoning, than if it is based upon a recital of certain cases in which such effects have followed on such causes. But in fact such a recital is inadequate for its purpose unless it is known that there were not present other causes which were capable of producing the effect. In order to decide that the effect is not to be ascribed to other causes, it is in general necessary to assume, openly or tacitly, certain general propositions as to their mode of operation. And perhaps no one of these propositions may be more certain, or more capable of being properly tested by the practical man than the original argument based on general reasoning as to the effect of the particular cause in question; although this argument was put aside in favour of that claimed to be based directly on specific facts. Such a rash and impatient use of history and statistics is doubly injurious. Not only can it be applied with almost as much apparent effectiveness in support of propositions that are false as in support of propositions that are true; but it also tends to throw unmerited discredit on the labour of those economists in Germany and elsewhere who are doing solid work in the investigation of facts. Their efforts are indeed chiefly directed towards the patient accumulation of materials that may enable future generations to proceed with more certainty and to deal with more complex questions than is at present possible. But their work has not been unfruitful of results which have been already available to extend our practical knowledge. Such of them as have done good work have not opposed the study of facts to the study of theory, but rather have made free use of the provisional doctrines which economic science has already obtained to interpret new facts; and have made use of new facts thus interpreted to suggest such modifications of their doctrines as may make them more nearly correspond to things as they are.[6]

[6] Even Mr. Bagehot seems not properly to distinguish the work done by these two sets of men. Compare *Fortnightly Review*. [This footnote, added in revision, probably refers to Bagehot's 'Postulates . . . ' which appeared in the *Fortnightly* for February and May, 1876. See Bagehot's *Economic Studies*, especially pp. 11–21.]

The first difficulty that we meet with in attempting to determine by direct induction the influence that foreign trade exerts on the steadiness of employment in a country arises from the fact that there exist at present no means of ascertaining exactly how many of the workers of a country are at any time out of employment. There are indeed in England a few important trades with regard to which data for this purpose, exact so far as they go, are supplied by the careful statistics of powerful trades unions. But such trades, though in some respects rightly called representative, have their work often interrupted by causes that do not affect agriculture or the smaller industries, and their statistics do not afford a trustworthy basis on which to found conclusions as to the total number of workmen out of employ in the country at any time. It may indeed be remarked that in the old trade guilds, masters used to cooperate with their men for collecting and for disseminating information on trade matters. There are indications that in some leading industries the combined efforts of master and man will produce thoroughly organised statistics: and if this movement should prosper and extend to all industries it will render possible to future generations many economic inductions which are now impossible.

In the next place if we were able accurately to compare the numbers of men that have been at various times out of employment in a country, we should have advanced but a little way towards determining the influence of foreign trade in the matter. For the growth of foreign trade is but one of many causes which affect the fluctuations of industry in a country: and it will be found that the method of direct induction will not enable us to separate from the total effect resulting from the combined action of all these causes, that particular portion which should rightly be ascribed to foreign trade.

It is impossible to infer the effects of foreign trade on the stability of industry by observation of the immediate consequences of each particular increase or diminution of a country's trade. For the influence which foreign trade exerts on the stability of industry is in great part dependent upon the economic habits prevalent in a country. Changes in these habits are produced slowly; while the oscillations in the amount of the foreign trade of a country are rapid. Therefore before the full effects of any passing increase of this amount have manifested themselves, the trade may have already moved so far in the opposite direction as to have shrunk to less than its normal dimensions. It will be impossible to separate the effects of the downward movement from those which linger on from the preceding upward movement. Of course whenever an improvement takes place in the foreign markets for a country's wares, a stimulus is likely to be given to her industries: and her workers are likely to be in full employment in those periods in which her foreign trade is in an ascending phase. But this fact throws no direct light upon the question whether the general effect of a large foreign trade is permanently to increase or diminish the steadiness of her industries.

There is more room for hoping that a satisfactory answer to the question may ultimately be obtained from an investigation of those changes which have come over the industries of various countries during periods of time in which their foreign trade has gradually undergone a large increase. But in almost every such period a number of causes of which foreign trade is but one, have concurred to produce vast changes in economic organisation and industrial habits. In order to arrive at a just estimation of the grave difficulties which surround the task of separating by direct observation and induction the influences due to the growth of foreign trade from those due to other causes, it will be advantageous to select some period during which the commerce of a particular country has rapidly increased and to enumerate with care the other changes which during that period have affected the steadiness of employment there. The transformation which England has undergone during the past hundred years has been aptly called by several continental writers the classic instance of economic development. It does not indeed illustrate clearly the operation of all the economic forces which have played or are playing an important role in the world. But it does exhibit clearly the operation of more numerous, more representative and more important economic forces than does any other single chapter of history. I proceed then to enumerate the chief changes which during the past hundred years have affected the steadiness of employment in England.

§ 5   Fundamental causes of these changes are to be found in extensions of knowledge and in developments of industrial organisations. Thus the progress of science and of mechanical invention has increased the advantages that attach to minute subdivision of labour and to production on a large scale: it has facilitated the transport of goods and the transmission of news, and has thereby promoted the localisation of particular branches of industry in special districts. Full scope has been given to each of these movements in consequence of the almost total cessation of the interference of revenue officers with the free action of the trader. While the growth of the system of banking has enabled borrowed capital to be obtained easily and on a large scale for all kinds of business.

It will be convenient while considering the various changes of which these are fundamental causes, to indicate the mode in which the operation of each of them has been influenced by foreign trade. For by this course we shall be led to see not only how we may not, but also how we may, proceed in order to determine the nature of the effects which the foreign trade of a country exerts on the steadiness of employment of her industries. We shall discover not only what difficulties lie in the way of the application of the method of direct induction from particular observations to problems of this class, but also what means for their solution can be obtained by systematic analysis and reasoning from general principles.

§ 6   During the past hundred years English employers and employed have moved apart from one another. This movement has been connected partly as consequence and partly as cause with changes in sentiment, in domestic habits and in social relations generally; but its chief cause is to be found in the advantages that modern improvements put within the reach of businesses that are conducted on a large scale. Thus annual hirings have gone out of vogue; and weekly hirings are generally substituted for them. Hence arises one great cause of unsteadiness of employment. A master who had to pay wages to his men, whether they were at work or not, had great inducements to employ them in working for stock at times at which he had no immediate prospect of a market for his wares; whereas a master can now in such a case dismiss at a short notice, without much injury to himself, at all events a considerable portion of his men. It is true that his men may consent during periods of depression to work for low wages, in order that he may continue his operations without loss. But they are generally unwilling to consent to a great reduction in their wages for this purpose. Under any circumstances they would indeed fear to glut the market for the ware which they produce, and so to prolong the period during which its price is low. But a new social discord, a new conflict between the immediate interests of the individual and the collective interests of society has been introduced by the fact that in such cases any concessions that they may make to their employer's need, may invite him to attempt reductions of wages which are not really necessary for the continuation of his work. On consideration, however, the reader will I think incline to the opinion that the tendency towards irregularities of industry which arises from this source is not likely to become greater in England than it already is; but may diminish.

Similarly the localisation of an industry tends to intensify interruptions of employment. When a particular industry is depressed, the workers in it may often find some makeshift occupation for their hands, provided their numbers are not large in proportion to the population which surrounds them. But in the cotton districts, or in the iron districts, of England it is difficult to find such occupation, when the cotton trade, or when the iron trade, is depressed.

The extent to which the system of production on a large scale prevails in a country depends directly on the peculiar genius of her people at least as much as it does on the extent of her foreign trade. For instance it would certainly prevail in the Northern States of America even if they had no foreign trade. Yet is is not uncommon to hear American manufacturers dilate on the advantages which a large export trade gives to this system. In fact the advantages which the system of production on a small scale has when competing for domestic custom find generally speaking no place in the competition for custom in foreign countries. This is the case with the advantages which small establishments scattered over a country have through incurring but slight expenses for the transport of the wares which they have made or repaired: and again with those advantages which the managers of such establishments have for establishing local connections and trade-acquaintance-ships, for accommodating themselves to local tastes and needs, and for estimating the solvency of their customers. Such establishments, deprived of their special advantages, have but small chance in competition with the superior resources and economies of large establishments or of localised trades. It is indeed true that in general industries have become to some extent localised and have made many of their most important advances in the art of production before they have been able to find any considerable sale for their wares in foreign countries. But a large export trade when it has once been obtained increases greatly the tendency which the industry has to fall into the hands of large capitalists or at all events to concentrate itself in special districts. We may then credit foreign trade with a considerable share of whatever benefits or evils are to be ascribed not only to the localisation of industry and to production on a large scale but also to the increased use of large fixed capitals in manufactures.

§ 7 The consequences of the application of expensive machinery in production are important for our present purposes: and we may consider them next. The owner of machinery incurs a loss whenever it is idle; and this loss is in many respects similar to that which suspension of work used to occasion to the employer who hired his men by the year. Thus although the progress of mechanical invention disturbs in many ways the even tenor of industry; yet a direct tendency to render employment steady is exerted by everything that increases the employer's outlay on account of machinery and other 'fixed capital' in comparison to the rest of his outlay. It is important to remark that while the disturbances arising from the invention of new machinery may probably not continue always to increase, fixed capital is likely to continue without any assignable limit to increase more rapidly than circulating capital.

Unfortunately the growth of fixed capital exerts an indirect effect in the direction opposite to that direct effect which we have just considered. For while the possession of expensive machinery tends to induce an employer to keep his own men constantly at work it tends also to make him exert an unsteadying influence on prices, and thereby indirectly to increase the difficulties which lie in the way of steady work on the part of others.[7] This point though sufficiently obvious to men in business is often overlooked. Let us consider a particular case. Suppose that one third of the total price that under normal circumstances a manufacturer receives for his wares is just sufficient to give him the average trade profits on his fixed capital, to cover the depreciation by time of this capital and to pay his rent. Looking only at the immediate effects of his action he will find that it will not answer his purpose to suspend production so long as he can sell his wares for more than two-thirds of the normal price, that is of the price which he must on the average obtain in order to make his business remunerative in the long run. It may even answer his purpose to continue to produce and to sell for a price considerably less than two-thirds of the normal price if, as is probable in a time of depression, he be able to purchase raw material and labour more cheaply than in ordinary times.

It is true indeed that various motives may deter him from this course. To begin with, his direct personal interest will cause him to weigh the probable effect of his conduct on the future demand for his wares by those purchasers with whom he is most brought into contact. But further he may probably consider that his comfort and his pecuniary interest will be promoted by his working to some extent in harmony with his neighbours in the same trade. He will fear the odium which will attach to him if he recklessly 'spoilt the markets' in which they were generally concerned. The force of this fear varies with circumstances, but it always exerts some tendency to produce tacit or open trade combinations for the purpose of moderating supply and sustaining prices. The efficiency of such combinations is in general increased by changes that tend to throw any branch of production into the control of a few large establishments. But trade combinations are in general weakened by improvements in the means of communication

---

[7] [The following deleted sentences were originally included here.] It is true that the price of manufactured wares is on the whole more steady than that of raw material. For this there are obvious causes: it is less than it would be if less expensive machinery were used in manufacture.

between distant markets; and by almost all extensions of foreign trade. For these tend to render effective the competition between men who have no personal knowledge of one another, whose interests are not in all respects similar, and who therefore have neither the opportunity nor the inclination to combine with one another. And, similarly they are weakened by every new facility for entering into the business that is offered to those who have but little capital of their own.

§8   A number of causes, of which her foreign trade has been the chief, have combined to develop the machinery of the English money market; until it has become, in Mr Bagehot's phrase 'by far the greatest combination of economical power and economical delicacy that the world has ever seen'.[8] Its power is shown in the promptness with which it affords fresh supplies of capital to any business that is able to turn them to profitable account, lending with an equal hand to those who have and those who have not capital of their own already invested in the business. Its delicacy arises from the fact that it allows only a small amount of capital to remain idle, so that in a time of pressure there is but little solid capital in reserve to be used to strengthen those portions of the economic system at which the tension is the greatest, or the power of resistance the least. The delicacy of the money market is one cause, though perhaps not the chief cause, of the severity of commercial panics, and of the distrust which remains for some years after these crises have passed: and has thus exerted a baleful influence on the steadiness of employment in England.

The efficiency and the power of the money market has had much influence in counteracting the strong economic forces that are tending to concentrate business in the hands of wealthy capitalists. Indeed the facility with which credit can be obtained in some classes of trades causes the stream to flow in the opposite direction. The conduct of business by men who are working chiefly on borrowed capital has several marked characteristics. Such men readily innovate, readily adapt themselves to supply a new want, readily avail themselves of each new invention and of each new process of production that

---

[8] [W. Bagehot, *Lombard Street* (Second edition; King, London, 1873) p. 3. Marshall's copy is preserved in the Marshall Library.]

promises well. Thus they are eminently efficient in preventing
the price of a commodity which can be produced quickly
from remaining long above that amount which is required for
defraying the expenses of its production. But they are not
inclined towards steady (or in American phrase, 'conservative') modes of action. They are, for instance, generally more
ready than old established firms to sell their wares 'at a loss',
i.e. at a price which allows them inadequate profit on their
fixed capital, either in order to attract to themselves new
customers, or for any other reasons. Thus their action tends
in many ways to increase the fluctuations of credit and mutual
confidence that occur in the commercial world; and to render
fluctuations of prices more violent than they otherwise would
be. All such fluctuations increase the difficulties which affect
the steady employment of a country's industries.

Much light has been thrown upon the question discussed in
the present chapter, by the masterly work contained in Mr
Bagehot's 'Lombard Street'. I shall venture here to introduce
from it a long quotation which illustrates not only the point
immediately at issue, but also generally the manner in which
economic and social changes affect each other. 'The increasingly democratic structure of English commerce is very un-
popular in many quarters and its effects are no doubt exceed-
ingly mixed. On the one hand, it prevents the long duration of
great families of merchant princes, such as those of Venice
and Genoa, who inherited nice cultivation as well as great
wealth, and who, to some extent, combined the tastes of an
aristocracy with the insight and verve of men of business.
These are pushed out so to say, by the dirty crowd of little
men. After a generation or two they retire into idle luxury.
Upon their immense capital they can only obtain low profits,
and these they do not think enough to compensate them for the
rough companions and rude manners they must meet in
business. This constant levelling of our commercial houses is,
too, unfavourable to commercial morality. Great firms, with a
reputation which they have received from the past, and which
they wish to transmit to the future, cannot be guilty of small
frauds. They live by a *continuity* of trade, which detected fraud
would spoil. When we scrutinise the reason of the impaired
reputation of English goods, we find it is the fault of new men

with little money of their own, created by bank "discounts". These men want business at once, and they produce an inferior article to get it. They rely on cheapness and rely successfully.'

'But these defects and others in the democratic structure of commerce are compensated by one great excellence. No country of great hereditary trade, no European country at least, was ever so little "sleepy", to use the only fit word, as England: no other was ever so prompt at once to seize new advantages. A country dependent mainly on great "merchant princes" will never be so prompt; their commerce perpetually slips more and more into a commerce of routine. A man of large wealth, however intelligent, always thinks, more or less – "I have a great income, and I want to keep it. If things go on as they are I shall certainly keep it; but if they change I *may* not keep it." Consequently he considers every change of circumstance a "bore", and thinks of such changes as little as he can. But a new man, who has his way to make in the world, knows that such changes are his opportunities; he is always on the look-out for them, and always heeds them when he finds them. The rough and vulgar structure of English commerce is the secret of its life; for it contains "the propensity to variation", which, in the social as in the animal kingdom, is the principle of progress.'[9]

§ 9 The same movement that has loosened the bond between the master and his men, has separated the producer from the consumer. The producer in old times could reckon upon a steady sale at customary prices to a particular set of purchasers whom he knew personally and whose wants he could gauge. But he cannot do this now. The new order of things, though it may on the whole be conducive to enterprise, yet causes great risk to be incurred by him who, without immediate orders for his wares, continues to produce for stock. This risk is increased by the spread of fickle habits in matters of fashion among all classes of society, and even by the growing rapidity of invention.[10] For these changes combine to increase the chance

[9] [Ibid., pp. 9–10.]
[10] [Similar passages will be found in Marshall's lecture 'Some Aspects of Modern Industrial Life' of 7 Oct 1878 (reproduced in *History of Political Economy*, Vol 4 (Spring 1972) pp. 53–61) and on pp. 114–15 of the *Economics of Industry*.]

that a large stock of wares, particularly, a large stock of almost any kind of implements, may become partially obsolete before it is completely disposed of. But of the causes which in the new order of things combine to increase this risk there remains yet to be described the subtlest and most important.

A vast and rapidly increasing portion of the industry of the country is devoted to producing things that are destined not for immediate consumption, but to be used as capital and afford a revenue. This fact is indeed a chief symptom and a chief cause of economic prosperity. But it involves a very wide separation between the original producer and the ultimate consumer of the wares for the making of which capital is required. The causes which determine the making of a new railway or a new dock, or the setting up of a new factory or new machinery, are highly complex. They depend only indirectly upon the demand of the ultimate consumer for those conveniences or commodities the supply of which is to be the remote result of the undertaking. Directly they depend upon the resources and the confidence of those who either actively or by the loan of capital contribute to the undertaking. It is a matter of vast difficulty to predict what these resources and this confidence will be. Those industries therefore which are largely concerned with the production of wares that are required for such undertakings are compelled to proceed with exceptional caution. They can rarely venture to produce in anticipation of a future demand. And in times of commercial depression the workmen attached to them are thrown in great part out of employment. Industries of this class have increased more rapidly than almost any others in the later stages of England's commercial development.

§ 10   On the other hand the recent developments of England's trade have opened to her markets, so wide and various, for the purchase of the necessaries of life, as to prevent great variations in the prices of these. A great rise in the price of the staple food of a country, is the most injurious of all economic changes. It causes much misery directly; and by preventing the people from purchasing their wonted supplies of the comforts of life, it tends to disorganise almost every industry in the country. The repeal of the corn-laws was unquestionably a necessary condition of the increased prosperity which England has seen during the present generation. She has gained greater benefits by availing herself of widely extended foreign markets in which to buy and sell, than it has been possible for any other country to gain in the same way. But every increase in the number of markets from which a country can obtain what she requires, or in which she can sell what she produces, must diminish the fluctuations of prices which are occasioned by local disturbances, must render the course of her industries more steady and equable.

It must, however, be remembered that the steadying influences thus exercised by the opening up of widely extended markets do not depend exclusively, or perhaps even mainly upon the improvement of the means of transport of goods. The easy communication of prompt, thorough and exact trade news is a condition of perhaps even greater importance. Without this it is not possible to buy in the cheapest market, and sell in the dearest; for the circumstances of each market change rapidly. The natural and direct action of commerce is to prevent prices from falling much below, or rising much above, their average level: since it offers high profits to those who divert wares from those markets in which the demand is abnormally low to those in which it is abnormally high. But such action, to be of avail, must be prompt. When the supplies of raw material, or the demand for the finished ware, in one set of markets becomes scanty a great fluctuation in prices and a great dislocation of industry are in general inevitable unless there is already an efficient organisation of the means of communication with other markets, not only for wares, but also for information. The dissemination of such information, in so far as it relates to public events, economic, social and political, is effected in part by the general press and by special trade publications, in part by private intelligence. Private telegrams are every day extending the scope of their action in respect to personal business details: they enable traders to obtain as they want it trustworthy information from their agents as to the business, the character, the manner of life, and generally the local reputation for solidity of other individual traders in another district, or in another country.

We thus find that the growth of England's commerce has brought with it two sets of causes which affect the steadiness of industry in opposite directions. One set tends to prevent the producer from obtaining an even and regular purchase of his wares by any particular group of customers. The other set is increasing his power of dealing readily and securely in remote markets. It appears, however, that the former set of causes has nearly reached its maximum, and cannot perpetually increase as fast as it has done during the past hundred years: but that the second set of causes is in the infancy of its strength and may go on increasing with unchecked growth for many generations to come.

§ 11   We have thus concluded a rapid sketch of some of the chief changes which, during the past hundred years, have affected the steadiness of employment of England's industries. We have seen them intimately and variously interwoven with one another; each event bringing about, after an interval, effects some of which tend in one direction and others in the opposite. The simple inductive method, the mere tabulation of Statistics, cannot afford us directly any appreciable assistance in the task of analysing these complex and intricate effects, and of assigning to each particular cause that particular portion of the total result, which it would have produced if acting alone. But indeed no such attempt at any scientific analysis is made by the greater number of those writers who found conclusions on the mere comparison of two short tables of statistics; who lightly infer that this or that economic or social event which has followed on a particular change in the magnitude of a country's trade, or in the height of her tariffs, is to be attributed to that change as its cause. They do not attempt to separate the various causes by whose joint action any result is brought about, before attributing to any one its share in bringing about that result. They fix their attention on the changes in one cause, they suppose it to produce its full effects either immediately or after such an interval as may be most favourable to the particular conclusion they desire to establish, and by this means they are enabled to find in almost any set of statistics support for the doctrines for which they are contending.[11]

---

[11] [The next paragraph was originally a footnote but on revision was to be incorporated into the text 'in small print'.]

A charge of this kind appears to me, as I have already hinted,[12] to lie against many American advocates both of Free-trade and of Protection. But though it may have been impossible for me completely to free my mind from bias in the matter, I am bound to record the conviction arrived at after much patient study that the worst instances of recklessness in this particular are to be found in the writings of the Protectionist school. Many of these have been exposed by Mr Grosvenor in his instructive work *Protection: does it protect?*.[13] He appears to me in general to be more careful than his opponents, and to pay more attention to the rules of scientific method. But even he has founded on the simple comparison of statistical tables many arguments which do not appear to me to be cogent.

§ 12   The analysis that has been given of the chief causes that during the last hundred years have affected the steadiness of employment in England does not only manifest the inadequacy of the direct inductive method for the solution of the complex problem of determining the influence that foreign trade has exerted in the matter. The analysis also puts us in a position for deciding with tolerable confidence what the nature of that influence must be. For it exhibits the growth of foreign trade as in general cooperating with, promoting and being promoted by most of the other chief factors of England's economic development. In particular it exhibits foreign trade as cooperating with other causes to exert influences some of which tend to increase and others to diminish the steadiness of employment. England's foreign trade has enabled her to obtain ample supplies of her staple food and has rendered its price tolerably uniform. Her trade has thereby conferred on her benefits which are beyond question far greater than any injuries with which it can possibly be credited. But leaving out of consideration this particular exceptional effect, we cannot I think escape the conclusion that the remainder of the influences which England's foreign trade exerts in the direction of steadiness of employment are

---

[12] [See § 4 above.]

[13] [W. M. Grosvenor, *Does Protection Protect?* (Appleton, New York, 1871). Marshall's copy, preserved in the Marshall Library, includes Marshall's list of 'Passages illustrating the province of statistics in economic science'.]

broader and more massive, have a greater capacity for further growth than those which it exerts in the direction of unsteadiness of employment.

But it must not be forgotten that all such analysis can refer directly only to the circumstances of a particular country at a particular time. The present circumstances of all civilised countries are so nearly alike, that in the absence of cause shown to the contrary, there is a strong presumption that an economic doctrine established for one of them is valid for others. But cause may be shown to the contrary. It may be argued, for instance, that the relative magnitude of the influences which foreign trade exerts on the stability of industry is in America altogether different from that which it is in England. If this argument can be sustained, America may justly claim that the conclusion just arrived at should not be applied to her, until her own case has been judged on its own merits. There are many practical questions with regard to which a country may insist that the applications of economic theory be constructed from the beginning specially for her, so as to take account of her own peculiar circumstances. In this matter British economists are not, in the opinion of foreigners, sufficiently tolerant. In the following chapter[14] some account will be given of exceptional circumstances in which foreign trade may probably exert on the whole a disturbing influence on a country's industries.

§ 13   We have next to consider the social and the indirect economic influences, which foreign trade may exert on a country by the manner in which it affects the variety of her industries and the relative magnitude of different groups of them. We have already seen[15] that if, in the free course of foreign trade, a country imports any ware, this fact proves that the country would incur an immediate economic loss by declining to purchase it from abroad. We have now to inquire whether the free course of foreign trade may not hinder from flourishing certain industries which are capable of conferring indirectly or ultimately an important benefit on the country.

[14] [This clearly refers to the unfinished Part I, Ch. VII, which appears to have been planned as Chapter VI at an earlier stage. See Section III.4, below.]
[15] [Probably in the missing Part I, Ch. I.]

We may commence by classifying the chief conditions under which a particular branch of industry, although it would not remunerate the capitalist who should undertake it, would yet afford to the country at large benefits more than sufficient to compensate for the direct pecuniary loss which would be involved in starting it. Such conditions are that the industry should tend to raise the mental and moral character of the people; that the industry requires masters and men to possess technical skill which is not immediately forthcoming, but which will be brought into existence by the industry itself after it has been carried on for some period; that the industry is one which is largely dependent on the organisation of auxiliary industries, or of facilities for transport; and that this organisation, though it will grow up gradually around the industry when it has once been started on a large scale, cannot be at once commanded by those who originate the industry. Let us consider these in detail.

§ 14 First let us consider the new industry as affecting the mental qualities and industrial faculties of the people. When a man works he produces two effects, one on his work, and another on himself. The former alone is of direct pecuniary interest to his employer. If in the course of a year's work a workman has received training in intelligence, in trustworthiness, in power of self control, and in technical skill and efficiency, the results of the training are the property of the workman and of the state; but not, save to a small extent and indirectly, the property of his employer. The workman can demand from his master an addition to his wages equivalent to the increased value of his services and in a free market his demand will be, within certain limits, successful. It is true that workmen are attracted towards occupations in which they can obtain training of such moral and economic advantages to themselves in the future. But they are likely to estimate such remote advantages at less than their full value unless they or their parents have already attained a somewhat high standard of intelligence and morality. But further, an industry which develops the higher qualities of those engaged in it benefits indirectly the character and condition of the neighbourhood in which it is. It improves the schools and the clubs, and raises the tone of society. The children of its own workers are likely, as their taste may lead them, to stray into other industries and to increase their efficiency; while its rewards may stimulate the better ambition of those engaged in other industries to educate their children up to its standard. It is possible therefore that there may be side by side in a country, two industries each of which is thoroughly well established, but that the one which is affording the higher profits to the capital and thus attracting capital to itself away from the other may be conferring on the country at large (including of course the capitalists concerned) less economic benefits than the other, and much less moral and social benefits. The importance of this case I conceive to be enormous on account of the vast industries to which it applies. But in economic discussions it has been to some extent thrown into the shade by the more striking case of the competition for capital in a country between what is called a [nascent] industry, and one which is already well established.

It is obvious on the smallest consideration that an industry, which if it once struck root fairly in a country might thrive there, may have great difficulty in striking root without some sort of external aid.

[§ 15]   British economists generally have abstained from laying stress on this fact. Their treatment of this question generally has been timid and weak: for it is impossible that those who are well acquainted with the circumstances of a new country can read their work without detecting and dwelling upon their omission and perhaps without exaggerating the importance of the argument which 'the orthodox' school has evaded.

The bold upright character of Mill is conspicuous when, in an often quoted passage, he says, 'The only case in which, on mere principles of political economy, protecting duties can be defensible, is when they are imposed temporarily (especially in a young and rising nation) in hopes of naturalizing a foreign industry, in itself perfectly suitable to the circumstances of the country. The superiority of one country over another in a branch of production, often arises only from having begun it sooner. There may be no inherent advantage on one part, or disadvantage on the other, but only a present superiority of acquired skill and experience. A country which has this skill and experience yet to acquire, may in other respects be better adapted to the production than those which were earlier in the field: and besides, it is a just remark of Mr Rae, that nothing has a greater tendency to promote improvements in any branch of production, than its trial under a new set of conditions. But it cannot be expected that individuals should, at their own risk, or rather to their certain loss, introduce a new manufacture, and bear the burthen of carrying it on until the producers have been educated up to the level of those with whom the processes are traditional. A protecting duty, continued for a reasonable time, will sometimes be the least inconvenient mode in which the nation can tax itself for the support of such an experiment. But the protection should be confined to cases in which there is good ground of assurance that the industry which it fosters will after a time be able to dispense with it; nor should the domestic producers ever be allowed to expect that it will be continued to them beyond the time necessary for a fair trial of what they are capable of accomplishing.'[16]

[§ 16]   Leaving for a following chapter[17] the discussion of the question what are the conditions under which 'a protecting duty . . . will be the least inconvenient mode in which a nation can tax itself for the support of such an experiment', I will quote a passage from an American writer bearing on the same subject. 'A well-organised system for carrying on a business, has very great advantages. All the auxiliary arts concerned in its prosecution, are near at hand; with frequent and cheap communication with the sources of supply of materials, stationary and travelling agents and correspondences, at home and abroad, for distributing the manufactured articles, and forcing them upon the attention of every consumer, civilised or savage, not merely at the commercial centres, but also in the remotest corners and obscurest recesses, where creatures possessed of anything to barter, can be found . . . .

---

[16] Pol. Econ., Bk V, Ch. X § 1. [J. S. Mill, *Principles of Political Economy*, pp. 918–19.]
[17] [See Section III.4, below.]

Another advantage of much greater importance in favor of
the party already exclusively possessed of the field, is the
organisation and skill of his artificers and workmen. The
difference between these, and those newly brought into an
employment, is the same as between regularly drilled troops,
and militia. "A sort of twist or gimp", made in Great Britain,
"which cost three shillings making, when first introduced, is
now manufactured for a penny, and this solely through the
increased dexterity of the workmen, without the intervention,
of any new machine." This is an extraordinary case and is,
therefore, the more striking illustration of a consideration of
momentous import in national economy. The manual dexterity acquired by practice in dispatching a greater quantity
of work of superior quality, avails much in all employments,
and in many predominates for years over competition. The
disadvantage of inferior manual skill cannot be overcome at
once by importing workmen from abroad. This is the first step.
Many foreign artisans come to us from Europe. So we send,
from time to time, a company of overseers and operatives in
cotton manufactories, to Mexico; and in like manner have
dispatched shipwrights and cotton cultivators to Turkey, and
machinists to Turkey and Russia. Intelligence and public
spirit, in the governments and their subjects of our times,
is doing for other arts, what brutal persecution on the continent, did for the woolen manufacture, in England, in the
seventeenth century.

But the importation of instructors in arts is an expensive
operation. Thus the English engineer first employed on the
Albany and Schenectady Railroad locomotive trains, had a
salary of three thousand dollars a year, for a service that now
costs sixty dollars a month. Then it requires some time to
introduce and thoroughly domesticate an art. The imported
artist often proves to be unskilful, vicious, conceited, turbulent,
or impracticable; and his faults will, perhaps, be aggravated
by the jealousy and antipathy of our own natives employed
with him, whereby the undertaker is subject to great vexation
and expense.'[18]

[18] *Propositions Concerning Protection and Free Trade* by Willard Phillips. [Little
and Brown] Boston. 1850. [The quotation comes from pp. 69–70, where the quotation
about the 'twist or gimp' is attributed to *Edinburgh Review* (Jan 1849) p. 81. Compare
J. S. Mill, *Principles of Political Economy*, p. 125.]

The importance of this last consideration, is, no doubt everywhere, diminishing. But it still remains true that it is extremely difficult to induce a steady first-rate workman to migrate by the promise of increasing his pay. Such a man's ambition is likely to be firm rather than daring: he is likely to enjoy the esteem of his neighbours and the affection of his relations; the increase in his pecuniary income which he may obtain in a foreign country must be very large indeed in order that the uncertain prospect of it may outweigh the certain possession at home of all those comforts for which the associations of his early life have led him to hope.

Conversations with workmen as well as with employers, chiefly in America, have convinced me that the attractions of a foreign country exert in general but slight influence on a workman who is not repelled from his own either by some accidental grievance, or by the consequences of some lack on his own part of social or industrial virtues. There are many minor difficulties in the way of those who pioneer in a country the course of an industry that may be ultimately beneficial to her. Some discussion of these may conveniently be included in the following chapter.[19] But one more remark of general application may be made with regard to the indirect economic effects which foreign trade may exert in causing one class of industries to prevail in a country rather than another.

[§ 17] Generally speaking, those industries which make an extensive use of fixed capital confer great benefits on all classes of the community, in so far as they are consumers, by cheapening the wares which they affect. And thus the working classes are ultimately benefited by almost every case in which 'circulating capital is converted into fixed'. But such a conversion does exercise injurious effects on the working classes at the time at which it is made. And of two modes of conducting an industry which are equally advantageous to the capitalist and to the consumer, that one which absorbs the least amount of fixed capital is more beneficial to the workman than the other. Now if a country employs ships to export cloth and bring back linen, the capital locked up in these ships is to be regarded as part of the fixed capital by means of which she obtains her

[19] [This again appears to refer to the unfinished Part I, Ch. VII.]

supplies of linen. Moreover the longer the period which is required for the making of any ware, the more injuriously does its production affect the supplies of the capital which is competing for labourers in the labour market. If then we are comparing the plans of making linen at home and of importing it in exchange for cloth, we must consider that the former plan is likely to be the shorter: since on the latter plan the capital is locked up and devoted to the obtaining of linen during the whole time which is required for the making of cloth, for the exporting it and for the importing of linen in return. In cases in which the capital locked up in ships is great in comparison with the value of the wares which they carry: and in cases in which foreign trade involves the locking up of capital in the wares themselves for long periods during their transport from one market to another: in these cases the benefits which foreign trade confers on the country may from the point of view of the working classes be subject to deductions, which however trifling they may be in practice, ought not to be ignored in theory.

There is thus some element of truth in Adam Smith's celebrated doctrine that 'the capital ... employed in the home trade of any country will generally give encouragement ... to a greater quantity of productive labour in that country' and increase the value of its annual produce more than an equal capital employed in the foreign trade of consumption'.[20] If this be taken to imply that foreign trade is injurious .to the growth of the wealth of the country it may be replied that 'the fact of capital being employed in the carrying trade' shows that the nett profits it yields are quite as great as any that could be obtained by employing it in agriculture or the home trade; and [that] ... the amount of such nett profits' is the measure of the influence exerted on the wealth of the country. The latter half of Adam Smith's doctrine, that relating to the annual produce of the country, is vague: some of the arguments which he gives in support of his doctrine are certainly fallacious. Moreover Adam Smith stated his doctrine without the conditions which are necessary to make it true and without an

---

[20] [*Wealth of Nations*, Book II, Ch. V (p. 166), which is also the source of the next quotation, which, however, comes from one of McCulloch's critical footnotes. See also Book IV, Ch. II (p. 199). (For Modern Library Edition, see pp. 352, 421.)]

adequate discussion of the indirect compensating advantages of foreign trade. Still there are elements, or germs of truth in this doctrine which Ricardo has overlooked in his famous and crushing attack on what Adam Smith has said about the employment of capital in foreign trade.[21] Ricardo's oversight is to be excused under the circumstances. But it is a matter of wonder that his followers, (including even Mill who was in general careful in such matters) have failed to observe the connection between the doctrine I have quoted from Adam Smith and Ricardo's own celebrated doctrine that 'an increase of the net produce of a country is compatible with a diminution of the gross produce, and that the motives for employing machinery are always sufficient to ensure its employment, if it will increase the net produce, although it may, and frequently must, diminish both the quantity of the gross produce and its value', and 'That the opinion entertained by the labouring class, that the employment of machinery is frequently' (or rather, as Mill has since shown, under circumstances of most rare occurrence) 'detrimental to their interests, is not founded on prejudice and error, but is conformable to the correct principles of political economy'.[22]

[§ 18]   The fear of the interruption of her foreign trade in time of war has controlled to some extent the willingness of each country to depend on foreign supplies of any ware, in particular of those which are in most urgent demand in time of war. Questions relating to this class of considerations cannot be treated generally: but must be discussed in detail with reference to the particular circumstances of each case. Of such discussions [history] has an abundant if not a superabundant supply. They cannot be thorough, unless they contain a thorough inquiry as to the extent to which the old melancholy maxim 'Si vis pacem para bellum' is valid in the case at issue. Such inquiries would be out of place here. And we may leave the subject with the remark that the glare which surrounds the events of war removes all danger that considerations arising from a country's military necessities may be overlooked or their importance underrated.

[21] [This probably refers to D. Ricardo, *Principles of Political Economy and Taxation*, Ch. XXVI, 'On Gross and Net Revenue'.]

[22] [Ibid., Ch. XXXI, p. 392.]

III.3 'Taxes on Foreign Trade for the Purposes of Revenue'

III.3.1 *Introduction*

The sixth chapter of Part One, which is reproduced in the present Section, was intended to deal with the revenue aspects of tariffs, leaving their protective aspects to be considered in the seventh and final chapter (Section III.4, below). The argument of this sixth chapter, like that of the two preceding it, follows a path so tortuous that its destination is not readily discernible, and Marshall's signposts are again inadequate. He passes through the following broad areas:

  (i) Introduction (§ 1).
 (ii) Effects on the rate of international exchange due to taxing foreign trade (§§ 2, 3).
(iii) Effects on consumers due to taxes on individual commodities (§§ 4–7).
 (iv) Effects due to the process of collection of taxes (§ 8).
  (v) General aspects of taxation policy (§§ 9–11).
 (vi) Bounties (§ 12).

The discussion under (ii) takes up points already considered in the earlier Essay on International Trade (Item II.8.1, above), and demonstrates once more that most of the reservations expressed by Marshall in later years about arguments for 'taxing the foreigner' were already present in his early work.[1] Some of the points raised in this connection are also taken up and refined in the final chapter of the *Pure Theory of Foreign Trade* (Section III.5, below).

The discussion under (iii) is a general treatment of indirect taxation. It introduces consumer's rent, and gives a verbal presentation of arguments that are rendered in more detail in the second chapter of the *Pure Theory of Domestic Values* (Section III.6, below). But it goes beyond this in hinting Marshall's theorem on direct versus indirect taxation, a formal version of which appears in the manuscript reproduced as Item IV.4.2, below. This manuscript was evidently drawn upon in preparing both the present chapter, and the *Pure Theory of Domestic Values.*

---

[1] See Vol 1, pp. 261, 277–8, above.

The brief discussion under (iii) is primarily a quotation from Cliffe Leslie, but the discussion under (iv) is the fullest available general statement of Marshall's early views on taxation.[2] Finally, the discussion under (v) looks forward to the argument in the *Pure Theory of Domestic Values* for subsidising industries operating under increasing returns.

A more detailed impression of the overall argument may be gleaned from the following table.

Analytical Table of Contents to Part I, Ch. VI: 'Taxes on Foreign Trade for the Purposes of Revenue'

§ 1   Modern protective duties are also important for the revenue they yield. The immediate and direct economic effects of taxes are to be considered in this chapter: the more remote and indirect effects of protection are considered in the next chapter. There are three immediate and direct effects:
(i) on the rate of exchange; (ii) on consumption; (iii) effects due to the mode of collection.
§ 2   Extent to which a country can impose part of the burden of an import tax on foreigners: extent likely to be limited.
§ 3   A tax on a particular export may give considerable gain: cases of English coal and American cotton: hypothetical case of corn. Development of rival sources of supply reduces the effectiveness of this. Domestic producers and politicians prefer import to export duties, and remainder of chapter concerned with the former.
§ 4   Adam Smith's fourth maxim on taxation: commodity taxes cause a loss to those who pay high prices, but an additional loss to those who no longer purchase the commodity. Fallacy of argument that state should not interfere with a man's spending of his income.
§ 5   The loss to consumers resulting from taxes which discriminate according to the mode or location of the production of a commodity.

[2] This discussion should be compared with the outline of the 1880 lectures on taxation (Section V.4, below). There was no decisive change in the transition to Marshall's later views on taxation, for which see *Official Papers*, pp. 327–420, and his 'National Taxation after the War', pp. 313–45 of W. H. Dawson (editor), *After War Problems* (George Allen and Unwin, London, 1917).

§6   A second type of loss: destruction of consumer rent. Generally should not tax commodities whose consumption falls off rapidly as price increases.

§7   The argument against discriminating taxes has chief application to import duties. The argument about consumer rent applies equally to Customs and Excise duties. England has abandoned discriminating duties: desirability of reducing duties on imported luxuries such as tea and coffee.

§8   The work of Customs and Excise officers necessarily hampers production and trade.

§9   The most appropriate tax system for a country not attempting to develop native industries would be like England's, but should have an increased reliance on income tax.

§10   A single tax cannot be condemned as inequitable, only a tax system. Difficulty of arranging customs duties so as to tax the rich more heavily. Disadvantages of *ad valorem* duties. Graduated specific duties.

§11   The need to take some account of effects on foreign countries.

§12   Bounties on exportation and production. Special case to be discussed in Part II.

III.3.2   *Text of Part I, Chapter VI:*
'*Taxes on Foreign Trade for the Purposes of Revenue*'

§1   Systems of finance which claim to be Protective of native Industries have often included taxes which practically prohibit the importation of certain wares. But such taxes are becoming rarer. The greater part of the Protective duties that are now levied by civilised nations are defended on the ground that they not only Protect the industries of the country in which they are levied, but also afford considerable revenue to the state. It is true that the most strenuous advocates of Protective taxation care but little for the immediate gain which it thus affords in comparison with the ulterior social and economic changes which they expect their policy to work in the country. But it is advisable before discussing the remote and indirect effects of this policy, to examine the immediate and direct economic effects of taxes upon the imports and exports of a country.

Facsimile of first page of manuscript of Part I Chap VI

These may [be] classified as Firstly the effects which are dependent on alterations in the rates of interchange with foreign countries; Secondly, the effects which are dependent on the particular nature of the commodity taxed: these are in general similar in character to those which would result from corresponding excise duties imposed on similar wares produced at home. Thirdly, the effects which are connected with

the special expenses and economic inconveniences inseparable
from the maintenance of the system of inspection of imports
and exports by customs officers. We may consider these in
order.

§ 2   It has already been shown[1] that when the price of a
commodity in a country is raised in consequence of her
imposing a tax on its importation her demand for that
commodity will diminish, and consequently the rate of
interchange will be altered in her favour excepting under
certain exceptional conditions. It will be shown hereafter[2]
that it is just possible that a diminution in her demand for
this ware may cause a diminution in the economy with which
it is produced, so that the country which exports it may not
be willing to supply it on a small scale at the old rate of interchange. In this case the country which imposes the tax may
have either to forgo the importation of the ware altogether,
or to pay for a smaller portion of it at a higher rate than before.
So that in this case the whole burden, and more than the
whole burden of the tax may fall upon her. But as already
observed,[3] this case is of so little practical importance directly,
and the treatment of it is so difficult that it may properly be
left to be dealt with by the apparatus of diagrams which will
be supplied in the second Part.

Generally then a country will succeed in throwing upon
foreigners a portion of the burden of the taxes which she
imposes upon her imports. But in almost every instance this
portion will be a very small one. The tax, it was argued,
would diminish the demand which she has for foreign wares,
would thus diminish the supply of her wares in foreign markets,
would therefore raise the price of these wares in foreign
markets; and would alter the rate of interchange in her favour.
The magnitude of this alteration depends upon the extent to
which a diminution in the supply of her wares in foreign
markets raises their price there: and we shall find on investigation that the rise in price that can thus be produced will in
general be very small. For although among the wares which a

---

[1] Part I, Ch. I § . [This refers to the missing first chapter.]

[2] Part II, Ch. II § . [This refers to Ch. II of the *Pure Theory of Foreign Trade*. See
Section III.5, below.]

[3] Ch. I § . [This refers to the missing first chapter of Part I.]

country exports there may be some which are in urgent demand abroad so that their price in foreign markets would rise much if the supply of them were diminished; yet she will derive no benefit from the urgency of this demand unless all the wares which she exports are in like demand. Now it must almost always happen that some of her wares are closely pressed by the competition of others and are only just able to retain their position in some markets. She will not be able to raise the price of these wares by diminishing the supply of them. Under these circumstances the effect of a diminution of her demand for foreign wares will be not to alter the rate of interchange to any considerable extent to her advantage: but to cause foreign countries to abstain in large part from purchasing from her those wares in the production of which she has no sort of monopoly. It may indeed happen that she has some sort of monopoly of all the wares which she is in the habit of exporting to some one other country; and it may seem that by taxing her imports from that country she may effect a considerable alteration to her own advantage in the rate of interchange with that country. But we have seen in Chapter II, how the machinery of Bills of Exchange unites together all the foreign consumers of a country's wares. The country attacked would in this case diminish her supply of the ware which the first country had taxed, and would obtain the means of purchasing the required amount of the wares of that country, by buying up bills on that country in other markets.

§ 3   It is scarcely possible then that a country can throw upon others a large portion of the burden of a tax which she imposes on her imports. But if she has and can retain a practical monopoly of the production of any ware which she exports, she may derive great gain at the expense of her neighbours by imposing a tax on the exportation of that ware.

There is little doubt but that England for instance could throw upon her neighbours some of the burden of an export duty on coal. Strong through not conclusive evidence that she could is furnished by the following facts. In the year 1871 Germany imported from England nearly 2,400,000 tons of coal; this amount fell to about 2,100,000 in 1872 and to less than 1,700,000 in 1873. Exclusive of what she paid for their being carried to Germany she gave us in return for them command over the produce of her own or other industries to the amount of only just over £1,000,000 in 1871, but her demand for coal being urgent and her domestic supplies being inadequate to her wants, she gave us more than £1,500,000 in 1872 and £1,700,000 in 1873. It may be granted that £1 represented command over somewhat less German produce in 1873 than in 1871: but the allowance to be made on this score is not very great; and it is certain that Germany gave us more of her produce in 1873 in return for 1,700,000 tons of coal than she did in 1871 in return for 2,400,000 tons.[4]

The American supply of cotton is another partial monopoly. America sold to foreign countries in the five years 1862–6 together about nine hundred million pounds of cotton for more than two hundred million (gold) dollars and in the year 1871 she sold for less than this amount nearly fifteen hundred million pounds. Again there are familiar stories of the monopoly of the spice producing islands. It is said that they used to burn a portion of their crop, when it was very heavy: since they obtained a greater total sum by the sale of a small crop than by the sale of a large one.

But the strongest case of all is that which we should obtain if we supposed the supplies of the necessaries of life which one country obtained to be limited to those which were exported to her from some one other country. For according to the celebrated calculations of Gregory King[5] a defect in the harvest may raise the price of corn in the following proportions: –

Defect		Above the common rate
1 tenth		3 tenths
2 tenths		8 tenths
3 tenths	raises the price	16 tenths
4 tenths		28 tenths
5 tenths		45 tenths

[4] [See Item II.8.1 above for a preliminary statement along these lines.]

[5] [This law is most probably attributable to Davenant rather than King. See W. S. Jevons, *Theory of Political Economy* (pp. 148–50 of first edition; pp. 154–6 of second edition) and G. H. Evans Jr, 'The Law of Demand – the Roles of Gregory King and Charles Davenant', *Quarterly Journal of Economics*, Vol 81 (Aug 1967) pp 483–92.]

Thus if the supply of corn were reduced by one half, the price would rise to more than five times the common rate. So that the country which supplied the other with corn might by halving the supply increase nearly three-fold the total amount of the wares of the other country which she obtained in exchange for it.

It is true as was hinted above[6] that the immediate practical importance of such facts as these is not so great as it at first sight appears. It is every day becoming more difficult for a country to obtain for a long period of time together high prices for her exports, by limiting their quantity. For instance when in 1862 the supply of American cotton fell off, there set in a rise in the quantity, and to some extent in the quality, of cotton grown in other countries. In so much that the low price at which American producers had to dispose of their cotton in England in 1871 was partly due to the fact that India and Egypt together were sending here more than half as much cotton as America was sending. The practical monopoly of raw cotton which America once had has been broken at all events as regards the coarser staples, and probably no vestige of it would long remain if she artificially limited her supply in order to sustain cotton at a high price. Thus the need which Europe has for American cotton is not therefore such as to enable America to shift off from her own shoulders any considerable portion of the taxes which she imposes upon her imports. For even if there were not many other portions of her produce which are already closely run by foreign rivals in European markets, she could [not][7] dispose of her coarser staples of cotton without overcoming a powerful competition. Neither could she throw upon other countries the main portion of the burden of any tax which she might impose on the exportation of the coarser staples of cotton. She might indeed for a time succeed in obtaining for herself the full amount of any tax she might impose on the exportation of the finest staples. But the high price of these staples would then offer a large premium to attempts to improve the staples of other

[6] Part I, Ch. I § 6. [This refers to the missing first chapter.]

[7] [The manuscript reads 'only'. Also, the previous sentence ends with 'imports of cotton'. The changes made seem to be required by the logic of the argument, although the variant 'exports of cotton' is probably to be preferred.]

countries. She would indeed be affording an artificial Protection to the industries of her rivals.

In fact the extension of means of communication is rendering it every day more easy for enterprise to obtain access in various quarters of the globe to soil from which rivals can be raised to almost all the old national monopolies. And though there may be movements in the opposite direction, the general tendency of progress is to render the cases more rare and less important in which any one of the exports of a country is of such a nature that a diminution of it would cause for any considerable period an increased amount of the produce of other countries to be obtained by the proceeds of the sale of it. The case of English coal is perhaps an exception. Coal cannot profitably be carried for very great distances. And if nature has not bestowed upon a country seams of good coal, no amount of perserverance will enable her to produce it. Moreover England in selling her coal to foreign nations, is in some measure selling to strangers the birthright of her children that are to come. There is therefore a strong case for the imposition of a duty on the exportation of coal from England. But such a measure would appear to many to be niggardly and illiberal.

A duty on the importation of any particular ware into a country is likely to be supported in the interests of those who produce similar wares in the country. But a proposal to impose a duty on the exportation of any particular ware is likely to have arrayed against it the opposition of all those who are [engaged] directly or indirectly in producing that ware. This opposition may in many cases become a powerful political force in the country. For this reason as well as because such a duty may act as an artificial Protection to rival industries in other countries, finance ministers are far more inclined to impose taxes on imports than on exports, even when they believe that their country has to some extent a monopoly of some of the wares which she exports. The theory of the incidence of taxes on exports has therefore but little direct practical interest. It has indirectly considerable practical interests; but inquiries with regard to this are reserved for the second Part; where will be supplied a fuller investigation of the theory than can be conveniently given without the aid of diagrams. With this we may dismiss for the present the subject of taxes on exports.

The rest of the chapter will be occupied with an inquiry into the effects of taxes on imports, starting from the position at which we have arrived. This is that a tax on any of the imports of a country will not in general effect a considerable alteration in the rate of interchange between her and other countries; but that whatever change is effected will be in her favour, in every case with which we need practically concern ourselves. So that the theory of foreign trade does not establish any *prima facie* objection to the imposition of a customs tax if the commodity taxed is one on which, if it were produced at home, it would be advisable to impose an Excise tax.

§ 4　The greater part of the objections to which taxes on particular commodities are liable are stated or hinted at in the fourth of Adam Smith's principles of taxation. This pregnant maxim runs as follows : –

'4. Every tax ought to be so contrived as both to take out and to keep out of the pockets of the people as little as possible, over and above what it brings into the public treasury of the state. A tax may either take out or keep out of the pockets of the people a great deal more than it brings into the public treasury, in the four following ways :– First, the levying of it may require a great number of officers, whose salaries may eat up the greater part of the produce of the tax, and whose perquisites may impose another additional tax upon the people.' Secondly it may divert a portion of the labour and capital of the community from a more to a less productive employment. 'Thirdly,... An injudicious tax offers a great temptation to smuggling.... Fourthly, by subjecting the people to the frequent visits and the odious examination of the tax-gatherers, it may expose them to much unnecessary trouble, vexation and oppression': to which Mill adds 'that the restrictive regulations to which trades and manufactures are often subjected to prevent evasion of a tax, are not only in themselves troublesome and expensive, but often oppose insuperable obstacles to making improvements in the processes.'[8]

It is with the second of these objections that we are at present chiefly concerned. Taxes levied on income, to whatever

[8] [See Adam Smith, *Wealth of Nations*, Book V, Ch. II, Part II (p. 372; Modern Library Edition, pp. 778–9); J. S. Mill, *Principles of Political Economy*, Book V, Ch. II, § 2 (p. 806).]

practical objections they may be liable have this advantage that the loss which they inflict on the community is limited to the amount of money which the tax-gatherer receives.[9] But the imposition of a tax on any particular commodity inflicts a loss not only on those who consume the commodity and pay the tax; but upon others also. For it causes detriment to those who in order to avoid paying the high price at which the taxed commodity is sold dispense with its use, consuming perhaps some substitute for it which is inferior in quality or less suited to their tastes or which is more expensive than the original commodity would have been if it had not been taxed.

Objections to taxes on particular commodities are often expressed by saying that the state has no right to interfere with the method in which a man spends his income: that it has no right to direct him to purchase one commodity rather than another. This is one of those metaphysical doctrines which trained thinkers shun, but which are frequently heard from others. For those who are most scornfully averse to the labour of philosophical analysis are those who are most completely enthralled by traditional commonplaces, in which are embedded dogmas concerning abstract rights, the distorted remains of obsolete metaphysical systems. Contentions of this fashion are much used by some of the more uneducated advocates of Free Trade, but the patient temper of modern science is averse to such crude dicta. It must be assumed as a basis of discussion that the State has a right to derive a revenue from taxation; that is to take away from the people some portion of their wealth. Whatever diminishes the wealth of the people diminishes their means, and therefore practically their liberty of gratifying their desires. A tax then is not condemned by the statement that it infringes the liberty of the consumer to satisfy his wants: for every tax does this.

A tax on a commodity is to be judged by weighing in the balance its advantages against its disadvantages. In calculating its advantages account must be taken of the revenue which it brings to the state and any beneficial influences which it may exert on the general social and economic condition of the

---

[9] [See Item IV.4.2, below, for Marshall's proof of this theorem on direct versus indirect taxation.]

people. In calculating its disadvantages account must be taken of the direct loss that it inflicts on those who continue to consume the commodity, the indirect loss that it inflicts on those who in consequence of the tax cease to consume the commodity, and lastly any injurious influences which it may exert on the general social and economic condition of the people. In the following chapter we are to discuss the ultimate social and economic tendencies of various schemes of taxation. Our immediate concern here is with the injury which a tax on a commodity inflicts on those whom it deters from consuming the commodity.

We have then to examine firstly what the nature of this indirect loss is, and secondly what are the conditions under which the taxation of any particular commodity involves this loss to an inordinately large extent. A full analysis of these conditions must be deferred to the second Part of the treatise; since it cannot conveniently be conducted without the aid of diagrams. But it will be possible here to indicate in outline the general nature of these conditions. I will first deal with a portion of the question which British economists have examined thoroughly. But I shall discuss it at some length because some intelligent people in England and many in other countries fail to recognise the exact bearing and the full force of the arguments in question.

§ [5]   Suppose that the price at which sugar of a certain quality made from sugar canes could be imported into England is 3d a pound. Suppose that the price at which the sugar equally fine and equally sweet could be produced in England from beet-roots is 5d a pound. Suppose then that a tax of 3d a pound is imposed on the importation of cane sugar; but that no tax is imposed upon beet sugar: and that as a consequence the consumption of beet-sugar is substituted for that of cane sugar. In this case so long as the state of affairs remained unchanged the government would derive no revenue from the tax but the consumer of sugar would pay twopence a pound more for each pound of sugar. He would in fact pay even more, because the traders who advanced the tax would require to be repaid by the consumer not only the amount of the tax but also profit on the advances they had made. We may however for the sake of simplicity neglect this additional charge in the present argument.

Something of this kind was done in France by the Edict of Napoleon followed up by a very high duty levied on imported sugar by Louis XVIII. The result has been to naturalise beet sugar in France, and to enable it to be produced at a much cheaper rate than when the tax was originally imposed. The advocates of Protection continually refer to this fact as affording a strong argument for their policy. One of them, Mr Greeley, has the candour to add without contradiction the calculation made in the *Free-Trader* that 'the French people have paid so much in the extra cost of their sugar that the sum total which they have *lost* would form a fund, the annual interest of which would supply them *gratis* with all the sugar they will consume to the end of time!'[10]

Next suppose that the tax on cane sugar was 2d per pound: and that as a consequence there were consumed twenty million pounds of beet sugar at 5d a pound and twenty million pounds of cane sugar at 5d a pound. The total loss to the consumer would be as great as before but the government would receive 2d a pound for one half of the total sugar consumed. If however it had imposed a tax of a penny a pound perhaps fifty million pounds of cane sugar would have been consumed at four pence a pound. By substituting a tax of a penny a pound for a tax of two pence a pound Government would thus increase its own revenue at the same time that it lowered the price which the consumer had to pay for sugar. Under these circumstances a tax of two pence a pound on cane sugar would be an eminently bad tax, at all events in its immediate effects. Such a tax could be excused only by a confident and well grounded expectation that it would cause a vast and rapid improvement in the production of beet sugar. It is important then to insist on the economic principle: –

A tax on a commodity is *prima facie* to be condemned if it causes the people largely to consume as a substitute some other

[10] [Horace Greeley, *Essays Designed to Elucidate the Science of Political Economy* (Fields, Osgood; Boston, 1870) pp. 210–11. Marshall's copy, preserved in the Marshall Library, has the marginal comment 'Greeley never answers this.' Greeley cites the *Free Trader* of July, 1868. Marshall's qualification in the text as to the interest payable on tax advances should come after this point, since the tax of 3d yields no revenue.]

commodity which is more expensive than the first would have been if the tax had not been imposed upon it. For such a tax takes from the pockets of the people much more than it brings into the public treasury.

In this principle is contained a *prima facie* condemnation of taxes on the importation of any commodity, such as wool or corn, the domestic supplies of which will be increased if the price to be obtained for them be raised. The tax might indeed cause the foreign producer who had already made his arrangements for supplying the commodity to be content with a lower price for a time. But he would soon alter his arrangements. So that before long the effect of the tax would be to raise the price of the commodity to the consumer by, at all events, nearly the full amount of the tax. But the amount which the Government would receive would be only the tax levied on that small amount of the commodity which continued to be imported. It is true that a large portion of this increased price of the domestic supplies would not represent a dead loss to the nation: for most of it would finally accrue to the landlords in the form of an increase of rent. But the additional supplies which were raised only in consequence of the rise in the price for which they could be sold, would in general only just repay the expenses of producing them and would afford no surplus profit to the farmer which could be claimed by the landlord as rent. The excess of the price which the consumers paid for this portion of the produce over that which they would have paid if no tax had been levied is a dead loss to them, and without corresponding gain to any one else. It may be repeated that the particular objection here urged against the tax is founded not on the fact that it is a tax on a commodity but on the fact that it is levied on one method of obtaining the commodity. The grounds of the objection would be removed if the domestic supplies of the commodity were subject to an excise duty equivalent to the customs duty on the imported supplies. Similarly there is on this particular ground no objection to be raised against a tax on the importation into England of such a commodity as tea. For a high price of tea would not cause large supplies of it to be produced at great expense at home. The tax would not take from the pockets of the consumers of tea anything in addition to the total amount paid to the tax-gatherers with the addition of course of the profits of intermediate dealers in tea.

All taxes which discriminate as to the mode in which a commodity has been produced, and are levied upon the community if it has been produced by one method, but not if it has been produced by others, are called 'discriminating duties'. It is obvious that taxes on the imported supplies of any commodity which are not balanced by equivalent taxes on the domestic supplies of it are to be included among discriminating duties. And the same applies to taxes upon foreign supplies of a commodity generally, when the supplies of it from some colony or some other favoured country are specially exempted from the operation of the tax. Taxes of the latter of these two classes played a very important role in the political and industrial history of the seventeenth and eighteenth centuries and of the earlier part of the nineteenth. Adam Smith's attacks on them may yet be read with interest but they have not an important bearing on the theory of foreign trade under its present conditions. The arguments against discriminating duties that have just been advanced have been duly discussed by British economists.

I proceed to say something of another injury which may be inflicted on the community by discriminating taxes as well as by some other taxes. It is closely allied to that which has just been discussed. But there is no explicit reference to it in the fundamental canon that a tax 'ought to take out of the pockets of the people as little as possible, over and above what it brings into the public treasury of the state':[11] and the matter has not hitherto been adequately investigated.

§ [6] Let us revert to the example of [the] last section. If the State imposed a tax of a penny a pound on cane sugar the tax-gatherer would receive the equivalent of all the additional expense to which the purchasers of sugar were put in consequence of the tax, with the exception of the profits which were required to remunerate the intermediate traders for advancing the money with which the tax was paid. But the resulting rise in the price of sugar would deter many persons from

---

[11] [This repeats the opening sentence of Adam Smith's fourth maxim, quoted earlier.]

purchasing their wonted supplies of it. Each of these persons would suffer an injury from the tax, but the public treasury would not derive any benefit corresponding to the loss of theirs. We suppose the tax to raise the price of sugar from threepence to fourpence a pound. Take then the case of a person who in consequence of the tax will be induced to curtail his consumption of sugar from 10 pounds to 8 pounds a year; but who would not have reduced his consumption if the price had only risen to three pence three farthings. That is to say the value in use of the tenth pound of sugar to him, the satisfaction that he derives from it, is worth considerably more than three pence to him, but somewhat less than four pence. The imposition of the tax therefore will take away from him the power of purchasing for three pence a commodity which would afford him a satisfaction nearly equal to that which he can obtain by spending four pence in other ways. It will inflict upon him a portion of the injury which he would have suffered from a total prohibition to purchase sugar. He derives a greater satisfaction from the sugar which he purchases than he would have done from any other commodities which he could have purchased with the same money. This excess or surplus satisfaction, of which the tax would take away a portion, will be called in the second Part of the treatise the 'Consumers' Rent' derived from sugar. The reader will then be introduced to means whereby, theoretically at least, an accurate measure of Consumers' Rent may be obtained and general principles will be laid down by which it may be decided whether a tax involves so large a destruction of Consumers' Rent that it is on this ground to be condemned. Such questions cannot be properly handled without the aid of diagrams. But the illustration that has been already given conducts us to the following general result, which may suffice for our present purposes.

The rise in price of a commodity consequent on the imposition of a tax on it must cause a diminution in its consumption. This diminution implies that consumers have been deprived of the opportunity of expending some of their money on the purchase of a commodity which could have afforded them a surplus of satisfaction and enjoyment over that which they can obtain by expending their money in other ways.

The destruction of this surplus satisfaction is a loss to the nation. It is not accompanied by any corresponding gain to the Treasury for the receipts of the Treasury fall off in just the same proportion as the consumption of the commodity falls off. The greater this diminution of consumption is the greater generally will this dead loss be. Hence we obtain an economic principle which may supplement that laid down in the preceding section: viz.:–

Generally speaking, a tax on a commodity is to be condemned as causing to the people a loss of satisfaction and enjoyment much greater than the equivalent of the revenue which it brings into the Treasury, if the imposition of the tax causes a great diminution in the consumption of that commodity.

Of course it may be advisable on special grounds to put hindrances in the way of the consumption of some particular commodities. For instance it may be held that the social and the indirect economic effects of a large consumption of ardent spirits are so injurious as to justify heavy taxes on them independently of any consideration of the revenue which such taxes afford to the State. It may be held that the interest which the State has in checking such consumption outweighs the immediate enjoyment which is forgone by those whom the tax induces to curtail their consumption. And there is much to be said in favour of the doctrine that even if it were possible to raise the whole of the required revenue by an income-tax equitably levied on all classes, the State would yet be right in imposing taxes on spirituous liquors. Such considerations as this enter into no opposition with the main argument of the text: but account must be taken of them before the conclusions arising from this argument can be properly applied in the treatment of practical questions.

§ [7]   The two economic principles that are enunciated in the two preceding sections apply equally to Excise and Customs duties. But there are at present few taxes which discriminate in favour of one group of domestic producers against others: while there are in many countries heavy taxes which discriminate in favour of domestic producers against foreign. So that the chief practical importance of the first of the two principles is in connection with its application to foreign trade. The second economic principle has perhaps as important application in connection with Excise as in connection with Customs. But the injurious effects of an injudicious Excise duty are in general more obvious; and more likely to have public attention directed to them by the energy of powerful groups of domestic producers than are those of an injudicious Customs duty. For this reason it is specially necessary to insist on a careful application of the second principle [to] Customs duties.

England has abandoned the policy of discriminating duties. The nearest approach to such duties in her system of taxation are those which are designed to discourage the consumption of alcohol when it is in the form of ardent spirits, more than when it is in the form of beer or wine. But the tax on imported spirits is balanced by a nearly equal tax on British spirits. The tax on imported sugar, when it existed was balanced by an almost equal tax on home produced sugar. And the British tariff contains no other taxes of any importance save those which are levied on commodities that England cannot produce and which therefore are not discriminating duties. It is sometimes said that England has completely adopted the policy of Free Trade. This is strictly true only with a somewhat forced interpretation of the phrase Free Trade. What is true is that she imposes no duties which discriminate against foreign producers, and that she imposes no taxes on imported commodities which she would not be likely to impose on these commodities if they were produced at home.

The taxes on tea, coffee and tobacco are defended as taxes on luxuries. It is argued that taxes on necessaries and on the raw material and implements of manufacture are on various grounds specially injurious. Consequently, that the needs of the State must be supplied by direct taxation so far as this can be levied equitably, and by such taxes upon luxuries as can be most easily collected. It must however be recollected that a luxury is generally speaking a commodity the consumption of which would be much diminished by an increase in its price: and that therefore a tax on a luxury is generally obnoxious to the second of the principles above laid down. Partly for this reason, partly on social grounds, it is much to be desired that the taxes on tea and coffee, which have recently been much reduced should be altogether removed.

§ [8]   The great advantage that the Excise officer has over the Customs officer in the collection of taxes consists in his being able to watch the process of production of the commodities which he intends to tax. So that although a commodity when it has once been produced in the country may easily elude his vigilance, he is in general able to discover how much is being produced by inspecting the places at which the production is carried on. But in order to obtain this advantage he is in some cases compelled to prohibit the use of processes which are of such a nature that he could not easily gauge the amount of the commodity which was being produced by them. The Customs officer is not compelled thus to interfere with freedom of action of producers. But on the other hand the Customs officer is compelled to make regulations which exert injurious restraints on the course of commerce. 'An inevitable consequence of customs duties', says Mr Cliffe Leslie[12]

> is to involve the State in a series of dilemmas, with only a choice of great evils. It must either grant unrestricted liberty of importation and exportation to every spot on the coast and along the rivers of the Kingdom, thereby entailing an enormous army of tax collectors and intolerable cost of collection, or it must limit direct foreign trade to selected places, thereby disturbing the natural order of things, and obstructing the development of numerous localities. It must either exact immediate payment of the duties on importation, thereby wasting capital, harassing merchants, and mulcting consumers; or it must establish

---

[12] Cobden Club Essays 1871–2 pp. 213–14. [T. E. Cliffe Leslie, 'Financial Reform', pp. 189–263 of *Cobden Club Essays, Second Series 1871–72* (second edition; Cassell, Petter and Galpin; London, Paris, New York; 1872). The quotation comes from p. 217 of the second edition. Marshall did not complete the quotation, leaving a lengthy blank space after the words 'is to involve' and giving the reference as pp. 213–14 (of the first edition). He can hardly have planned to include less than is given here, but might have projected a lengthier continuation. Marshall had also planned at one stage to include some figures on the costs and receipts of the Customs, Inland Revenue, and Excise taxes.]

the system of bonding, and encounter a fresh dilemma between covering the Kingdom with warehouses and customs officials, or confining the advantage of bonding unfairly to particular places.

§ [9]   That portion of the revenue of the State which has to be levied by taxes on commodities should then be raised as it is in England by heavy taxes on a few commodities which are consumed on a large scale by all classes of the community. If all attempts to develop native industries by artificial Protection be for the present put aside, it is certain that [the arguments against] every customs duty on a commodity which cannot be produced in the country, are, so far as we have yet seen, not greater, but are not in general much less, than would lie against an Excise duty on the same commodity if it were one of the natural products of the country. It happens that bulky commodities, i.e., those whose value is small in proportion to their bulk are as a rule commodities which for various social and economic reasons it is inexpedient to tax heavily. But a country which has a large land frontier cannot profitably impose heavy duties on articles of small bulk since such taxes would be evaded by smuggling, and she should therefore raise as small a portion of her revenue as possible by customs duties. The expedient of making the sale of tobacco a government monopoly has been adopted apparently with success by some countries.

Since great evils are inseparable from all taxes on particular commodities, every country should strive to prepare herself for a large increase of direct taxation levied equitably on the incomes of all classes. When the working classes are properly educated they will doubtless acquiesce in the adoption of this plan, since by its economy it would greatly diminish the total burden that they bear. But before taxes can be equitably levied on the incomes of the trading classes it will be necessary to effect a change in the opinions and sentiments that are current with regard to the extent of the right that a man has to secrecy with regard to his business affairs. It might be an injury to an individual trader to compel him under present circumstances to publish the exact condition of his finances. But if all men were compelled to do this, there would be inaugurated an era of solid credit and sound business in which economic progress could be at once more rapid and far more sure than it is at present. When this is effected the whole revenue of the country could easily be collected by direct taxes on income. For various reasons it might still appear advisable to retain taxes levied for the purposes of the central or of local government on real property, on alcoholic liquors, and perhaps on tobacco. There would however be a need for a careful discussion of the question whether it would not be better to relieve Customs and excise officers altogether from measuring the amount of alcoholic liquors and of tobacco which were imported or produced on private account; and to confine them to the easier task of totally preventing such importation or production. This question is becoming prominent in connection with the proposal to cause alcoholic [liquors] to be sold only under the control of local Government by officials who are so paid as to have nothing to gain from pushing their unhealthy consumption.

§ [10]   There remain to be considered two classes of objections that may be brought against a tax. It is customary to have a tax condemned on the ground that it is imposed or collected in an uncertain or arbitrary manner, and on the ground that its incidence is unequal or unjust.

With regard to the latter of these objections it must be remarked *in limine* that a single tax cannot be finally condemned on the charge that it presses with unequal weight on different classes of society: for in the system of taxation of which it is a portion there may be other taxes which press heavily where it presses lightly and vice versa. It is therefore impossible to decide whether the inequalities which exist in a system of customs duties constitute a serious evil without inquiring to what extent it is practicable to correct these inequalities by proper adjustments of the direct and indirect taxes which are included under the head of inland revenue. It must be conceded that any system of customs duties which claims to press equitably on the different classes of the community cannot but be complex: and that a complex system must involve heavy expenses of collection to the treasury and must seriously hamper the development of trade.

Considerations of equity have indeed inclined statesmen when levying a tax on the importation of the particular commodity so to adjust the tax that the finer qualities or those which are designed for the consumption of the rich are subject to a heavier tax in proportion to their weight or bulk than is paid on the coarser qualities or those which are designed for the consumption of the poor. There are two methods by which this result may be partially attained; but each of them is open to grave objection.

Firstly the tax may be levied *ad valorem*: that is it may be a certain fixed proportion of the value of the commodity. This value may be determined in each case by the officers of the Customs with or without an appeal to a body of experts: or it may be declared by the importer subject to penalties for false returns, one of which may be the compulsory sale of the commodity in question for the price at which he has valued them. But in any case this method is not only uncertain and arbitrary in its operation but it leaves large scope for fraud and to some extent tends to cause a deterioration of the commodities imported. Moreover it is open to the objection that when the commodity is at an exceptionally high price in foreign markets the tax is exceptionally high, to the great injury of the consumer at home. Also when the price of the commodity in foreign markets is exceptionally low the tax is exceptionally low; so that the public treasury reaps but little at the times when the consumer can most easily afford to pay much. For these reasons opinions adverse to *ad valorem* duties are making their way rapidly among the economists and statesmen of all nations, while in countries which retain duties that discriminate in favour of the domestic producer the system of *ad valorem* taxes [is] at a special disadvantage. For under this system the discriminating tax on which the domestic producer relies affords him the least assistance just when he is at his greatest straits. The advocates of Free Trade may concede to the advocates of Protection that if discriminating duties are to be levied at all, they should in the interest of the stability and steadiness of the industries of the country be levied not *ad valorem*; but in such a way that the tax levied on each particular quality of the commodity should be independent of the fluctuations of its price. We are thus conducted to the second of the two methods by which it is attempted to render equitable the taxes which are levied on the importation of particular commodities.

In this second method various qualities of the commodity to be taxed are arranged at the Customs house in groups or classes. Technical rules are laid down by which the customs officers may be guided in their task of classifying the imports of the commodities; and where practicable these rules are supplemented by standard samples with which the imports may be compared. When any portion of the commodity has thus been put in any class, the tax to be levied on it is absolutely determined by measuring its weight, or its bulk, without any reference to current prices. The system may be called the system of *graduated specific* duties. It evades many of the objections that have just been urged against the system of *ad valorem* duties. But it is very complex: it can scarcely be worked with uniform justice at any one port: and it is found practically impossible to prevent great divergences between the standards that are enforced at various ports. Moreover it to some extent fosters frauds and discourages improvements in production. Thus the English Government taxes at the same rate all qualities of tobacco also all qualities of wine that have the same alcoholic strength.

It cannot then be maintained that the English customs duties, when considered by themselves, constitute an equitable system of taxation. But it is urged that the inequalities of this system are redressed by means of income tax and other taxes which the inland revenue department levies almost exclusively on the wealthier classes. Arguments on this subject are apt to be distorted by partisan bias: the case cannot be discussed here: but it appears to the present writer that the poor man does not obtain from the inland revenue department sufficient relief to compensate him for the undue weight of the customs and excise duties which are levied on the luxuries which he consumes. It may however be shown that inequalities of this kind are of somewhat less importance than at first sight appears. For it is a general principle that taxes which have rested upon any particular class of society for a long period of years cease to be a special burden on that class.

For instance though a tax upon glass making would be paid at first almost entirely by glassmakers, it would reduce the inducements which capital and labour had to enter the business. It would thus cause the supply of glass in the country to diminish and its price to rise, so that ultimately the income which the capitalists and labourers engaged in glass making obtain will be sufficient to cover the payment of the tax as well as to remunerate them adequately for the skill and the endurance required for their work. No portion of a tax which had rested upon glassmaking for many generations would be paid by those engaged in the trade except the amount levied on the glass which they themselves consumed, the whole of it would be paid by the purchasers of glass. From this general principle it follows that the incidence of taxes which have been levied on the richer classes of the community for many generations is in part shifted on to the poorer classes and vice versa. Various incomplete portions of the system of doctrines here referred to have been laid down in the most trenchant manner by the two great schools of abstract economics: that founded in France by Quesnay and that founded in England by Ricardo. The more careful work of Adam Smith was directed towards a discovery of the difficulties which surround these doctrines, difficulties which are not even yet completely removed. The work of these taken together with that of Malthus and others has established two important results. The first is that a tax on wages or on necessaries tends to check the growth of the labouring population; to increase the competition of capitalists for workmen and diminish the competition of workmen for hire. So that the taxes, which have for many generations been levied on the working classes have had the effect of rendering less than they would otherwise have been the benefits which the rich and in particular the landowners derive from their property. The second result is that whatever diminishes the rate of profits tends to check to some, though not necessarily to a great extent, the accumulation of capital; and therefore of the means of supporting labour. Taxes on the rich fall to some extent on profits, so that the taxes which have for many generations been levied on the rich, have had the effect of making the position of the working classes less desirable than it otherwise would have been.

Since a tax on the production or importation of a particular commodity falls when first imposed with extreme severity on the traders who are concerned with that commodity, it is inexpedient to meet a sudden and transitional emergency by such taxes. This is one of many arguments for defraying so far as is possible the expenses of a war not by increased excise or customs duties, but by direct taxes levied equitably on all classes of the community. An income tax levied for this purpose cannot be assessed in the same manner as an income tax levied specially on the rich with the purposes of counter-balancing the unequal weight with which the English customs and excise duties fall upon the working classes. But there is no reason why there should not be levied at the same time two income taxes, one for each of these purposes. However it has been argued, perhaps with some slight show of reason, that those temperaments which lead men to advocate a policy that is apt to produce wars, are, generally speaking, the temperaments to which the pleasures derived from the con-sumption of alcoholic liquors are most grateful. So that, it is argued, a war tax upon these liquors will fall heavily, but not unjustly, on those people, who generally speaking are some-what more likely to be advocates of war than others.

§ [11]   The statesman before deciding whether any particular customs duty is expedient for a country, must inquire what influence the tax is likely to exercise on the foreign relations of that country. No foreign nation has just grounds for con-sidering itself aggrieved by taxes which conform to the prin-ciples on which the English tariff is based. For as has been said England abstains from putting the producers of any com-modities in a foreign country at a disadvantage relatively to the English producers of similar commodities and England taxes no important product which she would not in all probability tax if it were produced at home. But when a country imposes a tax on any commodity the chief supplies of which come to her from some other country, she may thereby raise temporarily at least angry feelings of which the statesman must take account. It cannot be denied that the language of some American statesmen with regard to the duties imposed upon goods imported from this country has often been injudicious and has tended somewhat to check the growth of friendship between the two nations. It were unreasonable for Englishmen to expect that America should abstain from imposing duties on their wares in cases in which it may be greatly to the interest of America to impose such duties. But some American statesmen have ostentatiously declared that in weighing the merits and demerits of such taxes, no consideration whatever ought to be had for the injury or annoyance which they might inflict on Great Britain. It will however be argued in the following chapter that this injury is in most cases less than at first sight it appears to be.

Commercial treaties belong rather to the domain of the practical politician than to that of the economist. There has been recently some agitation in favour of the position that England should impose discriminating duties on her imports from those countries who impose discriminating duties on her wares. It has been argued that foreign nations may be led by the fear of such retaliatory taxes to take some account of England's interest in the construction of their own tariffs. Some of the persons who have conducted this agitation contend further that by imposing such duties England would obtain additional means for employing her own people. Herein they are guilty of an old elementary fallacy which has already been discussed.[13] But the agitation has been viewed without disfavour by some persons who do not commit this error; and who even admit that by the imposition of such duties England would in the first instance injure herself. History however does not appear to afford much ground for the opinion that such action would in general attain its end. It is easier to begin than to end a war of hostile tariffs. The war calls forth angry feelings which rise rapidly and cannot be easily allayed. Other nations who are not yet convinced that tariffs which discriminate against the foreign producer are injurious to the nations that [impose][14] them, are likely to have their conversion to a free trade policy delayed if they observe that England can be easily induced to impose taxes that discriminate against foreign producers. This answer serves to prove that it is not England's interest to levy such taxes now. But those advocates of Free trade overstate their

---

[13] See Chap. I § . [This refers to the missing first chapter of Part I.]

[14] [The manuscript reads 'oppose', but 'impose' seems to fit much better, and a transcription error may be suspected.]

case who assert that in no conceivable case would countries be right in threatening to levy retaliatory taxes unless they abstained from so adjusting their tariffs as wantonly to vex and injure her.[15]

§ [12]   A word must be said with regard to bounties on exportation. The ordinary objections to them appear to be conclusive. These are that such bounties are apt to divert the industry of the country into channels for which it is not specially adapted; that in any case they alter the rate of interchange to the disadvantage of the country that gives them;[16] that the bounty is bestowed chiefly on foreign consumers; that the funds out of which it is paid must be provided by taxation and that since every method of taxation is in some measure wasteful and indirectly injurious, the total cost of a bounty to a country which gives it is very much greater than the sum which goes to the traders who receive the bounty.

There is indeed an exceptional case in which an argument of considerable force may be urged in favour of a bounty given on the production of a particular ware whether it be designed for consumption at home or abroad. This exceptional case cannot conveniently be handled without the aid of diagrams; and the reader must be referred to the third[17] Part of the book for an investigation of it. But whatever there may be to be said for a bounty on the production of a ware, there is no justification for a provision which limits the bounty to those portions of the produce which are exported. It happens however that those who are already engaged in a trade expect to be able to retain for themselves a greater portion of a bounty on the exportation of a ware than they could of a bounty on its production. For a bounty on production [is] a stronger inducement to men of small means who have no business connection to enter the trade. A bounty on exportation does not do this to the same extent. Indeed its immediate effect is of course

[15] [This sentence is so confused that it is hard to suggest an interpretation. The most straightforward is:... in no conceivable case would a country be right in threatening to levy retaliatory taxes against other countries who adjust their tariffs wantonly to vex and injure her.]

[16] See Chap. I § . [This again refers to the missing first chapter of Part I.]

[17] [Either this is a slip, or the *Pure Theory of Domestic Value* – which is clearly referred to here – was at one time planned as Part III, rather than a portion of Part II. See Section III.6, below.]

to relieve the home market from the pressure of excessive supplies; although it may after a time cause a glut in foreign markets which reacts on the home market. It was moreover thought desirable in old times to encourage the exportation of wares with the purpose of increasing the importation of the precious metals. Thus bounties on exportation have attracted more attention than they merit.

III.4 'Protection to Native Industries'

III.4.1 *Introduction*

The closing chapter to the main text of Marshall's international-trade volume was to have been his critical assessment of American protectionist doctrines. His views on these had taken firm shape in the wake of his visit to America in 1875. But, with the abandonment of the book, and with the non-appearance of the proposed *Economics of Trade and Finance*, the world had to await Marshall's judgement until 1890. In that year, in his Presidential Address to the British Association, he remarked:[1]

> In 1875 I went to America to study the problem of Protection on the spot. I discussed the Protective policy with several of its leading advocates, I visited factories in almost every first-class city, and compared as well as I could the condition of the workers there with that of similar workers at home, and I walked up and down some of the streets of nearly all the chief American cities, and said to myself as I went: 'The adoption of Free Trade, so soon as its first disturbances were over, would strengthen this firm and weaken that'; and I tried to strike a rough balance of the good and evil effects of such a change on the non-agricultural population. On the whole it seemed to me that the two were about equally balanced, and that the abandonment of Protection would injure the lower rather than the higher classes of manufacturing industries; that those metal and wood trades, for instance, which give the best scope for the special genius of the native American artisan would gain by the change.

---

[1] 'Some Aspects of Competition', *Memorials*, pp. 262–3. See also *Money Credit and Commerce*, Book III, Ch. XI; *Official Papers*, pp. 393–4; and *Industry and Trade*, pp. 782–4.

Taking account therefore of the political corruption which necessarily results from struggles about the tariff in a democratic country, and taking account also of the interests of the agricultural classes, I settled in my own mind the question as to which I had had some doubt till I went to America, and decided that, if an American, I should unhesitatingly vote for Free Trade.

A similar judgement is reflected in the fragments reproduced below, probably written in the immediate wake of the visit.

Marshall's discussions with American economists in 1875 are of some interest.[2] He started in Norwich, Connecticut, with D. A. Wells, once a disciple of Henry Carey, but now in the free-trade camp. Wells, he wrote

is said to have no practical power, & to be unfit for political life. But he is said, even by those who judge his tactics most severely, to possess more of just that kind of information which I am striving to obtain than any other man in America.[3]

After meeting Wells, Marshall recorded that

He told me an immense amount: but his time was valuable & he was not very well: so for a good part of the time he handed me over to 'Judge' Bowles: a man aged about 35, a student of Political Economy with his eyes open. He took me to see several factories.[4]

From Norwich, Marshall went to New Haven, where he 'called on two Professors of Political Economy Sumner and Walker at Yale'. He stayed with W. G. Sumner, who was, again, hardly a thoroughgoing protectionist, but rather a

[2] For the American background, see J. Dorfman, *The Economic Mind in American Civilisation* (Viking, New York, 1946–9) Vols II, III.

[3] Letter to Rebeccah Marshall, his mother, of 20 June 1875. Marshall Library, Marshall 3:68. The letter was written from Boston, where he stayed with C. W. Eliot, the President of Harvard College. There is no trace of any serious discussion of economic topics during Marshall's stay in Boston, although he met several literary figures, including Charles Norton, Dean Howells and Ralph Waldo Emerson, 'the greatest living transcendentalist'.

[4] Letter to Rebeccah Marshall, 5 July 1875. Marshall Library, Marshall 3:69. The 'Judge' was probably Samuel Bowles, editor of the Springfield (Mass.) *Republican*. See H. R. Ferlerger, *David A. Wells and the American Revenue System* (New York, 1942) p. 3.

conservative exponent of *laissez-faire*. Marshall observed 'I am not sure that he has the nature fitted for discovering epoch-making truths: but in every other respect he is a man of enormous ability.' Marshall found Sumner 'on the whole the most instructive companion I have had...he has not the enormous knowledge of America that Mr Wells has: but his training enabled him always to see what was the information I wanted, & to give it in clear, orderly form; he had mastery at once over principle & fact.'[5] Marshall subsequently recalled a lively discussion with F. A. Walker, mainly on American Indians.[6] Walker was at the time completing his book on *The Wages Question*,[7] so close on many points to Marshall's own thought on distribution theory. But this common interest does not seem to have been explored at any length.

After Yale, there seems to have been little opportunity for academic discussion until near the end of the visit, when Marshall spent a few days in Philadelphia, home of Henry Carey and the powerful Industrial League. Here, he expected to 'obtain the means of having American "Protectionist" doctrines expounded at me by the ablest expositors of them. Than which at the present moment there are few things which I more desire.'[8] Dental trouble cut short his stay, but he was able to report

> In Philadelphia I spent many hours in conversation with the leading protectionists. And now I think, as soon as I have read some books they have recommended me to read, I shall really know the whole of their case: & I do not believe there is or ever has been another Englishman who could say the same. I again missed some interesting people to whom I had brought notes of introduction, but who were not in town: but I could not have been much better off.[9]

[5] Ibid.

[6] See J. P. Munroe, *A Life of Francis Amasa Walker* (Holt, New York, 1923) p. 308. Marshall's retrospect, written late in life, misrecalled the meeting as in Boston. In 1885 Walker and his family visited the Marshalls in Cambridge (Ibid., p. 309).

[7] Indeed, the essential arguments had already appeared in Walker's article 'The Wage Fund Theory' in the *North American Review* for Jan 1875 (Vol 120, pp. 84–119). See F. A. Walker, *The Wages Question* (Holt, New York, 1876), especially p. 128.

[8] Letter to Rebeccah Marshall, 5 Sept 1875. Marshall Library, Marshall 3:74.

[9] Letter to Rebeccah Marshall, 23 Sept 1875. Marshall Library, Marshall 3:75.

The leading protectionist was, of course, Henry Carey, and Marshall recalled much later, as one of the most vivid recollections of the trip, 'Mr Carey's splendid anger, as he exclaimed that foreign commerce had made even the railways of America run from east to west, rather than from north to south.'[10] An amusing vignette of the forthright sage survives amongst Marshall's papers, dated 18 September 1875.

Comfortable House. Large Drawing room. Good pictures. Hale & hearty, age 83. In dressing gown. At previous (short) interview he had burst out with, 'England always goes in for whatever suits her own interest.' I said 'I should say at once that I am an Englishman & that I find a good motive for England's conduct when you can see nothing but what is bad' voice rather derb. He was somewhat staggered: but in the second interview avoided dropping into the original line. Had been a free-trader when young. Struck by fact people moved west: attributed it to free trade which caused exportation of manure. Struck again by remnants of houses, or orchards, 'a peach tree here, an apple tree there on barren hills'. This set him to criticising Malthus. With great trouble I nailed him to the question 'Do you reject the law of diminishing returns in an old country, the rate of agricultural progress, & the rate of emigration being given.' He could not give a direct yes: but he jumped off – why should people stay where they are born. Cairnes is diffuse & says nothing new except that things had a 'normal' value, McLeod talks nonsense. 'Oh! but English economists do not indorse McLeod.' 'Well but Chevalier does.' 'Chevalier is not trustworthy on such points.' 'Chevalier is a humbug: dishonest: a free-trader for gain in opposition to his convictions. McCulloch is even worse. Jevons too has written a book full of mathematical nonsense. He says value depends on utility. The jackass does not know that the utility is great only when the value is small. When Faraday first discovered how to produce electricity his methods were very expensive. There was very little of it, & therefore it did very little good: but its value was high.' 'Oh! but he does not mean total utility: he means utility per unit.' 'I don't know

[10] *Memorials*, p. 260 (also *Principles II*, pp. 280–2).

what he means' & he burst away to say something else.
I think it was that no one knew anything who could not
understand what was meant by value. 'Value depends on
cost of *r*eproduction.' I tried to nail him about this but could
not succeed. I nailed him on the question why do you
urge 'protection' for Ireland, & yet maintain that Alabama
has no right to erect custom houses round herself. He
winced: but said, 'Oh I do not *say* that Ireland ought to
have protection.' He spouted at me his old views at great
length. The interview lasted $2\frac{3}{4}$ hours: out of which he was
talking $2\frac{2}{3}$ hours.

He said his father had left Ireland because he found he
would spend so much time in prison if he did not: I understood him to say that his father was a protectionist but I do
not see how that is consistent with the fact that he himself
was at first a free trader.[11]

We do not know the names of the other protectionist writers
Marshall met in Philadelphia: leading possibilities would be
William Elder, Joseph Wharton and Robert Ellis Thompson,
Professor of Social Science in the University of Pennsylvania.
But we do know that he returned with a collection of protectionist books and pamphlets,[12] and with the conviction
that 'a Protective policy in fact was a very different thing from
a Protective policy as painted by sanguine economists, such as
Carey and some of his followers, who assumed that all other
people would be as upright as they knew themselves to be, and
as clear-sighted as they believed themselves to be'.[13]

---

[11] The note, of two pages octavo, is among some 'Sketches of Character' drawn
during the American trip. The punctuation has been edited slightly. Marshall's doubts
about Carey's father being a protectionist were unfounded. (See J. Dorfman, *The
Economic Mind* ..., Vol II, p. 790.)

[12] Marshall had copies of two of Wharton's pamphlets: J. Wharton, *International
Industrial Competition* (Baird, Philadelphia, 1870); idem, *National Self Protection*
(American Iron and Steel Association, 1875). Other books and pamphlets are cited
in the text below. Marshall was also familiar with the ideas of E. Peshine Smith, one
of Carey's earlier disciples. But these ideas were widely known through Smith's
successful *Manual of Political Economy* of 1853. The fact that Marshall quotes the
writings of D. Mason (Tariff Editor of the Chicago Inter-Ocean) and W. M. Grosvenor
(Editor of the St. Louis Democrat), suggests that he may have met them on his travels,
but there is no other indication of this.

[13] *Money Credit and Commerce*, p. 219. Also see *Official Papers*, pp. 365–420.

Among the books was Thompson's recently-published *Social Science and National Economy*,[14] which had been 'recommended . . . by leading American Protectionists as containing the best general account of their position which is to be had in a compact form'.[15] Marshall appears to have found the book very useful, and his Ch. VII on protectionist arguments was planned very much on the lines of a critical account of arguments which had been put forward by Thompson.[16] However, it seems that only the opening sections of the chapter were ever composed. They are reproduced in the text below. Although there is only a fragment, it is sufficiently extensive to give some indication of Marshall's approach. The scope and range of the discussion are indicated by the following table.

Analytical Table of Contents for Fragment of Part I, Ch. VII

§ 1   Protective and revenue duties: protective duties to be discussed with reference to America.
§ 2   Protectionism supported by some solid arguments, but also by many fallacious and careless ones.
§ 3   The main arguments of the protectionists.
§ 4   The argument that European traders would conspire to suppress unprotected American manufactures.
§ 5   Effect of a sudden change in tariffs: injurious for an increase and not only for a decrease.
§ 6   Conclusion on claims that protection diminishes fluctuations.
§ 7   Effects on the stability of American agriculture from protecting manufactures.

The form envisaged for the complete chapter can only be guessed. Various rough notes suggest that the main themes to be introduced were the following.

---

[14] Porter and Coates, Philadelphia, 1875.

[15] Below, p. 101. Also see *Industry and Trade*, p. 783 n.

[16] Marshall's interest appears to have been primarily in Thompson's Chapters XI and XII on 'The Science and Economy of Manufactures' (pp. 231–384). There are traces of Thompson's influence in other chapters of Marshall's manuscript too, as in the discussion of specific versus *ad valorem* duties in Part I, Ch. VI, § 10 (Section III.3, above), which is very similar to Thompson's discussion on pp. 240–7.

Economic arguments:

  (i) difficulties of nascent industries in competing on equal terms with established producers abroad;
 (ii) monopolistic behaviour of foreign producers who act to crush new rivals;
(iii) the uncertainty and instability produced by reliance on foreign markets;
 (iv) exporting agricultural products impoverishes the soil and restricts the crops that can be grown.

Social and political arguments:

  (i) the advantage of a diversified production in providing ample scope for the variegated skills and inventive talents latent in the people;
 (ii) the advantages and disadvantages of large towns ('[the] most shiftless emigrants stay there – but must stay somewhere and would probably not be put off emigrating even if U.S. more agricultural');
(iii) effects of high wages on present and future generations;
 (iv) monopoly and concentration of economic power;
  (v) effects of protection on home politics, especially through lobbying;
 (vi) effects on foreign relations.

Historical inductions:

'Conclude case about effect of Protection in reducing prices. Refer to and summarise what was said in Ch. V[17] about untrustworthiness of conclusions deduced from simple tables of statistics. Special unfairnesses (i) they quote generally cases in which many improvements have been introduced which without Protection would have occurred (ii) they select their own cases and quote falls in price due to accidental circumstances (iii) they quote cases in which the temporary fall in price has been occasioned by causes similar to those quoted above from Wells[18] (iv) when tariff cuts off market from English producers (a)

[17] [See Part I, Ch. V, § 4 (Section III.2, above). Also, compare a passage in Marshall's Inaugural Lecture, *Memorials*, p. 167.]
[18] [This possibly refers to D. A. Wells, *Wool and the Tariff: an Argument against Interference* (Privately printed, New York, 20 Mar 1873).]

some distress and consequent forced sales (b) large plant
requires to be occupied hence *temporary* fall. Conclude that
in the present condition of statistical science no direct
aid is to be obtained from this source towards solution
of general question of expediency of Protection.'

The only parts of the general scheme given detailed consideration in the fragment which survives are Economic arguments
(ii) and (iii).[19] It appears that this was the only part ever written,
but a rough sketch for the proposed conclusions reads:

Protection on the whole injurious to America because
though it may cause a few industries to take root and
flourish and may in some cases do good: yet on the whole it
happens that it protects the plague spots of America. It
does not tend to hinder the old-established centres of
manufacture from crushing out new ones. It renders export
trade difficult: England would in no case take very much
more corn, but she would take America's best manufactures and send her the produce of less intelligent labour.
It prevents highest development of American genius. It
demoralises politics.

But for very reasons that it injures America it probably
does not injure England as much as appears. In particular
[America's] policy of taxing heavily cheap products tends
to diminish English production of them for American
market: while difficulties thrown in way of American
producers of products requiring high skill help to enable
English producers to retain possession of all other markets
than American. [Moreover] it would be very injurious to
England to be very much dependent on one market for
corn.

Many of above arguments do not apply to countries
other than America: notably those [arguments] which
turn on importance of giving good market for products
requiring high skill. But in backward countries like Russia
another class of arguments comes in. If left alone they will not
become familiarised with the wants or means of civilisation.
Moreover distance is itself a strong protection for most

[19] There had already been some discussion of Economic argument (i) in Part I,
Ch. V, §§ 13–16 (Section III.2, above).

things. Still a government which has the means of knowing
what industries if once started will prosper: which is able to
prevent itself from being bamboozled by individuals: and
which can so manage matters as to prevent its legislators
and its custom-house officials from being bribed, may
perhaps protect industries. A government which is wise
enough and strong enough to do this may give bounties
in special cases. The plan of imposing a customs tax and
devoting proceeds to bounty on home-produced ware
has many advantages, and appears likely to grow in favour
among more enlightened and moderate advocates of
protection.

III.4.2 *Text of a Fragment of Part I, Chapter VII: 'Protection to Native Industries'*

§ 1 Every duty on imported commodities unless it be
absolutely prohibitive affords a revenue to the State. If however the duty be very high, the total revenue derived from it
may be less than would be derived from a lower duty: such a
duty can be defended only as affording Protection to native
industries; and it is agreed that, whether it succeed in its
aim or not, it shall be called a Protective duty. If the Customs
tax levied on an imported ware be no higher than the Excise
levied on similar wares produced at home, the tax is not
Protective: it may be condemned together with the corresponding Excise tax on the ground that it involves an
excessive interference with the free course of industry, but it is
not in opposition to the principles of Free-trade in the old and
narrower sense of the term. If however the Customs on an
imported ware be higher than the Excise on the corresponding
wares produced at home, but yet be such that if the rate of the
duty were lowered the total revenue received from it would be
diminished; then it is said to be at once a Revenue duty and a
Protection duty. Many of the most important duties which
enter into modern Protection systems of taxation are of this
class. A discussion of such a system must therefore be incomplete unless it contain an examination of the effects of
customs duties on the terms of international exchange, and
some inquiry into the merits and demerits of alternative
modes of raising the revenue in question. But, it will be

convenient in the present chapter to consider such taxes chiefly in relation to their effects on the industry of the country. Some account of their relations to the country's finances will be included in the following chapter.[1] That chapter is designed to point the way towards those intricate portions of the theory of foreign trade, which appear to require the complex apparatus that is supplied in the second Part of the treatise.

There is not in England any body of men considerable either on account of their numbers or their intelligence who hold that England at present can with advantage adopt a system of Protection duties. England's industries generally are in an advanced condition; she is dependent on foreign supplies of agricultural produce and the raw materials of manufacture; she has special facilities for acting as a depot for the commerce of the world. The adoption of a Protectionist system could confer on her scarcely any of the benefits which it may confer on other countries; and the injuries which it would inflict on her would be exceptionally numerous and far-reaching. For these reasons it is inexpedient that a discussion of the Protectionist system should have special reference to the conditions of England. But such a discussion can scarcely have sufficient definiteness, and so to speak, sufficient reality unless the reader has before his mind its applications to some particular country. The present chapter will in the main be occupied with an analysis of the advantages and disadvantages which may accrue from a system of Protective duties to the industries of the United States of America; or – as I shall say more briefly, in accordance with established usage – of America.

§ 2   It has already been stated that the policy of Protection is advocated by many men, upright and of great mental vigour, who are acquainted with the reasonings of British economists. It is true that, so far as I am aware, none of them have given evidence of that scientific precision of thought and accuracy of reasoning which have distinguished the best British economists. But their writings are free from the worst of those fallacies by which Protectionism used in its earlier stages to be defended throughout the world; and of which an ignorant or

---

[1] [This refers to Ch. VI of Part I (Section III.3, above) which had followed the present chapter in an earlier draft.]

unscrupulous use is yet made in speeches and writings addressed to the less educated portions of the people in America and other countries.[2] In particular the best advocates of Protection do not pretend that the exclusion of a foreign ware will cause the means of employing labour in the country to be increased by that amount which is required for producing this ware at home. They appear to be aware of the fact that the capital required for this purpose, if forthcoming at all, is likely to be that which would otherwise have been occupied in giving employment to industry in the production of the goods, which if the ware in question had been imported, would have been exported in exchange for it. They appear to be aware of this fact; but in general they do not state it explicitly.

On the other hand it has been conceded[3] that in so far as the conversion of circulating capital into fixed may be in extreme cases injurious to the labourer, [then] in so far the labourer may conceivably have an interest in opposition to the locking up of inordinate amounts of capital in the ships and the warehouses, etc., that are required for any particular branch of foreign trade. But while Ricardo and his followers have made an oversight in refusing to take any account of this consideration: there is probably no branch of trade of any

[2] As an instance of this I will quote a passage from one of a series of Editorial Articles which have appeared in the Chicago Inter-ocean during 1874 and 1875, and have been since republished under the title 'How Western Farmers are benefited by Protection'.

'Briefly stated, the general effect of Protective duties is to arouse the activities of production and to provide work and wages for labor. When we buy abroad an article which might have been manufactured at home, we take away from our own mechanics to bestow upon foreigners the employment and pay for services involved in the fabrication of that article. If this plan of purchase is carried on extensively, the result is that thousands of our own people are deprived of opportunities to earn a livelihood in the arts of reproduction. The circle of occupations being thus contracted, there ensues a more energetic competition within that narrowed area for the sale of services, with the necessary consequence of diminishing wages and the laborer's purchasing power. Now, it is the ability of the great masses of the people to buy that creates universal prosperity. It is the expenditure of their earnings that causes the rapid circulation of commodities – the thrift of manufacturing establishments, the enterprise of merchants, transportation by rail and water, the growth of cities, the rise in the value of real estate, and the whole series of movements involved in material advancement.'

[See D. Mason, *How Western Farmers are Benefited by Protection*, published by the author (Chicago, 1875) p. 71. A note indicates Marshall's intention to insert the present footnote in the text in small print.]

[3] Ch. V § [17]. [See Section III.2, above.]

importance which exerts by this means an injurious influence on the labourer comparable in magnitude with the benefits which it confers on him as a consumer of the imported ware.

American protectionists contend that profits and wages are so high in America, that unless Protected their manufacturers must be under-sold by Europeans. This contention contains truth; but it is in need of explanation. Nature has awarded liberal returns to capital and to labour employed in Agriculture in America:[4] capital and labour cannot in general be attracted to manufactures there unless by the hope of profits and wages equally liberal with those which can be obtained in Agriculture. Thus the argument in question comes to this: – If American manufactures were not Protected against the competition of European wares, capital and labour would obtain lower profits and wages by producing manufactured wares than they would by raising agricultural produce and devoting some of this to the purchase of European wares. Thus this contention is valid in so far as it states facts correctly: but it is nothing more than the fundamental truth on which the advocates of free trade insist, written in a somewhat disguised form. It proves that agriculture offers great attractions to American labour and capital. It does not prove that it is expedient to diminish these advantages by legislation.

With these remarks we may put aside the confusions which arise from careless or perverse reasonings and address ourselves to the solid arguments that can be put forward by able and thoughtful economists to prove that America may derive important social and economic benefits from the Protection of domestic manufactures.

§ 3   American Protectionists are fond of comparing their policy to that of a railway company which makes a tunnel in order to save a detour. The detour may be cheaper in the first instance; yet the tunnel may be cheaper in the long run: for it diminishes the distance to be traversed by every train that passes over the road. 'It overcomes the difficulty once for

---

[4] [A revised version continues from here with: 'The position of the American farmer working his own land has many advantages independent of the income obtained in it. So the capital and labour are not attracted ....']

all. It's', says an American writer,[5] 'like the tariff that makes us pay something for a few years to build up manufactories which then give us a more plentiful supply of cheaper goods than we could ever get in any other way.' They say that each nation should pass through a stage of Protectionism, even at the expense of diminishing for the time its productive efficiency : just as a boy should pass through a period of training and schoolwork instead of engaging at once in those pursuits in which his labour would be productive of the highest immediate pecuniary returns.

Professor Thompson, a recognised exponent of Protectionist doctrines, gives a summary of the grounds on which he maintains that the Protection of manufactures benefits in the long run the consumer of manufactured produce.[6]

The object and the effect of protective duties, then, is to enable the home producer to furnish the manufactured goods more plentifully and cheaper than before the duty was imposed . . . . What are the reasons for this final reduction in price? . . . (1) The lack of security deters the manufacturer from putting his capital into a large undertaking. He has to make great outlays, great sacrifices even, but he has no security that he will ever reap the fruits, unless the home market is secured to him. He fears the foreign competition more than that of his competitors at home, because the latter stand on an equality of power and capacity with him, while the former are able and ready to make large sacrifices simply to drive him out of the market and secure it to themselves . . . . (2) The inexperience of the laboring class is not to be overcome in a day . . . . And the captains of industry themselves need drill and experience as well as

[5] Cyrus Elder in *The Dream of a Free-trade Paradise* – a series of humorous tales in which the Protectionist policy is expounded with not less vigour and efficiency than the Free Trade Policy is in the celebrated tales of Bastiat. [Cyrus Elder, *Dream of a Free Trade Paradise and other Sketches*, with 12 illustrations by Henry L. Stephens. Published for the Industrial League by Henry Carey Baird (Philadelphia, 1873). The quotation comes from p. 13.]

[6] *Social Science and National Economy* by R. E. Thompson, Professor of Social Science in the University of Philadelphia [Porter and Coates, Philadelphia, 1875]. This book has been recommended to me by leading American Protectionists as containing the best general account of their position which is to be had in a compact form.

their workmen. The processes of a great manufacture are
not to be learnt in a day, even if no changes in method are
contemplated. But among the great advantages gained in
the acclimatization of new industries, not the least is the
gain in improved methods when an old industry is tried
under a new set of conditions.... (3) The complete organization of industry, and the accumulation of capital
that make it possible, are not effected in a day. It is a
commonplace of the economists that the products of
industry are cheapened by extending the scale of production.[7]

§ 4   Let us first consider the argument that European traders
are willing to sacrifice much capital in order to consummate
the ruin of those who are rising in competition with them. It is
of course possible that the foreign producers of a particular
class of wares might agree deliberately to sell at a loss in
American markets in order to prevent a rival industry from
taking root there. The compact organisation required for this
purpose is wholly impossible unless the main body of those
producers are resident in one country, and even in this case
can only be attained under exceptional conditions. But if
foreigners are kept off by Protection, there may be but little
difficulty in the way of an organisation sufficient to induce one
set of producers in, say, Pennsylvania to agree to undergo
some loss in order to crush out a rising branch of the manufacture in, say, Missouri or Alabama, and thereby retain for
themselves the monopoly of the home market. A similar
remark applies to the danger that a rising establishment may
be injured by the deliberate hostility of those particular
establishments with whose custom it is most likely to interfere.
It is urged that a wealthy manufacturer with an established
connection may, independently of any combination, be
willing to suffer some temporary loss in order to clear away
from the ground that he considered as his own a young rival
who was encroaching on it. Some cases in which rising
American firms have thus suffered from the set attacks of
English firms, have rankled in the minds of those who have

---

[7] [Ibid., pp. 263–7. Marshall intended a much fuller quotation but all the essential
points are in the pruned version given here.]

been brought into contact with them and have been used to good purpose by the advocates of Protectionism. But it appears that the set enmity of particular rivals in his own country is a source of more frequent and more serious danger to the first attempts of a manufacturer who is commencing business than is that of any rival in a distant country. And there are many reasons for believing that American men of business do not generally attach to this class of considerations a practical importance commensurate with the prominence which is given to it in Protectionist declamations.

But although a [producer] may not be specially likely to undergo absolute loss in order to injure a rival in a distant country, he may be less careful to avoid 'spoiling the market' there than at home. We have given above[8] some analysis of the causes which may induce a manufacturer in a business which makes large use of fixed capital, to reduce for a time the price of his wares much below its normal level; and of the motives which may restrain him from doing so. These motives depend in great part upon the extent to which he is anxious for the friendly regard of those particular manufacturers who would be injured by the spoiling of the market in question. And consequently when the supply of his wares is large relatively to the demand, he is likely to relieve himself by throwing his surplus on a foreign market rather than on the home market. But he is likely to be somewhat scrupulous about flooding those foreign markets with which he and his neighbours have intimate connections. So that in this matter a tariff which tends to sever the connection which English producers have with American markets works in two different directions. On the one hand it diminishes the facilities which the English producer has for throwing his surplus supplies in times of depression upon the American market: but on the other hand it causes him to be not disinclined to take advantage of such facilities as remain to him. With a view of further diminishing these facilities Protectionists desire that tariffs should be specific and not *ad valorem*. For under an *ad valorem* tariff the Protection afforded to the home-producer is least in times of general depression, when he is likely to be most in need of

---

[8] See Ch. V § 6. [The correct reference is to Part I, Ch. V, § 7 (Section III.2, above).]

it. In this matter they act wisely for their own purposes. They regard the benefit that consumers may derive from an influx of cheap goods, as of no importance to be compared with the benefits that the country will derive from sustaining its manufacturers in times of distress. It would not however be right to acquiesce in the treatment of the immediate interests of consumers as of no importance whatever.[9]

A high tariff has a second effect besides that of rendering it difficult for the foreign producer to get access to the American market. It also puts a large number of American industries into such a position that they cannot avoid the worst consequences of depression at home, by selling their surplus goods in foreign markets.

Take the case of an American industry that is Protected by a Customs tax of, say, forty per cent on the produce of rival industries in Europe, in addition to the charges which these industries must undergo in order to have their wares transported to the American market. Such an industry cannot compete with its European rivals in, say, the markets of South America, without submitting to receive [in] them a net price considerably more than 40 per cent lower than that which it has obtained at home: and this without making any allowance for the fact that at the times when American industries are specially anxious for a foreign market, European industries are likely to be offering their wares at less than the usual price. Thus the fluctuations to which a Protected industry is liable in consequence of great changes in the home market are generally speaking wider than those which could occur to the industries which are able to sustain themselves without the aid of Protection. This in any case is a serious evil. But the evil is gravest in the case of those industries which make large use of machinery and raw material on the importation of which a heavy tax is levied. For these taxes put them at a heavy disadvantage in competing with foreign producers whose machinery and raw material are not so taxed. The customs tax on the finished product may more than suffice to cover this disadvantage and may give the American manufacturer a decided advantage over the foreigner in the competition for

---

[9] [This sentence was deleted.]

the American market, but is of no avail for him when he is driven to sell some portion of his wares in other markets. Many New England manufacturers, especially in the cotton trade, are thus coming to the conclusion that the benefits which they derive from the partial exclusion of their foreign rivals from the American market, are of less importance than the injuries which the Protective tariff indirectly inflicts upon them. They argue that by raising artificially the price of their machinery, of their railway iron, and of the commodities which they and their workmen consume, the Protective tariff causes the whole of their business to be arranged according to a high scale of prices. So that they are not able to dispose of their wares in foreign markets in times in which the home demand is slack, except at a loss so severe as to entail if not ruin yet a suffering for which they are inadequately compensated by the high profits which in times of prosperity the Protection Tariff secures to them.[10]

The fact that an industry which is practically restricted to one market for the sale of its wares is unstable is insisted on by Protectionists as a reason why American manufacturing industries require Protection. What it proves is that a Protective tariff confers on the manufacturer but little solid benefit in comparison with the loss, that as regards its first effects at least, it inflicts upon the consumer. But as the matter is of importance it will be well to quote from a Protectionist authority.[11]

• But suppose the market for any such establishment to be confined to the country in which it is situated, say in this

[10] Mr Edward Atkinson of Boston is a prominent and worthy representative of a band of New England manufacturers who have been induced by this consideration and others based on broader grounds of public welfare to become advocates of Free-trade.

[11] Propositions concerning Protection and Free-trade by Mr Phillips 1850 pp. 74–6 [Willard Phillips, *Propositions Concerning* . . . . (Little and Brown, Boston, 1850)]. The Bulletin of the American Iron and Steel Association, an able Protectionist organ, gives (15 October 1875) with approval an abstract of an address just delivered by the Editor of 'Iron Age' to the New York society of practical engineering; in which the following passage occurs: – 'It is unnecessary perhaps to call attention to the relation which exists between economy and progress in manufacturing. It is enough to say that in the judgement of our wisest practical Statesmen the rapid industrial development of this country depends in a great degree if not wholly upon our ability to manufacture for export.'

country. For such one, let there be four similar ones in a foreign country, say Great Britain, whose market is not confined to that country, but extends also to this, and to Asia and Africa, South America, and Australia .... Each of those divers markets will be fluctuating, sometimes brisk, at others dull, and where either is dull, the current of their products will be turned towards the others, and by these compensations, their market, as a whole, will be more steady and uniform than if it were confined to any one country, however large.[12]

[§ 5]   We have hitherto discussed the effects of a high tariff on the supposition that it has been in steady operation without any important changes for a long period. All evils that arise from a change in the tariff are by the Protectionist school regarded as not properly attributable to the Protective System, but rather to be put to the account of the opposition that is offered to this system. They dilate on the social and economic evils which arise from the throwing out of employment of those engaged in Protected industries if the Protection were suddenly removed. They profess that no account of these evils is taken by their opponents. They insist with truth that even if the Free-trade system were admitted to be the best for the country in the long run, the evils which would arise from its sudden adoption might outweigh the benefits that it would ultimately confer. The charge is frequently made against the British school of economists that they overlook these facts, that they consider only the ultimate effects of each economic cause, without taking account of the evils which particular classes of society may have to undergo during the period of transition. Such charges may be valid when brought against some of the more popular writings of the school, but not when brought against the leaders of the school. The hardest of them all, Ricardo, has a careful chapter on the evil effects of 'sudden changes in the channels of trade':[13] and there is no foundation

---

[12] [Phillips, pp. 74–5 : Marshall gives only the first line. A missing page of the manuscript would account for the remainder, which was probably intended to be a more extensive quotation than is made here. The passage quoted is marked in Marshall's copy of the book, in the Marshall Library, with the comment 'The major premise for Atkinson's argument for free trade'.]

[13] [D. Ricardo, *Principles of Political Economy and Taxation*, Ch. XIX.]

for the charge implied by Protectionists that the leading
advocates of Free-trade in America demand that any change
should be made with violent rapidity. But the special evils
which are inseparable from change accompany a rise, as
surely as they do a fall in the Tariff: and the higher be the
normal scale of the Tariff, the greater will be the disturbances
of industry which will arise from increasing or diminishing in a
given proportion any of the taxes.

Experience in America has confirmed the predictions of
theory, with regard to the fluctuations occasioned by a great
increase in the customs levied on any particular ware. The
American capital specialised for producing this ware, whether
'fixed' in the trained skill of men, or embodied in machines is
inadequate to produce at a short notice a largely increased
supply. The masters and the men who are already in the trade
make for awhile, enormous wages and enormous profits. This
fact is quickly noised abroad, and capitalists and workmen
swarm into the trade. Some of the new comers are solid men
who would be likely to succeed under favourable conditions;
but the inordinate gains which the trade offers for a time,
attract in large numbers those restless and volatile men who
are without the genius necessary for successful speculation
but live under the constant illusion that they are fated to find
some short and easy road by which they may without effort
attain riches. Excessive production soon gluts the market.
Prices fall. Those engaged in the trade find a difficulty in
obtaining fresh loans or renewals of old loans: a few of them
may be able quietly to await better times, but many of them
are compelled to push the sales of their wares, while not a few
become bankrupt, whereby their stocks are thrown for sale
on the market without reserve. Gradually the surplus stocks
are disposed of, there are now perhaps again but few engaged
in the trade, and the price of the ware rises until abnormal
profits and wages are again made in the trade, and there is
a repetition on a smaller scale of the previous oscillation.

If, however, the ware be of such a nature that the total
value of the requisite annual supplies of it is not very large,
the effect of the imposition of a high import duty upon it may
be to give a practical [monopoly] to a few powerful firms. In
this case violent oscillations in the price of the ware will

probably be avoided so long at least as those already in the trade are able to prevent others from obtaining a footing in it. In such cases the monopolists are likely to sustain the price considerably above that amount which is required to cover the expenses of production of the ware and to amass large fortunes at the expense of the consumer.

[§ 6]   On the whole I conclude that no case has been made out to warrant the assumption which is frequently and boldly made that the system of Protection tends to diminish fluctuations of prices and of wages, and irregularities of employment. The balance of argument appears to incline decidedly towards those who maintain that the perturbations of industry are increased by a system which hinders, as the Protective system does, the ingress of foreign wares and the egress of native wares. But this conclusion is quite consistent with the belief that the special circumstances of a particular branch of industry may be such that wages and prices in it might be rendered more stable by a careful and temperate Protection. If a Government had unlimited wisdom, knowledge and power, if it were at once impartial and above the fear of being thought to be partial, it might be able to select for Protection at any time certain particular branches of industry which were in such a condition. To this point I shall return.

[§ 7]   It is necessary next to take some account of the fact that America's exports consist to a large extent of agricultural produce. The Protectionists affirm that the market which foreign trade offers to the American farmer is unstable. 'Distant markets' says Horace Greeley,[14] 'are all but inevitably inconstant, uncertain markets. Europe has deficient harvests one year, and buys Grain of us quite freely; but next year her harvests are bounteous, and she requires very little more food than she produces, no matter how freely we may be buying of her fabrics. Hence, our Wheat now sells very far below the prices which ruled here when Europe had a meagre harvest.' And he makes a characteristic quotation from a sermon

---

[14] *Political Economy* p. 137. [H. Greeley, *Essays Designed to Elucidate the Science of Political Economy* ... (Fields Osgood, Boston, 1870).]

preached in 1819.[15] 'No calamity is greater than a capricious market, baffling the sober, extended calculations of industry, and converting the husbandmen of a nation into a body of speculators, tempting at one time by high prices to adventurous purchases and lavish family expenses, and then, by the glut of the market and the fall of produce, dashing the hopes of thousands of families, and rearing upon their ruins a moneyed aristocracy.... [Manufacturers] afford employment also to classes of the community which would otherwise be idle or less usefully employed, call into action the diversity of talents with which God has endowed men, and lay open to the active mind of enterprise a greater choice of employment, and more powerful incitements to industry. But the vital utility of manufactures consists in their subserviency to agriculture, by affording to the husbandman a near and steady home market, and by diminishing the competition of exported produce in foreign markets, increasing the demand and the price.'

It is doubtless a true, and an important, doctrine that a farmer who is limited to one distant foreign market for the sale of his produce has an uncertain trade. Suppose that in the remote North-West of America the farmer is receiving at the rate of 20 shillings a quarter for wheat which is sent to Liverpool and sold at 60 shillings a quarter: then when the price in Liverpool falls to 40 shillings a quarter, his wheat will be of scarcely any value to him unless the freights to Liverpool are altered in his favour; for the prices in all the markets to which he has access are in the main ruled by the Liverpool price. It is true that in such a case the railways over which his wheat must travel will probably adopt a far-sighted policy, and reduce their freights; but it is contended that it is inexpedient that the farmer should be at the mercy of railway companies. But from this fact we cannot infer an answer to the question whether Protection to manufacturers tends to diminish the nervous and restless elements of American life, unless we assume further that it tends largely to increase the demand for

[15] [Ibid., pp. 142–4, where the source is identified as a 'Thanksgiving Sermon on "The Means of National Prosperity": Litchfield, Connecticut, December 2, 1819 by the Rev. Lyman Beecher'.]

agricultural produce in the American market. And Protectionists are as a matter of fact in the habit of assuming that their
System promotes immigration. Of course if that System increased the general prosperity of America it increases the
attractions which she offers to foreigners: but to assume this is
to assume the whole matter in dispute. It is indeed sometimes
boastfully said by them, that their tariff increases the difficulty which the English mechanic has in obtaining wheat at
home, and so brings him to America to seek food. But America
after all contains but a small portion of the wheat producing
surface of the globe: and the effect of the tariff in this direction
is not of much importance. So that we have not to inquire
whether the American farmer might not lead a less anxious
life if the population of America were largely increased and a
home market afforded him in lieu of a distant foreign market.
The question is whether the American farmer's career as it
is, is on the whole more anxious and uncertain than are those
manufacturing careers into which Protection seeks to drive
him. No writer, so far as I am aware, has ventured to maintain
that this is the case.

[It appears to have been argued next[16] that the existence
of an export trade in wheat stabilises American industry, for
a sudden change in American demand for wheat] is sufficient
to cause traders to retain for sale at home any portion that
may be required of the wheat which they had designed for
exportation. It has been already remarked[17] that a sudden
rise in the price of necessaries is among the greatest evils
which can befall a country. Such a rise inflicts grievous misery
on the poorer classes directly, and by causing almost all
classes suddenly to check their purchases of comforts and
luxuries it disturbs generally the markets throughout the
country. So that it does more than almost any other event can
do, to throw economic machinery out of gear, and to deprive
labour of steady employment. The Protectionists' plea that
the exportation of agricultural produce tends to increase the

---

[16] [The manuscript page which follows provides a fitting conclusion to the present
phase of discussion. It is, however, a rough draft, and there is no clear indication of
its purpose or position.]

[17] [See Part I, Ch. V, § 10 (Section III.2, above).]

instability of American industry may therefore be dismissed not merely as invalid, but as the reverse of the truth.

We shall at a later stage [have] to compare further the modes in which agricultural and manufacturing progress severally contribute to the general well-being of a country and to examine the influences which they exert on one another.

III.5   The Pure Theory of Foreign Trade

III.5.1   *Introduction*

Sidgwick chose Chapters II and III of Part II of Marshall's manuscript to print under the heading of 'The Pure Theory of Foreign Trade'.[1] Here, the closely-related Chapters I and IV are also included, so far as they survive, so that what has been known hitherto as Chapter I of the *Pure Theory* becomes Chapter II, and the old Chapter II becomes Chapter III. The Sidgwick chapters are reproduced without essential change. Footnotes have been amplified and obvious misprints corrected.[2] Also, the figures are spread through the text, rather than printed together on fold-out sheets. Otherwise the original has simply been reproduced.[3]

Marshall wrote of these four chapters to Cunynghame in April 1904:

[1] See Section I.4, above.

[2] Alterations which go beyond the correction of obvious misprints are shown by editorial square brackets. However, a few essential commas have been inserted silently.

[3] Some slight stylistic changes have been made. For example, 'fig.' is replaced by 'Figure', and some standardisation has been attempted in cases where the original did not adhere to a systematic treatment (as in the abbreviation of 'chapter'). But Marshall's haphazard capitalisation is left unchanged.

Fragmentary marginal notes, which appeared in the original printing, are not reproduced in the present text. These deleted notes read as follows, and were attached at the points indicated in parentheses:

The laws of the two curves are symmetrical. Laws relating to the Normal Class and Class I. A geometrical expression for the rate of interchange. (Ch. II, § 5)

Some technical terms are wanted. The scale of importation. Definition of Exchange-index. Definition of the phrases, 'to the right of *OE*', 'above *OG*'. (Ch. III §1)

The law of the forces which control the movement of the Exchange-index. (Ch. III, § 2)

Definition of Stable and Unstable Equilibrium. (Ch. III, § 3)

The first chapter was 'philosophical', on the abstract idea of an economic nation. Then came the chapters on foreign trade which Sidgwick printed (you know I was very ill and consented to his printing some chapters for private circulation, but left the selection to him); then came a chapter applying those curves to the incidence of import and export duties and bounties. He did not print that: I wish he had. It was quite finished. Some of the others were not.

But my case II, that of increasing returns, never seemed to me of much practical use; and in later years I warned people off it, on the ground that, if time was allowed for the development of economies of production on a large scale, time ought also to be allowed for the general increase of demand.[4]

The first chapter aimed to show how 'with modifications in detail the pure theory of Foreign Trade was applicable to many industrial and other problems'.[5] Marshall wrote to Edgeworth in March 1891:

I believe I told you that the first chapter of that part of my original MSS (printed by Sidgwick) was given to arguing that the

$$x = \text{amount} \Big\}$$
$$y = \text{amount} \Big\}$$

curves had perhaps more real applications to industrial groups and employer-employé-questions than to Foreign Trade. I have always intended to reproduce that in my vol. II and that is one reason why I have not discussed Trades Unions in vol. I.[6]

The analogy was obviously one to which Marshall was attached, but he never succeeded in making much of it in detail.[7]

---

[4] *Memorials*, p. 449. For other portions of the letter see Vol 1, pp. 63–4, 261, above.

[5] From the letter to Seligman quoted on p. 3, above.

[6] *Principles II*, p. 793.

[7] Schumpeter attributed the analogy to Edgeworth, but it is already clearly stated in Marshall's 1881 review of *Mathematical Psychics*. See Item IV.2.11, below, and J. A. Schumpeter, *History of Economic Analysis* (Oxford Press, 1954) p. 940.

The construction of a table of contents is perhaps the best way of briefly indicating the range and scope of the four chapters.

Analytical Table of Contents: The Pure Theory of Foreign Trade

§ 6   Quantitative laws of movement not at present discoverable.

§ 7   Irreversibility of certain movements, especially in Class II.

Ch. IV: *Variations of International Demand as Affecting the Rate of Interchange. The Incidence of Customs Duties*

§ 1   Causes of a change in international demand.

§ 2   Graphical representation of a change in demand.

§ 3   The imposition of a tax when both demands are Normal.

§ 4   Preliminary investigation of the cases where demands are not Normal.

§ 5   Applications to some particular cases: export taxes and relations between industrial groups.

§ 6   Effects of an increase in demand.

§ 7   General analysis of the effects of a reduction in one country's demand.

§ 8   The conditions for a large improvement in the rate of exchange (incomplete).

The leading ideas of Chapters II–IV are clearly stated in the earlier 'Essay on the Theory of International Trade' (Item II.8.1 above). They percolated out to the world, particularly through the writings of Pantaleoni, Edgeworth, Cunynghame, and Flux,[8] but it was only in 1923, after a delay of almost fifty years, that they were finally published under Marshall's own name. In 1904 his attitude had been thoroughly ambivalent: 'As to International Trade curves:– Mine were set to a definite tune, that called by Mill. It is improbable that I shall ever publish them: but I am not certain. I am rather tired of them.'[9] However, he was eventually unable to resist the temptation and Appendix J of *Money Credit and Commerce*

---

[8] M. Pantaleoni, *Principii di Economia Pura* (Barbèra, Florence, 1889). F. Y. Edgeworth, 'The Application of Mathematics to Political Economy', *Journal of the Royal Statistical Society*, Vol 52 (Dec 1889) pp. 538–76; 'The Pure Theory of International Values, I–III', *Economic Journal*, Vol 4 (Mar–Dec 1894) pp. 35–50, 424–43, 606–38. H. H. Cunynghame, *A Geometrical Political Economy* (Oxford Press, 1904). A. W. Flux, *Economic Principles* (Methuen, London, 1904).

[9] Letter to Cunynghame of June 1904: *Memorials*, p. 451.

is largely a paraphrase of these earlier chapters.[10] Indeed, some passages and diagrams were reproduced essentially unchanged, including much of what has been restored here as Chapter IV.[11]

The path-breaking lucidity of the *Pure Theory of Foreign Trade* has earned it a just fame, even in its hitherto abbreviated form. Any attempt at detailed commentary would seem both unnecessary and presumptuous. But attention might be drawn to the following points.

(i) The stability discussion of Ch. III is the first known application to economic theory of the phase-diagram method of handling a system of differential equations. Marshall's objections to a more formal mathematical analysis of such dynamic systems are cogent. Yet, when an analytical treatment was eventually assayed by Samuelson in 1948, it became clear that – though Marshall's results were largely vindicated – he had overlooked the possibility of oscillatory paths spiralling around the equilibrium point.[12]

(ii) In proving the fundamental Proposition VI (Ch. III, § 5), Marshall assumes that even when average production cost falls with output, because of increasing returns, total cost always rises. This restriction had already been introduced into the earlier 'Essay on International Trade', but not into

[10] This is pointed out in the footnote on p. 330 of *Money Credit and Commerce* which says that much of Appendix J had been 'designed to form part of an Appendix to a volume on International Trade, on which a good deal of work was done, chiefly between 1869 and 1873'. It adds that 'Somewhat later dates attach to attempts to assign definite measures, in abstract theory at least, to the elasticity of national demand; and to the total direct net benefit of a country's foreign trade to her. Subject to these exceptions, the main body of the present Appendix is reproduced with but little change in substance from that part of the MSS. which was privately printed and circulated among economists at home and abroad in 1879'.

However, see Sections II.8.1 and II.8.2 above for the suggestion that the period 1869–73 is probably too early for the actual composition of the *Pure Theory of Foreign Trade*, and for indications that the treatment of 'direct net benefit' was developed by the mid-seventies. Of course, as Marshall implies, the concept of elasticity is completely absent from the *Pure Theory*, since he did not discover it until 1882.

[11] The following are the main correspondences. Parts of Ch. III, § 7 reproduced on pp. 351–2. Parts of Ch. III, § 3 reproduced on p. 353. Ch. IV, §§ 4–7 reproduced on pp. 356–60. Figures 1, 6, 8, 9, 10, 14–17 reproduced as Figures 1, 22, 20, 23, 21, 24–27 respectively. There are too many close paraphrasings to make a list useful.

[12] See P. A. Samuelson, *Foundations of Economic Analysis* (Harvard Press, Cambridge, 1948) pp. 266–8. The 'oscillations' on p. 153 below are clearly fallacious.

the 'Essay on Value' (see Items II.8.1 and II.2.1 above). Subsequently it was introduced into the first edition of the *Principles*, but then deleted.[13]

(iii) Marshall's controversial notion of irreversibilities in supply (Ch. III, § 7) is discussed below in the context of the *Pure Theory of Domestic Values*.[14]

Marshall added complete marginal summaries only to Chapter I, and these read as follows.

§ 1   The pure theory of foreign trade, is interesting chiefly on account of its indirect applications to certain social questions. The scope of these is described in the present chapter.

§ 2   The pure theory of economics advances by successive approximations, towards the end, not of dictating practice, but of guarding men against some sources of prevalent error in practical matters.

§ 3   The practical engineer must commence his training by solving hypothetical problems. So must the economist. Thus for each of the practical problems of commerce, assistance is required from both the pure theories of 'domestic' and of 'international' values.

§ 4   The earlier disciples of Ricardo underrated the difficulties which obstruct the free competition between adjacent industrial groups. Mill was a leader of the reaction against this error. Mr Cliffe Leslie has worked in the same direction. The deficiencies of the theory of domestic values when taken alone, require to be made up by an examination of that hypothesis which is the basis of the pure theory of foreign trade.

§ 5   This hypothesis can be applied directly to the relations of groups that are organised. The arrangements of the old guilds were possible only under the domain of routine. But improvements of communication are overtaking the requirements of modern organisations of industry. And rough applications of the principles of the pure theory of foreign trade are habitually made by combinations of employers, and by combinations of workmen. Commercial

[13] See *Principles II*, p. 360.
[14] See p. 184 below.

wars and treaties between adjacent industrial groups.
Formal organisations of employers.

§ 6   Combinations of men are again setting themselves to
regulate trade, without recognizing the fundamental ethical
principle which applies to such regulations. The success
of a free-trade policy has caused men carelessly to regard
as universally applicable its fundamental doctrine.

III.5.2   Text of *The Pure Theory of Foreign Trade*
Ch. I: *The Scope of the Pure Theory of Foreign Trade*

[§ 1]   It has been seen that the chief practical questions to
which the theory of foreign trade has been applied are not
adapted for exact quantitative treatment in the present state of
economic science: and in the first part of this work no attempt
has been made at quantitative analysis. The second part of
the work is mainly occupied with the erection of an apparatus
fitted for the quantitative treatment of certain problems which
are directly suggested by the actual conditions of foreign trade;
and which may be included under the title 'the pure theory of
foreign trade'.[1] In the present chapter some account is given
of the position which this theory holds in the body of economic
science and of the services which it is designed to render. It
will be argued that the fundamental hypotheses and therefore
the results of the theory are capable of being so modified as to
be applied in the treatment of other portions of economic
doctrine besides those which directly relate to foreign trade.

§ 2   Let us first consider how the pure theory of foreign trade
or 'international values' supplements the pure theory of the
relative values of commodities produced under perfectly

1 [In a subsequent revision, the remainder of this paragraph was replaced by the
following passage.]

Some of the results thus obtained may appear of but slight importance if they be
considered only with reference to the regulation of customs-duties. But many of
them may be brought to bear on a large class of ethico-economical questions
concerning the relations between different industrial groups in the same country.
These applications of the pure theory of foreign trade will not be worked out in
the present treatise: but it may be well here to indicate their range. This chapter
is accordingly devoted to explaining the position which the pure theory of foreign
trade holds in the body of economic science, and in particular to describing the
scope of its indirect applications to the relations in which various industrial groups
of capitalists and labourers, stand to one another and to the rest of society.

free competition in the same country. The province of the pure or abstract theory of Economics, as of every other deductive science, is to deduce conclusions from hypotheses which correspond as closely as may be to the conditions that occur in fact. The greater the simplicity of the hypotheses the less close can be this correspondence; but the greater can be the exactness of the conclusions deduced from them. The hypotheses which are selected for the groundwork of the science are simple. Familiarity with the process of tracing conclusions from such hypotheses gives the power of dealing with problems based on hypotheses which gradually become more complex, and therefore capable of being made to approximate more closely to the facts of life. The number of problems to be worked out increases at each successive stage of the approximation, and before many stages have been passed the number becomes so vast as to be wholly unmanageable. Moreover, in the later stages of the work ethical and other social considerations must be introduced that are not strictly homogeneous with those which enter into the fundamental hypotheses. The pure science of economics therefore may not attempt to formulate a collection of problems which should contain cases closely resembling each of the questions which are likely to arise in the business of life. The claims and professions made by the chief authors of the science on her behalf are carefully limited and studiously humble. These authors have claimed to work out a number of hypothetical cases so chosen that in all predictions and in all practical proposals which have reference to the public well-being, the inquirer – whether he be an economist or not – must in *some steps* of his reasoning approach closely to some of these cases.[2]

§ 3   Mill has brought out the fact that there is a close analogy between the methods of economic science, and those of the science of mechanics.[3] The engineer knows that there is in

---

[2] Compare the definitions of Economics Pure and Applied given in the Index of Definitions at the end of the book. [No trace of such an Index survives.]

[3] [See J. S. Mill, 'On the Definition of Political Economy', the fifth of his *Essays on Some Unsettled Questions of Political Economy* (*Collected Works*, Vol IV, especially pp. 329–31); idem, *A System of Logic*, Book VI, Chs. VIII, IX.]

nature no string that is perfectly flexible, no rod that is perfectly rigid. But as a preparation for dealing approximately with the complex conditions of equilibrium of suspension bridges and of tubular bridges, he practises himself in the pure theory of mechanics. He seeks exact solution of problems that treat of the simple conditions of equilibrium, on the one hand of imaginary strings that are perfectly flexible and on the other of imaginary rods that are perfectly rigid.

So the economist is well aware that there are no two places between which capital and labour circulate with perfect freedom; and that there are no two places in the civilised world such that the supply of capital and labour in one of them is not directly or indirectly affected by the supply of capital and labour in the other. He is aware that no account at once simple and accurate can be given of the conditions of equilibrium of trade between Staffordshire and Yorkshire or between Russia and Italy. But as a preparation for dealing approximately with complex conditions of equilibrium he first practises himself in the 'pure' theory of economics – in the exact solution of problems that treat of simple conditions. He investigates the equilibrium of trade on the one hand for imaginary places between which there is a perfectly free circulation of capital and labour; and on the other hand for imaginary places between which capital and labour do not circulate at all. The first class of problems forms the basis of the pure theory of the relative values of commodities produced under perfectly free competition 'in the same country' – or, as I shall henceforth call it, 'the pure theory of *domestic values*'. The latter class of problems forms the basis of 'the pure theory of *international values*'.

§ 4   The last generation of economists were wont to apply directly to the solution of practical problems the results obtained by pure theory on the hypothesis that capital and labour circulate with perfect freedom. They were wont to assume that no great error is in general introduced by applying without modification these results to questions concerning the relations between wages and prices in different places which were *de facto* in the same country. In fact men were for a time dazzled by the splendid display of the power of deductive reasoning in economics which Ricardo exhibited. But latterly a reaction has set in towards the circumspect inductions of Adam Smith, which had been thrown into the shade by Ricardo's brilliant performance. It has been found that movements of labour from one occupation to another in the same town or from one town to another a few miles off are at all events in the Old World in practice subject to hindrances of which the earlier disciples of Ricardo took little or no account. During the past thirty years economists have been gradually getting to apprehend that the pure theory of domestic values is capable of direct application only within a very narrow range.

We shall find, if we look into the questions of applied economics that concern relative wages, profits and prices in different industries in the same country, [that] much less than was supposed can be derived from the pure theory of domestic values when taken alone; and that much more aid than was supposed can be derived from the pure theory of international values.

The importance of inquiry in this direction was indicated by Mr Mill. In his chapter on competition and custom he says,

> Political economists generally, and English political economists above others, have been accustomed to lay almost exclusive stress upon the first of these agencies; to exaggerate the effect of competition, and to take into little account the other and conflicting principle. They are apt to express themselves as if they thought that competition actually does, in all cases, whatever it can be shown to be the tendency of competition to do. This is partly intelligible, if we consider that only through the principle of competition has political economy any pretension to the character of a science. So far as rents, profits, wages, prices, are determined by competition, laws may be assigned for them. Assume competition to be their exclusive regulator, and principles of broad generality and scientific precision may be laid down, according to which they will be regulated. The political economist justly deems this his proper business: and as an abstract or hypothetical science, political economy cannot be required to do, and indeed cannot do, anything

more. But it would be a great misconception of the actual
course of human affairs, to suppose that competition exercises in fact this unlimited sway.... Our reasonings must,
in general, proceed as if the known and natural effects of
competition were actually produced by it, in all cases in
which it is not restrained by some positive obstacle. Where
competition, though free to exist, does not exist, or where it
exists, but has its natural consequences overruled by any
other agency, the conclusions will fail more or less of being
applicable. To escape error, we ought, in applying the
conclusions of political economy to the actual affairs of
life, to consider not only what will happen supposing the
maximum of competition, but how far the result will be
affected if competition falls short of the maximum.[4]

In his chapter on differences of wages in different occupations
[Mill] refers to the hindrances imposed both by competition
and custom on the choice of an occupation within a country.[5]
He reproduces the substance of this account in his chapters on
the cost of production,[6] in the course of which he also calls
attention to the analogy that exists between the wages-problem
and the theory of international values. Mr Cliffe Leslie in a
suggestive article published in 1868[7] insists on the fact that
the conditions on which the theory of international values is
based are to be found to a great extent in the hindrances
which lie in the way of free competition between groups of
labourers in different occupations and between the inhabitants
of different districts in England. In an article published in 1872
the same writer accumulates from the recent history of prices
in Germany 'evidence... that the principles which govern
the partition of the world's currency among different countries, and the scale of international prices, apply also to the

[4] [J. S. Mill, *Principles of Political Economy*, Book II, Ch. IV, §§ 1, 3 (pp. 239, 244).]
[5] [Ibid., Book II, Ch. XIV. Marshall included here the lengthy quotation from § 2 (pp. 386–8), commencing 'But independently of these or any other artificial mono-polies...' and ending '...is exposed to increased and increasing competition from at least the class immediately below it.']
[6] [Ibid., Book III, Chs. III, IV, XV.]
[7] [T. E. Cliffe Leslie, 'Political Economy and the Rate of Wages', *Fraser's Magazine*, Vol 78 (July 1868) reprinted as an Appendix to idem, *Land Systems and Industrial Economy of Ireland, England and Continental Countries* (Longmans Green, London, 1870).]

distribution of a national currency and the comparative prices of different places in the same country.'[8,9]

Thus it has become manifest that adjacent industrial groups even in a civilised country may receive remunerations which do not closely correspond to the difficulties of the processes of production in which they are engaged. Economists have never denied that passing changes may cause considerable fluctuations in the market prices of any ware, and in the wages and profits of those engaged in producing it. But it used to be contended that wages and profits could not long remain abnormally high, or abnormally low, in any industry: that is that they could not long remain much higher or much lower than in adjacent industries which had similar incidental advantages and disadvantages and which required natural qualities equally rare, and artificial habits equally difficult. It is now seen that custom, lack of information and other hindrances do for very long periods of time prevent the supply of labour, and to a less degree the supply of capital, from being properly adjusted to the demand. Insomuch that the wages of labour in a particular industry may remain for more than a generation considerably higher or considerably lower than the 'natural' or 'normal' amount. By this I mean, as has just been said, that amount which, according to the average rates current in the country, is an adequate return for the difficulties and expenses of the special education required as a preparation for the work, an adequate rent for rare natural qualities that may be required, and an adequate recompense for the fatigue and other disadvantages which the work involves – it being assumed that the work is performed up to a given standard of efficiency.[10]

---

[8] [Idem, 'The Gold Question and the Movement of Prices in Germany', *Fortnightly Review*, Vol 18 (Nov 1872) pp. 554–71, reprinted under the title 'Prices in Germany in 1872', *Essays in Political Economy* (Hodges Figgis, Dublin; Longmans Green, London; 1888) pp. 332–55, where the quotation comes from p. 339. (It is also on p. 333 of the first edition, published as *Essays in Moral and Political Philosophy*.)]

[9] Latterly some of the results thus obtained by others have been appropriated, but not developed, by Professor Cairnes. [This footnote, subsequently deleted, presumably refers to J. E. Cairnes, *Some Leading Principles of Political Economy Newly Expounded* (Macmillan, London, 1874), Part III.]

[10] If this condition is omitted the discrepancies appear to be far greater than they really are. Compare Part I Ch. § . [The most likely cross-reference is to Ch. IV, § 12.]

The pure theory of domestic values cannot then be applied directly to the complete solution of questions concerning relative wages, profits and prices in the same country. Its shortcomings must be supplied by means of an examination of the various modes in which the price that an industry obtains for its wares may be affected by changes in the amount which it offers for sale, or what is generally the same thing by changes in its demand for the wares produced by other industries. And this is precisely the problem with the solution of which the pure theory of foreign trade is occupied.

§ 5   Much is to be learnt from the applications of the pure theory of foreign trade to the circumstances of the relations between the supply of and the demand for the wares produced or the services rendered by any unorganised industrial group. But this application becomes of vital moment in the case of those industrial groups which are formally organised and which set themselves deliberately to regulate the supply of their wares or of their services so as to dispose of them on terms as advantageous as possible to themselves.

In the Middle Ages the Teutonic spirit had made men prone to guilds and other industrial brotherhoods. These were welded together under staid conditions, and Precedent (das Hergebrachte) exerted almost undisputed sway over them. But the discovery of the New World and the second birth of mechanical science instituted a new order of things. The Era of change came with irresistible force upon industry. The old organisations would not and could not bend to it, and therefore they were broken to pieces by it. Efficient organisations could not again arise until it became possible for them to accommodate themselves rapidly to each new change. It had become necessary that they should be able not only to make continual readjustments in matters of detail, but also quickly to modify their purposes: they required frequently to review their principles of action as well as to decide promptly on questions of tactics. The railway, the printing press and the telegraph have increased the rapidity with which the requirements of industry have changed but the means of communication which they have developed during the present generation are rendering possible organisations of industry adapted to the circumstances of the new era.

When ironmasters or coalmasters or cotton manufacturers meet together in formal assembly and discuss whether it be not for their common interest that they should agree partially to suspend their operations they proclaim the fact that they constitute for some purpose 'a nation'. The principles which govern their conduct relatively to the community at large are closely akin to those by which the government of a country is guided when considering to what extent the burden of any of her import duties will be borne by other countries.

It is indeed true that informal combinations of masters were in some sort of working order in Adam Smith's time. But the same cannot be said of the complementary combinations, the trades unions. Until recently conferences of workers in a trade from distant parts of the kingdom were scarcely possible, but now they are frequent. It is possible now for the officers of a large Trades-Union, without incurring inordinate expense, to distribute to every member a full copy of the arguments for or against a particular decision. A direct and true vote is thus frequently collected from men scattered throughout the length and breadth of the country.

In fact the present generation has seen the birth of many of the agencies which are necessary for the existence of the great industrial republics of modern England. These agencies have rendered it possible now, as it was possible in the middle ages, for the tie of common occupation to bind men together into a kind of 'nation', just as they are bound together by the tie of geographic neighbourhood or of supposed community of descent. We have not now to discuss how much of evil enters into the 'patriotic' spirit which induces a working man to submit to grave hardships rather than act in opposition to the policy on which his trades-union has resolved. It is enough for our purpose that this feeling is sufficiently strong to enable the officers of a union to engage in war and make treaties of peace with confidence that their plans will be adopted and their decisions effectively carried out.

Again the history of every board of Arbitration and of Conciliation affords illustrations of the manner in which the masters and the workmen of a particular trade in any district regard themselves as, for many purposes, separate nations. They may be seen applying with more or less insight, the principles of the pure theory of foreign trade to questions concerning their commercial relations to one another, as well as to the great body of the consumers of their wares and to rival industrial groups who are engaged in producing similar wares.

It is advisable to dwell upon the close analogy which the politico-commercial relations which exist between two organised industrial groups bear to those which exist between two nations. The trades-guilds had continual quarrels with one another. In France a lawsuit between the second-hand clothiers and the tailors lasted three hundred years. The saddlers quarrelled with the wheelwrights, the makers of hardware with the blacksmiths, the nailers with the locksmiths, the publishers with the second-hand booksellers. Some of these hostile trades spent a million a year in law proceedings against their rivals.[11]

In recent times the bricklayers', the plasterers' and the masons' Unions have quarrelled as to the proper boundaries between their respective provinces. Episodes of alternating alliances and jealousies are to be found in the history of the relations between men engaged in iron-works and the colliers who supply the iron-works with coal; two groups of workers whose interests are, with regard to some questions, in harmony, and with regard to others, at variance.

In most parts of Lancashire the brickmakers' and bricklayers' associations are in alliance, offensive and defensive, one consequence of which is that within certain arbitrarily fixed limits, no bricks can be laid that have not been made within the same limits.... In one or two of the northern counties, the associated plasterers and associated plasterers' labourers have come to an understanding, according to which the latter are to abstain from all plasterers' work, except simple white-washing; and plasterers in return are to do nothing, except pure plasterers' work, that the labourers would like to do for them, insomuch that if a plasterer wants laths or plaster to go on with, he must not

---

[11] See *Fortnightly Review*, Vol XV, p. 515. [J. C. Morison, 'Two Chapters on the Reign of Louis XIV, Ch. II A.D. 1679–1715', *Fortnightly Review*, Vol 15 (Apr 1874) pp. 496–516.]

go and fetch them himself, but must send a labourer for them.[12]

Indeed almost all contests in support of the regulations by which each trade seeks to protect its own interests are faint echoes of the old commercial wars. The principle in each case is the same: one nation of men submit to be taxed in order that their government may wage successful war so as to control in their interests the manner in which their wares are sold to other nations. The action of the Grangers, or farmers unions, in America has proclaimed the fact that agriculturists are for some purposes a compact nation having interests distinct from those of the manufacturing classes. The formation with us of the Federation of Employers has proclaimed the fact that those who bring into the market the power of superintending industry regard themselves as, for some purposes, a 'nation' which carries on commerce with the rest of the community. While a corresponding fact with regard to the labouring classes as a whole is evidenced by the quiet but steady movements towards unity of organisation among Englishmen; and by the more ambitious schemes which find favour among some classes on the Continent.

Some years ago I attended a meeting advertised as of 'the working man's party' in Frankfort. There were present several hundred men whose countenances were remarkably intelligent. The strictest order prevailed, and there was no excitement which could urge the speakers into unusually strong language. But they persistently spoke of capital as 'the Enemy'.[13]

---

[12] Thornton on Labour Book III Ch. V. [W. T. Thornton, *On Labour*... (Macmillan, London, 1869) pp. 322, 325 of the first (1869) edition; pp. 344, 347 of the second (1870) edition.]

[13] [The manuscript includes here a long quotation (of 3 manuscript pages) 'from an article by Mr. Lloyd Jones on the Federation of Trade Societies' as 'characteristic of the views of working men with regard to the relations in which labourers as a body stand to capitalists as a body'. No reference is given. The following sentences are perhaps the most notable: 'The employers... can get, what is of great use in warfare of any kind, prompt decisions; and, therefore, more immediate and more effective action. On the other hand they have the great drawback of being competitors in the common markets in which they sell their goods... whilst the men have all one common interest.... the men as well as the employers recognize the doctrine of supply and demand. Only very foolish and inexperienced unionists think of striking in a declining trade.... We know that by the help of [a] union wages rise sooner in a rising market, and decline later in a falling market.']

There are signs that employers will set themselves to meet the powerful organisation of the Trades Unions by attempting to copy that organisation. Such attempts are subject to great difficulties and have not as yet been generally successful.[14]

§ 6   At one time the masters and workmen engaged in producing any ware used in some measure to take counsel together with a view to limiting the production of it. But after the breaking up of the guilds the workmen ceased for a long time to take any share in 'the regulation of trade' in this regard.[15] Recently, however, several Trades Unions have shown signs of an inclination, and to some extent of a power, to control the supply of the wares in the production of which they are specially interested. Trades Unions indeed frequently avow that in this matter they are guided solely by a consideration of the interests of their members. They seldom set themselves to consider the fundamental ethical question by which must be tested the principles of action of any industrial group which artificially limits the amount of its produce. This question is: Would the general adoption of these principles of action by each branch of industry be beneficial? Would it have the effect of steadying the course of industry, without to any considerable extent diminishing the aggregate supply of the means of subsistence and comfort, of physical, mental and moral improvement? Or would it so diminish these as seriously to injure the total happiness of the world and to check human progress? Nor is it reasonable to blame them without measure for not pondering over this question. This question has been in great measure ignored by capitalists

[14] [The manuscript includes here a lengthy quotation (of two manuscript pages) from *Capital and Labour* (The organ of the National Association of the Federated Employers of Labour) for 22 July 1874, so that 'the reader should have a clear notion of the form these attempts are taking.' The quotation deals with the formation of The South Yorkshire and North Derbyshire Coal Owners' Association, whose Articles required that 'no advance in the rate of wages payable to workmen ... or an alteration in the number of their hours, shall be made or agreed to be made by any member without the previous consent of the Board, except in the case of growing boys.']

[15] [A marginal note of later date appears at this point of the manuscript: 'Note the next six pages to be somewhat changed in form and transferred to Part IV'. Since only three further pages remain, it appears that at least three pages have been lost. None of Marshall's published writings is identifiably based on the following paragraphs.]

in their combinations and by statesmen in their tariffs. It is indeed true that many statesmen in old times and some statesmen in modern times have openly denied the existence of any obligation to make any sacrifice whatever with the purpose of promoting the welfare of other countries. And doctrines almost equally immoral have been avowed by some capitalists in defence of their adoption of a course of action which has inflicted on society an injury great in comparison with the benefit which has accrued to themselves from it. But the ethical considerations in question are neglected also by many men in all classes of society who would not adopt a low moral standard for their conduct; such men frequently justify to themselves the course which they pursue by the consideration that their conduct is in accordance with the doctrines of Political Economy.

The policy of Free Trade in England had to contend during several generations against a resolute force of combined ignorance and selfishness. The intelligence and public spirit of the country were enlisted on its side; and when at length it was adopted Englishmen were proud of having achieved an important step in the progress of civilisation. The increase of prosperity which followed has acted powerfully on men's imaginations; and the same habits of intellectual sloth which had caused men before to reject the doctrines of Free Trade without examining them, cause many men now to shun the labour of inquiring what are the exceptions to which these doctrines are liable. So that workmen and employers, merchants and statesmen, are under the impression that economic science teaches not only that as a rule 'each man in pursuit of his own direct interests is led to adopt that course in which he will be of the greatest service to society at large', but also that the exceptions to this rule are of trifling importance. A certain school of economists have indeed acquired the habit of regarding this doctrine as of almost absolute universal validity and are reckless in the applications they make of it. For instance they determine what course of action on the part of some particular group of working men would be most beneficial to society at large; and then set themselves to prove that every other course of action . . . .[16]

---

[16] [The manuscript ends here. For an earlier, but related, argument see Section V.2, below.]

Ch. II : *The Premises of the Pure Theory of Foreign Trade.*
The Method of Diagrams. The Fundamental Laws of Curves
which Represent International Demand

[§ 1]   The function of a pure theory is to deduce definite conclusions from definite hypothetical premises. The premises should approximate as closely as possible to the facts with which the corresponding applied theory has to deal. But the terms used in the pure theory must be capable of exact interpretation, and the hypotheses on which it is based must be simple and easily handled.

The pure theory of foreign trade satisfies these conditions. This theory is based upon the hypothesis that two countries, say England and Germany, carry on trade with each other but only with each other. It is assumed that they are not under any obligations to make foreign payments excepting those arising from trade, so that in equilibrium the exports of each country exchange for her imports. It is assumed that the pure theory of domestic values has provided the means of measuring the value in England of all the various wares exported by England in terms of any one of them. Suppose cloth of a definite quality to be one of them; then the value, in England, of all the wares which England exports may be expressed as that of a certain number of yards of cloth. So the value in Germany of all the wares which Germany exports, may be expressed as that of, say, a certain number of yards of linen.

We may for brevity use the phrase 'a certain number of yards of cloth,' as a substitute for the complete phrase 'English wares the equivalent of a certain number of yards of cloth': and so for linen. Further we may consider that the processes of producing the cloth and the linen are not completed until the cloth and the linen are delivered in Germany and England respectively. By this means we shall avoid the necessity of specially mentioning the expenses of transport; so that we shall find no occasion to follow Mill in making the assumption that the expenses of transport may be neglected.

We may apply this method of speaking to express the conditions under which trade is in equilibrium; i.e. is such that there is no tendency for the imports and exports of the countries in question to increase or to diminish. Thus: – In equilibrium a certain number, say ten million, of yards of cloth are exported annually to Germany and sold there for a price which covers the expenses of producing a certain number, say fifteen million, of yards of linen. Vice versa, fifteen million yards of linen are exported to England and sold there for a price which covers the expense of producing ten million yards of cloth.

We are now in a position to give a definite interpretation to the phrase 'the rate of interchange between two countries' in place of the inexact account sometimes given. We may measure the rate of interchange between England and Germany by the amount of linen which England obtains in return for each yard of cloth which she exports.

It seems on the whole best thus to represent the value of the wares which England exports as equivalent to that of a certain number of yards of cloth. But we might measure it as equivalent to a certain number of units of English capital and labour, or as we may say as equivalent to a certain number of units of English cost of production.[1] We should then measure the rate of interchange between England and Germany by the number of units of German cost of production which England obtains in return for the produce of a given number of units of her cost of production. This latter method of measurement has several advantages, and there is no reason why it should not be adopted in the treatment of some portions of the pure theory of foreign trade. But for the general purposes of the theory the method of measurement first given will be found to be the most convenient.

The theory of foreign trade is necessarily difficult. Mill when introducing it says, 'I must give notice that we are now in the region of the most complicated questions which Political Economy affords; that the subject is one which cannot possibly be made elementary; and that a more continuous effort of attention than has [in the earlier portions of the science] been required, will be necessary [in order] to follow the series of

---

[1] For a solution of the ambiguities connected with the use of this phrase see Appendix I. [No trace of this appendix survives, but the treatment was probably intended to be on lines similar to that in the essay on 'Mr. Mill's Theory of Value', which Marshall published in the *Fortnightly Review*, Apr 1876 (*Memorials*, pp. 119–33).]

deductions'.[2] The unavoidable difficulties of the subject are
great: but students frequently fall into errors which they may
easily avoid if they will resolve that when discussing the pure
theory they will not speak of the imports or exports of a
country as measured in terms of money.

Suppose that the fact to be expressed is that England has
increased her demand for the wares of Germany; and has
thereby caused the rate of interchange to be altered to her
disadvantage.

It is found by experience that students commencing the
subject have a tendency to describe this fact thus: – England
used to import (say) ten million pounds worth of German
wares, giving for them (after allowing for carriage) ten million
pounds worth of English: but her demand for German wares
increases so that she purchases twelve million pounds worth;
and, the rate of interchange being altered to her disadvantage
she has to give in return for them (after allowing for carriage)
thirteen million pounds worth of her own wares.

This statement is inaccurate because it ignores the changes
that will meanwhile have occurred in the standards of prices in
the two countries. After, as well as before, the change in
England's demand, each million pounds worth of English
goods will be exchanged (allowance being made for the cost
of carriage) for a million pounds worth of German goods,
prices being measured according to the new standard. But the
change will have caused gold to flow from England to Germany,
so as to raise prices in Germany and lower them in England.
So that the above statement should have been: – England
imports an amount of German wares which according to the
old standard of German prices was worth twelve million
pounds, but according to the new standard of prices is worth
(say) twelve and a half millions. In exchange England exports
an amount of her own wares which according to the old
standard of her prices was worth thirteen million pounds, but
according to the new standard is worth twelve and a half
millions. This statement is accurate but uselessly complex.
And the complexities of which this is an instance, increase till

---

[2] [J. S. Mill, *Principles of Political Economy*, Book III, Ch. XVIII, § 1 (p. 596). The
insertions and capitalisations are Marshall's.]

they become wholly unmanageable if the attempt is made to proceed far into the pure theory of foreign trade on the plan of measuring exports and imports in terms of money.

§ 2   We may now proceed to consider the laws which govern the demand of one country for the wares of another. The explanation of these laws is tolerably simple, so long as we are dealing only with the normal conditions of foreign trade. Under ordinary circumstances, a decrease in a country's exports will cause her to obtain her imports on terms more advantageous, but not much more advantageous than before. There will be increased competition for her wares in foreign markets, and consequently their price will tend to rise; but as some at least of her wares will be closely pressed by the rivalry of foreign producers, the rate of interchange will not be altered in her favour sufficiently to prevent a decrease in the amount of her imports. Similarly any increase in her exports will cause her to obtain an increase in her imports, though she will obtain them on somewhat less advantageous terms. So long, then, as we assume these normal conditions to exist, we may trace the changes of foreign trade by means of the ordinary processes of general reasoning, without the aid of any artificial apparatus. But such a treatment becomes very difficult, if not impossible, when we pass to consider exceptional cases in which these normal conditions fail: and it is the special task of the pure theory of foreign trade to deal with such exceptional cases. The only apparatus which Ricardo and Mill brought to bear on the problems of pure economic theory was that of arithmetical illustration. But this is inadequate to the work. The use of numerical examples will perhaps enable the investigator to ascertain some of the consequences which may arise from the causes into whose operation he is inquiring: but it affords no security that he will discover all of these consequences or even the most important of them. Moreover when he has deduced certain conclusions from a particular set of numbers which he has chosen to illustrate certain general premises, he is not unlikely to infer that these conclusions follow necessarily from the premises he has laid down: whereas these conclusions may be latent in the particular choice of numbers that he has made, and may not be capable of being deduced from every set of numbers which satisfy the conditions laid down in the general premises. Experience proves that even powerful thinkers are liable to be thus led into error in spite of their being well aware that the legitimate use of numerical examples is only to illustrate and not to prove general rules.[3] The weakness and inefficiency of this apparatus will be demonstrated in the course of the present examination of the theory of foreign trade. For the free use of numerical examples has not enabled Ricardo and Mill to discover the conclusions which follow necessarily from their hypothesis.

The pure theory of economic science requires the aid of an apparatus which can grasp and handle the general quantitative relations on the assumption of which the theory is based. The most powerful engines for such a purpose are supplied by the various branches of mathematical calculus. But diagrams are of great service, wherever they are applicable, in interpreting to the eye the processes by which the methods of mathematical analysis obtain their results. It happens that with a few unimportant exceptions all the results which have been obtained by the application of mathematical methods to pure economic theory can be obtained independently by the method of diagrams.

Diagrams present simultaneously to the eye the chief forces which are at work, laid out, as it were, in a map; and thereby suggest results to which attention has not been directed by the use of the methods of mathematical analysis. The method of diagrams can be freely used by every one who is capable of exact reasoning, even though he have no knowledge of Mathematics. The reader, who will take the trouble to assure himself that he thoroughly understands the account of the curves given in the following paragraphs, will not find difficulty in following the reasoning to which they are afterwards applied.

§ 3   The most convenient mode of procedure will be to commence by examining the conditions of the first of the exceptional cases to which reference has been made;[4] then

---

[3] [On this point, compare Item II.7.2 above.]

[4] [This reference presumably occurred in one of the earlier missing chapters of Part I – probably Ch. I (compare Part I, Ch. VI, § 1, in Section III.3 above).]

to interpret the normal conditions of the problem as well as these exceptional conditions into the language of diagrams; and afterwards to treat the second exceptional case, which is of minor importance.

The first exceptional case is that of a group of problems in which it is assumed that a diminution of the total exports of a country may cause these to be in such urgent demand abroad that she obtains in return for her diminished exports an increased instead of a diminished supply of foreign wares. The results of an investigation of this exceptional case are capable of being applied in the partial and indirect solution of some practical problems connected with the trade that is carried on between existing countries; particularly in connection with duties on exportation. But the chief importance of these results arises from the fact that they may be applied to the trade that a compact industrial group carries on with its neighbours. We shall refer to this class of problems as 'Class I'; and shall give the name of 'Class II' to the second exceptional case to which reference has been made; the case, namely, in which an increase in the amount of wares which a country produces for exportation effects a very great diminution in the expenses at which she can produce them; so that the consequent fall in their value diminishes the total amount of the imports that she receives in exchange for them.[5] When we are considering the circumstances of trade from which both these exceptional cases are excluded, we may for brevity say that we are discussing the 'Normal class' of problems.

Applying this classification to the special case of the trade in cloth and linen which we have supposed to be carried on between England and Germany, we may say: – Every increase in the amount of linen which is thrown annually on the English market will necessitate a cheapening of the terms on which it is offered for sale. The effect of this cheapening will (save in problems of Class II) cause each yard of linen to exchange for the means of producing and exporting a smaller amount of cloth than before: that is, will alter the rate of interchange in England's favour.[6] In the Normal Class this alteration will be

---

[5] [As the later discussion shows, this should read 'in exchange for a yard of cloth.']

[6] An examination of the extraordinary circumstances in which this may not be true will be found in §§ 5, 6.

slight, so that every increase in the amount of linen imported will occasion an increase in the amount of cloth exported. But in Class I an increase in the amount of linen imported will depress the price at which it can be sold in England, and it will alter the rate of interchange in England's favour to so great an extent as to cause the amount of cloth exported not to increase but diminish. A precisely similar statement of course applies to Germany's demand for cloth. Class I may be illustrated numerically thus: – Suppose the sale of 10 million yards of linen in England to afford the means of purchasing and exporting 10 million yards of cloth, the rate of interchange being thus, one yard of cloth to one yard of linen. An increase in the amount of linen to 15 million yards may perhaps cause the amount of cloth to increase to 12 million: while it is possible that a further increase in the linen to 20 million may so force down its price in the English market as to cause the rate of interchange to become two yards of linen for one of cloth; in which case the amount of cloth which Germany obtains will fall to ten million yards.

§ 4   Let us now commence to interpret the laws of international demand into the language of diagrams. Let distances measured along a fixed straight line Ox (Figure 1) represent numbers of yards of cloth. Let distances measured along a straight line Oy at right angles to Ox represent numbers of yards of linen. Let a curve OE be drawn as follows: – N being any point upon Oy, let it be determined from a knowledge of the circumstances of England's demand for linen, what is the number of yards of cloth, the expenses of producing and exporting which will be covered annually by the proceeds of the sale in England of an amount of linen represented by ON. From Ox measure off OM, equal to this number of yards of cloth. Draw lines through M and N at right angles to Ox and Oy respectively, meeting in P; then P is a point on the required curve, OE. If N be moved from O gradually along Oy, P will assume a series of positions, each of which corresponds to one position of N; the continuous string of points thus formed will be the curve OE. (In other words, OE will be the locus of P.) If we were applying the method of diagrams to the trade that is actually carried on between two countries,

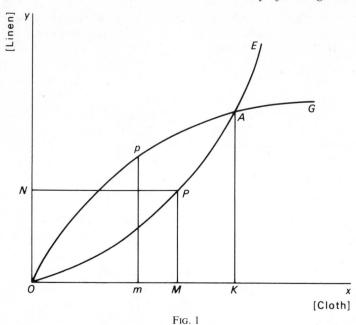

Fig. 1

we could not indeed obtain trustworthy data for drawing more than a limited portion of the curve. For it is not possible to conjecture with any approach to certainty what would be the terms on which it would be possible to sell in a country an amount of imports, either very much greater, or very much less, than that which is actually sold there. But for the purposes of the pure theory we are at liberty to suppose that the curve is properly drawn throughout its entire length. We may call *OE* 'England's demand curve'; and bearing in mind that *PM* is equal to *ON*, we may describe it thus : –

England's demand curve is such that any point P *being taken on it, and* PM *being drawn perpendicular to* Ox; *OM represents the amount of cloth which England will be willing to give annually for an amount of linen represented by* PM.

In exactly the same way we may construct a curve *OG* which may be called Germany's demand curve, and which may be described thus : –

Germany's demand curve is such that any point p being taken upon it and pm being drawn perpendicular to Ox; *pm represents*

the amount of linen which Germany will be willing to give
annually for an amount of cloth represented by Om.

It may not be superfluous to state explicitly that the period
for which the supplies of cloth and linen are reckoned is taken
as a year only for the purposes of definiteness and brevity. If
the phrase 'in a given unit of time' were not cumbrous, it
might be substituted throughout for the word 'annually.'

The terms in which the curves are described imply that there
is no change in the circumstances which govern the amount of
linen that England is willing to take at each particular rate of
interchange: and similarly that the circumstances which
govern the German demand for cloth remain constant. As a
matter of fact the causes which govern the demand of a country
for foreign wares do vary from time to time. They are altered
by every change that affects her power of raising on the one
hand the wares which she exports, and on the other domestic
rivals to the wares which she imports; by almost every invention, and almost every change of fashion. But, as has been
already said, we should aim at simplicity in our first approximations, in order that they may be easily manageable. Therefore,
we are to neglect for the present all consideration of the disturbances arising from such variations; leaving account to be
taken of them in the applications of the results of the pure
theory to practical issues.

§ 5   We may now interpret into the language of curves the
laws of international demand. The first proposition to be
laid down requires no proof. It is that corresponding to every
statement that can be made with regard to the terms on which
England may be willing to export cloth in exchange for linen,
there is a similar statement with regard to the terms on which
Germany may be willing to [ex]port linen in exchange for
cloth. Or in other words: –

PROP. I.   *Every statement as to the shape which it is possible*
for OE *to assume, has corresponding to it a similar statement as*
to the shape which it is possible for OG *to assume; but wherever*
Ox *occurs in the former statement,* Oy *will occur in the latter,*
and vice versa; whenever reference is made to a horizontal
straight line in the former, there must be made reference in the
latter to a vertical straight line, and vice versa.

If the reader should be unaccustomed to such a process of substitution, he may be helped to realise its validity, if he will draw any one of the figures that belong to the pure theory of foreign trade, with a broad pen on thin paper. He should then hold the paper between him and the light, with the reverse of the paper to him, with Oy horizontal, and Ox pointing vertically upwards. He will see through the paper, the two curves OE and OG with their places interchanged. Whatever proposition the figure has been used to prove with regard to OE, will now apply without any change or substitution to OG; when he has gone through this proof, he may turn the figure back again to its old position. He will observe that this proposition does not affirm that in any particular state of the trade, the shape of OG will be similar to the shape of OE: but only that whatever be the limits within which the possible variations in the shape of OE are confined by the fundamental laws of foreign trade, there exist precisely similar limits for OG.

It will suffice therefore to examine at length the laws which relate to the shape of OE. We may first lay down some laws which hold in the Normal Class and Class I, but not in Class II.

Let us suppose N to move from O along Oy, and let us watch the corresponding changes in the magnitude of OM and in the ratio of ON to OM. We find : –

PROP. II. *For the Normal Class and Class I: if* P *be a point moving along* OE, *and* PM, PN *drawn perpendicular to* Ox *and* Oy *respectively, every increase in* PM *is accompanied by an increase in the ratio of* PM *to* OM.

For the greater the amount of linen that has to be disposed of annually in England, the less will be the general purchasing power over which each yard of it will give command: and therefore, the less the amount of cloth that will be given in exchange for each yard of linen. The only exception to this is in the problems of Class II, in which an increase in the amount of cloth made for exportation may conceivably so increase the economy of its production as to enable a yard of cloth to be obtained by a less amount of general purchasing power than before. From this proposition we obtain at once,

PROP. III.   *In curves of the Normal Class and of Class I
if* P *be any point in* OE, *every point in that portion of* OE *which
is between* O *and* P *must lie below the straight line* OP*; and
every point in the remaining portion of* OE *must lie above the
straight line* OP *produced. Similarly if* p *be any point in* OG
every point in that portion of OG *which is between* O *and* [p]
must lie to the left of the line Op, *and every point in the remaining
portion of* OG *must lie to the right of the straight line* Op
produced. Hence we obtain at once,

PROP. IV.   *If either of the curves belongs to the Normal
Class or to Class I it cannot cut twice any straight line through*
O.

This result may be expressed in another form which will
be more convenient for some purposes thus:

Let *P* be a point such that *PM* being drawn perpendicular
to *Ox*, *PM* is the amount of linen which Germany is actually
sending to England at any time in exchange for *OM* cloth.
(We shall hereafter (see Ch.[III]) call this point *P* the 'Exchange-
index.') Then the rate of interchange is indicated by the ratio
between *PM* and *OM*. This ratio will be constant whatever
position *P* may have on any given straight line through *O*.
So that the rate of interchange is determined by the magnitude
of the angle which the straight line joining *P* and *O* makes
with *Ox*:[7] the greater this angle is, the more advantageous the
rate of interchange is to England, and the less advantageous it
is to Germany. Therefore Prop. IV may be put in the form,

PROP. IV. COR.   *If the demand curve of a country belong to
the Normal Class or to Class I, the amount of foreign wares
which she will import is determined when the rate of interchange
is known.*

Again, in the Normal Class and in Class I when the amount
of linen offered for sale in England is very small, it will be disposed of on terms advantageous to Germany, so that the

---

[7] It is measured mathematically by tan *POx* from the point of view of England, and
by cot *POx* from the point of view of Germany. The mathematical reader will observe
that in the Normal Case and in Case I the curves may have points of contrary flexure.
That is, if $y = f(x)$ be the equation of *OE*, $f''(x)$ may change sign at any point on the
curve. But $d(y/x)/dy$ must remain positive: i.e. $x - y(dx/dy)$ must remain positive;
i.e. every straight line which touches *OE* must cut *Ox* to the right of *O*. There is an
obvious geometrical proof of this result.

amount of cloth exported in exchange for it will be proportionally large. Thus where *PM* is small, the ratio of *PM* to *OM* is small: and a point moving from *O* along *OE* will keep at first close to *Ox*. So a point moving from *O* along *OG* will keep at first close to *Oy*.

It can hence be inferred, or it can be proved directly from Prop. IV, that:

PROP. V.   *In the Normal Class and in Class I that portion of* OE *which is adjacent to* O *lies below that portion of* OG *which is adjacent to* O.

Thus we may not invert the positions which *OE* and *OG* have in Figure 1 in the neighbourhood of *O*.

Under Class II we shall have to discuss the forms which *OE* may assume if the production of cloth on a large scale for exportation renders possible important economies that would otherwise be impossible. But however extensive these economies may be, they cannot cause the total expenses of producing any given amount of cloth to be less than the total expenses of producing a smaller amount. Hence the general condition of the arts of production being assumed, we know definitely the expenses of producing any given amount of cloth in England for exportation.

Therefore *OE* cannot bend downwards towards *Ox* after the manner of the curve in Figure 2. For if *OE* could assume a shape such that a horizontal line *AB* could be drawn cutting it in *A* and *B;* then, *AC* and *BD* being drawn perpendicular to *Ox*, the shape of the curve would imply the following statement: – *AC* linen is just capable of being sold for the expenses of producing *OC* cloth: and also *BD* linen (which is the same as *AC* linen) is capable of being sold for the expenses of producing *OD* cloth. But this is impossible. Thus we obtain a fundamental law which is valid for the Normal Class and for Classes I and II and is the only law to which the curves must conform under all circumstances: viz.

PROP. VI.   OE *cannot in any case be cut more than once by a horizontal line. Similarly* OG *cannot in any case be cut more than once by a vertical line.*

§ 6   Let us next investigate the laws which bind the curves if they belong to the Normal Class, but not if they belong to

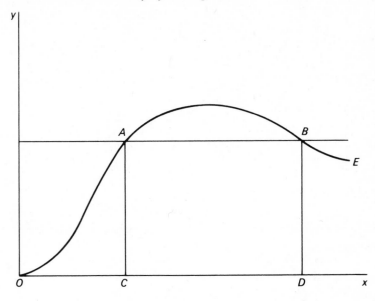

Class I. For the Normal Class, but not for Class I it is assumed that every increase in the amount of linen offered for sale annually in England increases the total proceeds of the sale, and consequently increases the amount of cloth that is exported in exchange for it. That is to say: if from N, any point in Oy, NP be drawn at right angles to Oy to meet the curve OE in P, then the greater be ON the greater also is NP. But in Class I, as N moves from O along Oy the increase in ON though it is at first accompanied by an increase in NP, yet when N arrives at a certain point (V in Figure 3) NP ceases to increase and begins to diminish, and the curve bends round towards Oy. These and corresponding results may be put in the following convenient form:

PROP. VII.   *In the Normal Class* OE *cannot cut the same vertical line more than once: but it may in Class I. So in the Normal Class* OG *cannot cut the same horizontal line more than once; but it may in Class I.*

In Figure 3 the curves cut one another only in one point; but consistently with the conditions of Class I they may cut one

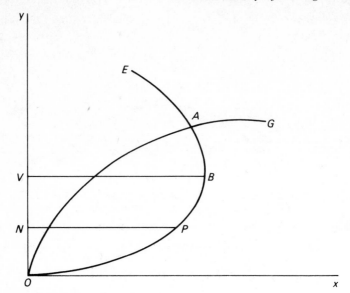

FIG. 3

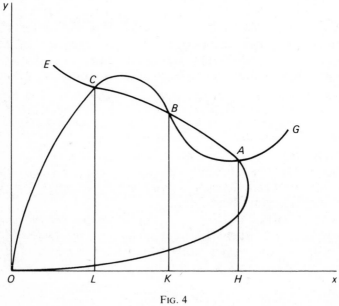

FIG. 4

another several times, as represented in Figure 4. It may be well formally to prove that:

PROP. VIII.   *In the Normal Class* OE *and* OG *cannot cut one another in more than one point* (*besides* O).

Let A be a point of intersection of the curves (see Figure 1); then AE must lie entirely above OA produced, by Prop. [III]; and AG must lie entirely to the right of OA produced: consequently AE and AG cannot cut again. Nor can AE cut the portion of OG which lies between O and A. For by Prop. VI the portion of OG between O and A must lie entirely to the left of a vertical straight line through A; and by Prop. VII AE must lie entirely to the right of this straight line. Similarly AG cannot cut the portion of OE which lies between O and A. Therefore OE and OG cannot meet except in O and A.

PROP. IX.   *Every point in which the two curves cut one another corresponds to an equilibrium of the trade.*

Let AH, BK, CL be drawn perpendicular to Ox.[8] Then since A is a point on OE, AH linen can be sold annually in the English market for a price which will just cover the expenses of producing (and exporting to Germany) OH cloth: and since A is a point on OG, OH cloth can be sold annually in the German market for a price which will just cover the expenses of producing (and importing to England) AH linen. That is, when OH cloth is exchanged for AH linen, there is no force present either to increase or diminish England's exports or imports: trade is in equilibrium. A precisely similar proof shows that trade is in equilibrium when OK cloth is exchanged for BK linen. In the following chapter it will be proved that the equilibrium of the trade is *stable* in each of the positions represented by A in Figure 3 and by A and C in Figure 4: but that it is unstable in the position represented by B in Figure 4. The possibility of more than one position of equilibrium in such cases as this has been noticed by Mill. His treatment of the matter is certainly inadequate: for he has failed to discover the laws which determine whether any particular position of equilibrium is stable or unstable. It is, generally speaking, true of Mill as of Adam Smith, that much of his work which appears at first sight to contain error, proves

---

[8] [This refers to Figure 4, but may also be applied to Figure 5.]

itself on further investigation to be only incomplete or incompletely expressed. This is however one of the few instances in which careful study has failed to convince me that Mill's work is right as far as it goes. The reader who may care to inquire into this matter is referred to the Note at the end of the present chapter.[9]

§ 7   We may proceed to the discussion of problems of Exceptional Class II. The case does not yet appear to have much direct bearing on questions relating either to the trade that is actually carried on between existing countries, or to the terms on which any compact industrial group is able to sell its wares or its services. But it claims attention on the ground that it is not logically excluded by the hypothesis on which the pure theory of foreign trade has been constructed since the time of Ricardo. Moreover history shows that the practical applications of the work of pure science have in general been discovered after, and not before, that work was done; advances in that applied knowledge which gives us direct command over nature have never been made with rapidity except when men have been willing to expend some pains on completing the solution of problems suggested to them by pure science, even although the practical purposes which the various portions of their work would subserve could not be discovered beforehand. Finally no great amount of additional trouble will be involved in working out this exceptional case.

This case has its origin in the fact that the wares which a country exports may be such that the difficulty of producing them diminishes very rapidly when their amount increases. It is indeed true, as has been said,[10] that in general the production of a commodity on a large scale for home consumption precedes the development of any considerable foreign trade in it. Still the extent to which division of labour in the production of it can be carried, is enlarged by every extension of the foreign markets for it. For instance, there exist in England large groups of works each of which groups is filled with expensive machinery that is adapted exclusively for making the special machinery that is required in some one class of

---

[9] [See p. 148 below.]
[10] [This seems to refer to one of the missing chapters of Part I.]

manufactures, and the growth of such works has been very greatly promoted by foreign trade. Adam Smith mentioned as one of the chief advantages of foreign trade that 'By means of it, the narrowness of the home market does not hinder the division of labour in any particular branch of art or manufacture from being carried to the highest perfection.'[11] And it is certain that in the century which has followed the publication of Adam Smith's work England's export trade has exerted a quiet but constant influence in developing broad inventions and economies in manufacture. These have benefited foreign countries in the first instance by causing England to sell them her manufactured goods on cheap terms, and in the second instance by passing over to those countries and assisting them to manufacture for themselves.

Thus it is possible, to revert to our old hypothesis, that an increase in Germany's demand for English cloth may to so great an extent develop the facilities which England has for producing cloth as to cause a great and permanent fall in the value of cloth in England. It is true that in order to obtain this cloth Germany will have in general to force a sale here for an increased amount of her own products, and consequently to lower their price. But it is conceivable that under exceptional conditions the increase in the amount of English cloth required for exportation to Germany may cause an increase in the economy of producing cloth so rapid and extensive that the fall in the price of cloth in England may be greater than the fall in the price of linen. Thus it is possible that an increase in Germany's demand for English cloth may cause each yard of linen to be sold here on such terms as to give command over a larger amount of cloth than before; it is possible that an increase in Germany's demand for English cloth may cause her to obtain an import of English cloth increased *in a greater ratio* than is her export of linen to England.

The introduction of the economies which were requisite in order to render possible such cases as this on a large scale have seldom been effected within a short space of time. The lapse of generations has been required for that development of England's invention and economies in manufacture which was

---

[11] [*Wealth of Nations*, Book IV, Ch. 1, pp. 195–6, (Modern Library edition, p. 415).]

above attributed in part to her export trade. And the practical importance of such cases as have occurred on a somewhat small scale is in general less than at first sight appears. Let us examine one such case. The agricultural implements which England makes for herself are not always adapted for use in countries where the population is sparse. Eastern Europe wants field steam engines in which straw can be used as fuel; she wants mowing and reaping machines that can be used on uneven ground. Special knowledge, special skill and special machinery are to a great or less extent required for the manufacture of these implements. For some time England played a very poor part in the work; partly because she had to compete with America who had organised this manufacture for her own market. At length the steady increase in the volume of the demand for these implements is enabling Englishmen to produce them with rapidly increasing economy. But their present success arises in great measure from their having had experience in the manufacture of wares of similar kind; and the main body of the work in which this experience has been obtained, is directed to the supply of the home market.

Let us proceed to interpret problems of Class II in the language of diagrams. Let P, Q (Figure 5) be two points on OE such that PM and QR being drawn perpendicular to Ox, QR is greater than PM. We found that in the Normal Class and in Class I the ratio of QR to OR must be greater than the ratio of PM to OM (Prop. II). But in Class II it is possible for an increase in the amount of cloth produced in England so to diminish the expenses of producing each yard, that an increase in the amount of linen imported, although it will cause the value of each yard of linen in England to fall, may yet cause each yard of linen to give the means of purchasing a greater amount of cloth than before: so that the exports of cloth increase not in a less ratio, but in a greater ratio than the imports of linen. So that the ratio of QR to OR may be less than the ratio of PM to OM. Hence,

PROP. X.　　*In Class II the curves do not necessarily conform to the laws which are enunciated in Prop. II, III, IV, V and VII as valid for the Normal Class and for Class I.*

Thus for instance OE and OG may lie as in Figure 5; and may cut each other at A, B and C. The proof given in Prop. IX

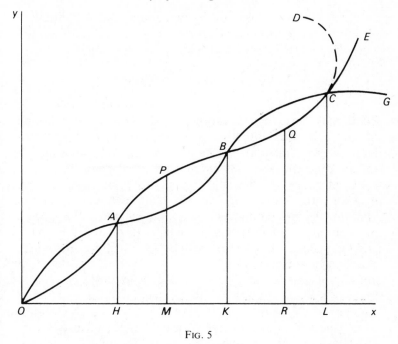

Fig. 5

that every point of intersection of the curves corresponds to a
position of equilibrium of the trade applies to this case. It
will be proved in the next chapter that *A* and *C* correspond to
stable, and *B* to unstable, equilibrium. It must be remembered
that it has been proved in Prop. VI that in no case whatever
can *OE* cut any horizontal line twice, nor can *OG* cut any
vertical line twice. It is possible for *OE* in Figure 5, ultimately
to bend back towards *Oy*, as does the dotted portion *CD*,
if it happen that a very large amount of linen is incapable of
being sold in England except on terms extremely advantageous
to England.

The reader may exercise his fancy by drawing various forms
which the curves may have, consistently with the fundamental
laws that have been laid down, and combining them in pairs
so as to observe their possible points of intersection. After
reading the next chapter he may interpret the points of intersection; of course the positions of the curves in Figure 5 are
capable of being inverted. They would then represent a case

in which the trade between the two countries could not grow up gradually; but could be carried on with profit to both if it were once started on a large scale by any external cause.

Note on Mill's Treatment of an Exceptional Case[12]

In § 6 of Ch. XVIII of Book III Mill attempts to deal with difficulties in the theory of foreign trade, of which a solution is offered in the Examination of Class I in the present Essay. He has seen that under certain circumstances there may be several different positions of equilibrium of trade: so that the problem arises of determining at which of these several positions the trade will remain. Mill has undertaken to illustrate by an example the method in which this general problem may be solved. But it appears to me that the special example which he has chosen does not illustrate the general problem in question. For I understand him to mean that the amount of cloth which England will expend on the purchase of linen is a given quantity, independent of the rate of interchange, say OV; and that the amount of linen which Germany is willing to expend in the purchase of cloth is a given quantity; say OW. On this hypothesis the trade has only one possible position of equilibrium; viz. that in which OV cloth is exchanged for OW linen. Mill has proved, what indeed is obvious, that the division of the total benefits of the trade between the two countries depends upon the relative magnitudes of OV and OW.

Mill's example may be represented in a diagram thus. Draw (Figure 6) VPQ and WRS at right angles to Ox and Oy respectively, cutting one another in A. Let VP be the amount of linen which England could make for herself with the expense to which she is put in order to make and export OV cloth, then PQ is a portion of England's demand curve, which in this case has 'degenerated' (in mathematical phrase) into a straight line. Similarly if WR be the amount of [cloth] which Germany could make for herself with the expense to which she is put in order to make and export OW linen, then RS is a portion of Germany's demand curve. These two straight

[12] [This note refers to J. S. Mill, *Principles of Political Economy*, Book III, Ch. XVIII, § 6 (pp. 607–9).]

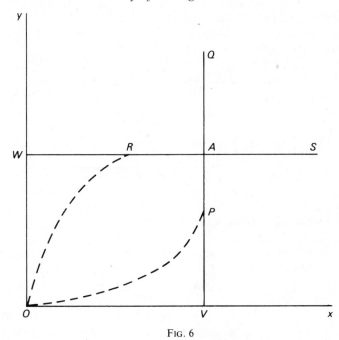

lines *PQ* and *RS* cannot intersect in more than one point. Mill's example therefore does not afford any aid towards the solution of the class of problems which are suggested by the intersections of the curves in Figure 4. With regard to division of the benefits of the trade between the two countries it may be remarked that if *A* coincides with *P* England has to pay for her imported linen the full equivalent of what it would cost her to make it herself; and therefore she derives no benefit from the trade. So if *A* coincides with *R*, Germany derives no benefit from the trade. The further *A* is above *P*, the greater is the benefit that England derives from the trade: the further *A* is to the right of *R*, the greater is the benefit that Germany derives from the trade. Of course, by the conditions of the problem, *A* cannot lie below *P*, or to the left of *R*.

Ch. III :   *Stable and Unstable Equilibrium of Foreign Trade*

§ 1   It will be convenient to have a name for the point which corresponds to the actual position of the trade between

England and Germany at any time. It generally happens in fact that the exports and imports of a country are not distributed evenly all over the year. Allowance must be made for these irregularities before the results of the pure theory can be applied to practice. But for the purposes of the pure theory it is allowable to assume that the importation and the consumption of foreign wares is distributed evenly all over the year.

Thus we may say that cloth is at any time being imported into Germany on the scale of OM annually (or in a given unit of time); meaning thereby that the scale on which it is being imported is such that if it were to continue, the amount imported in the year (or unit of time) would be OM.

We have then the following: −

DEFINITION. If at any time cloth be exported from England on the scale of OM annually, in exchange for linen on the scale of ON annually; and MP, NP be drawn at right angles to Ox, Oy respectively, meeting in P; then P is the exchange-index at that time.

It has been proved in Prop. IX that the trade is in equilibrium when the exchange-index is at any point of intersection of OE and $[OG]$. In the present chapter it will be shown that some points of intersection correspond to stable equilibrium of the trade and others to unstable: and a fundamental law will be laid down by which the one set may be distinguished from the other. It will be convenient to commence by supposing that the exchange-index is not at A: but that some external disturbing force, as a war, or a bad harvest, has jerked the exchange-index to some position such that the trade corresponding to it is not in equilibrium; and to investigate the forces which will govern its motion.

We know from Prop. VI that OE cannot cut a horizontal straight line through P more than once: and that OG cannot cut a vertical straight line through P more than once. We may have therefore the following:−

DEFINITION. A point P is said to be *to the right* or *to the left* of OE according as it is to the right or the left of the point in which OE is cut by the horizontal straight line through P: and the point P is said to be *above* or *below* OG according as it is above or below the point in which OG is cut by a vertical straight line through P.

§2   The greater part of the pure theory of foreign trade
consists of a series of corollaries from the laws with regard to
the shapes of *OE* and *OG*, which were laid down in the last
chapter, together with the following law: –

PROP. XI.   *If the Exchange-index be at any time to the right
of* OE *it will tend to move to the left; if it be to the left of* OE
*it will tend to move to the right. Similarly, if the Exchange-
index be at any time above* OG *it will tend to move downwards;
if it be below* OG *it will tend to move upwards.*

Such interpretation as this proposition may require will be
contained in the proof of it. It must be remembered it is
assumed throughout that the export trade of each country is
conducted by private traders competing against one another.
So that when the terms on which a country's foreign trade
is conducted are such as to afford a rate of profits higher than
the rate current in other industries, the competition of traders
to obtain these higher profits will lead to an increase in the
exportation of her wares: and *vice versa* when the rate of
profits in the foreign trade [is] exceptionally low.

Let the exchange-point *P* be to the left of *OE*, as in Figure 7,
and let *NP* produced cut *OE* in *Q*. Then since *Q* is a point

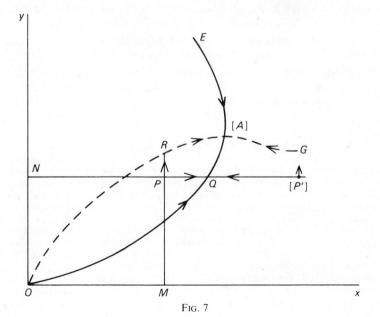

FIG. 7

on OE, ON linen is capable of being disposed of annually in England in exchange for the means of producing and exporting NQ cloth. But at the time in question linen is being imported on the scale of ON annually, and cloth is being exported in exchange for it on the scale of only NP annually. Consequently the exportation of cloth in exchange for linen must be a trade which affords abnormally high profits. Consequently, since competition in the trade is supposed to be free, the exportation of cloth will increase. Therefore when the exchange-index is to the left of OE it will tend to move to the right. So if the exchange-point lay at P' in NQ produced, it would show that cloth was being exported at the rate of NP' annually in exchange for an amount of linen ON, which could be disposed of in England only for the expenses of producing and exporting NQ cloth: consequently the exportation of cloth would tend to diminish, *i.e.* when the exchange-point is to the right of OE, it will tend to move to the left.

Similar proofs apply to the second part of the proposition which relates to OG.

In order therefore to determine the directions in which the amounts of the exports of cloth and linen are tending to change at any time, it is requisite only to determine the position of the exchange-index at that time, and through it to draw arrowheads – an arrowhead pointing towards the right if the exchange-index lies on the left of OE, towards the left if this point lies on the right of OE; and an arrowhead pointing upwards if the exchange-index lies below OG, downwards if this point lies above OG.[1]

---

[1] Thus the motion of the exchange-index is in every respect similar to that of a material particle moving freely under the action of forces which attract it towards OE and OG. Suppose OE to be a rigid wire which exerts attractions only in a horizontal direction and always towards the right when the particle is, according to the definition in the text, on the left of OE, and vice versa. Similarly suppose OG to be a rigid wire which exerts attractions only in a vertical direction, and always upwards when the particle is, according to the definition in the text, below OG, and vice versa. Then this particle will move exactly in the same manner as does our exchange-index, so that if we chose to assign to these horizontal and vertical forces any particular laws, we should obtain a differential equation for the motion of the exchange-index. This equation when integrated would give us the path which on this particular supposition the particle would describe. Such calculations might afford considerable scope to the ingenuity of those who devise mathematical problems, but as we shall see further on (§ 6) they would afford no aid to the Economist.

The exchange-index will in each case tend to move in some direction within the angle made by the arrowheads. Thus, if the exchange-index be at P (Figure 7), it will tend to move in some direction lying within the angle RPQ. So that, unless some external event should arise to disturb the trade relations between the two countries, the exchange-index must soon strike either OE between Q and A, or OG between R and A. But, as we cannot tell the relative magnitude of the horizontal tendency along PQ, and of the vertical tendency along PR, we cannot predict which of the two curves it will strike first. Suppose it strike OE first: when it is on OE there will be no force tending to make it move either to the right or to the left. But there will be a force attracting it upwards. It will therefore tend to oscillate along QA towards A. For we may use this brief phrase to express the fact that the exchange-index will not necessarily remain on QA during the whole of its motion to A, but may oscillate first on one side of QA and then on the other: under the action of the forces which urge it to the right whenever it is to the left of OE, and to the left whenever it is to the right of OE. It will, however, unless its movements be disturbed by some powerful cause extraneous to the ordinary circumstances of the trade, in general adhere somewhat closely to QA. It will be convenient also to place at each of several points on the curve an arrowhead, to indicate the direction in which the exchange-index, if at that point, would. be made to oscillate along the curve on which it is by the force exerted on it by the other curve. Similarly, if the exchange-index moving from P had struck the curve OG first, it would have oscillated along RA towards A.

Exactly in the same way it may be proved that if the exchange-index were at any time at P' it would be impelled by the forces acting on it to move upwards to the left: that if it struck OE first it would oscillate along QA towards A; and that if it struck OG first it would oscillate along GA towards A. And similarly for the points P'' and P'''.[2]

Finally, if the exchange-index coming towards A shoot beside it or beyond it in any direction, or if the exchange-

---

[2] [The points P', P'', P''', A are not shown in the original Figure 7, even in the copy which appears to have been drawn by Marshall. The locations of P' and A may be clearly determined, and have been included, but those of P'' and P''' may only be conjectured.]

index be displaced by any disturbing event from *A* in any direction, the forces acting upon it will bring it back to *OE* or *OG*, and cause it to oscillate along that curve which it strikes first toward *A*.

§ 3   It will be convenient to speak of the equilibrium of the trade between England and Germany corresponding to a point of intersection of *OE* and *OG* as the equilibrium at that point. We may now give a formal

DEFINITION.   The equilibrium at a point of intersection of *OE* and *OG* is *stable*, provided that when the exchange-index strikes either of the curves in the neighbourhood of that point, the forces acting on the index tend to make it oscillate along the curve *towards* that point. In other cases the equilibrium is *unstable*.

It will be seen hereafter that the equilibrium at every point in which *OE* and *OG* cut one another, if it is unstable for displacements in any direction, is unstable for displacements in every direction. But this result does not hold of points in which the curves meet but touch without cutting one another.

We may now enunciate the fundamental rule for deciding whether any particular point of intersection of the curves corresponds to a stable or to an unstable equilibrium of the trade. But, in order that this may be given in a convenient form, it is necessary to have some handy means of distinguishing the various directions in which different parts of the curves may lie.

If a point moves from *O* along *OE* in Figure 8, it at first increases its distance from *Oy* at the same time that it increases its distance from *Ox*. It continues to do so until it arrives at *R* when the direction of the curve is vertical. If the point continues its motion from *R* onwards to *C* and *B*, it will continue to recede, but it will approach towards *Oy*. It will be convenient to express the difference between the portions of *OE* by saying that between *O* and *R* the curve is inclined *positively*; and that from *R* to *B*, and for some distance beyond *B*, the curve is inclined *negatively*. Or more generally : –

Whatever portion of a curve lies in such a direction that a point, which moves along it so as to recede from *Ox*, recedes also from *Oy*; that portion of the curve is said to be *inclined*

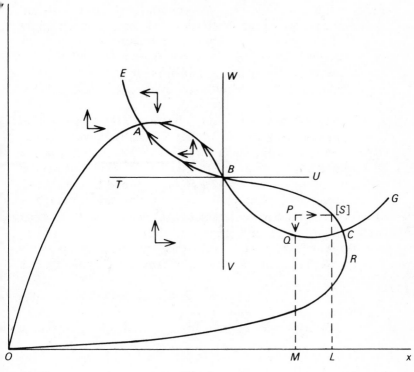

FIG. 8

positively. Conversely, whatever portion of a curve lies in such a direction that a point which moves along it so as to recede from Ox approaches Oy; that portion of the curve is said to be *inclined negatively.*

Using these terms we may enunciate

PROP. XII.   *The equilibrium is stable at every point of inter-section of* OE *and* OG, *excepting those at which both curves are inclined positively, but* OG *is more nearly vertical than* OE, *and excepting those at which both curves are inclined negatively, but* OG *is more nearly vertical than* OE.

In accordance with this Proposition, the equilibria at A and C in each of the Figures 8 and 9 (which are repetitions of Figures 4 and 5 respectively) are stable, and the equilibrium at B in each of these figures is unstable, as has been already indicated. The most convenient mode of establishing this

Proposition is perhaps to draw a number of figures representative of every position in which the curves can lie at a point of intersection. Arrowheads should then be inserted to indicate, in conformity with Prop. XI, the directions of the forces which would act upon the exchange-index at different points in the figures, so as to exhibit the motion of the exchange-index.

If through B in Figure 8 there be drawn the straight lines TBU from left to right, and VBW vertically upwards, then, if the exchange-point be displaced to a position within the quadrant TBW, it will tend to move to A. If displaced to a position within the quadrant VBU it will tend to move to C. If displaced to a position in either of the quadrants TBV, WBU, it will tend to move to A or C, according to whether the forces acting upon it bring it into the quadrant TBW, or into the quadrant VBU. In this last case it is just possible that the exchange-index may on its way back strike B. This

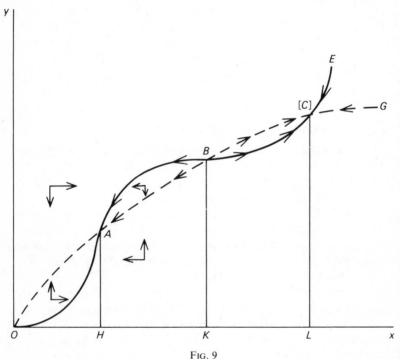

Fig. 9

possibility is worthy of note. But the motion of the exchange-
index is not likely to be arrested at *B*; and if disturbed from
B ever so little along either of the curves it would tend to
move off to *A* or *C*. Therefore it is not inaccurate to describe
the equilibrium at *B* as unstable. Indeed precisely analogous
cases occur in Mechanics. A body displaced from equilibrium
may pass through a position of unstable equilibrium on its way
towards a position of stable equilibrium. Similar remarks
apply to the unstable equilibrium at *B* in Figure 9.

The informal proof of the Proposition that has already been
suggested might perhaps suffice. But it seems advisable to
indicate the manner in which a formal proof of it may be
given.

Let then *D* be any point of intersection of *OE* and *OG*.
Let horizontal and vertical straight lines *TDU*, *VDW* be drawn
as in Figure 10.

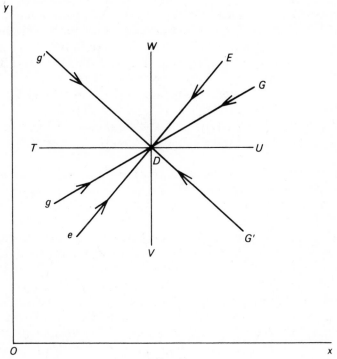

Fig. 10

Firstly let England's curve be inclined positively at D: let it point at D in the direction of the straight line eDE. Then will the equilibrium be stable provided that at D Germany's curve either (i) be inclined positively but make a greater angle with the vertical than eDE does, pointing at D for instance in the direction of gDG; or (ii) be inclined negatively, and pointing at D for instance in the direction of $g'DG'$: or in other words provided that Germany's curve lie within the angles eDW, EDV.

For suppose the exchange-index to strike OE just below D, then it must be below OG, whether OG lie in the direction gD or $g'D$; because eD lies below both gD and $g'D$: therefore it must be attracted upwards. Therefore the arrowhead on eD must point towards D. So it may be proved that the arrowhead on DE points towards D: and that the arrowheads on gD and DG, and on $g'D$ and DG' all point towards D. Which proves that under the stated condition D is a point of stable equilibrium.

In exactly the same manner it may be proved that the equilibrium at D will be unstable if while England's curve lies at D in the direction eDE Germany's curve is positively inclined and makes a smaller angle with the vertical than eDE does, and lies therefore in the angles eDV, WDE.

In the same manner also it may be proved that if OE is inclined negatively at D, the equilibrium at D is stable unless OG be inclined negatively at D and be more nearly vertical than OE is, which completes the proof of the Proposition.

§ 4   It may promote clear conceptions with regard to the drift of the above reasoning if some portion of it be expressed directly in terms of the motives which govern the exportation of cloth and of linen. Let us take for this purpose the case in which the exchange-index has been jerked by some disturbance from OC to the point P in Figure 8 within the loop BC. This may mean that some abnormal event such for instance as a passing difficulty in the English cloth producing trade, has checked the supply of cloth, so that cloth is imported into Germany on the scale of OM yards annually instead of OL annually. Although Germany would be willing permanently to purchase this amount only by giving linen in return for it on the scale of QM yards annually; yet being taken by surprise,

and unprovided with a substitute for cloth, or for some other
transitional cause she pays for it on the scale of *PM* yards of
linen annually. Let us then inquire what tendencies there will
be, as soon as the disturbance is past, to increase or diminish
the scales on which cloth and linen are sent from one country
to the other.

Let us look first at Germany's side of the case. As soon as
the disturbing causes have ceased to operate, cloth imported
on the scale of *OM* yards annually will be capable of being disposed of in Germany only on terms so disadvantageous to
England as not to enable linen to be exported in exchange for
it on a scale as great as that of *PM* annually. Consequently
those who export linen from Germany will find it unprofitable
to carry on an extensive trade until they are able to obtain
cloth on more favourable terms of interchange. Therefore there
will be a diminution in the scale on which linen is exported
from Germany.

England's side of the case is the reverse of this. Linen
imported on the scale of *PM* annually will be capable of being
disposed of in England on terms which will enable cloth to be
exported in exchange for it on the scale of more than *OM*
annually. Consequently the exporters of cloth from England
will find that their trade affords at the present rates of interchange abnormally high profits. These traders are supposed
to act not in combination, but in free competition with one
another; so that each of them will strive to obtain for himself
as large a share as possible of this profitable trade and will
push the sale of his cloth to Germany even if in order to do so
he should be compelled to submit to a slight reduction of the
price on which he disposes of it. Therefore there will be an
increase in the scale on which cloth is exported from England.
That is to say the exchange-index will move from *P* downwards
to the right until it strikes *OE* or *OG*. Suppose it to strike
OG first in the point *F*. At this time cloth is being imported
from England on the scale of *OZ* annually, and linen exported
in exchange for it on the scale of *FZ* annually: and with this
state of the trade Germany is just satisfied. The terms on
which cloth can be sold in Germany are just sufficient to
sustain the trade in this position. But linen imported into
England on the scale of *FZ* annually can be disposed of there

on terms more than sufficiently advantageous to cover the expenses of exporting cloth on the scale of OZ annually: consequently the exportation of cloth will continue to increase. So long as the exchange-index remains on OG the only force tending to change its motion will be a horizontal force to the right. But if the index falls below OG the exporters of linen from Germany will have an inducement to extend their sales to England; and *vice versa* if the index rises above OG they will at once contract their sales to England. Whereby the index will be compelled to oscillate along OG towards C. So if the index had struck OE first, it would have been compelled to oscillate along OE towards C. Therefore the equilibrium at C is stable.[3]

In the course of the proof of Prop. XII, it was proved implicitly that if at a point of intersection of the two curves, the equilibrium was stable for displacements in any one direction it was stable for displacements in all directions: and similarly for unstable equilibrium. Of course these results are capable of an easy independent proof.

But if the curves touch without cutting one another, those arrowheads on the curves which are on one side of the point of contact will be directed towards that point and those which are on the other will be directed away from it as in Figure 11. In fact the position of OE in this figure is obtained from the position which it has in Figure 8 by pressing it downwards so that the two points of intersection B and C in Figure 8 run together to make the point of contact D in Figure 11. So that D is really two coincident points of intersection one of which corresponds to stable and the other to unstable equilibrium.

Of course, since disturbances of equilibrium occur in every direction, a point at which equilibrium is unstable for displacements in any direction is a point at which trade cannot rest and therefore has no practical importance. An investigation of the many various conditions under which the curves may touch one another will afford to the reader some curious amusement; but so far as at present appears, it is devoid of any practical utility.

---

[3] [The point F is not shown, but must lie on OG between Q and C. The point Z lies on Ox so that the line FZ is perpendicular to Ox. The point S is labelled R in the original, which thus has two points R.]

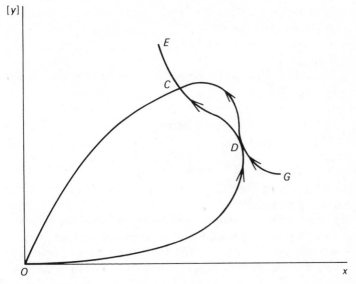

Fig. 11

§ 5   PROP. XIII.   *If from a point of intersection of* OE *and* OG *at which the equilibrium is stable we proceed along either of the curves in either direction until we arrive at another point of intersection, this second point must be one of unstable equilibrium, and vice versa.*

This proposition is obviously true. For if we proceed from a point of intersection along that portion of *OE* which lies above *OG*; and place arrowheads on *OE* on our way, these must all point downwards until we come up to the next point of intersection, therefore that point of intersection is unstable. And a precisely similar proof applies, mutatis mutandis, to every other case. It may be an interesting exercise to attempt to draw diagrams in which one of the curves shall be represented as passing through two points of stable equilibrium consecutively, or through two points of unstable equilibrium; and to notice how each attempt is foiled by the necessity of conforming to the fundamental laws of the curves. Of course the Proposition is capable of a direct geometrical proof.

It was proved in Prop. V that if *OE* belong to the Normal Class or Class I, that portion of *OE* which is adjacent to *O* lies below that portion of *OG* which is adjacent to *O*. Therefore arrowheads placed on *OE* in the neighbourhood of *O* must point upwards and those placed on *OG* must point to the right. Therefore the first point of intersection at which we arrive if we proceed along either of the curves from *O* must be a point of stable equilibrium. In other words, *O* is a point of unstable equilibrium if both the curves belong to the Normal Class or to Class I. But if either of them belong to Class II, *O* may be a point of stable equilibrium, and the first point of intersection at which we arrive when we pass along either of the curves from *O* may be a point of unstable equilibrium.

In this last case the total number of points of intersection (*O* not being included) will be two or some other even number. But in every other case the total number must be one or three, or some other odd number. For it is obvious that if we proceed from *O* along either of the curves, the last point of intersection that we arrive at must be one of stable equilibrium.

§ 6   We have seen how the position of the exchange-index relatively to *OE* and *OG* determines the directions of the horizontal and of the vertical force which act on it: but there are no general laws by which the magnitude of each of these forces can be determined. Therefore even if we knew exactly the shapes which the curves assumed in any particular problem, we should not have data on which to base a calculation of the precise path which the exchange point would describe.[4]

The task of discovering laws by which the shapes of the curves may in any case be approximately determined does not appear to transcend the resources which the science of statistics at present affords us. It will indeed, be a long time before this task is achieved: when it is achieved, it may be

---

[4] For the mathematical functions introduced into the original differential equation could not, in the present condition of our knowledge, be chosen so as to represent even approximately the economic forces that actually operate in the world. And by integrating them we should move further away from, instead of approaching nearer to the actual facts of life. For this reason, among others, the method of diagrams seems to me to be generally speaking of greater use to the Economist, than the methods of mathematical analysis. For when using the former method we have continually before us those assumptions which are justified by economic facts, and no others. Whereas the use of mathematical analysis has been found to tempt men to expend their energy on the elaboration of minute and complex hypotheses, which have indeed some distant analogy to economic conditions, but which cannot properly be said to represent in any way economic laws.

worth while to hand over the curves to be manipulated by the processes of analytical mathematics: but until then, the mathematical treatment of the curve cannot lead us to any results which cannot be at once obtained from inspection of the diagrams. Even then the methods of mathematical analysis will not be able to afford any considerable assistance in the task of determining the motion of the exchange-index. For a large amount of additional work will have to be done before we can obtain approximate laws for representing the magnitude of the horizontal and vertical forces which will act upon the exchange-index in any position.

Finally, even when this is done there will yet remain a further difficulty in the way of the mathematical treatment of the problem. It is necessary to inquire with considerable care into this difficulty; because it extends so far as even to impair to some extent the efficiency of the treatment of the problem by the method of diagrams.

§ 7   It has been remarked, that in economics every event causes permanent alterations in the conditions under which future events can occur. This is to some extent, the case in the physical world, but not to nearly so great an extent. The forces that act on a pendulum in any position are not to any appreciable extent dependent on the oscillations that the pendulum has already made. And there are many other classes of movement in the physical world, which are exact copies of movements that have gone before. But every movement that takes place in the moral world alters the magnitude if not the character of the forces that govern succeeding movements. And economic forces belong to the moral world in so far as they depend upon human habits and affections, upon man's knowledge and industrial skill. Where, for instance, any casual disturbance increases the amount of English wares of any kind that are consumed in Germany it leaves behind it a permanent effect in an increased familiarity on the part of German consumers with English wares; and in this and other ways occasions permanent alterations in the circumstances of demand. An alteration of the shape of Germany's demand curve is rendered necessary by any change which alters the amount of German wares that can be exported annually with the proceeds of the sale in Germany of any given amount of English wares. Consequently, every movement of the exchange-index entails some alteration in the shapes of the curves, and therefore in the forces which determine its succeeding movements. If the curves belong to the Normal Class, or to Class I, the alterations thus required are not likely to be extensive. At all events, the general character of the curves will seldom be changed: and though the positions of equilibrium may be slightly shifted; the general tenor of the reasonings that have been based on the assumption that the shapes of the curves remain rigid and unchanged, will not be thereby invalidated.

But these reasonings may be frequently invalidated if either of the curves belongs to Class II. For suppose that an increase in the amount of cloth produced for exportation leads to the introduction of extensive economies. Such economies when they have once been obtained are not readily lost. Developments of mechanical appliances, of division of labour, and of organisation of transport, when they have once been effected are not readily abandoned. Capital and skilled labour which have once been devoted to any particular industry, may indeed become depreciated in value when there is a falling off in the demand for the wares which they produce; but they cannot quickly be converted to other occupations. So that for a time their competition will prevent a diminished demand from causing an increased price of the wares.

Thus for instance the shape of OE in Figure 12 implies that if cloth were produced for exportation on the scale of OU annually, the economies introduced into its production would be so extensive as to enable it to be produced and exported for a total price which would be covered by the sale in England of linen on the scale of TU annually. If these economies were once effected the shape of the curve would probably cease to represent accurately the circumstances of England's demand. The expenses of production, for instance, of OV cloth would no longer be much greater proportionately than those of OU cloth: so that cloth on the scale of OV annually could be produced and exported by means of the proceeds of the sale of linen imported on a scale considerably less than that of RV. Thus in order that the curve might again represent the

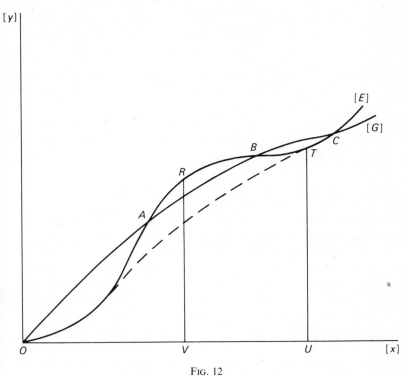

Fig. 12

circumstances of England's demand it would be necessary to draw it lower down; possibly so much lower as to make it fall in the position of the dotted curve in the figure, so as to have only one point of intersection with *OG*. And generally if the circumstances of the production of cloth are such that an increased production of it for exportation, within certain limits, cause greatly increased economies in its production; then the curve between these limits will require some special treatment. For it can be taken to represent the conditions of England's demand only before and up to the occurrence of any event which renders it profitable to produce cloth on a large scale for a time sufficiently long for the introduction of these economies. After the occurrence of such an event, the curve must be, partially at least, re-drawn. Thus if at a point just to the right of this portion of the curve there be drawn,

in accordance with the rules laid down, an arrowhead pointing
to the left; this arrowhead will indicate a resistance that must
be overcome before the exchange-index can move to this
point. But if by any means the exchange-index is brought to
this point, the existence of the arrowhead will not justify us in
assuming without investigation that in the corresponding
practical problem there will be in operation a force tending to
make the exchange-index move toward the left. Conclusions
based upon the assumption of the rigidity of the curves may be
applied to practical problems coming under Class II in so far
as the conclusions relate to the resistances which must be
overcome before there can be effected an increase in the scale
on which cloth or linen is exported: but not in so far as they
relate to the forces which may operate to diminish this scale.
Therefore the account of positions of unstable equilibrium
which has been deduced from an examination of the curves
in Class II may not be applied to practical problems generally
until a careful inquiry has been instituted in each particular
case as to the probability that economies which had once been
introduced, would be quickly lost. It is chiefly for this reason
that as has already been said the results obtained from the
curves in Class II are of less importance than those obtained
in the Normal Class and in Class I. But though they cannot so
far as at present appears be largely used for the immediate
deduction of conclusions in matters of practice, there seems
to be large scope for the use of them in the suggestion of new
practical problems.

Ch. IV: *Variations of International Demand as Affecting the
Rate of Interchange. The Incidence of Customs Taxes*

[§ 1]   The changes which may alter a country's demand for
foreign wares are numerous. Among them is to be included
every change in the facilities which she has for producing any
class of wares, whether they be wares which she exports, or
wares which she produces for home consumption and which
may enter into competition with those which she imports.
Among them again is to be included every change that affects
her resources generally, and as a consequence affects the
amount of wealth which she is ready to expend on foreign

wares. And among them is to be included every change in the
cost of transport of her imports and exports, every change in
the taxes which she imposes on her foreign trade and every
change in the bounties which she awards to it. When the
doctrines of the pure theory are applied to practical questions,
account must be taken of the fact that each of these causes will
produce indirect and remote results which may be important,
and are likely to differ in character from those which will be
produced by any other of these causes. But the pure theory
will be performing its proper function if it conducts the inquiry into the effects which any one of these causes will have in
altering the rate of interchange, and does not for the time being
take account of any other effects. If this be done it will be
found that all these various disturbing causes act in a similar
manner, and that an account of their operation is capable of
being contained in our investigation.

§ 2   Let us first investigate the operation of those causes
which will cause a diminution in England's demand for linen.
Let P be any point on OE, [with] PM drawn perpendicular to
Ox, so that before the change OM is the amount of cloth which
can be obtained for exportation by the proceeds of the sale of
PM linen annually.

   If (i) the price of linen in England is lowered in consequence
of an increase in England's facilities for producing linen, or
wares the consumption of which can be substituted for that
of linen; there will be occasioned thereby a diminution in the
amount of English wares generally and therefore of cloth
that can be produced and exported with the proceeds of the
sale in England of any particular amount of linen. The same
result will be caused by (ii) a diminution in England's facilities
for producing cloth; or (iii) a diminution in England's wealth
and power of purchasing generally; or (iv) the imposition
of a new tax, or the increase of an old tax, upon the importation
of linen into England; or (v) the imposition of a new tax or
the increase of an old tax upon the exportation of cloth from
England; or (vi) the diminution of an existing bounty upon
the importation of linen; or (vii) the diminution of an existing
bounty upon the exportation of cloth: if any of these changes
occur, the importation from Germany of PM linen annually

will give traders the means of exporting in return an amount of cloth less than *OM*. Let this amount be *OM'* (Figure 13). From *M'* draw *M'P'* at right angles to *Ox* and equal to *MP*; then *P'* is a point on the curve which represents England's new demand. We may call this curve *OE'*. Since this reasoning is independent of the position of *P*, it follows that corresponding to every point upon *OE* there will be a point at the same distance from *Ox* and nearer to *Oy* which will be on England's new demand curve; and this curve *OE'* in the figure is the aggregate of the new points thus obtained.

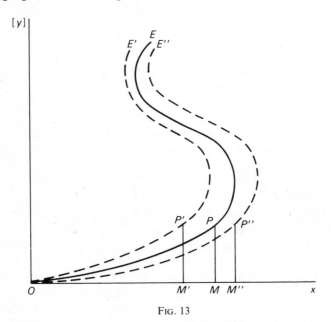

Fig. 13

In some special cases the ratio of *OM'* to *OM* will be the same for every position of *P* on *OE*. And in general this relation may hold approximately for considerable portions of the curve: but it will not as a rule hold accurately or universally. We may however in any case speak of England's demand curve as being *pushed to the left* by any of the changes just mentioned.

It is conceivable that the change may cause England's curve to move from one Class to another. But the circumstances under which they can occur are so rare and unimportant that it will not be advisable to complicate the discussion by taking account of them. Any special case of this kind which the reader may be curious to investigate may be treated without difficulty on the general principles of the reasonings which follow. But in these reasonings it will be assumed that if before the change a curve belongs to the Normal Class, or to Class I, it will belong to the same Class after the change.

England's demand curve will be *pushed to the right*, as into the position OE'' [Figure 13], by any change similar in character, but opposite in direction to any of those by which it would be pushed to the left. For any of these changes will enable each particular amount of linen to afford to the importers of it the means of exporting in exchange a larger amount of cloth than before the change.

Similarly Germany's demand curve will be *pushed downwards* by every change that diminishes Germany's demand for cloth, upwards by every change that increases this demand. It may be noted that if a tax is levied in England on the trade, whether on the importation of linen or on the exportation of cloth it pushes England's demand curve to the left, but does not affect Germany's curve. For Germany's curve is concerned only with the question how much linen traders can afford, and by competition will be forced to export from her, in exchange for a given amount of cloth. It is not concerned with the question whether the whole of the proceeds of the sale of the linen in England are expended in the purchase of cloth for exportation or a portion of these proceeds are absorbed by a tax levied in England. Similarly if the tax were levied in Germany it would not affect England's curve; but would push Germany's curve downwards.

§ 3   We may commence with a preliminary examination of the simple results which are produced by the imposition of a tax on the importation of linen into England or by any other change which pushes England's demand curve towards the left in the case in which both curves belong to the Normal Class. These results are represented in Figure $13\frac{1}{2}$. Before the change the exchange-index was in stable equilibrium at A. At the change England's demand curve assumes the position

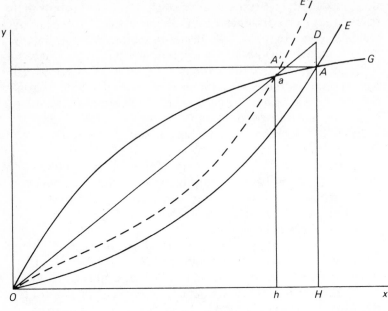

OE', and the exchange-index is at once attracted towards the new position of stable equilibrium at *a*. Consequently England instead of obtaining *AH* linen for *OH* cloth, obtains *ah* linen for *Oh* cloth. The amount of linen which she obtains is less; but the rate of interchange is altered in her favour. For let *HA* and *Oa* be produced to meet in *D*: it is then obvious that at the rate of interchange at which *ah* linen is given for *Oh* cloth, there would be given *DH* linen for *OH* cloth; and therefore that the rate *ah* linen for *Oh* cloth is more favourable to England than that of *AH* linen for *OH* cloth. And generally it is obvious that the extent to which the rate of interchange is altered by the tax in England's favour is measured by the excess of the angle *DOx* over the angle *AOx*. In this simple case it can be easily proved that this excess will be the greater the smaller be the angle which *OE* makes at *A* with the straight line *OA* and the greater be the angle which *OG* makes at *A* with *OA*. Or to put the same thing in other words, the alteration of the rate of interchange in England's favour which is effected by the

tax will, other things being equal, be the less, the less be the
rise in the price of linen in the English market which is occasioned by any given diminution of the amount of it offered
for sale there; and the greater be the rise in the price of cloth
in the German market which is occasioned by any given
diminution of its supply there. A formal proof of this result
will be contained in a solution that will be given further on
of a general problem of which the above is a particular instance.[1]

[§ 4]   We have now to examine the effects which may be
produced by the imposition of [a] tax on the importation of
linen into England, or any other change which pushes
England's curve to the left in cases in which the curves are not
restricted to the Normal Class. But before doing this it will be
convenient to obtain a general notion of these results by the
inspection of diagrams.

In Figure 14 both curves belong to Class I; in Figure 15
England's curve belongs to Class II. The movement of
England's curve from the position OE to the position OE'
corresponds to the imposition of a small tax, the movement
of it to OE'' corresponds to the imposition of a larger tax.

First let us consider the results which arise if England's
curve is pushed from the position OE to the position OE'.
Then in both figures the exchange-index, if before the change
it is at A, will after the change move to a; and if before the
change it is at C it will after the change move to c. It will be
noticed that in both figures a is nearer to Oy than A is, and c
nearer than C. That is, in each of the four instances in which the
exchange-index moves from A to a or C to c in either of the
figures the amount of cloth exported is diminished. Also the
amount of linen imported into England is diminished in three

---

[1] [See Proposition XIV below. The remainder of this chapter, as far as it survives,
appears with minor changes and deletions as Section 11 (pp. 356–60) of Appendix J
of *Money Credit and Commerce*. The section heading is 'Summary of the curious
results of the imposition of general import taxes by one of two countries, trading
exclusively with one another, under all conceivable conditions of reciprocal demand
and supply'. According to a note on the manuscript, the version used for *Money
Credit and Commerce* was typed by Miss Pate direct from the original in 1910, the
amendments being indicated on the manuscript in pencil. Here the original version
is restored, and errors which mar pp. 359–60 of *Money Credit and Commerce* are
corrected.]

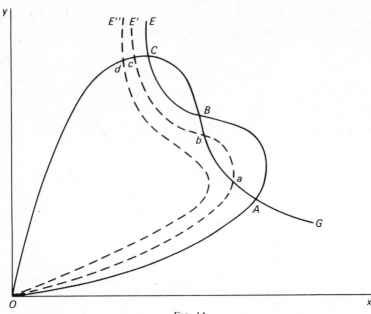

Fig. 14

out of the four instances, but is increased in the instance
in which the exchange-index is by the change made to move
from *A* to *a* in Figure 14. Also if straight lines be drawn from
O to *A*, *a*, *C*, *c*, the angle *cOx* is greater than the angle *COx*
and the angle *aOx* is greater than the angle *AOx* in both
figures. That is in each of the four instances the rate of interchange is altered to England's advantage.

Of the above cases, that which has the greatest general
interest is that in which the exchange-index moves from *A*
to *a* in Figure 14. For in this instance the imposition of the
tax causes the rate of interchange to be altered in England's
favour to so great an extent that she obtains an increased
amount of linen in exchange for a diminished amount of
cloth. A more striking result of this class is, however, obtained
when England's curve is pushed further to the left to the
position *OE''*. For then the exchange-index will move away
[from *A*] to *d*, and England will obtain more than twice the
old amount of linen in exchange for less than half the old
amount of cloth.

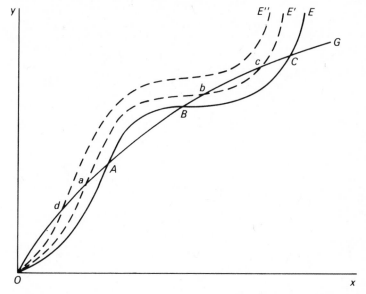

Fig. 15

Such cases as that represented in Figure 14 have but little direct practical bearing. For as a rule one at least of the curves belongs to the Normal Class.

[§ 5]   By giving a special interpretation to the curves in Figure 16 we may cause them to correspond closely to the actual circumstances of some important practical problems.

Instead of using distances along Ox to measure cloth as representative of the whole of England's exports to Germany, let us use these distances to measure only one of the wares which England exports, viz. coal.

OE can no longer be called England's demand curve but may be called England's coal export curve; and OG may now be called Germany's demand curve for coal. OE will now be a curve such that if any point P be taken on it and PM drawn perpendicular to Ox, OM represents the amount of coal which England is willing to export annually in exchange for an amount of Germany's wares represented by PM. So OG will now be a curve such that if any point p be taken on it and pm drawn perpendicular to Ox, pm represents the amount of her

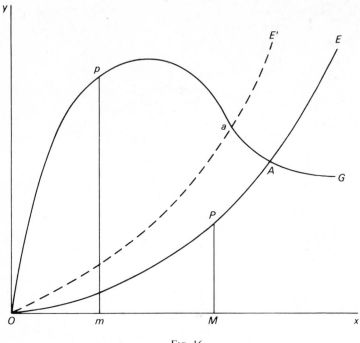

own wares which Germany is willing to export annually in exchange for *Om* coal.

Recent history[2,3] shows that Germany's demand curve for coal may take the form which is given to it in Figure 16. But England's coal export curve cannot belong to Class I; it cannot bend around and approach *Oy*. For the amount of Germany's wares which can be bought with the proceeds of the sale of English coal in Germany cannot be very great and no increase of this amount that could occur would be sufficient

---

[2] See Part II, Ch. II, § [3]. [This refers to Ch. II, above. A more appropriate reference would be to Part I, Ch. VI, § 3 (Section III.3 above).]

[3] [*Money Credit and Commerce* replaces this footnote with the following one: 'P.S. 1921. This refers to events which culminated in 1873. When writing this (about 1871), I had carelessly dropped into the practice of using money as a measure of the value of exports and imports: and the subsequent debacle of prices, illustrates well the dangers of such a course. But it seems best to let the passage remain.' The substance of this note appears in the 1910 revision of the manuscript. The date of 1871 that is here suggested for the manuscript appears too early by several years: see Vol 1, p. 260, above.]

so to increase the total supply of these wares as to glut the English market with them and cause a very great diminution in the rate at which they could be disposed of.

Looking at the Figure [16] we see that any cause which pushed England's coal export curve to the left from the position OE to the position OE' might cause the exchange-index to move from A to a, i.e., might cause England to obtain a larger amount of Germany's wares than before in exchange for a smaller amount of coal than before. But, as has been already remarked,[4] although England may bring about this result by imposing a special export duty on coal, she cannot do it by imposing an import duty on German wares. For Germany's demand for English wares generally is to be classed under the Normal Class. Though she cannot easily dispense with English coal there are many other wares which she is just induced to purchase at the present rate of interchange, but which she would obtain either from her own producers or from those of some other country if England endeavoured by imposing an import duty to alter the rate of interchange to her own advantage. In the same way it may be true that the demand curve of European nations for the finest staples of American cotton is of the character represented by OG in Figure 16, so that America might derive immediate gain from a special export duty on these particular staples. But the burden of the import duties of America cannot be made to fall in the main on European countries so long as a large portion of America's exports of cotton and other goods are closely run by the competition of rivals from other countries.

The cases in which the circumstances of a small portion of the trade which one country carries on with another correspond to the curves in Figure 16, though by no means unimportant, are not very common. But the circumstances of the trade which any industrial group carries on with the rest of the community may very often be represented by these curves. Thus the circumstances of the demand of the community for new houses may at certain times and places correspond pretty closely to the shape of OG in the figure.

---

[4] [See Part I, Ch. VI, §§ 2, 3, (Section III.3 above).]

The conditions under which the building trades are willing to dispose of their services may be represented by OE: and the claims which their Unions make when written out in exact terms may be such as to be rightly interpreted by the assertion that they can push this curve to the left into the position OE': and thereby obtain an increased amount of the wealth of the community at the expense of a diminished amount of their own labour. I must leave this remark to be developed on another occasion.

It is in connection also with the circumstances of the commerce of particular industrial groups rather than with those of the trade between two countries that interest attaches to the position of OE'' in Figure 15. It is a curious result that if in this figure the exchange-index be at C, and England's curve is pushed into the position OE'' the exchange-index will move off to d, and the trade will be nearly destroyed.

[§ 6]   We have considered hitherto only those changes which push England's curve to the left. We may trace some results of a change which acts in the opposite direction, if we suppose that England's demand originally coincided with OE'' or OE' in Figures 13, 14, 15 and 16; and that, in consequence of the change, it is pushed to the right into the position of OE' or OE.

Of course there is no use in making a separate inquiry into the results of the changes which may push OG downwards or upwards. For *mutatis mutandis* these correspond in every respect to those which have been found to occur when OE is pushed to the left or to the right respectively: and they may be traced directly, if in accordance with a previous suggestion[5] the figures of the present chapter be drawn on thin paper and held to the light so that the reverse side of the paper is towards the spectator, and Ox points upwards.

[§ 7]   The results that have just been deduced from inspection of particular shapes of the curves are included in the investigation with which the rest of this chapter is occupied. Much of this investigation is somewhat difficult: and though it systematises and completes our knowledge of certain exceptional cases, it will not furnish any new active principles.

---

[5] [See Ch. II, § 5, above.]

Therefore it may be omitted by those readers who are not specially inclined to abstract reasonings.

In the present section the curve OE' is to be taken to be the position assumed by England's demand curve after the imposition of a tax on the importation of linen into England, or some other event which diminishes England's demand for linen and pushes England's curve towards the left, but does not alter the position of Germany's curve. This event will for brevity be referred to as 'the change'.

PROP. XIV.   *The change will cause a diminution in the amount of cloth exported to Germany.*

In other words, if the exchange-index be, before the change, in equilibrium at A, and F be the intersection of OE' and OG to which the index moves after the change, then F must lie on the left of A. The exchange-index is taken to be at A at the time at which England's curve assumes the position OE'. From this time the forces acting upon the index will tend to make it move towards the right or left according as it is to the left or the right of OE'. But by construction A is to the right of OE'. Therefore if the exchange-index is at A at the time of the change it will after the change move from A along OG towards the left.

In the above reasoning it has not been assumed that the intersection at A was one which corresponded to stable equilibrium. Hence it results that if OG has several points of intersection with OE and also with OE' those two sets are distributed along OG in pairs. That is if we pass along OG from any one intersection of OG with OE to any other, we must pass through an even number (0, or 2 or 4, etc.) of intersections of OG with OE': and if we pass along OG from any one intersection of OG with OE' to any other we pass through an even number of intersections of OG with OE. Of course an independent geometrical proof can be given of this result.

Next let us assume that A is a point of stable equilibrium for the curves OE and OG: and that F is the point of stable equilibrium for OE' and OG to which the exchange-index moves after the change. And let us inquire what are the positions in which it is possible for F to lie. Let straight lines be drawn as in Figure 17. That is let the horizontal line $TA'AR$

be drawn through A cutting Oy in T and OE' in A'. Let the vertical line $HASV$ be drawn cutting Ox in H and the straight line OA' produced in $[S]$: and let the vertical line $H'UA'V'$ be

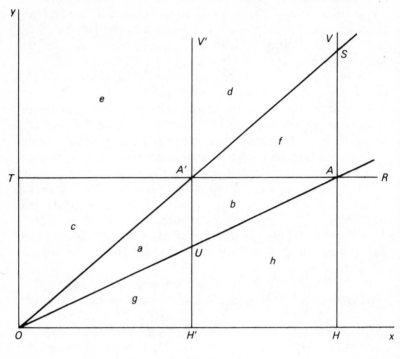

Fig. 17

drawn cutting Ox in H' and the straight line OA in U. We obtain then, directly from the Propositions established in Chapter II, the following results:

If OG belong to the Normal Class, F must lie within the triangle OAT (Prop. III, VII); if to Class I, F must lie in the space $yOAV$ (Prop. III, VI); if to Class II, F may, so far as this condition is concerned, lie anywhere to the left of HV (Prop. VI).[6]

[6] [The Proposition numbers have been attributed to fill in blanks in the manuscript.]

Similarly, if OE' belong to the Normal Class, F must lie somewhere in the spaces $OA'H'$, $V'A'SV$; if to Class I, F must lie within the spaces $OHAA'$, $yTA'SV$; if to Class II, F may, as far as this condition is concerned, lie anywhere to the left of HV. Combining these conditions we have:

Firstly on the supposition that OG belongs to the Normal Class

(i) let OE' belong to the Normal Class, then F must lie within the triangle $OA'U$ as for instance a;
(ii) let OE' belong to Class I, then F may lie anywhere within the triangle OAA', as for instance a or b;
(iii) let OE' belong to Class II, then F may lie anywhere within the triangle OAT, as for instance a, b or c.

Secondly on the supposition that OG belongs to Class I

(i) let OE' belong to the Normal Class, then F may lie anywhere within the spaces $OA'U$, $V'A'SV$, as for instance a or d;
(ii) let OE' belong to Class I, then F may lie anywhere within the spaces $OA'A$, $yTA'SV$, as for instance a, b, d or e;
(iii) let OE' belong to Class II, then F may lie anywhere within the space $yOAV$, as for instance a, b, c, d, e or f.

Thirdly on the supposition that OG belongs to Class II

(i) let OE' belong to the Normal Class, then F may lie anywhere within the spaces $OA'H'$, $V'A'SV$ as for instance a, d or g;
(ii) let OE' belong to Class I, then F may lie anywhere within the spaces $OHAA'$, $yTA'SV$ as for instance a, b, d, e, g or h;
(iii) let OE' belong to Class II then F may lie anywhere to the left of HV as a, b, c, d, e, f, g or h.

These results cannot be recapitulated in a short Proposition; but they may be conveniently displayed thus:[7]

---

[7] [The first part of the table is slightly obscure: it should be read, for example, as: If OE' is Normal, then for quantities of linen less than OT, OE' will lie in the area contained in the angle $OA'H'$; if OG is Normal, then for quantities of cloth less than OH, OG will lie in the area contained in the angle OAT; and so on.]

OE' Normal lies in $\angle OA'H'$ OG Normal lies in $\angle OAT$
OE' Class I lies in $OA'A$ OG Class I lies in OAS
OE' Class II lies in $OA'A$ or $OA'T$ OG Class II lies in OAS or OAH

If Germany's curve belongs to class	While England's belongs to class	F may move to the points
Normal	Normal	a
Normal	I	a or b
Normal	II	a, b or c
I	Normal	a or d
I	I	a, b, d or e
I	II	a, b, c, d, e or f
II	Normal	a, d or g
II	I	a, b, d, e, g or h
II	II	a, b, c, d, e, f, g or h

The amount of cloth exported from England is diminished in every case. The rate of interchange is altered in England's favour in every case in which Germany's curve belongs to the Normal Class or to Class I. The amount of linen is diminished in every case in which Germany's curve belongs to the Normal Class. Positions c and f can be reached only when England's curve belongs to Class II; positions g and h only when Germany's curve belongs to Class II.

[§ 8]   Next follows a Proposition which is very important.

PROP. XVI.[8]   *If neither of the curves belongs to Class II, the alteration in the rate of interchange will be the more favourable to England the less be the extent to which England's willingness to purchase linen is stimulated by any given alteration of that rate in her favour and the less the extent to which Germany's willingness to purchase cloth is checked by any alteration of the rate to her disadvantage.*

The amount of foreign wares which a country will import is determined for the Normal Class and Class I when the rate

---

[8] [There can be no doubt as to the numbering of this Proposition, or that the preceding one was numbered XIV, although the number was afterwards deleted. There is no hint of a gap in the manuscript that would account for the missing Proposition: conceivably the tabular results were meant to stand as Proposition XV, but more probably Marshall made a simple error.]

of interchange is known (see Prop. IV cor.). If then a given alteration of the rate of interchange favourable to her would cause a large increase in her demand . . . .[9]

III.6   The Pure Theory of Domestic Values

III.6.1   *Introduction*

The two chapters printed by Sidgwick under the heading 'The Pure Theory of Domestic Values' are reproduced here without essential change. The footnotes have been amplified, and a large number of obvious misprints in Ch. I, §§ 3, 5 and Ch. II, §§ 4–6 have been amended. Also, the figures have been corrected where necessary and are spread through the text, rather than printed *en bloc*. But otherwise the original is simply reproduced unchanged.[1]

The scope of these chapters may be indicated best through the table of contents:

Analytical Table of Contents: The Pure Theory of Domestic Values

Ch. I: Domestic Values [untitled in original].
   § 1   The theory of domestic values: general approach to its diagrammatic representation.

[9] [The manuscript of this chapter breaks off here. It is not clear just how much is lost. The first Proposition of the succeeding chapter (Ch. I of *The Pure Theory of Domestic Values*) is numbered XVII, while the first figure referred to there is Figure 20 (see Section III.6, below). Hence, two figures and accompanying discussion are missing. A complete set of the international trade Figures 1 to 17 (including $13\frac{1}{2}$) that survives in the Marshall Library has at the end two further unnumbered figures. One is similar to Figure 17, but with A and A' reversed. To secure continuity in the numbering of figures, these unnumbered figures are reproduced as Figures 18 and 19 on pp. 182–3. They suggest that the analysis of tax incidence was developed further and that consideration was also given (Figure 19) to the special case introduced into the 'Essay on International Trade' (Item II.8.1, Figure 10 above). But this cannot be established with any certainty.]

[1] Alterations which go beyond the correction of obvious misprints are shown by editorial square brackets. However, a few essential commas have been added silently.

Fragmentary marginal notes, which appeared in the original printing, are not reproduced in the present text. These deleted notes, which were attached to Ch. I, § 5, read as follows:

The extent to which the economies derived from manufacturing on a large scale depend on the amount of the total production. Characteristics of industries which may properly be called manufacturing. The advantages which a large industry, particularly if it be localised, may have even if it be not conducted in large establishments. Subsidiary industries. The education and economy of technical skill. The intercommunication of ideas.

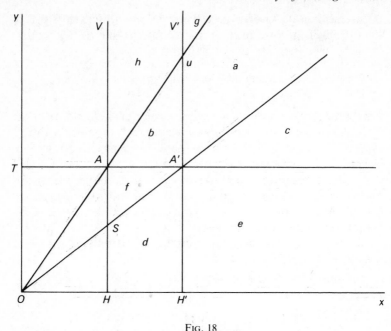

Fig. 18

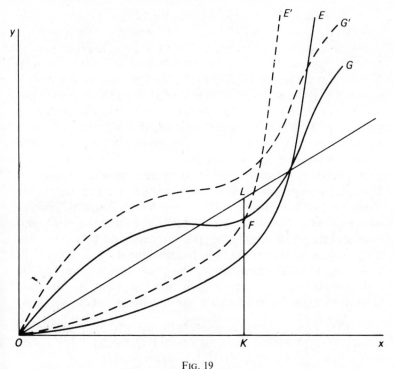

§ 4   The effects on consumers' rent of a tax or bounty on a commodity whose expense of production is independent of the quantity produced.

§ 5   The same for a commodity whose expense of production increases with quantity produced: the effects of the change on landlords' rent.

§ 6   The same for a commodity whose expense of production decreases with quantity produced.

§ 7   The possible gain to consumers from taxing a commodity with an increasing expense of production in order to subsidise a commodity with a decreasing expense of production.

§ 8   Comparison of this scheme with an income tax.

§ 9   Falsity of the argument that the Government has no concern with how a man spends his income.

The foundations for Chapter I are clearly laid out in the early 'Essay on Value' (Item II.2.1, above), which is in many ways more elaborate and complete. The beginnings of Chapter II are less clearly discernible, but fragments may be seen developing in Items IV.2.1, IV.3.5 and 6, and IV.4.1 and 2, below. Of all the chapters in Part II of Marshall's international-trade volume, Ch. II of the *Domestic Values* is the closest to the text of Part I and should be studied in conjunction with Part I, Ch. VI (Section III.3, above) which deals with the revenue effects of customs duties.

When the *Principles* came to be written, the *Pure Theory of Domestic Values* was largely incorporated into it, forming the basis for most of Chapters III, V and VII of Book V.[2] Subsequently, Marshall's treatment of increasing returns and irreversibilities of supply became increasingly tentative, but his position remained essentially unchanged.

Again, detailed commentary on these chapters would be presumptions in the light of their just fame, but the reader's attention might be drawn to a few specific points.

(i) Marshall's earliest unambiguous statements of the doctrines of external economies and quasi-rent are to be found in Ch. I, § 5, and Ch. II, § 5, respectively.

(ii) In treating irreversibilities of supply under increasing return,[3] Marshall in effect makes supply price a function of two variables – current output and past-peak output. The latter admits a ratchet effect, reflecting scale economies that are 'not readily lost'. Quite distinct alternative rationalisations of this may be suggested. The pioneering to unprecedented output levels may yield new skills and knowledge which, once gained, are retained perpetually at no cost. Alternatively, the long-run may be much longer for declines in output scale than for increases, since fixed capital and skilled labour do not readily leave the industry to which they are committed. The learning effect is a genuine irreversibility: the friction is,

---

[2] This refers to the first edition (cf. *Principles II*, pp. 38, 84). The nearest analogues in the variorum edition would be Chs. III, XII and XIII of Book V, and Appendix H. There is also a brief reliance on the earlier work in Book III, Ch. VI (see *Principles II*, p. 261).

[3] The discussion in Ch. I, § 7, reiterates that of Ch. III, § 7, of the *Pure Theory of Foreign Trade*.

strictly speaking, an *asymmetry*, which becomes an irreversibility only by taking the long-run for scale decreases as infinite i.e. by assuming that friction is so great that some resources *never* leave. (Of course, this last assumption can be defended as an approximation if resources leave only slowly, relative to the length of period relevant for equilibrium.)

Marshall appears to rely on both kinds of argument, but to place chief reliance on the second. His procedures seem defensible, but have caused considerable confusion amongst commentators – partly because of the obvious inadequacy of static analysis for exploring such irreversible phenomena.

(iii) Marshall referred to his treatment of consumers' rent in a letter to J. N. Keynes of 2 December 1889.

I hope I did not imply that you confused hedonics and economics. ... What I meant is that the very fact that my protest against Jevons' systematic confusion between the two has been (deliberately) a silent one, makes me very anxious that my consumers Rent should not be sewn up into his Total Utility. I had that prominently in mind when writing on the burden of a tax in my old treatise on Foreign Trade. I wanted to make clear that economic statistics have nothing to do with Utility but only with its rough money measure.[4]

The treatment of consumers' rent deserves careful reading, as there is every reason to think that Marshall meant here *exactly* what he said. Attempts to discern, at this stage of Marshall's work, a subtler underlying theory, of which this verbal exposition was a mere gloss, seem misguided.

(iv) The tax-subsidy argument of Ch. II, § 7, was the progenitor of a long line of controversy, aptly summed up and resolved in 1943 by Ellis and Fellner.[5] Marshall cannot be convicted of outright error, but his suggestion proved fruitful of confusion. Another, less-noticed, source of difficulty (discussed in detail in the Introduction to Item IV.4.2, below)

[4] Marshall Library, Keynes 1 : 93. The version in *Principles II*, pp. 260–1, omits without warning the phrase 'in my old treatise on Foreign Trade'.
[5] H. S. Ellis and W. Fellner, 'External Economies and Diseconomies', *American Economic Review*, Vol 33 (Sept 1943) pp. 493–511. Reprinted in G. J. Stigler and K.E. Boulding (editors), *Readings in Price Theory* (Blakiston, Philadelphia, 1943; for the *American Economic Association*).

arises from attempts to apply Marshall's partial-equilibrium approach to the general-equilibrium problem of choosing an optimal tax *system*.

II.6.2.   Text of The Pure Theory of Domestic Values

Ch. I: *Domestic Values*

§ 1   In the present part of the treatise we are concerned with the causes which determine the relative values of commodities produced in the same country under the action of free competition. This theory is called by Mill and others the 'theory of Value,' but I prefer to call it 'the theory of Domestic values.' For the term 'theory of value' is a generic term, and ought, I think, to be interpreted so as to include the theory of Domestic values and the theory of International values. The apparatus of diagrams which was best adapted for the investigation of the latter will not be of service here; where another apparatus must accordingly be supplied.

The necessity of this change can be easily seen. For in the theory of international values it is important to bring out the similarity between the positions in which the country that buys and the country that sells any particular ware stand to one another. And, to refer to the example of foreign trade which was discussed in the previous Part,[1] the economic causes that govern Germany's willingness to exchange her linen for English cloth are in every respect homogeneous with those that govern England's willingness to exchange her cloth for German linen. It was expedient, therefore, that the curves which represented the respective demands of England and Germany should be drawn on the same principle. This would not have been effected if we had taken distances along Ox to represent numbers of yards of cloth, and distances measured along Oy to represent the exchange value of cloth in terms of linen. Such an arrangement of the diagrams would have some advantages; but it would have involved the laying down of two complete sets of laws for the construction of the curves; so that, in fact, the laws which governed the shape of Germany's

---

[1] [This appears to refer to the *Pure Theory of Foreign Trade*, and is a further indication that the *Pure Theory of Domestic Values* may have been planned as Part III of the original trade volume.]

curve would have been in no respect similar to or symmetrical with those which governed the shape of England's curve. This want of symmetry would have marred, though it would not have rendered impracticable, the application of the method of diagrams to the more elementary portions of the theory; but in other portions it would have led to unmanageable complications.

In the theory of Domestic values on the other hand, the causes that determine the price at which producers are willing to bring into the market any given amount of a commodity are, in most respects, of a different character from the causes which determine the price at which consumers are willing to buy any given amount. There is not in the nature of the case any symmetry between these two sets of causes. Therefore it is useless to attempt to express the operation of these two sets of causes by curves, the laws of which shall be symmetrical.

It may at first sight seem that in consequence of the absence of symmetry the diagrams which interpret the pure theory of Domestic values must be very complex. But it is not so; for this theory, although in one respect it is at a disadvantage relatively to the pure theory of International values, yet has a compensating advantage. In the theory of Domestic values it is not necessary to consider at one time the special circumstances of more than one commodity; whereas in the theory of International values, with the partial exception of a certain portion of it, to be discussed hereafter,[2] it is necessary to consider together the circumstances that govern the demand for at least two commodities, as e.g. cloth and linen. The importance of this advantage is so great that the application of the method of diagrams to the former theory involves on the whole less difficulty than does its application to the latter theory.

§ 2   The progress of the theory of Domestic values has been much hindered by contentions as to the relation in which value stands to 'cost of production,' and the meaning which is to be attributed to this phrase. The phrase is used in two different senses. Sometimes it means the sum total of the efforts and abstinences which have been undergone by the various

---

[2] [This probably refers to the uncompleted final chapter.]

labourers and capitalists who have had share in the production. At other times it means the economic measure of
these efforts and abstinences, i.e. the price that must be paid by
any person who wishes to purchase them.

In the present investigation we are concerned with cost of
production only in its latter use, or, as I prefer saying, with
'expenses of production.' We have to deal only with the
machinery of exchange. We have not to estimate the fatigue
or discomfort which must be undergone by those who perform
any given task; we have only to consider the price which must
be paid to them in order to induce them to perform it. We
have to consider the consequences which result from the
great central law of economic science.

This law is that 'producers, each governed under the sway
of free competition by calculations of his own interest, will
endeavour so to regulate the amount of any commodity which
is produced for a given market during a given period, that this
amount shall be just capable on the average of finding purchasers during this period at a remunerative price. A remunerative price is to be interpreted to be a price which shall be
just equal to the sum of the exchange or economic measures of
those efforts and sacrifices which are required for the production of the commodity when the amount in question is produced. These economic measures are the expenses which must
be incurred by a person who would purchase the performance
of these efforts and sacrifices.'[3]

Accordingly, we take as before two fixed straight lines Ox
and Oy at right angles to one another. But while we take
distances along Ox to represent amounts of the commodity in
question, we must take distances measured along Oy to represent values of a unit of the commodity; as e.g. a ton, if the
commodity be coal; a yard, if the commodity be cloth, &c.
These values must be measured in terms of some other
commodity; in general it is convenient to measure them in
terms of money, or, which is the same thing, in terms of command over commodities in general, so that distances measured
along Oy represent prices. The curves are capable of being

---

[3] From an article by the present writer in the *Fortnightly Review* for April, 1876.
[This refers to the essay on 'Mr. Mill's Theory of Value'. The passage 'quoted' – it is
in fact paraphrased – occurs on *Memorials*, pp. 126–7.]

applied in the solution of many problems concerning market values. But here they will be applied only to average values.

§ 3   Let us consider first the curve which represents the circumstances of the average demand in a given market for a particular commodity; say for coal, supposed to be all of uniform quality. The market may be a district of any size; it may be the whole of a country. The amount of coals which will be bought or 'demanded' in a given time, say in a year, will depend upon the average price at which they are offered for sale. Thus, if it is possible to dispose of, say, a million tons annually in this market, at an average price of 25s. a ton; it would not have been possible to dispose of eleven hundred thousand tons annually, save at a lower price, say at an average of 23s. a ton. Let us suppose that we know the price at which each several amount of coals can be disposed of annually. If then we measure numbers of tons of coals along Ox and the number of shillings in the price of a ton of coals along Oy, we may draw what may be called 'the Demand curve,' thus: Let M_1 be any point on Ox (Figure 20), and let the price at which it is possible to dispose of OM_1 coals annually be estimated and found to be equal to ON_1. Draw M_1P_1 and N_1P_1 at right angles to Ox and Oy respectively to meet in P_1. Then P_1 is a point on the curve. By causing M_1 to move continuously from O along Ox, and finding the position of P_1 corresponding to each position of M_1, we can obtain a continuous series of positions for P_1; i.e. we can make P_1 describe the curve which we are seeking.

Of course it may not be possible to conjecture, with any approach to accuracy, the price at which it would be possible to dispose of a quantity of the commodity, either very much greater or very much less than that amount which is wanted to be sold in the market in question. Consequently in the discussion of any particular practical problem the demand curve can be regarded as trustworthy, only within somewhat narrow limits on either side of this amount. But this difficulty is of importance only in connection with Applied Economics. In Pure Economics, with which alone we are concerned here, we may suppose the curve to be properly drawn throughout its whole length.

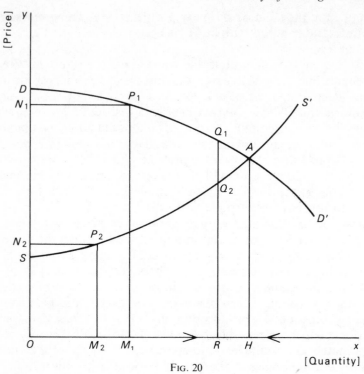

Fig. 20

Recollecting that P_1M_1 is equal to ON_1 we may define the Demand curve thus:

The Demand curve DD' for a commodity in the market is such that if any point P_1 be taken on it, and P_1M_1 be drawn perpendicular to Ox, P_1M_1 represents the price per unit, at which an amount of the commodity, represented by OM_1, is capable of being sold in the market in each year (or other given period).

Since every increase in OM_1 causes a decrease in P_1M_1, a point moving from D along DD' will continually increase its distance from Oy and diminish its distance from Ox. We may here recall a definition already given.[4] It has been said:

Whatever portion of a curve lies in such a direction that a point which moves along it so as to recede from Ox recedes also from Oy; that portion of the curve is said to be *inclined*

[4] [See Ch. III, § 3, of the *Pure Theory of Foreign Trade*.]

positively. Conversely, whatever portion of a curve lies in such a direction that a point which moves along it so as to recede from Ox approaches Oy; that portion of the curve is said to be *inclined negatively.*

With this definition we may enunciate

PROP. XVII.   *The Demand Curve is throughout inclined negatively.*

§ 4   On similar principles we may draw the curve which represents the circumstances of the average supply of the commodity: or as we may say, 'the Supply Curve.' It may be that every increase in the amount supplied involves a more than proportional increase in the expense of producing it. Thus we may suppose that if a million tons annually can be raised and brought into the market at a price of 25s. a ton, the requisite allowance being made for traders' profits of various kinds; that for an annual supply of nine hundred thousand tons, a price of 23s. would be sufficient; but that for an annual supply of eleven hundred thousand tons, a price of 27s. would be required. Let us suppose that we know the price which is sufficient to cover the expenses of production of each several amount of coal supplied annually in the market. We may then draw the Supply curve thus:

Let M_2 be any point on Ox, Figure 20. Let the price which will just cover the expenses of producing and bringing into the market OM_2 tons of coal annually be calculated and found equal to ON_2. Draw M_2P_2, and N_2P_2, at right angles to Ox and Oy respectively to meet in P_2. Then P_2 is a point on the curve. By causing M_2 to move continuously from O along Ox, and finding the position of P_2 corresponding to each position of M_2, we can obtain a continuous series of positions for P_2: i.e. we can make P_2 describe the curve which we are seeking.

The calculations necessary for drawing the Supply curve in any particular practical problem, are in general trustworthy only for amounts [neither] very much greater [nor] very much less than that which is wanted actually to be sold in the market in question. But as has been already remarked with reference to the Demand curve, this difficulty does not prevent us from reasoning in pure Economics on the supposition that the curve is properly drawn throughout its whole length.

We may then define the Supply curve thus:

The Supply curve SS' for a commodity in a market is such that if any point P_2 be taken on it, and P_2M_2 drawn perpendicular to Ox, P_2M_2 represents the price per unit at which a supply of the commodity of which the amount is represented by OM_2 can be remuneratively produced and brought into the market in each year (or other given period).

The law which governs the shape of this curve is not so simple as the corresponding law for the Demand curve. Some remarks will be made in the following section as to the manner in which an increase in the total production of any commodity affects the price at which its producers can afford to offer it for sale. For the present we may assume that in general an increase in the production of a raw commodity can be effected only at a more than proportionately increased expense: while an increase in the demand for manufactured commodities in most cases tends to a diminution of the price at which they can be offered for sale. Thus if SS' be the Supply curve for a raw commodity, the law in most, but not in all, cases will be, that if a point moves from S along the curve it will increase its distance from Ox at the same time that it increases its distance from Oy: or in other words, that the curve is inclined positively throughout. If, however, SS' be the Supply curve for a manufactured commodity, the law in most, but not in all, cases will be that if a point moves from S along the curve, it will while increasing its distance from Oy diminish its distance from Ox. But after the point has moved in this way for a certain distance, it may cease to approach Ox, and begin to recede from it. For it may happen that a further increase in the amount produced will not render possible any important further economies in the production; and that in consequence of the increasing expense to which manufacturers are put in obtaining additional supplies of the raw material or of labour, any further increase in the amount produced can be profitably effected only at an increased price. But again, the production of an amount considerably larger than this may render possible further economies of such magnitude as to outweigh the tendency which the expense of obtaining additional supplies of labour and of raw material has to increase the price at which the commodity can be produced. So that as the point continues to move along SS' it may, while continuing to recede from Oy, again commence to approach Ox, and so on. Thus SS' may have the shape that is given to it in Figure 21. This result may be expressed by saying that it is possible that some portions of the supply curve may be positively inclined and others negatively. It is, however, obvious that the Supply curve cannot bend backwards after the manner of the curve drawn in Figure 22. For the circumstances on which the difficulty of production of any given amount OM_2 of the commodity depends, being definite; it cannot be true that each of two prices P_2M_2 and Q_2M_2 is just sufficient to render remunerative the production of the same amount OM_2. Hence we obtain the only law to which the Supply curve must in all cases conform, viz.:

PROP. XVIII. *The Supply Curve cannot cut twice any vertical straight line.*

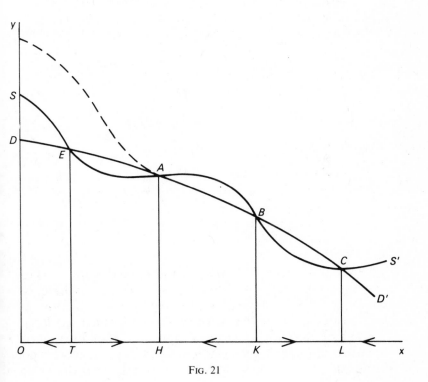

FIG. 21

It may be observed that the law that has been given with regard to the shape of the Demand curve includes the law:

The Demand curve cannot cut twice either any vertical straight line or any horizontal straight line.

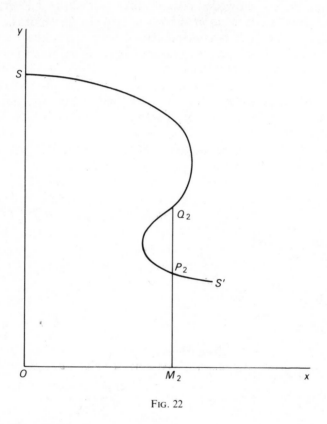

FIG. 22

§ 5   No attempt can be made in the present work fully to investigate the data which would be required for the construction of the supply curve in any particular case. For in such an attempt it would be necessary to work over a very large portion of the ground covered by the science of applied Economics. Enough has been said to indicate to those who are already acquainted with that science the general character of the required investigation.[5] But I would venture to remark that the customary method of treating the advantages of division of labour and of production on a large scale appears to me to be in one respect defective. For the manner in which these advantages are discussed in most Economic treatises is such as to imply that the most important of them can as a rule be obtained only by the concentration of large masses of workmen in vast establishments. If this were the rule, it would be reasonable to object that the introduction of economies into the process of manufacture does not depend directly and in the main on the magnitude of the total amount of the commodity produced. It may indeed be argued that an industry which gives employment to only some twenty thousand men altogether may happen to be concentrated in the hands of a few large firms, and may thus have command over most of the more important advantages of production on a large scale. And it may be argued that industries of far larger dimensions may be conducted almost entirely by small masters. Such, for instance, is the case with some of the metal trades and with the trades of boot-making and tailoring in England. The answer to this objection is twofold.

In the first place it must be insisted that such industries as the two last mentioned are not fairly to be classed as manufacturing industries. For in them the producer who is brought into immediate contact with the consumer is generally in a position of great advantage relatively to the manufacturer, who lives at a distance from the ultimate purchaser of his wares, and who has to make them to fit a number of lay models. But even in trades of this class, when the progress of invention renders possible important economies of which none but large establishments can avail themselves, such establishments will rise more speedily and more surely if the total demand for the produce of the industry is great than if it is small. I may quote, in illustration of this principle, the history of the boot-making trade in America: in which the growth of

[5] But compare the Appendix on Mill's *Theory of Value*. [This is possibly the Appendix I referred to in Ch. II, § 1, of the *Pure Theory of Foreign Trade*. Or it may be Appendix II, as to which there is no information. It seems improbable that Marshall's intention was simply to republish his 1876 essay on 'Mr. Mill's Theory of Value', as this would have been indicated in § 2 above.]

large establishments and a localised industry has been
simultaneous with the development of various forms of the
sewing machine and of other great economies in manufacture.
And the clothing trades in America and elsewhere appear to
be entering upon a similar phase.

We may then properly limit the title of manufacturing
industries to those the produce of which is adapted for being
dealt with wholesale, which do not require the producer to be
brought into immediate contact with the consumer; which
are not concerned with raising raw produce from the earth;
and which give scope for various forms of specialised skill and
specialised machinery.

The term manufacturing industries when thus limited will
include the metal trades which have been referred to as being
mainly in the hands of small masters. This brings us to the
second portion of the answer to the objection with which we
are dealing. For in these trades the advantages of production
on a large scale can in general be as well attained by the
aggregation of a large number of small masters into one district as by the erection of a few large works. It is true that the
disadvantages under which the small masters lie in the competition with large firms are increasing more rapidly than are
their peculiar advantages; and that in most though not in all
directions there is a tendency for small masters to be sup-
planted. But in the metal trades in question, and in many
others, the advantages which are generally classed under the
heads of division of labour and production on a large scale
can be attained almost as fully by the aggregation into one
district of many establishments of a moderate size as by the
erection of a few huge factories. The customary method of
treating the advantages of division of labour appears to me
to be defective, inasmuch as it takes but little account of this
fact. I cannot, however, do more here than indicate in outline
an explanation of it.

Firstly, with regard to many classes of commodities it is
possible to divide the process of production into several stages,
each of which can be performed with the maximum of economy
in a small establishment: though the larger capitalists have
even in these cases superior advantages as regards the buying
of materials, and occasionally as regards the selling of that

which they produce. If there exist a large number of such small establishments specialised for the performance of a particular stage of the process of production, there will be room for the profitable investment of capital in the organising of subsidiary industries adapted for meeting their special wants. The most important of these subsidiary industries fall chiefly into two groups.

One of these groups is occupied with making the special tools and machinery required for this stage of the production. Such a task offers large scope for enterprise both in other ways and in particular in the invention and erection of machinery designed for making these special tools and machinery. But in order that such a task may be efficiently performed, it is necessary that the total demand for these tools and machinery should be very great.

The other group of subsidiary industries is occupied with collecting and distributing the various materials and other commodities which are required by the small establishments in question, and with collecting and distributing the produce of their work. This task will be performed partly by carriers, including those who make and manage railways and canals: partly by intermediate traders, some on a small scale and some on a large. In this class of subsidiary industries are to be reckoned also the trade newspaper and other agencies for collecting and disseminating information relating to particular trades.

Secondly, among the most important of the economies which are available in the production of many classes of commodities are those which are concerned with the education of specialised skill. When large masses of men in the same locality are engaged in similar tasks, it is found that, by associating with one another, they educate one another. To use a mode of speaking which workmen themselves use, the skill required for their work 'is in the air, and children breathe it as they grow up.' Moreover, a man who has the faculties required for the work of a foreman, or for any specially difficult class of manual work, is likely soon to be put to the best work for which he is fitted, if there are in his neighbourhood many workshops in which he may seek a berth. Thus nascent talent is quickly and surely developed. Again, the large extent of the market in which employers can seek skilled labour makes it easy for them, when they want to extend their business, to obtain additional supplies of ready trained workmen. And they escape that disorganisation of their business, which would arise if they could not easily fill up the gap occasioned by the illness or death of a foreman or other highly skilled workman.

Thirdly, if the total number of firms engaged in a particular industry is small, there are but few men in a position to make improvements in the processes of manufacture, to invent new machines and new methods. But when the total number of men interested in the matter is very large there are to be found among them many who, by their intellect and temper, are fitted to originate new ideas. Each new idea is canvassed and improved upon by many minds; each new accidental experience and each deliberate experiment will afford food for reflection and for new suggestions, not to a few persons but to many. Thus in a large localised industry new ideas are likely to be started rapidly: and each new idea is likely to be fertile of practical improvements.

This inter-communication of ideas has in recent times been rendered possible to a considerable extent, even in trades that are not localised, by the trade newspapers, to which reference has already been made. But such a newspaper cannot have an adequate supply of able editors and correspondents unless the trade interests with which it deals are on a sufficiently great scale to enable it to obtain a large circulation.

It may then be concluded that an increase in the total amount of a commodity manufactured can scarcely fail to occasion increased economies in the production, whether the task of production is distributed among a large number of small capitalists, or is concentrated in the hands of a comparatively small number of large firms.

§ 6   We shall want to represent geometrically the scale on which the total production of the commodity in question is being actually carried on at any particular time. For this purpose we have the following

DEFINITION   *R* (Figure 22A) being a point on *Ox*, let *OR* measure the amount of the commodity which would be

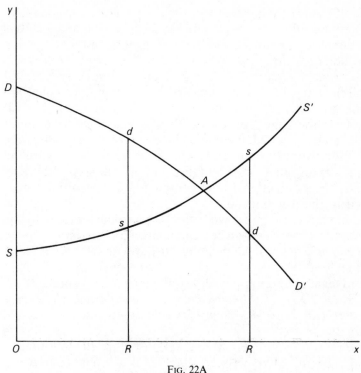

Fig. 22A

produced in a year if the scale on which the production is carried on at a given time were continued uniformly. Then R is the *Amount*-index at that time.[6]

With this definition we may enunciate the fundamental

PROP. XIX. *Let a vertical straight line drawn through the Amount-index cut the Demand curve in* d, *and the Supply curve in* s. *If* d *is above* s *the Amount-index will tend to move to the right. If* d *is below* s *the Amount-index will tend to move to the left. If* d *coincides with* s, *as at* A, *the Amount-index will be in equilibrium, tending to move neither to the right nor to the left.*

For, R being the Amount-index, an amount OR can be produced just at the price Rs, and can be disposed of at the price

[6] Compare the definition of the term 'Exchange-index' and the remarks on it in the *Pure Theory of Foreign Trade*, Ch. [III]. § [1]. [The reference in the Sidgwick version is Ch. I, § 9, which would be Ch. II, § 9, in the present version. There is no such section. However, the exchange-index is briefly mentioned in Ch. II, § 5.]

Rd. If then Rd is greater than Rs, the producers will make at an expense Rs what they can sell at the price Rd; and will thus obtain over and above the ordinary profits on their capital a profit sd on each unit of the commodity they produce. The trade will therefore be exceptionally profitable, and capital will flow into it. Thus an increased amount of the commodity will be produced; or in other words, the Amount-index will move to the right. Again, if Rd, the price at which the amount OR can be disposed of annually in the market, be less than Rs, the price which is required to enable the business to return the ordinary profits to the capitalist, capital will leave the trade. Thus the production of the commodity will be diminished; that is, the Amount-index will move to the left. But if Rd be equal to Rs, the trade will return the ordinary profits to the capitalist; and there will be no tendency for the Amount-index to move either to the right or to the left. Of course Rd is equal to Rs when R is vertically below a point of intersection of the Demand and Supply curves. We may then formulate

PROP. XX.   *The Amount-index is in equilibrium whenever it is vertically below any point of intersection of the Demand and Supply curves.*

It follows from Prop. XIX, that if in Figure 20 the Amount-index be anywhere between O and H it will tend to move to the right; if anywhere beyond H it will tend to move to the left. So in Figure 21 if the Amount-index be between O and T it will tend to move to the left; if between T and H, to the right; if between H and K, to the left; if between K and L, to the right; if beyond L, to the left. These results are indicated in each figure by arrowheads placed along Ox. They may be expressed by saying that A in Figure 20 and A and C in Figure 21 are points of stable equilibrium. But E and B in Figure 21 are points of unstable [equilibrium]. For we may give the following

DEFINITION. If the Amount-index on being slightly displaced from any position in which it is at equilibrium tends to return to that position, the equilibrium is said to be *stable*: if not, it is said to be *unstable*. Thus, as an immediate consequence from Prop. [XIX], we obtain

PROP. XXI.   *The equilibrium of the Amount-index corresponding to any point of intersection of the Demand and Supply curves is stable or unstable according as the Demand curve lies above or below the Supply curve just to the left of that point.*

If the curves touch one another at any point, the equilibrium corresponding to it will be stable for displacements in one direction, and unstable for displacements in the other. No practical interest attaches to the investigation of this case.[7]

It is obvious that if we move along either of the curves in either direction from one point of stable equilibrium to the next, we must pass through a point of unstable equilibrium. In other words, in cases in which the curves cut each other more than once points of stable and unstable equilibrium alternate.

Also the last point of intersection reached as we move to the right must be a point of stable equilibrium. For if the amount produced were increased indefinitely the price at which it could be sold would necessarily fall almost to zero: but the price required to cover its expenses of production would not so fall. Therefore if a point moves to the right along the Supply curve it must ultimately rise and remain above the Demand curve.

The first point of intersection arrived at as we proceed from left to right may be a point either of stable or of unstable equilibrium. If, as in Figure 21, it be a point of unstable equilibrium, this fact will indicate that the production of the commodity in question on a small scale will not remunerate the producers. So that this production cannot be commenced at all unless some passing necessity has caused temporarily an urgent demand for the commodity of a character similar to that represented by the dotted curve in the figure. But the production, when once fairly started, could be carried on profitably.

§ 7   In discussing the unstable equilibrium which was met with in the theory of foreign trade some remarks were made (Part II. Ch. III. § 7)[8] with regard to the fact that in Economics every event causes permanent alterations in the conditions under which future events can occur. To these the reader is

---

[7] Compare the remarks on the analogous case, *Pure Theory of Foreign Trade*, Ch. [III] § 4.

[8] [That is, Ch. III, § 7, of the *Pure Theory of Foreign Trade*.]

referred. It was argued that in the theory of foreign trade an unstable equilibrium is met with which conforms completely to the conditions which are fulfilled by the unstable equilibrium of mechanics. This case was discussed in connection with curves of Class I, and is illustrated in Figure 4. But it was remarked that these conditions are not completely conformed to by the so-called unstable equilibrium, which depends upon the diminution of the expenses of production that arises from an increase in the amount produced.

It was argued that when any casual disturbance has caused a great increase in the production of any commodity, and thereby has led to the introduction of extensive economies, these economies are not readily lost. Developments of mechanical appliances, of division of labour and of organisation of transport, when they have been once obtained are not readily abandoned. Capital and labour, when they have once been devoted to any particular industry, may indeed become depreciated in value when there is a falling off in the demand for the wares which they produce: but they cannot quickly be converted to other occupations; and their competition will for a time prevent a diminished demand from causing an increased price of the wares. Precisely similar remarks apply to what I have called unstable equilibrium in the present theory: and *mutatis mutandis* they may be reproduced here.[9]

Thus for instance, the shape of the Supply curve in Figure 23 implies that if the ware in question were produced on the scale OV annually, the economies introduced into its production would be so extensive as to enable it to be sold at a price TV. If these economies were once effected the shape of the curve SS' would probably cease to represent accurately the circumstances of supply. The expenses of production, for instance, of an amount OU would no longer be much greater proportionately than those of an amount OV. Thus in order that the curve might again represent the circumstances of Supply it would be necessary to draw it lower down; possibly

---

[9] [It is literally the case that the next two paragraphs repeat *mutatis mutandis* the last paragraph of Ch. III, § 7 of the *Pure Theory of Foreign Trade*. At three points the appropriate emendations are not made, so that references to OG, the Exchange-index, and the scale on which cloth or linen is exported remain uncorrected. The reference to OG has been replaced by the appropriate reference to DD', but the others are left unchanged.]

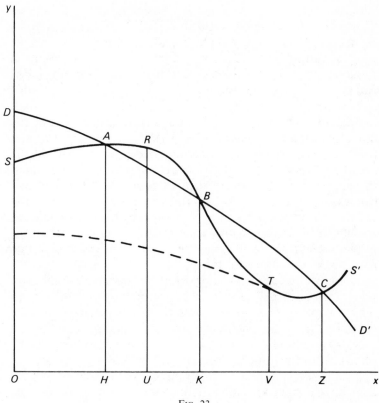

FIG. 23

so much lower as to make it fall into the position of the dotted curve in the figure and make only one intersection with [*DD'*]. Thus we may lay down a general principle to the effect that if the process by which a ware is manufactured be of such a nature that an increase in the scale of production within certain limits causes great additional increased economies to be introduced into the manufacture, then the Supply curve for the ware between these limits will require some special treatment. For this portion of the curve can only be taken to represent the circumstances of Supply before and up to the occurrence of any event which renders it profitable to produce the commodity on a large scale for a time sufficiently long for the introduction of these economies. After the occurrence of such an event, the curve must be, partially at least, re-drawn. Thus if at a point on Ox below this portion of the curve there be drawn in accordance with the rules laid down, an arrow-head pointing to the left; this arrow-head will indicate a resistance that must be overcome before the Amount-index can move to this point. But if by any means the Amount-index is brought to this point, the existence of the arrow-head will not justify us in assuming without investigation that in the corresponding practical problem there will be in operation a force tending to make the Exchange-index move towards the left. Conclusions based upon the assumption of the rigidity of the curves may be applied to practical problems concerning domestic values in so far as the conclusions relate to the resistances which must be overcome before there can be effected an increase in the scale on which cloth or linen is exported: but not in so far as they relate to the forces which may operate to diminish this scale.

Therefore the account of positions of unstable equilibrium which has been deduced from an examination of the curves may not be applied to practical problems generally until a careful enquiry has been instituted in each particular case as to the probability that economies which had once been introduced, would be quickly lost. But though as far as at present appears they cannot be largely used for the immediate deduction of conclusions in matters of practice, there seems to be large scope for the use of them in the suggestion of new practical problems.

§ 8   In applying the curves of Demand and Supply to the solution of any particular problem we must determine definitely what is the length of the period with the average circumstances of which the problem deals. For this purpose much care is required. Even the best writers on Economics have sometimes failed clearly to discriminate the various senses in which they have used the word average in such phrases as average supply,' 'average demand,' 'average value.'

Let us consider for instance the case of wheat. The supplies of wheat come almost exclusively from the northern hemisphere, and are therefore harvested at about the same time of year. Consequently if all the facts of the harvest were known, and their bearings properly estimated by all dealers, there need be no important fluctuations in the price of wheat during the year; or at all events none until the prospects of the next harvest had begun to declare themselves. The great fluctuations that do occur even in the winter months, are not to be regarded as the effects of economic causes in the narrower use of the phrase. Their causes are rather to be sought among mental phenomena; in the insufficiency of men's knowledge and the fallibility of men's judgements.

With reference to market prices for markets of long duration some care is required in order to discover the average price or the level about which the market price oscillates. For in comparing prices obtained at two different dates allowance must be made for the interest due on the price obtained at the earlier date. Thus if interest be reckoned at 5 per cent. per annum, the price of 60s. for a quarter of corn sold in January would be on the same level as a price of 61s. 6d. for a quarter sold in the ensuing July.

A list of the monthly prices of wheat since 1793 (Tooke's *History of Prices*, II. p. 390, and *Statistical Abstracts*) exhibits in many cases two oscillations, in some even three, in the course of a single harvest year.[10] Not nearly all these oscillations can be accounted for by variations in the prospects of a good harvest in the coming year. After allowing for these variations and also for the effect of partial and temporary combinations open or tacit among dealers, we find a large margin of irregularities which has to be put to the account of the difficulty of obtaining rapidly the requisite data. This difficulty has been increased by the growing complexity of

---

[10] [See T. Tooke, *A History of Prices and of the State of the Circulation from 1793 to 1837* (Longman, Orme, Brown, Green and Longmans; London; 1838; two volumes). Vol. II, p. 390 is a 'Table of the Monthly Average Price of Wheat per Winchester Quarter in England and Wales from 1793 to 1837 inclusive'. Marshall's copy, in the Marshall Library, has on this page the annotation 'Highest prices in each 'Harvest Year' marked. From the above it may be inferred that the practice of taking the harvest year from 1 Sept to 31 Aug is open to objections. When a dear year is followed by a cheaper the price in Sept is in general the highest in that year. Sept should be omitted altogether.' The *Statistical Abstract for the United Kingdom in each of the Last Fifteen Years* was published annually. The Twentieth was published in 1873 (Eyre and Spottiswoode, London, for H.M.S.O: *c.* 833) and covered 1858 to 1872. The First (for 1840–54) was reprinted in 1870 (*c.* 145) with additions covering 1855 to 1869.]

these data almost as much as it has been diminished by our improved means of transmitting information. It is true that the average price for July for the last 80 years is at least as much in excess as it ought to be – by about 3*s*. 6*d*. – of the average price for January. But so tardily are facts ascertained, that when a scanty harvest is followed by an abundant one, not only is the fall in price exhibited in the September column in general comparatively small, but in many cases the progress of the fall is protracted throughout the greater part of the harvest year. For the last 30 years the price has been lower on the average for February than for November; and but little higher for April than for October. The causes that determine the relations of the average price of wheat to the market prices, when the term 'average' means average during six winter months, are of an entirely different character from the causes which determine these relations when the period for which the average is taken is long enough to include several harvests.

The periods with which we are concerned in the present discussion are of the latter character. They are sufficiently long to eliminate the casual disturbances which arise from the failure of producers so to adjust the supply to the demand, that the amount supplied may be just sold off at a remunerative price. But they are sufficiently short to exclude fundamental changes in the circumstances of demand and in those of supply. On the side of demand for the ware in question it is requisite that the periods should not include (i) any very great change in the prosperity and purchasing power of the community; (ii) any important changes in the fashions which affect the use of the ware; (iii) the invention or the great cheapening of any other ware which comes to be used largely as a substitute for it; (iv) the deficiency of the supply of any ware for which the ware in question may be used as a substitute, whether this deficiency be occasioned by bad harvests, by war, or by the imposition of customs or excise taxes; (v) a sudden large requirement for the commodity, as e.g. for ropes in the breaking out of a maritime war; (vi) the discovery of new means of utilising the ware, or the opening up of important markets in which it can be sold.

On the side of Supply it is requisite that the periods should not include (i) the opening up or cutting off, as e.g. by a war, or a tax, of any important source of supply of the ware itself or of the material of which it is made; or (ii) the invention of any fundamentally new process or machine for the manufacture of the ware. But the period may include such extended applications of known processes and machinery, and such economies in conveyance and distribution as are direct consequences of an increase in the scale of production.

Thus, to revert to the case of wheat, the supply and demand curves cannot, at all events as applied in the present discussion, be made to exhibit the operation of causes which govern the changes in the value of wheat which have occurred in the course of many generations. Recent controversies render it expedient to examine this point somewhat carefully. British economists have enunciated a Law of Diminishing Return. They assert that a considerable increase in the amount of wheat raised from a given area in a country which is already thickly peopled can be raised only at the cost of an amount of labour increased more than proportionately. American economists assert that in a new country, at all events, and often even in an old country, the growth of population brings with it such improvements in agricultural skill, such new knowledge of processes and implements, such near access to good markets for buying and selling, and such developments of communication by road and railway, that an increased supply of food can be produced at the cost of labour increased less than proportionately. In particular they insist that the amount of labour which has to be expended in order to raise a quarter of wheat under the most unfavourable circumstances in which wheat is grown in England is less than it was many centuries ago. These statements on which British and the American economists severally lay stress are doubtless both true. But they do not traverse one another. The law of diminishing returns may be expressed by a Supply curve for wheat which is throughout inclined positively as in Figure 20. The complementary fact which the special circumstances of America have made prominent may be expressed by a Supply curve for wheat, some portions of which are inclined positively and

others negatively, as in Figure 21. It would however be necessary in this case to measure the value of the corn produced in
terms of a unit of some particular kind of labour; while in the
former case the value may be expressed either in this unit or
in terms of a unit of the precious metals. But the two Supply
curves thus drawn would correspond to wholly different
problems. Each curve would represent changes in the cost,
measured in money or labour, of raising corn which would be
occasioned by changes in the amount produced. But the
former curve would refer to an interval of time so short as to
include no fundamental change in the general condition of the
country, in the development of the arts of cultivation, of the
means of locomotion, and generally of the industries subsidiary to agriculture. Corresponding to this curve there
might be drawn a demand curve roughly representing the
circumstances of average demand for the wheat during the
same period. The position of the point of intersection of the
two would then represent approximately the average amount
which would be produced and the average price about which
the mean price would oscillate. But in the second case the
supply curve would refer to a period so long as to include
fundamental changes in the character of the various industries
of the country. In drawing the curve, allowance would be made
not only for those economies which spring directly from the
increase in the amount produced, but also for those inventions
and other improvements which were caused by the growth of
civilisation that was concurrent with the increase of population. A supply curve can be thus drawn to express the result of
statistics as to past history or of conjectures as to future history. But it is obvious that we cannot properly pair this curve
off with a corresponding demand curve, and determine by the
intersection of the two an average value about which the
market value has oscillated.

We might indeed add together the prices of wheat in the
various years, and divide the sum by the number of years, in
order to find an arithmetic mean of the prices. But this mean
would not be rightly called an average result of economic
causes. For such a phrase cannot be strictly interpreted without
assuming some uniformity at least in the general character of
the causes operating. And we could not make any assumption

of this kind which would correspond even approximately to the facts of the case. Malthus indeed has made[11] some instructive investigations as to the relations which in the course of English history have existed between the average price of corn, the average wages of labour, and the growth of population. It is true that the statistics at his command were not thoroughly satisfactory, but he made good use of such as he had; and more recent investigations have on the whole tended to confirm his conclusions. He concludes, 'that during a course of nearly 500 years, the earnings of a day's labour in this country have probably been more frequently below than above a peck of wheat; that a peck of wheat may be considered as something like a middle point, or rather above the middle point, about which the market wages of labour, varying according to the demand and supply, have oscillated; and that the population of a country may increase with some rapidity, while the wages of labour are even under this point.'

But he finds that average corn wages were not far short of two pecks during the latter part of the fifteenth century, and that in the seventeenth century they were generally under three quarters of a peck. 'From 1720 to 1750 the price of corn fell and the wages of labour rose, but still they could command but little more than the half of what was earned in the fifteenth century. From this period corn began to rise, and labour not to rise quite in proportion; but during the forty years from 1770 to 1810 and 1811, the wages of labour in the command of corn seem to have been nearly stationary.'

'It appears then that, making a proper allowance for the varying value of other parts of the wages of labour besides food, the quantity of the customary grain which a labouring family can actually earn, is at once a measure of the encouragement to population and of the condition of the labourer; while

---

[11] Political Economy, Ch. IV. [T. R. Malthus, *Principles of Political Economy Considered with a View to their Practical Application* (Murray, London, first edition 1820). Marshall's quotations came from the first edition (pp. 284, 558–9 and 290–1 respectively) and are not to be found in the second (Pickering, London, 1836), except for a reworded version of the first quotation which appears on p. 254. Marshall's slight stylistic changes are retained.]

the money price of such wages is the best measure of the value of money as far as one commodity can go.'[12]

These facts may, perhaps with some little violence to words, be made to represent supply of and demand for employment as determining the average wages of labour. This is how Malthus endeavoured to use them. But they cannot fairly be made to represent the way in which the average price of corn is determined by economic causes.

§ 9   The reader will have no difficulty in drawing for himself diagrams representing the alterations in the curves and in the positions of equilibrium which may arise from any general change in the circumstances either of supply or of demand. The principles on which he will have to proceed are in every respect similar to those on which the investigation of the corresponding problem in the theory of international values has been conducted. We may follow the analogy of the terms used there in describing the alteration of the supply curve which is required when any event causes an increase in the expenses of producing each several amount of the commodity. We may say that such an event, whether it be a tax, or the cutting off of any sources of supply, or any other difficulty, 'pushes upwards' the supply curve.

For let P be any point on the curve (Figure 24), so that PM is the price which is necessary to cover the expenses of production of the commodity when the amount OM is produced. Then after the change some larger price pM will be required in order to cover these expenses. Thus as P is made to move along SS', the old supply curve, p will trace out ss', the new supply curve. If the change be the imposition of a tax which bears a fixed ratio to the selling price of the commodity, the ratio of pM to PM will be constant for all positions of P.

Similarly the supply curve may be 'pushed downwards' by the remission of a tax or the awarding of a bounty, by the opening up of new sources of supply, or by the invention of an

---

[12] Cairnes, *Leading Principles*, Part I. Ch. V. § 3, apparently in ignorance of this investigation and of the conclusive evidence that corn wages have been higher in some centuries than in others, assails the brief reference that Mill has made (*Pol. Econ.* Bk. III Ch. XV. § 2) to this evidence. [See J. E. Cairnes, *Some Leading Principles of Political Economy Newly Expounded* (Macmillan, London, 1874); J. S. Mill, *Principles of Political Economy*, pp. 579–80.]

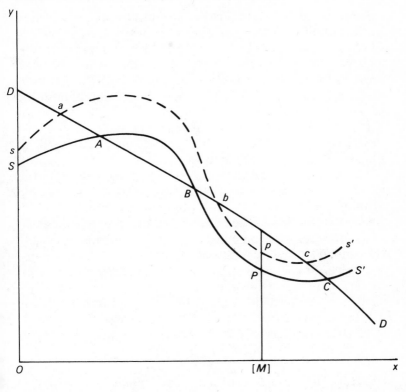

FIG. 24

improved method of manufacture. For, as has been said
already, any substantially new invention is a change in the
circumstances of supply which invalidates the old supply
curve. An increase in the scale of production will necessarily
lead to increased economies in consequence of the scope which
it will offer for the application of already known methods and
machinery. In drawing the original supply curve it was
assumed that these economies could be predicted; and that
allowance could be made for them. But new inventions and
other improvements which are not directly caused by an
increase in the scale of production are not capable of being
predicted; and when they occur they render it necessary to
draw a new supply curve from new data.

In the same way the demand curve will be moved upwards by the discovery of any new purpose to which the commodity in question can be applied; and generally by every change that increases the demand for it. A diminution of the demand, arising perhaps from a change in fashion, or from the invention of some substitute for the commodity, will similarly push the demand curve downwards.

It may be noticed that a considerable movement of the supply curve upwards or of the demand curve downwards in Figure 24 will reduce the number of the points of intersection of the curves from three to one; and this one will lie to the left of *A*. Thus the amount-index may be moved from stable equilibrium at a point vertically below *C* to a point not very far from *O*. But it must be remembered that the hypothesis on which this result is obtained does not, generally speaking, correspond to the actual facts of important practical problems. For as has already been argued at length, the indications given by a negatively inclined portion of the supply curve are completely trustworthy only so long as the amount-index is moving under it from left to right; they cease to represent accurately the facts of the corresponding practical problem so soon as this movement has once been made.

Ch. II: *The Total Burden of a Tax. Consumers' Rent*

§ 1   It has already been insisted that the burden which a tax on a commodity inflicts on the consumers does not consist only of the pecuniary loss which they undergo in paying an increased price for the commodity.

It was argued that the money that they used to expend on the commodity brought in to them a greater satisfaction than they could obtain by expending that money on other things; for if any other mode of expenditure had seemed preferable to them, they would have chosen it. The tax diminishes in two ways the satisfaction which they derive through their facilities for purchasing the commodity. Firstly, in so far as they continue to purchase the commodity, the tax causes them to pay a higher price for it; secondly, the tax deters them from consuming as large an amount of it as before.[1]

---

[1] [See Part I, Ch. VI, § 6 (Section III.3, above).]

In the present chapter a more careful investigation will be given of the amount of this pleasure or satisfaction which a person derives from being able to purchase a particular commodity at a given price; or, in other words, of the amount of the excess or surplus satisfaction which he derives from his purchases of the commodity over the value to him of the money he pays. Now that which a person would be just willing to pay for any satisfaction rather than go without it, is, as will be explained further on, the 'economic measure' of the satisfaction to him. The economic measure of that excess or surplus satisfaction into which we are inquiring will be called 'Consumers' Rent.' Diagrams similar to those of the preceding chapter will be applied in estimating the amount of the total consumers' rent derived by all the several purchasers of the commodity in the market: and in inquiring into the diminution of this consumers' rent which will be caused by a tax on the commodity. It is somewhat difficult to discern clearly the nature of this surplus satisfaction and of its economic measure: but when this difficulty has been overcome, the apparatus of diagrams that is here supplied will be found to be easily handled, and to be capable of achieving important new results.

§ 2   In order to give definiteness to our notions, let us consider the case of coals purchased for domestic consumption. Let us assume also for convenience, that it is not practicable to sell less than a ton of coals at a time. Let us take the case of a man who, if the price of coals were £10 a ton, would just be induced to buy one ton annually; who would just be induced to buy two tons if the price were £7, three tons if the price were £5, four tons if the price were £3, five tons if the price were £2, six tons if the price were £1. 10s., and who, the price being actually £1, does purchase seven tons. We have to investigate the consumers' rent which he derives from his power of purchasing coal at £1 a ton.

The fact that he would just be induced to purchase one ton if the price were £10, proves that the total enjoyment or satisfaction which he derives from that ton is as great as that which he could obtain by spending £10 on other things. In other words, the satisfaction derived from, or 'the value in use' to him of, a single ton a year, is economically measured by £10.

Therefore his power of purchasing one ton of coals for £1 gives him a surplus satisfaction of which the economic measure is £9 in excess of that satisfaction, command over which he gives up by parting with the £1; that is to say, it gives him a consumers' rent of £9.

Again, if the price were £7 a ton, he would just be induced to purchase a second ton; so that the value in use to him of a second ton is measured by £7. The consumers' rent that he derives from his power of purchasing this ton for £1 is therefore £6: and so on. Thus the whole consumers' rent which he derives from the power of purchasing coal at £1 a ton is £9+6+4+2+1+$\frac{1}{2}$, i.e. £22$\frac{1}{2}$.

We may put the same thing in another way. The economic measure of the total value in use, or, as Mr Jevons says,[2] of 'the total utility of the coal,' is the sum of the prices that he would be just willing to give for each successive ton: i.e. £10+7+5+3+2+1$\frac{1}{2}$+1, i.e. £29. 10s. He has to pay for them seven times the value in exchange or market-price of a ton of coal. This value in exchange is of course equal to the measure of the value in use to him of the last ton of coal which he purchases, or in Mr Jevons' phrase, to the measure of the final utility of a ton of coal to him. For he will not pay for a thing more than it is worth to him: and if he can get a thing for less than it is worth to him, he will increase his purchases of it. So that the last ton of coals which he buys, i.e. the ton which he is only just induced to buy, must be worth to him just what he pays for it.

Thus the Consumers' rent measures the surplus or excess of the total value in use to him of the seven tons of coal which he purchases, over the value in use of the commodities which he could have obtained by expending in other ways the £7 which are the value in exchange of those seven tons.

We are as a rule unable to obtain the facts necessary for measuring the value in use of a commodity to any individual who purchases it; for we cannot estimate the quantity which he would purchase at a given price. But, as was argued in the preceding chapter, the statistics of trade will generally enable us to draw the Demand curve of the commodity for the whole

---

[2] [W. S. Jevons, *The Theory of Political Economy* (Macmillan, London, 1871). The quotation is illustrative rather than direct.]

market; that is, will enable us to estimate the total amount of the commodity which could be sold at a given price to the whole body of consumers.[3] And by this means we are enabled to find the economic measure of the value in use of the commodity to the several members of the community.

The measure of human satisfaction thus obtained is indeed a rough measure. For in this as in many other portions of economic reasoning it is necessary, as a first approximation, to treat a pleasure that is worth a shilling to one man as equivalent to a pleasure that is worth a shilling to any other man. Assumptions of this nature have indeed to be made in almost every branch of statistical science. For all social and therefore all economic statistics deal with aggregates of human feelings and affections. It is not possible to add together arithmetically any two pleasures without some more or less arbitrary mode of measuring them. Now the economic measure of the satisfaction which a man derives from any source is as has been said the amount of money which he will just give in order to obtain it. The economic measures of various satisfactions can be represented in statistical tables; and these may be used in establishing economic laws.[4] But such laws will contain only a portion of the whole truth of the matter to which they relate. And before deductions from these laws can be used for practical purposes, allowance must be made for the fact that a satisfaction which a rich man values at a shilling is slight in comparison with one for which a poor man will be willing to pay a shilling.

To take an extreme case. Suppose a poor woman who would manage to purchase one pound of tea in a year, even if she had to pay 5s. for it; she will derive vast surplus satisfaction from purshasing several pounds of tea at 2s. a pound. Then suppose a comparatively rich man who would buy only one bundle of asparagus at the price of 5s.: but who, the price being 2s., purchases several bundles. The surplus satisfaction that the rich man derives from his asparagus at 2s. a bundle is much less than that which the poor woman derives from her power of purchasing tea at 2s. a pound. But the two

---

[3] [No such discussion is to be found in Ch.I.]

[4] For a more general account of Economic measures the reader is referred to Appendix III. [Nothing further can be ascertained about Appendix III.]

satisfactions have the same economic measures, in other words the consumers' rents in the two cases are equal. Bearing in mind then that the economic measure of a benefit which the people receive is only a first approximation towards its real importance, we may proceed to estimate the total consumers' rent which is derived from the purchase of a commodity in a market.

The analogy on which the term 'consumers' rent' is based is tolerably obvious. The term 'rent,' or, as we may say, 'landlords' rent,' is applied to the excess of the value of the total produce of land over the amount which is just required to remunerate the farmer for the outlay involved in raising the produce. So consumers' rent is the excess of the value to a man of the total amount of a commodity which he purchases over the outlay which he has to make in order to obtain it. The farmer endeavours to apply to his land as much capital as can be profitably expended upon it. He expects the last portion of it which he applies, i.e., that portion which he is only just induced to apply, to give a return that at the current price will just remunerate him: he does not expect to obtain from this portion of his outlay any surplus, or rent. So the amount of the outlay made by the purchaser of any commodity is such that the value to him of the last portion of his purchase, i.e. of that portion of the commodity which he is only just induced to buy, is just equal to the value to him of what he pays for it at the current price; it affords him no surplus or consumers' rent. This analogy will be brought out clearly by a comparison of the diagrams given in this Chapter with those given in the Appendix on rent.[5] But the analogy between the two theories of landlords' rent and of consumers' rent, though close so far as it goes, does not extend far.

§ 3   Let us consider then the demand curve *DD'* (Figure 25) for a commodity in a given market. Let *OH* be the amount which is sold there at the price *HA* annually, a year being taken as the unit of time for the market. Taking any point *M* in *OH* let us draw *MP* vertically upwards to meet the curve in *P* and cut a horizontal line through *A* in *R*. We suppose all the

---

[5] [This was possibly the Appendix II, not otherwise mentioned. The diagrams on landlords' rent were obviously those of Section II. 7 above.]

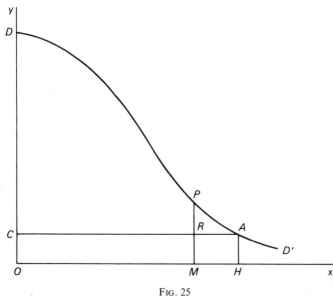

Fig. 25

several units of the commodity, say all the tons of coal, to be of like quality; so that it does not matter which unit is sold to any particular purchaser. It will however be convenient in order to give definiteness to our ideas to suppose the units numbered in the order of the eagerness of the several purchasers: the eagerness of the purchaser of any unit being measured by the price he is just willing to pay for that unit. The figure informs us that OM units can be sold at the price PM; but that at any higher price not quite so many units can be sold. There must be then some individual who will buy more at the price PM, than he will at any higher price. We are then to regard the OMth unit as sold to this individual. Suppose for instance that PM represents £2 and that OM represents a million tons. The purchaser described in the last section was just willing to buy his fifth ton of coal at the price £2. The OMth or millionth ton of coal may then be said to be sold to him. If AH and therefore RM represent £1, the consumers' rent derived from the OMth ton is the excess of PM or £2, which the purchaser of that ton would have been willing to pay for it, over RM, the £1 which he actually does pay for it. Let us suppose that a very thin vertical parallelogram is drawn of which the height is *PM* and of which the base is the distance along *Ox* that measures a single unit or ton of coal. It will be convenient henceforward to regard price as measured not by a mathematical straight line without thickness, as *PM*; but by a very thin parallelogram, or as it may be called a thick straight line, of which the breadth is in every case equal to the distance along *Ox* which measures a unit or ton of coal. Thus we should say that the total satisfaction derived from the *OM*th ton of coal is measured by the thick straight line *MP*; that the price paid for this ton is represented by the thick straight line *MR* and the consumers' rent derived from this ton by the thick straight line *RP*. Now let us suppose that such thin parallelograms or thick straight lines are drawn for all positions of *M* between *O* and *H*, one for each ton or unit of coal. The thick straight lines thus drawn, as *MP* is, from *Ox* up to the demand curve will each measure the total satisfaction derived from a ton of coal. The sum of these satisfactions taken together is the total satisfaction derived from the consumption of coal; and these thick straight lines taken together occupy and exactly fill up the whole area *DOHA*. Therefore we may say that the area *DOHA* measures the total satisfaction derived from the consumption of coal. Again each of the thick straight lines drawn as *MR* is from *Ox* upwards as far as *AC* represents the price that actually is paid for a ton of coal. These thick straight lines together make up the area *COHA*: and therefore this area represents the total price paid for coal. Finally each of the thick straight lines drawn as *RP* is from *AC* upwards as far as the Demand Curve represents the Consumers' rent derived from the corresponding unit or ton of coal. These thick straight lines together make up the area *DCA*; and therefore this area represents the total consumers' rent that is derived from coal when the price is *AH*.

It has already been remarked that it will seldom be possible to obtain the data necessary for drawing the Demand curve accurately throughout any large portion of its length.[6] If *A* is the point on the curve corresponding to the amount that is wont to be sold in the market, data may be obtained sufficient for drawing the curve with tolerable correctness for some

[6] [See Ch. I, § 2.]

distance on either side of A; but it will scarcely ever occur that the curve can be drawn with any approach to accuracy right up to D. It happens however, that the practical applications of this as of other portions of the theory of Domestic values require a knowledge of the shape of the Demand curve only in the neighbourhood of A. At all events in the present discussion we shall not be much concerned to ascertain accurately the total area DCA; it will be sufficient for most of our purposes to know the changes in the magnitude of this area that would be occasioned by moving A through small distances along the curve in either direction. Nevertheless it will be convenient to continue to assume, as in the pure theory we are at liberty to do, that the curve is completely drawn for us.[7]

§ 4 We may proceed to investigate the increase or diminution of Consumers' Rent which will in any particular instance be occasioned by a rise or a fall in the prices at which various amounts of the commodity can severally be produced. According to the phraseology explained at the end of the preceding chapter such a rise or fall will push the supply curve upwards or downwards respectively. An account has already been given of the various causes which may make it necessary to draw a new supply curve.[8] For brevity and for convenience it will be convenient to select from these a tax and a bounty as representing the two classes which may push the supply curve upwards and downwards; and during the present chapter to consider every change in the position of the Supply curve as due either to a tax or to a bounty. The reader will be able at once to make the alterations in the propositions which follow which are necessary in order to adapt them to the case of any other change which may disturb the position of the supply curve.

Let us first consider the effects of the imposition of a tax. Let us commence with the special case in which the expenses of production of the commodity in question are supposed to

---

[7] The mathematician will notice that if $y = f(x)$ be the equation to DD' and (a, b) the coordinates of A; the consumers' rent is

$$\int_0^a f(x)\,dx - ab.$$

[8] [See Ch. I, § 9.]

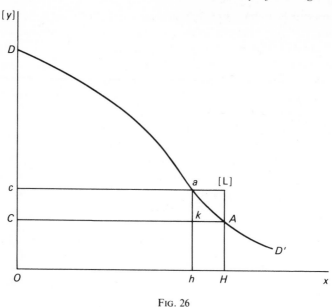

FIG. 26

be independent of the amount produced: or in other words of the special case in which the Supply curve is a horizontal straight line, at all events for some distance on either side of its intersection with the Demand curve. Let then a horizontal straight line CA (Figures 26 and 27) be the supply line before the imposition of the tax. Let the tax be $[Cc]$ per unit of the commodity: so that the new supply line is the horizontal straight line ca. Let the Demand curve cut the old and the new Supply lines in A and a respectively, so that A and a are the old and the new positions of equilibrium. Draw AH and ah perpendicular to Ox: let ah cut CA in k. Thus the tax diminishes the Consumers' Rent from the amount DCA to the amount Dca: the loss of the Consumers' Rent is $CAac$. Also the government collects a tax of Cc on each of Oh, or which is the same thing on each of Ck units of the commodity: the total tax which it collects is therefore $cCka$. The amount which the government receives from the tax is less than the resulting destruction of Consumers' Rent by the amount akA. In a complete estimate of the total burden which is inflicted on the

people by a tax which affords a given revenue to the government, account must be taken of the cost of collection of the
tax and of the annoyances and interferences with the freedom
of the trade which it occasions. But if these considerations be
for the time put aside, we may conclude that the immediate
economic effects of the tax will be good or bad according as
the loss of Consumers' Rent akA is, or is not, small as compared with the amount collected $cCka$. This area akA may for
our present purpose be taken as convertible with the triangle
formed by three straight lines joining a, k and A. It is indeed
true that if the curve aA be convex towards k the area in
question will be less than if aA be concave towards k. But
this consideration does not appear to be practically important
and it may be hereafter neglected.

We have then to consider the tax to be for our present
purposes good or bad according as the triangle akA is great or
small in comparison to the parallelogram $cCka$; that is
according as kA, the amount by which the consumption is
diminished, is small or great in comparison with Ck the
amount of the remaining consumption. The nature of the
demand curve represented in Figure 26 is such that a given
rise in price will not induce consumers to curtail their consumption much. The commodity for which this curve is drawn
therefore may be a necessary. If not it must be a comfort or
a luxury which consumers cannot be easily induced to forgo;
perhaps because those particular persons who are in the habit
of consuming it are wealthy and do not concern themselves
about small changes in the expense of their wonted gratifications. But whatever the commodity be, there is one statement that may be made with certainty with regard to it. This
statement is that there is no available substitute for the
commodity which escapes the tax that is imposed on it: or in
other words, that the tax in question is not a 'discriminating
tax.' Thus for example, Figure 26 may perhaps represent the
circumstances of the market for butcher's meat in a new
country in which an increase in the supply can be obtained
without involving an increase in the expenses of production.
Such a tax, to whatever other objection it might be liable,
would not involve a loss of consumers' rent which would much
exceed the receipts of the tax gatherer. But the effects of a tax

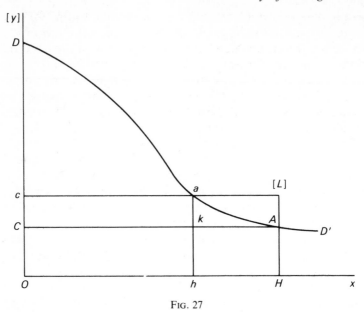

F<small>IG</small>. 27

levied on mutton and not on beef would be of a wholly
different character. They may be represented by Figure 27, if
the Demand curve in that figure can be taken to represent the
various amounts of mutton which it would be possible to
dispose of at various prices, the price of beef being assumed
to be stationary. For any considerable increase in the price of
mutton under these circumstances would occasion a very
great diminution in the consumption of it. Such a tax therefore
would be in effect a discriminating tax. And it would bring
into the state a very small revenue in proportion to the injury
that it inflicted on the consumers.

The results thus obtained admit of being explained with
sufficient clearness without the aid of diagrams. But the exact
analysis which has just been applied to the simple case in
which the Supply curve is a horizontal straight line, was
required as an introduction to the more complex cases to
which we shall soon proceed. Before leaving the present simple
case, however, it will be well to consider the manner in which
the awarding of a bounty on the production of a commodity
would affect Consumers' rent. For this purpose we may use

Figures 26 and 27, if we take Oc to represent the price at which the commodity would naturally be offered for sale; and that the awarding of a bounty of cC on the production of each unit of the commodity causes the price to fall to OC. Let HA and ca be produced to meet in L. The total bounty which the state will pay, will be Cc on each of OH units of the commodity: it will therefore be represented by the parallelogram $cCAL$. The bounty will have caused Consumers' Rent to increase from the amount Dca to the amount DCA. So that the increase of Consumers' Rent is measured by the area $cCAa$; and this is less than the total amount of the bounty which the Government pays by the area aLA. Thus if we consider a commodity the expenses of production of which are fixed, that is independent of the amount produced; we have the following pair of results which are valid independently of all allowances that have to be made on account of the expenses and indirect evils which are involved in collecting a tax or awarding a bounty, viz.: –

A tax on the commodity brings in less to the tax gatherer than it takes from Consumers' Rent; and

A bounty on it takes from the Government more than it adds to Consumers' Rent.

§ 5   We may next examine the change that is made in consumers' rent by a tax on a commodity, the expenses of production of which increase with every increase in the amount produced. This case is represented by pushing the Supply curve in Figure 28 upwards from the position SS' to the position ss'. If the tax be 'Specific,' i.e., independent of the price of the commodity, the vertical distance between any point on SS' and the corresponding point on ss' will be constant throughout the curves: if the tax be *ad valorem*, this distance will bear a constant ratio to the distance of either point from Ox. But the investigations which follow are independent of any particular assumption as to the principles on which the tax is levied. As before, the position of equilibrium is transferred from A to a; AC and ac are drawn horizontally, $akEh$ is drawn vertically, cutting AC in k, SS' in E and Ox in h; and EF is drawn perpendicular to Oy. The tax levied on each unit of the commodity is represented by aE; and the total amount

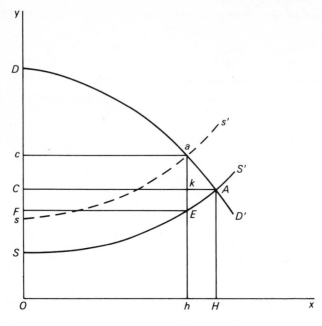

FIG. 28

of the tax collected is the parallelogram *cFEa*. The loss of consumers' rent is as before *cCAa*. In the preceding case we found that this loss must be greater than the amount collected by the Government. But in the present case the loss of consumers' rent will be less than the total sum which the tax collectors receive if the triangle *akA* is less than the parallelogram *CFEk*. As the figure shows, this may easily occur. This result has important practical bearings which will be discussed in a later section.

But bearing in mind that we are here treating of commodities that are produced at home, and not with imported commodities, we must examine the effects which the tax may have upon landlords' rent; that is, upon the rent of the land from which the commodity or the raw material of it is raised. It will be convenient to introduce this examination by first investigating the increase of rent which will follow on an increase in the demand for the commodity, and a consequent rise in its price.

Suppose then that the amount produced is originally Oh for the production of which Eh is remunerative, and that it is increased to OH for the production of which AH is required. Generally speaking, the amount Oh will now be produced with as little difficulty as before; or even with less if the increase in the scale of production renders possible improvements in the methods of production, or in the organisation of transport. The production of the amount hH is a matter indeed of proportionately greater difficulty. But the increase in price is obtained for the whole amount OH. Whence it follows that this rise in price must occasion either a higher rate of remuneration to those who are engaged in the production, or else an increase of the rent which is obtained by the owners of land or of other natural agents which may be employed at some stage in the production; or a combination of both these results. No general rule can be laid down as to the division of the benefits between these two classes. This division will depend not only upon the nature of the commodity in question, but also upon the length of the period for which its average price is estimated. If the work of production requires specialised skill and habits which cannot be acquired rapidly, a sudden increase in the amount produced will necessitate the employment of unhandy workers. It will be necessary to pay these men well in order to induce them to enter upon an occupation that is new to them. The price of the commodity must be sufficient to remunerate the employers who hire this expensive but unskilled labour. It must therefore be sufficient to cause a strong competition among employers, resulting in their offering a very high wage for skilled labour. This increased wage may itself be regarded partly as a rent of scarce personal qualities, and partly as exceptionally high profits on the investment of capital in the technical education of the worker. Similar causes will raise the 'wages of superintendence' of employers and others engaged in the task of management much above their usual level. Also the profits derived from buildings, machinery, and other capital specialised to the trade, will be abnormally high. But the exceptional wages and profits thus obtained by specialised capital and specialised skill can generally speaking endure only for a few months or years. So that if we are considering the causes which determine average prices during long periods of time, we may suppose that an increase in the demand for the commodity will occasion sufficient increase in the supplies of appropriate skill and capital to keep wages and profits down to their normal level. On this supposition the total expenses which have to be allowed for on account of the capital and labour employed in the production of the amount Oh will not be affected by the fact that an additional amount hH is produced. The whole of the increase in price from Eh to AH will go as rent to the owner of the land on which the raw material of the commodity is produced.

We may now turn back to the case in which the imposition of a tax causes the amount produced to diminish from OH to Oh; the price which the consumer pays increasing from AH to ah, but the price which the producer receives decreasing from AH to Eh. The skill and capital specialised to the production will be in excess of the requirements of the market and will obtain for a time diminished wages and profits. But gradually the surplus supply of skill and capital will dwindle away, until wages and profits rise to their normal level. So that if the periods of time for which we are making our calculations are long we may say that the total expenses which have to be allowed for on account of the capital and labour employed in the production of the amount Oh will not be affected by the fact that the amount hH is no longer produced. The whole of the diminution in the price which the producer receives from AH to Eh will fall upon the owner of the land on which the raw material of the commodity is produced.

In fact there is a certain class of problems referring to agricultural produce in which the total landlords' rent will be measured before the imposition of the tax by CSA, and afterwards by FSE.

For let us make the supposition that the expenses which have to be allowed for capital and labour on account of the production of any given unit of the commodity, as, e.g., the Ohth, are not affected by the fact that additional units are produced. That is to say the expenses of production exclusive of rent of the Ohth unit will be a fixed amount hE. Therefore, when the price HA, that is hk, is obtained for this unit, the landlord will be able to claim as his share that portion Ek of the vertical line hk which is intercepted between the Supply curve and the price line CA. Applying to this case the same method of reasoning that has been applied above to the case of consumers' rent we find that the total landlords' rent is measured by the sum of those vertical thick lines corresponding to successive units of the commodity up to the OHth, which are intercepted between the Supply curve and the price line CA. And the sum of these thick lines exactly makes up the area CSA.

On this supposition the tax diminishes landlords' rent by the amount $FEAC$. This together with $cCAa$, the loss of consumers' rent makes up the whole area $cFEAa$, which exceeds the total receipts of the tax gatherer by the amount EAa.

This method of measuring landlords' rent illustrates the analogy which exists between it and consumers' rent. It is possible to erect by this method an apparatus of curves which shall contain a complete exposition of the pure theory of the rent of land. But another apparatus of curves which is practically more convenient for this purpose is supplied in an Appendix to the present volume.

As in the previous case we may represent the results of awarding a bounty to the production by supposing that SS' is the original position of the Supply curve and that in consequence of the bounty it is pushed downwards into the position ss' (see Figure 29). Let ha be produced to meet SS' in L and let LG be drawn perpendicular to Oy. The bounty will have caused the amount produced to increase from OH to Oh, the price to the consumer to decrease from HA to ha, and the expenses of production to increase from HA to hL. The total bounty paid by Government will be cG on each of Oh units of the commodity: and will be represented by the area $GcaL$. It will thus be necessarily much larger than the increase of consumers' rent, which will be only $CcaA$.

But here again allowance must be made for the increase that the bounty would occasion in landlords' rent. We have just seen that in the case of agricultural produce we may suppose the Supply curve SS' to be so drawn that when the price is HA the total landlords' rent is represented by the area CSA. On this supposition the total landlords' rent after the awarding of the bounty will be represented by the area GSL; that is, it will be increased by the area $GCAL$. Thus the

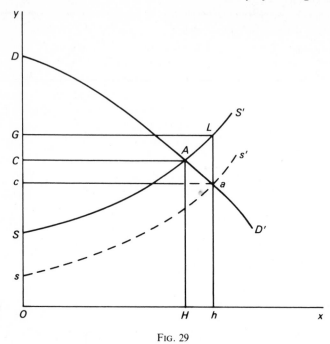

Fig. 29

increase of consumers' rent together with the increase of land-lords' rent will be less than the total bounty which Govern-ment pays by the area *LAa*. If the commodity in question had been an imported commodity the increased price which was required to obtain an increased supply would in general have been a benefit to the foreign producer at the expense of the consumer at home. The Government by levying a tax would intercept some of this benefit, but as has been already indicated it could not in general intercept much of it. A more full examination of this matter is given elsewhere.[9]

§ 6   We have lastly to consider the case in which the Supply curve is inclined negatively in the neighbourhood of *A*, its points of intersection with the Demand curve. That is to say, we have to suppose that the greater be the amount produced, the less will be the expenses of production; provided this amount be neither much greater nor much less than that

[9] [See Part I, Ch. VI, § 2 (Section III.3, above).]

amount *OH* which actually is produced when the trade is undisturbed. The figure (Figure 30) may be constructed as before. The Supply curve is pushed upward by the tax to the position *ss'*, and cuts *DD'* in *a*; *ah* drawn vertically cuts *SS'* in *E*. The total receipts of the tax gatherer are represented as before by the area *cFEa*: and the loss of Consumers' Rent is represented by the much larger area *cCAa*. The diminution of the demand for the raw material of the manufacture will probably cause some diminution of landlords' rent. We must remember the indications given by such portions of the Supply curve as are inclined negatively are not completely trustworthy when they relate to movements of the amount-index towards the left, as in the present case. We must remember that the tax may act tardily in crushing out such economies as have already been introduced into the manufacture. But when every due allowance has been made, it will remain true that a tax imposed on a commodity for which the Supply curve is

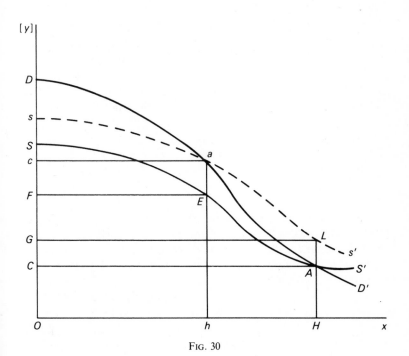

Fig. 30

inclined negatively, involves a wasteful destruction of Consumers' Rent.

We may as before represent the results of awarding a bounty to the production by supposing that ss' is the original position of the Supply curve; and that in consequence of the bounty it is pushed down into the position SS'. Thus the amount-index will move to the right from h to H; and the indications given by the curve may be trusted. Let HA be produced as before to meet $[ss']$ in L, then the total bounty paid by the Government is represented by the area $GCAL$; and the gain of Consumers' Rent by the area $cCAa$; the latter area will often be, as it is in the figure before us, much larger than the former area. Moreover, allowance must be made for an increase of landlords' rent which may have accrued from an increased demand for the raw material of the manufacture. For the increased demand for the raw material will probably have caused its price to rise; at the same time that, in consequence of the economies introduced into the manufacture, it causes the price of the finished product to fall.

Figure 31 represents a remarkable, though of course also an exceptional, instance of the case, a less striking instance of which is represented in Figure 30. If the awarding of a bounty push downward the Supply curve from the position SS' into the position $S_1S'_1$, equilibrium would pass from A to A_1; and from A_1 it might probably pass to C_1, on the occasion of some temporary increase in demand. If the Supply curve be pushed downward into the position $S_2S'_2$, equilibrium will necessarily pass to C_2, and thus an enormous increase of Consumers' Rent will be effected by a bounty, the total cost of which to Government will not be very great.

§ 7   If we compare the results of the last three sections, we shall obtain a conclusion of great importance. Let us suppose then that Figures 28 and 30 are drawn to the same scale. That is, let the distances along Ox, which represent units of the commodity, be equal in the two figures; and let the distances along Oy, which represent any given price, be equal in the two figures: so that equal areas represent equal sums of money in the two figures. Let us suppose also that the area $cFEa$ in Figure 28 is just equal to the area $GCAL$ in Figure 30; so that

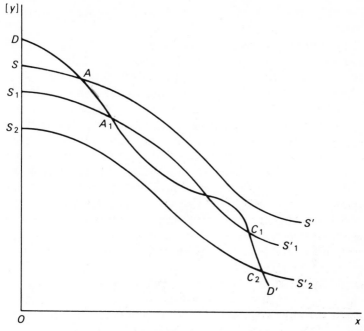

Fɪɢ. 31

Government by levying a tax of cF in Figure 28 on each unit of the commodity represented there would obtain the means of awarding the bounty of CG in Figure 30 on each unit of the commodity represented in that figure. It would thus diminish Consumers' Rent by $cCAa$ in Figure 28, and would increase it by the much larger area $cCAa$ in Figure 30. It is true that the tax in Figure 28 will have caused a diminution of landlords' rent; but this will not necessarily be much greater than that increase of landlords' rent which will arise from the increased demand for the raw material of the manufacture in Figure 30. It is, however, possible to suppose that the loss of landlords' rent in the one case is considerably greater than the gain in the second; it is possible also to make liberal allowance for the cost of working of the Government departments that manage the collection of the. tax and the awarding of the bounty; and yet to conclude that by the scheme in question

Government may have conferred a great economic benefit on the nation as a whole.

But before a practical rule be based upon this result of the pure theory, it is necessary to take account of other classes of considerations. For the purposes of pure theory we have been at liberty to argue as though the knowledge and the probity of Government were unlimited. We have assumed that Government knowledge is sufficient to enable it to draw the Supply and Demand curves for the commodities in question; or at least such portions of the curves as lie in either figure between *ah* and *AH*. Thus we have assumed Government not only to know the present circumstances of the markets for various commodities, but also to forecast changes in the expenses of production which would result from changes in the amount produced. We have also assumed that Government officials will not be in any manner imposed upon or corrupted by those who desire to avoid the payment of the tax, or to obtain the bounty. The practical statesman, before venturing on such a scheme as that here suggested, will have to take account not only of the mishaps that may arise from errors in his calculations, but also of the deterioration of public morals which is likely to ensue when it is to the interest of wealthy classes of producers to bribe legislators or public officers. He will also have to take account of the injustice which may be involved in taxing one set of consumers in order to give a bounty to another. But it should always be observed that a single tax cannot rightly be condemned as unjust; such a condemnation can attach only to a system of taxation taken as a whole.[10]

§ 8   It has just been argued that Consumers' Rent may possibly be increased by the plan of bringing a tax on some commodities in order to provide the means of awarding a bounty on others; but that such a scheme would be likely to work mischief indirectly. The analysis of the present chapter leads us, however, to a practical result of great importance: for we have seen that a much larger destruction of Consumers' Rent will be involved in levying a given amount of revenue by taxes on commodities of which the expenses of production

[10] [See the discussion in Part I, Ch. VI, § 10 (Section III.3, above).]

diminish as the amount produced increases, as in Figure 30, than by taxes on those for which the opposite rule holds, as in Figure 28. It is true that the destruction of landlords' rent is likely to be somewhat greater in the latter case than in the former; but it will not in general be much greater. Consequently it appears that account being taken of the interests of consumers and landlords together, it is not expedient that the revenue should be derived from taxes levied equally on all commodities; but that such revenue as is derived from taxes on commodities should be obtained almost exclusively from commodities the expenses of production of which increase, or at least do not diminish, as the amount produced increases.

The whole of a man's income is expended in the purchase of services and of commodities. It is indeed commonly said that a man spends some portion of his income and saves another. But it is a familiar economic axiom that a man purchases labour and commodities with that portion of his income which he saves just as much as he does with that which he is said to spend. He is said to spend when he seeks to obtain present enjoyment from the services and the commodities which he purchases. He is said to save when he causes the labour and the commodities which he purchases to be devoted to the production of wealth from which he expects to derive the means of enjoyment in the future. It is possible to devise a plan by which taxes on raw materials and implements and on finished commodities and personal services should be so adjusted as to take from each man the same percentage of his total income. But such a plan will be complex, and it would involve too long a digression to investigate it here. Moreover, all economists are agreed that it would be expedient, if it could practically be done, to exempt from taxation that portion of a man's income which he saves. They would prefer to levy taxes only on the remainder of his income; or, as we may hereafter say, in conformity to popular usage, only 'on his expenditure.' And it is obvious that such a tax would be convertible with a tax levied equally on every percentage taken by taxation from every sum which he expends on the purchase of labour or commodities for his own immediate consumption and not for the purposes of trade. Next it is obvious that the analysis of the Consumers' Rent which has been applied to the demand for and supply of commodities of any kind may be applied with only verbal alterations to the demand for and the supply of services of any kind. A Demand curve for any class of services may be drawn on just the same principles as Demand curves for any commodity. And when the market-price of such services is known, the Consumers' Rent which accrues to the purchasers of them is determined in just the same manner as before. We arrived recently at the conclusion that it is not expedient that the revenue should be derived from taxes levied equally on all commodities. We now see that this principle may be extended: but the enunciation of it in its extended form is a matter of some difficulty. We must in this case also commence by putting aside for the present all considerations relating to the expenses and other difficulties involved in collecting. We have then to compare the advantages of two systems of taxation in each of which taxes are levied on all purchases [of] commodities and services which are designed to afford gratification directly, and are not made in the course of trade or intended to be used as capital. According to the first system, a certain amount of revenue is supposed to be collected exclusively from commodities the expenses of production of which increase as the amount produced increases. According to the second, the same revenue is collected by taxes on all purchases of commodities and services for the purposes of direct gratification. We find that the first system is more advantageous than the second: that the second is convertible with what we have called a tax upon expenditure: and since this tax has unquestionably superior advantages to those possessed by an income-tax, we obtain the important result that the expenses and other difficulties of collection being neglected, the first system of taxation is more advantageous than an income-tax.

This principle does not prove that on the whole an income-tax is inexpedient. For in levying other taxes customs and excise officers are compelled, as has been already observed, to worry and hamper by their inspection the trader and the producer.[11] Moreover, they levy the tax in the first instance from capital that is being productively employed, and the

---

[11] [See Part I, Ch. VI, § 8 (Section III.3, above).]

consumer is compelled ultimately to pay not only the amount of the tax, but also a high rate of interest, or traders' profits, upon it. The income-tax evades these evils; and though the income-tax assessments cannot in the present state of public morality be made with tolerable accuracy, there is no reason why public opinion should not be gradually so acted upon as to enable the tax to be levied equitably. The general tenor of the arguments of the present treatise points to the conclusion that every effort should be made thus to act upon public opinion with the purpose of ultimately raising nearly the whole of the revenue by direct taxation.

But the principle that has just been laid down is subversive of one particular that has not been unfrequently urged in favour of the substitution of an income-tax for taxes on particular commodities.

This argument is, that if each man's contribution is taken from him directly in the form of an income-tax; the Government leaves it entirely to his own discretion to decide what commodities or other sources of satisfaction to himself he can most conveniently give up in order to obtain the means of paying the tax. But that Government wantonly infringes individual liberty if it levies taxes on particular commodities, with the effect of inducing the individual to curtail his consumption of them rather than of others. It is urged that in so doing Government claims for itself the power of judging better than the individual can, what is the relative value to him of the various gratifications which he purchases.

This argument is fallacious because it takes no account of the fact that every individual, and therefore the whole state, has a direct interest in the character of each man's expenditure. For brevity let us suppose A to be a commodity the expenses of production of which continually increase as the amount produced increases: and B to be a commodity for which the opposite law holds. Then if a person increases his purchases of B, he helps to increase the scale on which it is produced, and thus to lower its price; so that he confers a benefit on all others who may wish to consume B. But if he increases his purchases of A, his action tends to raise the price of A, he injures those who desire to purchase A. By purchasing A rather than B, he will probably add more to landlords' rent in one direction than he takes from it in another, but not in general much more. Therefore it would be to the interests of the state that each man should be directed to devote less of his income to the purchase of *A* and more to the purchase of *B* than he would if he took no account of the interest of any person except himself in the matter.

We are not at present concerned to estimate the probability that any Government will possess sufficient knowledge, judgment and power to enable it to perform such a task with any tolerable success. It is sufficient to establish here that a Government which should levy its revenues by a tax on income or expenditure would cut itself off from the attempt to use a power which it theoretically has of promoting the common weal. Theoretically it has the power of so adjusting taxation as to cause each individual on the one hand to contract his consumption of those commodities, a diminution of the demand for which will benefit those who continue to purchase them; and on the other hand, somewhat to augment his consumption of those commodities, an increase in the total demand for which will lower the price at which they can be produced.

PART IV

Miscellaneous Notes on
Economic Theory

Miscellaneous Notes on Economic Theory

IV.1 Introduction

This Part reproduces various notes or fragments which are of interest either intrinsically, or for the light they throw on Marshall's thinking and its development. The notes fall into three groups and are presented in sections with the following headings (see the Table of Contents for a detailed listing):

IV.2 Notes on other economists, *c.* 1868–81
IV.3 Pages from a mathematical notebook, *c.* 1867–72
IV.4 Miscellaneous notes on economic theory, *c.* 1873–87
IV.5 Fragments for the *Principles*

Datings are approximate. The notes in Sections IV.2 and IV.3 have, to a considerable extent, the role of appendixes to Sections I.2 and II, whilst IV.5 is essentially an appendix to Section I.6. The notes in IV.4 have, however, considerable independent interest, as they show Marshall pioneering in hitherto unexpected areas in the process of dealing with questions of indirect taxation, economic growth and social welfare. We also find him developing original results on marginal-productivity theory.

The notes are numbered within each Section, and each is given a title – which is only original if enclosed in quotation marks. Every note is prefaced by an Introduction, in which any quotations are explicitly indicated, after which follows the Text. Editorial insertions in the text are enclosed in the usual square brackets, as are editorial footnotes to the Text or editorial additions to original footnotes.

IV.2   Notes on Other Economists, c. 1868–81

IV.2.1   *Annotations of Cournot*

Introduction   Marshall apparently first read A. A. Cournot's *Recherches sur les Principes Mathématiques de la Théorie des Richesses* around 1868.[1] He reread it in 1882[2] – quite possibly for the last time – and probably recurred to it on occasion during the intervening years. Marshall's annotated copy of the original 1838 edition of Cournot is preserved in the Marshall Library and the annotations are continued on a separate manuscript. It seems quite probable that the notes were written before 1870.[3] A particular feature supporting this is Marshall's failure to follow his usual practice, adopted quite early, of showing price on the vertical axis of his supply-demand diagrams. It is true that he may simply have been following Cournot's precedent.[4] But Cournot's diagrams are not at all closely related to Marshall's, and – as the reader will doubtless discover – there is a strong temptation, for anyone well versed in Marshall's now-standard convention, to redraw the diagrams in order to make the argument more accessible to intuition. If it could be established, a pre-1870 dating would be of considerable significance. Marshall develops Cournot's monopoly analysis and introduces the device of a grid of rectangular hyperbolae for finding monopoly equilibrium graphically.[5] He also extends Cournot's analysis of competitive supply and demand. But, most significant, is the replacement of Cournot's rather unsatisfactory measure of the welfare effects of a stipulated change by a proper measure of consumer surplus, in annotations 2 and

---

[1] Published by L. Hachette, Paris, 1838. A translation into English by N. T. Bacon was published in 1897 as *Researches into the Mathematical Principles of the Theory of Wealth by Augustin Cournot* (Macmillan, New York, 1897). Marshall's claim to have read Cournot around 1868 is recorded above (see Vol 1, p. 40).

[2] See Vol 1, p. 85, above.

[3] There is an annotation in different style which says: '$\phi(D)$ being total expenses of production $d\phi(D)/dD$ = final expenses of production = price, note ye anticipation of Jevons.' This is inappropriately attached to Cournot's § 29 (Ch. V) rather than § 50 (Ch. VIII) where it belongs. There is nothing to indicate that it was not added on a later (possibly careless) reading.

[4] Cournot's Figures 1 and 6 have this characteristic. His Figure 6 is somewhat related to the figure that Marshall uses in Annotation 4 below.

[5] Marshall published an account of this device in 1873 – see Item IV.4.1, below.

5, and a proper measure of producer surplus in annotation 5.[6] Indeed, annotation 5 is extraordinarily close in conception to the analysis stemming from Fleeming Jenkin's 1870 paper on 'The Graphic Representation of the Laws of Supply and Demand'.[7] It is unfortunate that evidence on dating is insufficient to justify Marshall's claim that he anticipated Jenkin, but there is nothing in the annotations making such a claim inherently implausible.

There is, however, one general puzzle which can appropriately be aired here. Marshall claimed to have learned from Cournot early, but also to have 'worked a good deal at the mathematical theory of monopolies', as well as on international trade, during the period 1870–4, adding on another occasion that the monopoly diagrams 'were the last to be developed'.[8] It has always seemed improbable that anyone acquainted in 1869 with both Cournot and the differential calculus should have taken four years to develop Marshall's monopoly diagrams, and the annotations confirm such doubts. There is evidence suggesting that Marshall had a grasp of the monopoly problem in 1870 or 1871,[9] so that the above phrases do pose a puzzle. A plausible solution is that Marshall took his work on monopolies also to cover his use of surplus analysis in welfare economics. The latter figured prominently in the *Pure Theory of Domestic Values* and must have been well advanced by 1874, while the concept of 'compromise benefit' is clearly hinted in the 1873 paper to the Cambridge Philosophical Society.[10] It may be conjectured that it was to these deeper aspects of the analysis that Marshall referred when speaking of the monopoly analysis as the last to be developed.

[6] It is true that Cournot has an adequate measure of producer surplus in § 52, while Marshall goes off the rails in annotation 2. But Cournot always measures cost to consumers by the extra expenditure of those who continue to consume, whilst Marshall adds to this the loss of those who have ceased to consume.

[7] Originally published in Sir Alexander Grant (editor), *Recess Studies* (Edmonston and Douglas, Edinburgh, 1870). Jenkin's full surplus analysis is to be found in his paper 'On the Principles which Regulate the Incidence of Taxes', *Proceedings of the Royal Society of Edinburgh*, 1871–2, whose existence escaped Marshall for many years. (See Vol 1, p. 45, above.)

[8] See *Memorials*, p. 416; *Principles II*, p. 69n.

[9] See Vol 1, p. 152, above.

[10] See Item IV.4.1, below.

Text

1. [*Taxing a monopolist*][11]

> [D = amount demanded]
> x = amount [sold]
> p = total price
> $\phi(x)$ = total expenses of production
> xy = monopolist's profit
> [i = tax per unit sold]

We have $D = f(p)$ or

$$x = f\left(y + \frac{\phi(x)}{x}\right)$$

or

$$y = \psi(x)$$

When

$$yx = \text{maximum}$$

therefore

$$\psi(x) + x\psi'(x) = 0 \tag{1}$$

and

$$2\psi'(x) + x\psi''(x) < 0 \tag{2}$$

In the curve

$$y^0 = \psi(x^0) - i$$

[after a tax is imposed] we have [from $y^0 x^0 = \text{maximum}$]

$$\psi(x^0) - i + x^0\psi'(x^0) = 0 \tag{3}$$

Now put

$$x^0 = x + \Delta x$$

---

[11] [This relates to § 38 (Ch. VI) of Cournot's text, but reference should also be made to § 31 (Ch. V). To ease the reader's task, slight changes have been made in notation and equation numbering. The opening definitions appear to have been added at a later date.]

Then[12]

$$\psi(x) + x\psi'(x) + \{2\psi'(x) + x\psi''(x)\}\Delta x - i = 0$$

Therefore, from (1) and (2), Δx must be of opposite sign to i. Cournot has assumed this, but has not referred to (2). It might be worthwhile to put in a note this mathematical proof on the ground that Cournot has omitted it, but a proof without mathematics may be shortly given as follows.

Let P [Figure 1] be the point for which xy is a maximum. That is, the curve touches from the inside a hyperbola at P. Now if $PP' = i$, the tangent to the locus of P' at P' is parallel to the tangent to the locus of P at P and therefore more inclined to the axis of x than the tangent at P' to the hyperbola through it. Therefore P' is not a maximum point.

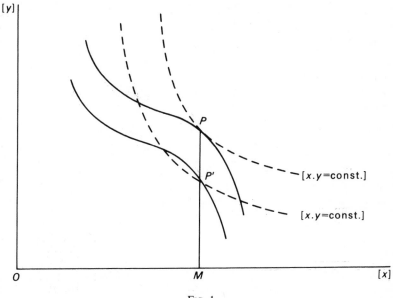

Fig. 1

2. [*The welfare effects of subsidising a monopolist*][13]

Draw the curve $x = f(y + \phi(x)/x)$ [where] $y + \phi(x)/x = p$: xy = monopolistic class and xy = maximum, $x = OM$

---

[12] [Expanding (3) about x and neglecting all terms above the first order.]
[13] [This also relates to § 38 of Cournot's text.]

[Figure 2]. Now draw $x = f(y + \phi(x)/x + i)$. $xy =$ maximum gives $x = OM'$ [Figure 2, where $P'PP''$ is the demand curve]. Now let i be negative i.e. instead of a tax let there be a bounty. Gain of producer $= OQ' - OP$ [i.e. $ORQ'M'' - ONPM$]. Loss of state $= OQ' - OP''$ [i.e. $ORQ'M'' - ON''P''M''$] and OP is always $< OP''$, therefore $OP'' - OP$ [i.e. $ON''P''M'' - ONPM$] is positive.[14] But the gain to the consumer is $PP''N''N$ therefore the total gain is PSP'' [not shown].[15]

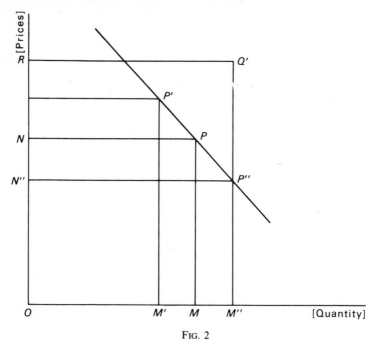

Fig. 2

[14] [This reflects the fact that, from the fact of profit maximisation, P must be a point on the demand curve at which the demand elasticity exceeds one. Incidentally, it is remarkable that Marshall failed to come up earlier with the concept of elasticity of demand. He comments on Cournot's § 24 (Ch. IV) '... at [a] point for which $pf(p) =$ maximum ye demand curve has tangent which cuts off equal lengths from Ox and Oy (i.e. which is tangent to a rectangular hyperbola with Ox and Oy as asymptotes).' Also: 'Commodities fall into two classes according as their current price is above or below. that price which makes $pf(p)$ a maximum.']

[15] [Note that the bounty rate is $Q'P''$ and that the bounty lowers the price paid by consumers from MP to $M''P''$, increasing output from OM to OM''. Since Marshall neglects the cost of producing the extra output he should find the sum of consumer and producer gains exceeding total subsidy cost by the area $MPP''M''$. Instead, he could take average cost as constant at $M''P''$, so that the welfare gain would be the triangle with hypotenuse PP''.]

3. [*On Cournot's analysis of duopoly*][16]

The method of dealing with the problem given here seems to be unnecessarily cumbersome. The cases in which there are two or more rival monopolists in competition is not without interest but it takes a very subordinate place in economic theory and it seems unwise to make the general theory of competition dependent on it.

4. [*A graphical analysis of competitive equilibrium*][17]

Let the producers be able to produce respectively

$$P_1 M_1 \text{ at price } P_1 N_1$$

$$P_2 p_2 \text{ at price } P_2 N_2$$

$$P_3 p_3 \text{ at price } P_3 N_3$$

[see Figure 3]. Demand equals RS at price RT. Equilibrium is at U.

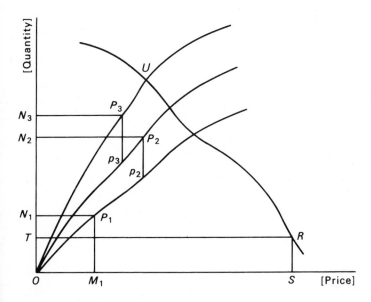

FIG. 3

[16] [This refers to Cournot's Ch. VII.]
[17] [This also refers to Cournot's Ch. VII.]

5. [*The removal of a prohibition on trade*][18]

Following Cournot's notation:

In country A, D_a of a commodity M is sold at price p_a. In country B, D_b at price p_b, p_b being greater than p_a and the importation of M into B being forbidden.

The prohibition is removed.

In A, D'_a is produced; price equals p'_a; Δ is consumed at home; ε is exported.

In B, D'_b is produced; price is p'_b.

Supposing that in A at price OM_1, P_1M_1 can be produced [see Figure 4]; at price OM_2, P_2M_2 can be sold [domestically]; and after the change at price OM_3, P_3p_3 can be sold.

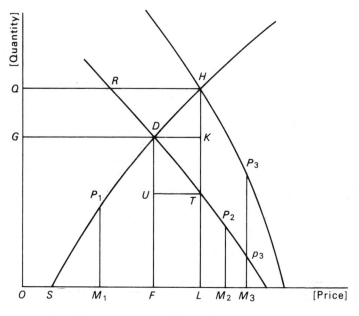

Fig. 4

The old equilibrium is at D; profits of producers are DSF. After the change [equilibrium is at H and] profits of producers are HSL. But at the price OL only TL can be sold in A. Thus

[18] [This relates to Cournot's Chs. X and XII. Unlike Cournot, Marshall ignores transport costs.]

consumers in *A* lose *TLFU* and also *TUD*, corresponding to
the loss incurred by those who cease to consume. Therefore
the net gain equals *HDT*.

In country *B*, [referring to Figure 5] at price OM_1, P_1M_1
can be produced; at price OM_2, P_2p_2 can be imported after
the removal of prohibition; at price OM_3, P_3M_3 will be
consumed. Originally equilibrium [was] at *D*; *DEF* equalled
the profits of producers. After the change equilibrium is at *G*;
HK is produced at home, *GH* imported. Producers have lost
HKED but consumers have gained *DEKL* in money, besides
DLG representing satisfaction of new consumers. The net gain
equals *GHD*.

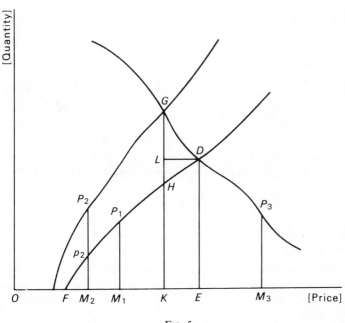

It is worthwhile to draw the figures on the supposition that
in each country cost of production is independent of quantity.
[Figure 6 shows the] gain of *A* is zero [and Figure 7 shows the]
gain of *B* is *GKED*: a remarkable result especially in connection

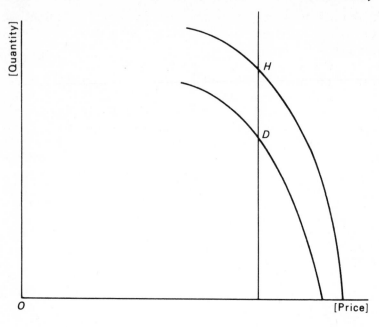

FIG. 6

with the question of the comparative advisability of encouraging the importation of raw and manufactured materials respectively.

IV.2.2 *On von Thünen*

Introduction Throughout the whole of Marshall's early manuscripts, letters and publications, the name of von Thünen is mentioned only in this note, which appears to date from an early stage of Marshall's work. It relates to Volume Two, Part One of *der Isolierte Staat*, which was published in 1850, shortly before Thünen's death.[1] Marshall clearly perceives Thünen's marginal-productivity approach to interest[2] and corrects an expositional slip. He also corrects a blunder in Thünen's derivation of the 'natural wage', more

---

[1] A Translation of Volume Two is given in B. W. Dempsey, *The Frontier Wage* (Loyola University Press, Chicago, 1960). Marshall's notes refer to Chs. 8–11 and 15 (Dempsey, pp. 249–64 and 288–94).

[2] Marshall describes this fairly fully in *Principles I*, p. 522.

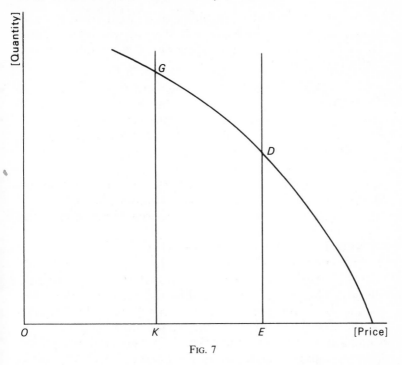

Fig. 7

appropriately described as 'a proposition concerning the rational level of accumulation of capital'.[3] However, Marshall perceives, even at this stage, the 'fanciful and unreal assumptions as to the causes that determine the accumulation of capital'.[4]

There is little here to suggest why Marshall came to feel that he had been strongly influenced by Thünen.[5] One is

[3] H. D. Dickinson, 'Von Thünen's Economics', *Economic Journal*, Vol 79 (Dec 1969) p. 899. A similar correction had been made in 1865 by G. F. E. Knapp (see Dickinson, p. 899n; Dempsey, p. 92).

[4] *Principles I*, p. 522n.

[5] In a manuscript note dated 11 December 1919 that is preserved in the Marshall Library, Marshall characterises Thünen as follows: '... von Thünen, though not so profound a mathematician as Cournot, had been led by systematic studies of agriculture to anticipate, in some degree at all events, some of the leading doctrines of twentieth century economics as to the distribution of resources among various methods of expenditure which would afford the most desirable harvest of gratifications.' He adds 'My own obligations to [Thünen] are greater than to any other writer excepting only Adam Smith and Ricardo.' See also *Principles I*, p. x, and *Memorials*, pp. 359–60.

tempted to guess that what Marshall really derived was the perception of the possibility of a symmetrical treatment of capital and labour. In a retrospect of the distribution theory of the 1879 *Economics of Industry*, he observed:

> Von Thünen worked out his theory with several curious subtleties, and some perversities but he gave a good lead by suggesting symmetrical relations between labour and capital; the earnings of each being defined by the last profitable application of each at the margin.[6]

Text[7] Let a labourer's necessaries for a year, sufficing for the bringing up to full age of two children, be 100. Let A represent the wages of a day labourer under any given circumstances.

First take the case of the tropics where without any capital the product of a year's labour is 110. Let capital of A (i.e. 110) turn this into $150 = 110 + 40$. Let capital of $2A$ (i.e. 220) turn this into $186 = 150 + (9/10)40$. For the extra 110 the extra produce being only 36 the capitalist can get only 36 as profits for the first 110. Therefore the wages must be [the] gross product less 72, or 114. After this v. Thünen supposes a third A to be applied and to produce an extra $(9/10)^2\ 40 = 32\cdot4$. But he renders part of his calculation wrong by supposing that the A is not the same as before, i.e. that $3A$ does not equal 330 but equals $342\ [= 3 \times 114]$.

He afterwards gives (Table B)[8] the corresponding results for countries in which, without some capital to start with, the year's produce is less than enough to support a labourer. He then proceeds to calculate what is the real interest of the labourer. He does not do this by supposing the capitalist's savings to depend on his profits and determining the extras which the labourer can obtain for any given amount of capital (as in Table three).[9] But assuming the amount of capital with which the labourer works to be given, the produce of his

---

[6] *Principles II*, pp. 232–3.

[7] [Two paragraphs, which add little of interest, have been deleted and Thünen's rather cumbersome notation has been simplified in the first passage, where originally 100 is 100*c* and A is *IA* (Jahres Arbeiterlohn) etc.]

[8] Dempsey, p. 268.

[9] Presumably the untitled table, Dempsey, p. 290.

labour p is given; the necessaries which he has are called a, the extras which he has are called y, the amount of capital with which he is set to work is Q and the unknown rate of profit is z.

Now v. Thünen makes the arbitrary assumption, without apparently knowing it, that under all circumstances the labourer saves the whole of the y and is not in the least interested directly in its magnitude; that he employs it as capital and gets of course yz income out of it, that he consumes this under any circumstances and is consequently interested exclusively in its amount without any reference to the profits to be made out of it.

Thus we have yz = maximum where

$$p = a + y + Qz$$

p, a and Q being constant, therefore

$$y \, dz + z \, dy = 0; \qquad dy + Q \, dz = 0$$

therefore $y = Qz$ and $p = a + 2y$ so that

$$a + y = \frac{a + p}{2}$$

This is the result which v. Thünen *ought* to get, but does not. For while assuming that p is constant and that the value of p depends on that of Q he takes Q not constant but equal to $q(a + y)$ where q is constant. Thus

$$p = (a + y)(1 + qz)$$

So
$$y \, dz + z \, dy = 0, \qquad (1 + qz) \, dy + (a + y)q \, dz = 0$$

Therefore $y(1 + qz) = (a + y)qz$, [or] $y = aqz$, [and]

$$ap = (a + y)^2$$

[and so $a + y = \sqrt{ap}$].

He has got into his confusion about $q(a + y)$ by trying to express everything in terms of barley. He then considers a certain amount of capital to be measured, not by a corresponding amount of barley, but by the barley wages of the labourer who made it. Thus, absolutely arbitrary as are his assumptions, he has to make another (of inferior importance) in order to get his result natural wage = $\sqrt{ap}$.

It is worth remarking that, whether we take Q or q as constant (v. Thünen points it out for the latter case), our results $a + y = (a + p)/2$ and $a + y = \sqrt{ap}$ respectively are independent of the values of Q and q.

IV.2.3 *On Turgot*

Introduction The next six notes are selected from a mass of what appear to be Marshall's lecture notes. These quote from and comment on the works of many earlier authors, but are too diffuse, incomplete and limited in interest to justify any attempt at reproduction *in extenso*. However, it may be of value to select a few highlights. It seems almost certain that the whole mass of notes was written in the late 1860s and early 1870s.

The present note is on Turgot and refers to his *Réflexions sur la Formation et la Distribution des Richesses* (1770).[1] It views Turgot as a predecessor of the British Classical Economists.

Text He assumes[2] that every one is at starvation door except landowners and capitalists: and he assumes[3] that any tax on profits of capital will cause such an enormous diminution in capital that the state will suffer more than it gains. It is true that he does not know clearly what he is assuming: that his assumptions are implied rather than expressed: and that he would probably have rejected them if they were distinctly proposed to him. On these assumptions his conclusion that a tax on anything but rent will have to be paid by the landowners together with charges of collection is *true*. It is to be noted that the more reckless Ricardians make all these assumptions with one exception. They recognize the existence of a number of highly salaried individuals who could be taxed. These are the people to whom, whether consciously or not, reference is chiefly made when a tax is spoken of as falling on consumers, but as not being a tax upon wages. The definite step made [by the Ricardians] in advance of Turgot and Adam Smith was

---

[1] A translation in the Economic Classics series, edited by W. J. Ashley, is *Reflections on the Formation and Distribution of Riches* (Macmillan, New York, 1898).

[2] [*Reflections*] § vi, vii etc.

[3] [*Reflections*] § xcv.

the recognition of the population principle.[4] Turgot says the competition of other artisans limits the means of each artisan to his own subsistence. Adam Smith says the reason of this is that 'men, like all other animals, naturally multiply in proportion to the means of their subsistence.'[5] The distinction between Adam Smith and Ricardo is that Ricardo knew clearly what he was assuming: and Smith did not. Thus if a more productive crop be introduced, as potatoes instead of corn, Adam Smith says the landlord will get a larger share of this larger produce,[6] tacitly and probably not quite consciously basing his conclusion on the previous assumption. Ricardo says this result will be ultimately true basing his conclusion consciously on this assumption and arguing that in the meanwhile the reverse consequences will exist for a time.[7]

IV.2.4   On Adam Smith's Treatment of Rent

Introduction   This commentary on the treatment of rent in Book I, Ch. XI of Adam Smith's *Wealth of Nations* leads to an interesting consideration of the possibility of expressing rent in opportunity-cost terms. As explained in the Introduction to the preceding Note, the source for the present Text is a body of Marshall's early lecture notes.

Text   His position seems to be this:[1]

'land, in almost any situation, produces a greater quantity of food than what is sufficient to maintain all the labour necessary for bringing it to market, in the most liberal way in which that labour is ever maintained.'

---

[4] I have since discovered that the Physiocrats knew the population principle. [Note added at a later date.]

[5] [*Wealth of Nations*, Book I, Ch. XI, p. 67 (Modern Library, p. 146). This and the succeeding Note (Item IV.2.4) are cross referenced by Marshall.]

[6] [Ibid., p. 73.]

[7] [Ricardo's treatment of agricultural improvements (*Principles of Political Economy and Taxation*, Ch. II, pp. 79–84) is discussed in Appendix L of Marshall's *Principles*.]

[1] [Marshall's loose quotations have been corrected. His page references coincide with the McCulloch edition of the *Wealth of Nations*. They come from, in turn, p. 67, p. 66, p. 67, p. 67, p. 73 (Modern Library, pp. 146, 144, 146, 146, 159).]

and since

> 'Rent, considered as the price paid for the use of land, is naturally the highest which the tenant can afford to pay in the actual circumstances of the land'

therefore if land is devoted to the production of food

> 'Something ... always remains for a rent to the landlord.'

He clearly recognizes that this depends on the fact that

> 'men, like all other animals, naturally multiply in proportion to the means of their subsistence.'

But he goes on to argue

> 'that the rent of the cultivated land, of which the produce is human food, regulates the rent of the greater part of other cultivated land.'

Of course the rent of any land affects the rent of any other. But he does seem to imply a further special truth – land is cultivated for the sake of *necessaries* in general up to that limit at which the necessaries produced will just support the requisite labour. By this means the margin of cultivation and the gross population are determined for any given state of agriculture (using the phrase in a broad sense to include police regulations and modes of transport, though these last are not important as far as necessaries are concerned). The surplus products of more favourable soils form a stock which is divided according to the requirements of its owners among different classes of labourers (in a broad use of the term). These according to their requirements portion it out among other labourers and so on. Let an acre of land be capable of producing α gallons of wine (say) by labour which can be supported by necessaries in amount β. Then if there remain people who are willing to give tickets for β in exchange for α gallons, but none who are willing to give more, this land will be on the margin of cultivation and may be cultivated for wine, though not for corn if it would produce less than $\beta(1 + r)$ necessaries.[2] The rent of any other vineyard per acre, supposing

---

[2] [Since r is presumably the profit rate, this implies that 'tickets' involve the delivery of necessaries at the beginning of the year and the receipt of wine at the end. Only thus would necessaries and wine exchange at the end of the year in ratio $\beta(1 + r):\alpha$.]

the same amount of capital employed per acre, equals produce per acre less α gallons. But A. Smith would seem to wish to go further and to say that the rent of a vineyard was determined by the rent which it could pay as a cornland: this is confused rather than false. The rent of a field as a vineyard being given as above, its rent as cornland being also given, it is made a vineyard or a cornland as the one rent or the other is the greater. It is true that if the corn rent of a corn land is known, also its gross produce, also the corn price of wine, then if we know the total produce of a vineyard which employs the same number of labourers we know the rent of the vineyard in corn. This might be inverted: but the difference is that the rent of the cornland if corn were the only necessary would be the one datum, the one primitive fact given by external circumstances, and supplying the basis of calculation.[3] The special difficulty is that the daily necessaries of a labourer cannot be determined as regards either kind or quantity *a priori*. We must express them empirically as a function of time and place.

IV.2.5 *On Adam Smith on the Importation of Corn*

Introduction This note comments on the following passage by Adam Smith:

> The trade of the merchant importer of foreign corn for home consumption evidently contributes to the immediate supply of the home market, and must so far be immediately beneficial to the great body of the people. It tends, indeed, to lower somewhat the average money price of corn, but not to diminish its real value, or the quantity of labour which it is capable of maintaining. If importation was at all times free, our farmers and country gentlemen would, probably, one year with another, get less money for their corn than they do at present, when importation is at most times in effect prohibited; but the money which they got would be of more value, would buy more goods of all other kinds, and would employ more labour.[1]

---

[3] [This is because corn wages are given as a datum by the subsistence requirements of labourers.]

[1] *Wealth of Nations*, Bk IV, Ch. V, p. 239 (Modern Library, pp. 501–2).

In destroying Smith's arguments, Marshall demonstrates his own mastery of classical modes of reasoning.

As explained in the Introduction to IV.2.3, the source for the present Text is a body of Marshall's early lecture notes.

Text   The rate of profit of farmers is in the long run the same, allowing for special advantages, as in other trades. Still, if profits fall in the farming trade, capital will owing to friction leave it but slowly and for the time at least farmers will suffer. In the main a fall in the value of corn as measured by other commodities will press upon the landlords whom A. Smith probably means when he speaks of 'country gentlemen'. If we look forward far enough the growth of population will have brought back corn to its old real value.[2] (Whether corn would have its old price or not it is impossible to say without knowing the details of financial history in such matters as the number of banks, clearing houses etc. as well as ratio of the increase of the total amount of gold in circulation to that of the total wealth in existence.)

But Adam Smith obviously does not intend us to look forward. He is speaking of immediate results. The immediate effect is that the production of corn is confined to those places in which, and within those limits within which, it can be produced with a comparatively small amount of labour. That is the last quarter of corn produced, the quarter which can only just pay its expenses and can contribute nothing to rent, is the produce of less labour than before. Therefore the value of every quarter of corn is that of a less amount of labour than before: consequently it will purchase less of the labour of an artisan than before. For the wages of the artisan cannot have fallen relatively to those of the agricultural labourer. (Indeed, if we look at the case from another point of view we shall see that there would be caused rather the opposite effect. Capital which had been employed in producing corn directly will be employed in producing manufactures to be exchanged for corn: this will cause an increased competition for artisans' labour and a diminished one for agriculturists' labour. And until the friction has been overcome which resists the

---

[2] [The real value of corn is its purchasing power in terms of labour.]

transference of labour from one occupation to another, artisans' wages will be abnormally high as compared with those of agriculturists. But this point is of course not important.)

Thus corn will have fallen in value relatively to all other commodities: and the real rent will have fallen more than the corn rent. There is no special reason for believing that money would have altered its value relatively to commodities in general, or that the money value of corn will bear a very different relation to its real value from that which it bore before.

We must not forget that for long periods it is approximately true that the corn value of commodities is an excellent measure of their real value, on the whole perhaps the best we have. But A. Smith is distinctly not talking of long periods, and he argues that in consequence of the change the corn values of other commodities fall relatively to other real values.

IV.2.6 On Ricardo's Discussion of Bounties on Production

Introduction This note comments on Ch. XXIII of David Ricardo's *On the Principles of Political Economy and Taxation*, the chapter entitled 'On Bounties on Production'. Marshall brings out very clearly his perception of the 'violently strained' assumptions that underly Ricardo's discussion. As explained in the Introduction to IV.2.3, the source for the present Text is a body of Marshall's early lecture notes.

Text The whole of this chapter rests on the tacit assumptions underlying the whole of Ricardo's theory of taxes on necessaries: viz. that on the one hand the population remains stationary and the amount of corn produced remains stationary: and, on the other hand, that wages are at such a low level that the smallest pressure on them causes a tendency in population to fall off, and that this tendency causes real wages to rise to their old level. That is to say he (i) neglects the period during which the pressure upon population is causing misery to the people in comparison with the period during which, according to the probable stability of social, economical and fiscal circumstances, the bounties, taxes and modes of production of the country may be expected to endure without great and decisive change: and (ii) assumes that a check to population insufficient to make an appreciable alteration in 'the margin of cultivation', will be sufficient, by diminishing the competition of labourers, to throw the whole burden of the tax upon capital (or to give to capital the whole benefit of the bounty). With these *tacit* assumptions and the further *explicit* assumption that the country is entirely cut off from foreign trade he has no difficulty in proving that

(α) a tax on necessaries to give a bounty on luxuries, lowers corn rent, does not affect money rent (real rent), raises wages, lowers profits, leaves capital and labour where it was

(β) a tax on luxuries to give a bounty on necessaries, raises corn rent, does not affect money rent, lowers wages, raises profits, leaves as before everything unchanged

(γ) taxes on some necessaries and on some luxuries combined with equivalent bounties on other necessaries and other luxuries have a combination of the effects of (α) and (β): i.e. of two no-effects: i.e. produces no effect.

(This last point is not put in so general a form as that here given.)

It may be replied that if he intended to assume wages and the margin of cultivation unchanged he might have [immediately] obtained his result, viz. that labour, capital, and real rent are unaffected by the proposed cumbrous financial operations (except of course insofar as the officials required to superintend the collection of the tax and the management of the industries affected caused expenses direct and indirect). But to this again there is the reply that for the benefits of the more sluggish intellects an investigation of some sort is required to convince them of the differences between this case and that in which a portion of the commodities which have received the bounty may be exported. If this might be done the 'measure might entirely alter the natural distribution of employments; to the advantage indeed of the foreign countries, but ruinously to that in which so absurd a policy was adopted.'[1] He moreover contrasts the effect of a cheapening of corn due to a bounty

[1] [D. Ricardo, *On the Principles of Political Economy and Taxation*, Ch. XXIII, p. 326.]

raised by a tax, with that of a cheapening due to an improvement in the arts of production. This last raises profits. It gives the capitalist command over the fruits of more labour, while the labour itself is more effective. He takes occasion also to point out how from the converse of the present results we obtain a confirmation of the position that a tax upon necessaries does not (as A. Smith declares)[2] take more from the wealthy classes than would be taken by levying the same amount by any other kind of tax. (It must be borne in mind that the whole case rests on violently strained assumptions which neglect a possible checking of population and of division of labour.)

The general propositions that a bounty takes more from the state than it gives to the consumer, and that a tax takes more from the consumer than it gives to the state are rendered devoid of application here by the assumption, following from his fundamental assumptions, that there is no change in the amount produced and consumed of any commodity.

IV.2.7   *On Ricardo on Supply and Demand*

Introduction   This note considers the following passage from Ricardo's discussion of supply and demand in Ch. XXX of *On the Principles of Political Economy and Taxation*.

If the natural price of bread should fall 50 per cent. from some great discovery in the science of agriculture, the demand would not greatly increase, for no man would desire more than would satisfy his wants, and as the demand would not increase, neither would the supply; for a commodity is not supplied merely because it can be produced, but because there is a demand for it. Here, then, we have a case where the supply and demand have scarcely varied, or if they have increased, they have increased in the same proportion; and yet the price of bread will have fallen 50 per cent., at a time, too, when the value of money had continued invariable.[1]

---

[2] [Adam Smith, *Wealth of Nations*, Bk V, Ch. II, p. 394 (Modern Library, p. 824).]
[1] D. Ricardo, *On the Principles of Political Economy and Taxation*, p. 385.

The chief interest in Marshall's discussion lies in the close parallels with his early Essay on Value (Item II.2.1 above), which suggest that the two are roughly contemporaneous. As explained in the Introduction to IV.2.3, the source for the present Text is a body of Marshall's early lecture notes.

Text 'Supply' thus does not mean amount to be sold at any particular price: but simply amount produced and which may be sold. 'Demand' does not mean amount bought or which would be bought at any price: but probably if pressed he would give as a measure of its quantity the amount of desire for it. But then proportion between demand and supply is nonsense: because they are heterogeneous. In speaking of hats he had admitted that the law that the commodities 'fall in proportion as the sellers augment their quantity, and rise in proportion to the eagerness of the buyers to purchase them'[2] (notice the heterogeneity) is true of monopolised commodities and indeed of the market prices of all other commodities for a limited period. [In these cases] 'price has no necessary connexion with their natural value: but the prices of commodities, which are subject to competition, and whose quantity may be increased in any moderate degree, will ultimately depend, not on the state of demand and supply, but on the increased or diminished cost of their production.[3]

His position indeed is not absolutely devoid of meaning, assuming that the supply is of such a nature that it will not answer the purpose of the sellers to hoard any of it. Suppose for instance that the African tribes to whom Livingstone sold his muskets knew that he would sell all of them for whatever he could get. Then the price would be determined solely by competition of buyers: the sole things to be known would be supply i.e. amount to be sold independent of price, and demand i.e. eagerness to buy. But if the words be thus used we cannot talk of proportion between supply and demand. I is at all events after a certain point a vertical straight line [Figure 1]. But in assuming the people to sell we have assumed a certain eagerness to sell.

---

[2] [Ibid.]
[3] [Ibid.]

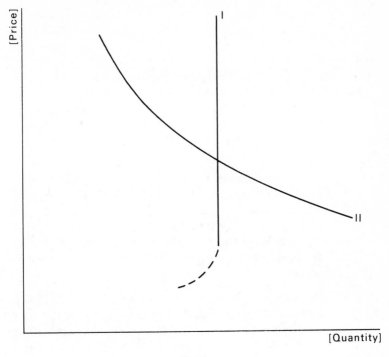

Fig. 1

IV.2.8   *On McLeod on Value*

Introduction   Henry Dunning McLeod (Marshall refers to him here as McCleod) never succeeded in being taken quite seriously by his contemporaries, despite his voluminous, if opinionated, writings on economic topics.[1] But Marshall cited him as a progenitor of the quasi-rent theory, or at least as a stimulator of its development,[2] and also as a precursor of Jevons, Walras and Menger.[3] In the present note he outlines McLeod's strictures on classical value theory and gives his

[1] On McLeod see the article in the *Dictionary of National Biography*.

[2] *Memorials*, p. 414: quoted in Vol 1, p. 49, above. Although McLeod was given credit on this point, we have Foxwell's 1879 assurance (to Jevons) that Marshall did not generally hold McLeod in high esteem. See R. D. C. Black, 'W. S. Jevons and the Economists of his Time', *Manchester School*, Vol 30 (Sept 1962) p. 206.

[3] *Principles I*, p. 821.

own reaction to them. The book referred to is McLeod's *Dictionary of Political Economy*, Volume I of which first appeared in 1863 and covered the letters A–C.[4] The treatment was as eccentric as all McLeod's work, and it is hardly surprising that the remaining volumes never materialised.

As explained in the Introduction to IV.2.3, the source for the present Text is a body of Marshall's early lecture notes.

Text　He makes a great raid on Mill and Ricardo. But according to him

> 'we have the whole subject summed up in these two laws:
> 1. The relation between supply and demand is universally the only regulator of Value.
> 2. In such cases as production can be increased without limit, people learn to adjust the supply to the demand, so that the value of the article will nearly agree with its cost of production'.[5]

It is equally true that the demand adapts itself to the supply. In fact the advantage that McCleod obtains is that he can give as his main definition one which is universally valid when explained by the other. Mill's main definition gives in the cases to which it does apply a mode of estimating from limited data the value of anything; but it does not apply in all cases. It seems possible to combine the advantages of the two methods.

IV.2.9　*'Thornton on Labour'*

Introduction　W. T. Thornton's book, *On Labour; its Wrongful Claims and Rightful Dues. Its Actual Present and Possible Future*,[1] has a small place in the history of economic thought as the vehicle of John Stuart Mill's recantation of the strict wages-fund doctrine. It also seems to have had an influence on

---

[4] H. D. McLeod, *A Dictionary of Political Economy*, Vol I (Longmans, Green, Longmans, Roberts and Green, London, 1863). The kind of statement leading Marshall towards the concept of quasi-rent is exemplified by: 'when the price of a manufactured article rises, wages often rise too, when the price falls wages fall too. Hence, even adopting the Ricardian phraseology, it is just as often value that regulates cost of production as the reverse.' Ibid., p. 53.

[5] *Dictionary* Vol I, p. 55. [Article on 'Axioms and Definitions', pp. 39–57 – also see Article on 'Cost of Production', pp. 558–66.]

[1] Macmillan, London, 1869. Second edition 1870.

Marshall rather similar to that of McLeod. That is, it did not so much suggest particular ideas as provoke certain lines of thought. In Thornton's case, the most important provocation was the claimed subversion of the laws of supply and demand as a sufficient determinant of value – a point which also drew Jevons's attention.[2] In his 1876 essay on 'Mr. Mill's Theory of Value', Marshall described the influence of Thornton in the following way:

> The theory of market values was considered by economists as of slight importance, until Mr. Thornton's book *On Labour* appeared. Mr. Thornton's work is not free from faults; but he has not received his due meed of gratitude for having led men to a point of view from which the practical importance of the theory of market values is clearly seen.[3]

The present Text is of a prefatory note in Marshall's hand attached to the inner cover of a copy of the 1870 edition of Thornton. It seems very probable that the book was intended for the use of the women students taught by Marshall in the early 1870s.[4]

Text   The chief fault in this book is its length. But in general it is attractive in style; and until Brentano's account of Trades Unions (Arbeiter-Gilden II^te Theil) is translated, will remain possibly the best book on the subject for English readers; at all events for such as do not study Blue-books. Like most people of his class, Thornton overrates the importance of what he has done, and in many of his attacks upon Mill he has overstated his case: but what he says constructively is in the main good. The whole book with the exception of Chapters II and III of Part II should be read. Ch. I of Part II may be omitted by those who have no time for any but very light reading.[5]

A.M.

[2] See W. S. Jevons, *The Theory of Political Economy* (Macmillan, London, 1871) pp. 106–7.
[3] *Memorials*, pp. 130–1.
[4] The book (now held in the Marshall Library) was at one time in the Library of Newnham College. The 'women students' formed the nucleus from which this college was formed in 1880. (See Vol 1, p. 10, above).
[5] [Thornton's Book II, Ch. I is entitled 'Of Supply and Demand, and of their Influence on Prices and Wages'. Chs. II and III are entitled 'The Claims of Labour, and its Rights' and 'The Rights of Capital'.]

IV.2.10   *On Richard Jones*

Introduction   The economic writings of the Reverend Richard Jones were referred to respectfully by Marshall when he observed in 1897 that

> [Jones's] influence, though little heard of in the outer world, largely dominated the minds of those Englishmen who came to the serious study of economics after his works had been published by Dr. Whewell in 1859.[1]

The present text is a prefatory note in a copy of Whewell's edition of Jones's work.[2] The note, like that on Thornton, was probably intended for the guidance of the women students taught by Marshall in the early 1870s.[3]

Text   Although there is not much in this book which will be new to anyone who has read Mill carefully, time may be spent not unprofitably in reading somewhat rapidly the prefatory notice, and pp. 281–351 of the book.[4] For

(i) the systematically inductive habit of Jones may exercise a healthy influence on those who have given most attention to the Ricardian or deductive portion of Mill's book

(ii) the book contains many important and suggestive facts which are not otherwise easily accessible. See in particular pp. 281–335, and 362–72.

(iii) The careful analysis contained in the remainder of the selected passages, may give even to advanced students important suggestions as to method, but are likely to be of greater use as aids in teaching children or unlettered persons who must be led to analyse systematically before they can reason constructively.

A.M.

---

[1] *Memorials*, p. 296.

[2] The Reverend Richard Jones, *Literary Remains Consisting of Lectures and Tracts on Political Economy*, edited with a Prefatory Notice by the Reverend William Whewell (John Murray, London, 1859).

[3] The book is now held in the Marshall Library. Unlike the Thornton volume, it does not bear the Newnham book plate.

[4] The pages mentioned cover the following: The Anglo-Indian Revenue Systems (281–90); Primitive Political Economy in England (292–337); Text Book of Lectures on the Political Economy of Nations, delivered at the East India College, Haileybury, (Lecture I, Of Labour, 339–57; Lecture II, Of Capital, 358–90).

IV.2.11 *The Review of Edgeworth's 'Mathematical Psychics'*[1]

Introduction Marshall's second and last book review (his first being that of Jevons)[2] appeared in *The Academy*, 18 June 1881 (p. 457). According to J. M. Keynes, it led to an acquaintance between Marshall and Edgeworth which ripened into a lifelong friendship.[3] It seems worthwhile reproducing it here, as it has never been reprinted and remains relatively inaccessible. The argument about the application of barter curves to labour bargaining had already been made by Marshall in Part II Ch. 1 of his unpublished trade volume.[4] The argument on the preferability of a price-quantity approach to value, over a quantity-quantity or barter one, had been suggested in the 1876 essay on 'Mr. Mill's Theory of Value'.[5]

Text This book shows clear signs of genius, and is a promise of great things to come. It is called 'An Essay on the Application of Mathematics to the Moral Sciences.' But the moral sciences are various and vast; and a goodly volume might be filled with a mere enumeration of the openings which they offer for the use of mathematical language and mathematical method. The essay before us attempts no such task, but is mainly devoted to the fundamental problem of the mathematical rendering of the 'Calculus of Pleasure'; and this is regarded from two points of view, as the 'Economical Calculus' and as the 'Calculus of Utilitarian Ethics'.

The discussion of this problem is introduced by an argument tending to show that 'mathematical reasonings are possible without numerical *data*'.[6] It is well put, but there is a certain air of unreality about all such arguments. To a person who thinks that mathematics are a complex kind of arithmetic, a sort of highly involved double rule of three, argument is useless. While to a person who does know the meaning of the

---

[1] F. Y. Edgeworth, *Mathematical Psychics: an Essay on the Application of Mathematics to the Moral Sciences* (Kegan Paul, London, 1881).

[2] In *The Academy*, 1 Apr 1872 (see *Memorials*, pp. 93–100).

[3] See Vol 1, p. 23, above.

[4] See Section III.5, above.

[5] *Memorials*, pp. 128–9.

[6] [Not, apparently, a direct quotation, but see *Mathematical Psychics*, pp. v, 2, 83.]

terms used, it seems but a truism to say, in words which Mr.
Edgeworth quotes from Cournot: –

> 'L'une des fonctions les plus importantes de l'analyse
> consiste précisément à assigner des relations déterminées
> entre des quantités dont les valeurs numériques, et même
> les formes algébriques, sont absolument inassignables.'[7]

The real question is not whether it is *possible*, but whether it
is *profitable* to apply mathematical reasonings in the moral
sciences. And this is a question which cannot be answered
a priori; it can be answered only from the experience of those
who make the attempt. When a man has cleared up his mind
about a difficult economic question by mathematical reasoning, he generally finds it best to throw aside his mathematics
and express what he has to say in language that is under-
standed of the people.

The general aim of Mr Edgeworth's 'Economical Calculus'
is to investigate the conditions under which the terms and
extent of a contract between two people can be determined
beforehand, the utility to each of them of the things with
regard to which the contract is made being known. He
considers this problem – firstly, when each of the two dealers
stands alone; and, secondly, when he is one of a number of
competing dealers. He supposes that if X exchanges an
amount x of his commodity for an amount y of the commodity
which Y has to dispose of, the total gratification which X will
get from what is left of his commodity after subtracting x from
it, together with that which he will get from an amount y of
the other commodity, may be represented by $P = F(x, y)$.
This total gratification he calls, rather awkwardly, 'the utility
of X.' In like manner he represents the utility of Y by $\pi = \phi(xy)$.
He then seeks for 'the contract curve' – that is, the locus of
points corresponding to contracts, which, when once made,
are settlements, in this sense that no change of the terms can
be proposed which will be acceptable to both parties; its
equation is, of course,[8]

---

[7] [*Mathematical Psychics*, p. 83 (quoted from p. 51, § 21, of the 1838 edition of
Cournot's *Recherches*; p. 48 of the Bacon translation).]

[8] [The derivatives are clearly partial, whilst $\pi = \phi(xy)$ should be interpreted as
$\pi = \phi(x, y)$.]

$$\frac{dP}{dx} \cdot \frac{d\pi}{dy} - \frac{dP}{dy} \cdot \frac{d\pi}{dx} = 0$$

This equation is, as Mr Edgeworth points out, almost the same as Mr Jevons's celebrated equation of exchange. But he gives it a new interpretation, and applies it to new uses; and by reasonings which, partly from the frequent use of unexplained metaphor, are rather hard to follow, he deduces a list of cases in which the terms of contract are unstable or indeterminate. He argues, for instance, in one of his numerous appendices, that contracts between employers and workmen, and between Irish landlords and cottier tenants, are not generally made under the conditions which enable the terms of the contract to be determined beforehand; the terms depend to a great extent upon the advantageous position with regard to bargaining, and the skill in bargaining, of the several parties concerned. This is, of course, not entirely new, but it is put in a new way.

His readers may sometimes wish that he had kept his work by him a little longer till he had worked it out more fully, and obtained that simplicity which comes only through long labour. But, taking it at what it claims to be, 'a tentative study', we can only admire its brilliancy, force, and originality.

It will be interesting to watch the development of his theory, and, in particular, to see how far he succeeds in preventing his mathematics from running away with him, and carrying him out of sight of the actual facts of economics. For he has adopted a mode of expressing the problem of exchange which gives him at once a wide grasp and great freedom of movement, but which has the disadvantage of not being very easily translated so as to express the conditions of ordinary mercantile transactions. He takes barter as his typical bargain, and lets x and y represent, as we have seen, quantities of the two things bartered. No doubt this is the right way of treating some problems of international trade, and what is nearly the same thing, of the trade between the members of different compact industrial groups, whether the groups are formally organised or not. But there are many reasons for thinking that the greater part of economic theory can be dealt with most easily by letting x represent the amount of the commodity dealt in, and *y* the price of the unit of that commodity expressed in the terms of money, which is supposed provisionally to have a uniform purchasing power.[9] This method certainly lends itself most easily to the task of interpreting the past and directing the future of statistical enquiries – a consideration of the first importance. If, however, Mr Edgeworth can prevent his theories from becoming too abstract he may do. great things by them.

There is little room left to discuss his Calculus of Utilitarian Ethics; but this is the less to be regretted because the greater part of the substance of it has been published by him before.[10] Suffice it that he starts from the position that different men have different capacities for happiness and different capacities for work, and applies mathematics with great originality and suggestiveness to the enquiry how work and wealth must be distributed so as to give the greatest possible happiness. Perhaps the problem which he attacks is incapable of a complete solution; but it may be safely said that no one can read his discussion of it without profit.

IV.3 Pages from a Mathematical Notebook, c. 1867–72

Introduction A manuscript notebook, preserved in the Marshall Library, contains what, from both content and physical appearance, appear to be some of Marshall's earliest exercises in economic analysis, perhaps retained for sentimental reasons. It seems likely that some of the entries date from 1867 or 1868, but others are probably later, though almost certainly prior to 1873.[1] The pages appear to have been utilised in a haphazard manner, so that the order of the notes selected for reproduction here has been rearranged in a rough estimate of temporal sequence. The notes are presented with a minimum of commentary, as their chief interest lies in the insight they give into Marshall's mental processes. But attention should be drawn to the last two, in particular, as

[9] [This is Marshall's standard assumption. Compare p. 188, above; Vol 1, p. 128; *Economics of Industry*, pp. 68–9; *Principles I*, p. 62.]

[10] [See F. Y. Edgeworth, *New and Old Methods of Ethics* (James Parker and Co., Oxford and London, 1877). Also see F. Y. Edgeworth, 'The Hedonical Calculus', *Mind*, Vol 4 (July 1879) pp. 394–408.]

[1] Very similar diagrams appear in a notebook of H. S. Foxwell's inscribed 'Pol. Economy. A few of Marshall's curves. 1870?' (Generously made available by R. Freeman.)

they contain significant anticipations of later work and show a full mastery of the consumer-surplus concept.

IV.3.1 *Rent*

Introduction This note sketches very clearly the conceptual foundations for Marshall's treatment of rent in Section II.7 above. It goes on to consider the metayer system, under which half the product, rather than a fixed rent, goes to the landlord. For simplicity, the metayer landlord is assumed to supply no working capital.

Text Let us consider a given acre of ground in a given condition i.e. with a given amount of capital sunk in it. The profits on the capital we shall include under rent. Let w be the week's wages of a labourer: r the rate of profit which a farmer expects for the period for which he has to advance wages on the average i.e. for half a year. Let an amount of capital $= w(1 + r)$ applied to the land (whether directly or indirectly in the form of labour) be called a *lot* of capital and be represented by an area of height OC and breadth unity [see Figure 1].

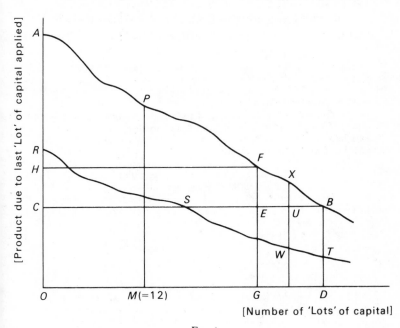

Fig. 1

Let the additional produce due to the application of the 12th 'lot' of capital be represented by an area of height *PM* and breadth unity. If *PM* is greater than *OC* such an application of capital will be made and an area of breadth = unity and height = 'the difference between *PM* and *OC*' will be the corresponding rent.

If *AB* be the locus of *P* and be cut by a horizontal line through *C* in *B*, then *ACB* will be the total rent: *ODBC* will be the produce that replaces with profit the farmer's outlay.

Let now (from a rise in *r* or *w* or both) $w(1 + r)$ increase from an area of breadth unity and height *OC* to one of the same breadth and height *OH*. The number of weeks spent on the land will be diminished from *OD* to *OG*, and the gross produce will be diminished [by] *FGDB*, the gross rent being diminished by *HCBF*, measured in produce. But as the price of produce will in consequence of the diminution rise in a greater proportion than the average diminution in the gross produce ([although the diminution] will sometimes, particularly in the case of poor lands, be very great) [money] rent will on the whole probably rise.[1]

A Tithe will have similar effects.... A rent charge will alter the rent,... [but] will not alter prices.[2] The line *RST* bisecting

---

[1] [Marshall here asserts, as an empirical matter, the inelasticity of demand for the product. He does not intend to assert that the money value of gross product cannot fall on any piece of land. But he overlooks a basic difficulty at this point. The rest of his analysis may be regarded as conducted with respect to a particular piece of land, on the assumption that the product price is *given*. But when he turns to consider all the land producing a particular product, the rest of his analysis remains valid only if the wage rate is expressed in terms of the product. But now a change in product price changes the effective wage rate, leading to a change in the output from each piece of land. What is needed is a process of *simultaneous* determination. This, Marshall did develop (as in Section II.7, above), but he shows no recognition of the need for it here. However, the following fragment from a neighbouring note is of some interest. A_i (the gross product of land *i*) falls by δA_i because of a change in the wage rate. The product price, p, is a function of $\sum A_i$ hence the increase in product price δp is determined by $\sum \delta A_i$. Marshall says:

'We know from experience

$$\sum A_i p < \sum (A_i - \delta A_i)(p + \delta p) \quad \text{i.e.} \frac{\delta p}{\sum \delta A_i} > \frac{p}{\sum A_i},$$

How near he came to the elasticity concept!]

[2] [The curves showing these results are omitted from the diagram to avoid overcomplication. A tithe lowers the curve *APB* in ratio 9:10. A 'rent charge' is a proportional tax on rent.]

all the ordinates of *AB* divides off the rent on the Metayer system. Naturally cultivation will cease at *S* and the landlord will lose enormously. If the cultivator however has nothing to do with his spare time he may expend on the land labour which does not bring him full wages. But he cannot do this further than the point *U* where $SUW = SCR$.[3] The rent is now $ACUX$ (since $SUW = SCR$) and is less than on the English system. For a case in which *SU* is greater than *SB* see [Figure 2, where $RCSr = STWU$].

$$[\text{Metayer] rent} = ACBb + STWX - RSCr$$

$$= \text{rack [English] rent} - BXU$$

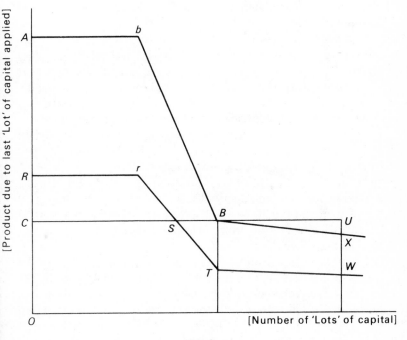

Fig. 2

---

[3] [Marshall assumes here that the tenant will in no circumstances push his efforts beyond the point where the *average* return repays the market value of his outlay i.e. beyond the point where the *average* return per 'lot' is $w(1+r)$, the marginal return on the English system. For further discussion of metayage see *Principles I*, pp. 644–5.]

Therefore the metayer rent is under every conceivable circumstance less than the rack rent: but the gross produce is conceivably (though the case could never occur in practice I should think) greater on the metayer than on the rack-rent system.

If we take into account the fact that the landlord supplies cattle etc. we have simply to alter the ratio $OR:OA$ and this will not affect the results.[4]

IV.3.2   *Triangular Barter*

Introduction   This note is included, not for its intrinsic interest, which is slight, but because it illustrates to perfection the groping, intuitive way in which Marshall often tackled his problems – not at all what one would expect from an erstwhile Second Wrangler.

The note also has interest because Marshall uses in it the convention of drawing price on the horizontal axis, suggesting an early date of composition, and also tending to confirm that the Annotations on Cournot (IV.2.1 above) are of early date.

Text   England sends cloth to Germany: Germany linen to Russia: Russia furs to England. Russia may be supposed to sell furs to England in exchange for a bill on cloth and sell this bill to Germany for linen.

We learn from [curve] III [Figure 3] how many furs Russia is willing to exchange away at a given rate of interchange of furs for linen. We have to discover from [curves] I and II [Figures 1 and 2] how many furs she can get rid of at a given rate of exchange.

Let us see what results I and II give us corresponding to the different amounts of cloth for which the supposed bill is drawn. Let e.g. this amount be 6,000,000. From I we learn that Germany is willing to adopt the rate 16 linen for 10 cloth and $9,600,000:6,000,000 = 16:10$. From II we learn that England is willing to adopt the rate 15 furs for 10 cloth[1] and $9,000,000:6,000,000 = 15:10$. Therefore at the rate 15 furs for

---

[4] [This presupposes that the landlord takes a further fractional share from the tenants' half of the gross produce equalling the fraction that the landlord supplies of every 'lot' of capital.]

[1] [The numerical example does not correspond exactly to Figures 1–3.]

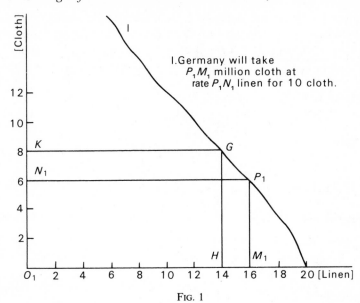

I.Germany will take
P_1M_1 million cloth at
rate P_1N_1 linen for 10 cloth.

FIG. 1

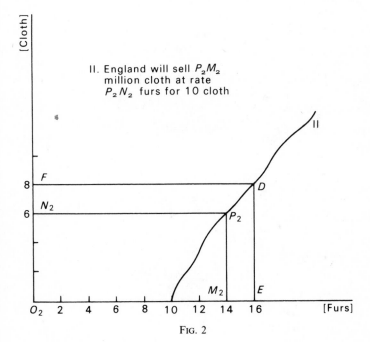

II. England will sell P_2M_2
million cloth at rate
P_2N_2 furs for 10 cloth

FIG. 2

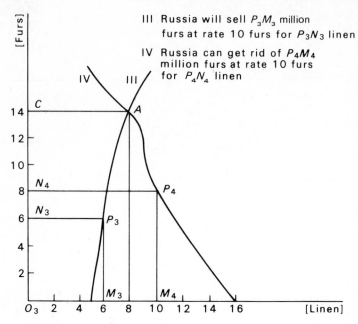

III Russia will sell P_3M_3 million
furs at rate 10 furs for P_3N_3 linen

IV Russia can get rid of P_4M_4
million furs at rate 10 furs
for P_4N_4 linen

FIG. 3

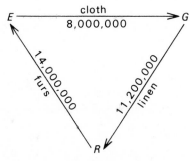

10 cloth = 14 linen = $17\frac{1}{2}$ furs
∴ 10 furs = 140 ÷ $\frac{35}{2}$ linen
= 8 linen

FIG. 4

16 linen i.e. 10 furs [for] $10\frac{2}{3}$ linen Russia can get rid of 9,000,000 furs. Draw then $O_3M_4 = 10\frac{2}{3}$, $M_4P_4 = 9$; the locus of P_4 will be a curve such that Russia can get rid of P_4M_4 million furs at rate 10 furs for P_4N_4 linen.

Let III and IV cut at A. A is the point of equilibrium. For Russia can with 14 million furs get a bill for 8 million cloth (at rate 10 cloth for $17\frac{1}{2}$ furs) and with a bill for 8 million cloth can get 11,200,000 linen (at rate 10 cloth for 14 linen); thus she can get 11,200,000 linen for 14,000,000 furs (at rate 8 linen for 10 furs) and at rate 8 linen for 10 furs she is willing to sell 14,000,000 furs Q.E.D. [See Figure 4.]

N.B.   The conditions that equilibrium should be stable are that

I   If England can get more furs she will sell in exchange more cloth

II   If Germany can get more cloth she will sell in exchange more linen

III   If Russia can get more linen she will sell in exchange more furs.

IV.3.3 'Wages'

Introduction   This note deals with a very simple model in which the amount of capital, K, is a function of the rate of profit, r, expressed as a percentage. Gross output less rent is $\frac{1}{4}K$ and the wage bill is

$$(1) \qquad W(r) = \tfrac{1}{4}K(r) - \frac{r}{100}K(r)$$

Workers are allowed to influence the profit rate through bargaining, and the wage bill is maximised when

$$(2) \qquad 100\frac{dW(r)}{dr} = -K(r) + \frac{dK(r)}{dr}\left(\frac{100}{4} - r\right) = 0$$

Text   Let the amount of capital in the country be PM (20) million when the customary rate of profit is OM (10) per cent. After paying rent and replacing in the hands of every capitalist the [amount he] had before let the remaining produce be PQ: we may suppose the proportion which this bears to PM to be constant and to be equal to $\frac{1}{4}$ [so that $PQ = 5$]. Then $PR = 20 \cdot 10/100 = 2$ million represents the profits and the remainder RQ [$= 3$] represents wages. [See Figure 1.]

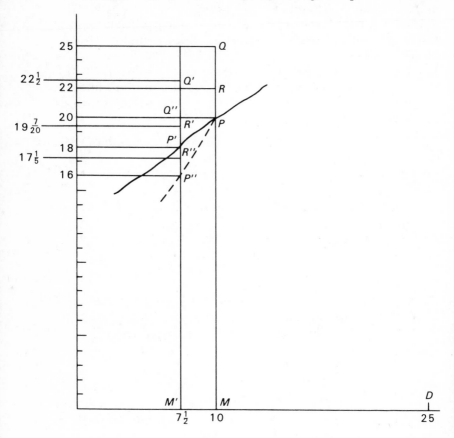

FIG. 1

Now let the rate of profit be diminished to $7\frac{1}{2}$ per cent and the remaining part of the produce obtained as wages by labourers. At this rate of profit OM' the amount of capital which will exist when equilibrium has been obtained is $P'M'$ (18). Then $P'Q' = 4\frac{1}{2}$ while $P'R' = 1\frac{7}{20}$, therefore $R'Q' = 3\frac{3}{20}$; $RQ = 3$: thus labourers have gained by the manoeuvre 150,000.

Had the curve taken the form PP'' we should have had $P''M'' = 16, P''Q'' = 4, P''R'' = 1\frac{1}{5}, R''Q'' = 2\frac{4}{5}$ and the labourers have lost 200,000.

It will be found that if OD be taken equal to 25 then if the angle DPM is greater than the angle the tangent at P makes with PM, labourers will lose by forcing down profits and vice versa: a maximum or minimum of wages will be given when these two angles are equal.[1]

To the injury of the labourers must be set the rise in food which might follow on increased demand and render their real rise in wages less than their actual. To the benefit of labourers must be set that increased wages might (i) induce them to save some capital themselves and (ii) by raising their physical and mental vigour increase the gross produce.

IV.3.4 'Money'

Introduction This note develops the argument in Book III, Ch. 9, § 3 of J. S. Mill's *Principles*, where Mill attempts to reconcile the quantity-theoretic and cost-of-production approaches to the value of money. Marshall's note serves as a kind of graphical appendix, or forerunner, to his Essay on Money, reproduced above (Item II.2.1).[1]

Text Mill supposes the gold and silver used for manufacturing purposes to be put out of the question. Then, supposing the amount of change people [want] to be at any time given, we have a rectangular hyperbola to represent the value at which gold can be bought. Suppose the amount of gold in a country to be 10 million ounces (other countries excluded) and that the change required in the country corresponds to the work of a labourer for sixty million weeks, we of course find that in equilibrium one ounce of gold corresponds to six weeks' labour. [See Figure 1.]

---

[1] [To verify this rule, note (from equation (2) of the Introduction) that if the wage bill is to be maximised at P then $dK/dr = K/(25-r) = 20/(25-10) = 1\frac{1}{3}$ is required. This will be the case only if angle $P'PM$ equals angle MPD (P' being taken for the moment as a point on the tangent to $K(r)$ at P).]

[1] For a related diagrammatic illustration see Appendix C of *Money Credit and Commerce*.

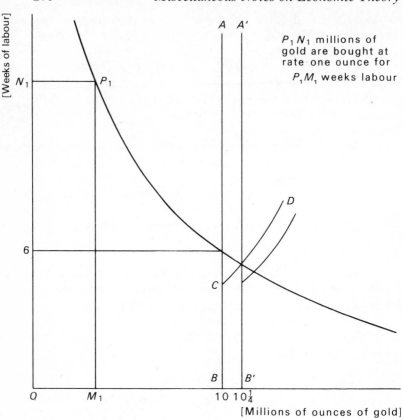

Fig. 1

If gold cannot be produced at less cost in labour than this of course it will not be produced at all. If it can we shall have for the year's production a curve of the kind *CD* [Figure 1]. At the end of the year the supply of gold will be $10\frac{1}{4}$ million and the intersection of the curve with $A'B'$ will give the new value of gold. This supposes the amount of change required by the country to have remained constant. But we may of course suppose it to be increased, as by cash payments to cooperative stores, or diminished as by making of a new bank.

IV.3.5   'Influence of Taxation'

Introduction   This remarkable note is a fully-fledged derivation of the consumer-surplus measure. Its outline definition
of an optimal structure of indirect taxes was developed in a
later note (Item IV.4.3 below).

Text

$y = \phi(x)$ is demand curve
$y = f(x)$ is supply curve before tax of a pence
$y = f(x) + a$ is supply curve after tax of a pence
$PN = \alpha;$ $P'N' = \alpha'$

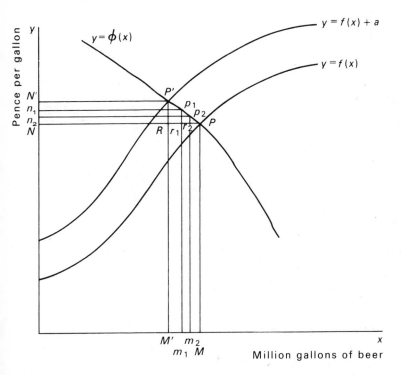

The tax [revenue] $= a\alpha' \equiv \psi(a)$. If p_1, p_2 be two points very
near together, purchasers to the extent of $m_1 m_2$ millions would
have paid up to a price $p_1 m_1$ i.e. the loss on each gallon which

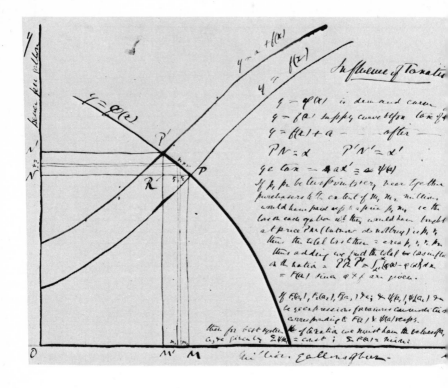

Facsimile of manuscript for 'Influence of Taxation'

they would have bought at price PM (but now do not buy) is $p_1 r_1$. Thus the total loss to them equals the area $p_1 r_1 r_2 p_2$. Thus adding up we find the total loss inflicted on the nation $= PRP' =$

$$\int_{\alpha'}^{\alpha} \{\phi(x) - \phi(\alpha)\}\, dx = F(a)$$

since ϕ and f are given.

If $F_1(a_1)$, $F_2(a_2)$, $F_3(a_3)$ etc. and $\psi_1(a_1)$, $\psi_2(a_2)$, $\psi_3(a_3)$ etc. be the expressions for various commodities, corresponding to $F(a)$ and $\psi(a)$ respectively, then for the best system of taxation we must have the values of a_1, a_2, a_3 etc. given by $\Sigma\psi(a) =$ constant and $\Sigma F(a) =$ minimum.

IV.3.6 '*Tolls (and Railway Fares)*'

Introduction The reader who follows this condensed note with pencil and paper will find in it a truly remarkable statement of cost-benefit analysis, covering questions of both optimal production and optimal investment for a public utility, as well as the theory of private monopoly. The note contains all the essential ideas of the chapter on 'The Theory of Monopolies' in the *Principles* (i.e. Book V, Ch. XIV) and goes beyond it in the explicit consideration of investment decisions. The reader might note that, in the *Principles*, Marshall takes the view that the government should *not* treat £1 of consumers' surplus as equally desirable with £1 of tax revenue, since

> Even a government which considers its own interests coincident with those of the people has to take account of the fact that, if it abandons one source of revenue, it must in general fall back on others which have their own disadvantages. For they will necessarily involve friction and expense in collection, together with some injury to the public, of the kind which we have described as a loss of consumers' surplus...[1]

It is on these lines that the fraction $n < 1$ of the present note is probably to be interpreted.

The question naturally arising is whether Marshall's ideas here were influenced by the work of Dupuit. Marshall expressly denied any influence, and it seems quite likely that Dupuit's work was completely unknown in England until Jevons came upon it in the later 1870s.[2]

Text When the toll equals PM let OM tolls be paid on a certain bridge. The amount levied will be greatest when $OM \cdot MP$ is greatest (i.e. if a rectangular hyperbola with Ox and Oy as axes touch the curve in P, the amount levied will be greatest when the toll equals PM). Let the equation to the locus of P be $y = f(x)$.

---

[1] *Principles I*, p. 488.
[2] See Vol 1, p. 39, above and *Principles II*, p. 263. Also see W. S. Jevons, *The Theory of Political Economy* (Second edition, Macmillan, London, 1879) pp. xxviii, xxix. W. Jaffé (ed.), *Correspondence of Léon Walras and Related Papers, Vol. I. 1857–1883* (North Holland, Amsterdam, 1965) p. 533 (letter of 28 February 1877).

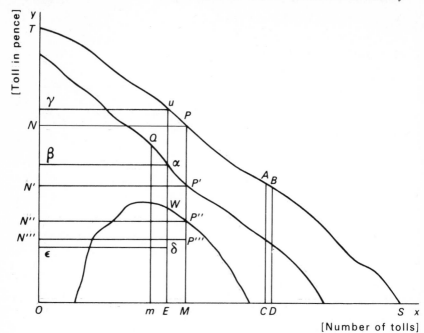

Fig. 1

When OM carriages pass over the bridge let the damage done by each of them equal PP'. Let the equation to the locus of P' be $y = f(x) - \phi(x)$, i.e. $PP' = \phi(x)$. A toll should now be levied such as to make $Om \cdot mQ$ a maximum i.e. Q should be chosen so that at Q the curve touches one of [the] above series of hyperbolas.

The number of people who would pay a toll BD, but not a toll AC is equal to CD when CD is very small; and the loss to those people in consequence of the tolls being greater than they will pay is $ACDB$; thus the whole loss which people who do not pay the toll PM undergo is equal to PMS [for example]. We may suppose that this loss causes to the state a loss equal in amount to n times it, where n is less than unity but dependent for its value on OM. Make $P'N'N''P'' = n \cdot PMS$. Then the net gain to the state resulting from a toll PM is $OMP''N''$. The toll should be levied so as to make this a maximum i.e.

if one of the above series of hyperbolas touches [the locus of P''] in W, then uE is the tax which should be levied. (The locus of P'' is $y = f(x) - \phi(x) - \chi(x)$ where

$$\chi(x) = \int_{OM}^{OS} f(x)\psi(x)\,dx$$

$\psi\,(x)$ being equal to n.)

The total advantage which people gain from the bridge after deducting the tolls which they pay is TPN, when the toll is PM. As before let the state gain from this an advantage n times its amount. Then if $(\alpha\beta OE) + n \cdot (T\gamma u)$ is greater than the interest on the bridge's cost (allowing for its being perishable) the bridge ought to be built.

If $n = 1$ and $E\delta$ be taken equal to $u\alpha$ then the bridge must be built provided $T\varepsilon\,\delta uT$ be greater than the interest on the cost of the bridge. Had we measured off MP''' equal to PP' and made $TN'''P'''PT$ a maximum we should have got for the right toll uE as before.

IV.4   Miscellaneous Notes on Economic Theory, c. 1873–87

Introduction   The present section contains an interesting assortment of notes on theoretical topics, many dealing with questions that Marshall did not pursue in later years, and so did not embellish in his later work. The notes have in common a mathematical form of argument, and are arranged in rough chronological order.

IV.4.1   'Graphic Representation by Aid of a Series of Hyperbolas of Some Economic Problems Having Reference to Monopolies'

Introduction   This abstract of a paper that Marshall presented in 1873 to the Cambridge Philosophical Society was published in the Society's *Proceedings*.[1] The background is explained in the footnote to the Preface of the First Edition of the *Principles*:

> Mr. Henry Cunynghame who was attending my lectures in 1873, seeing me annoyed by being unable to draw a series of rectangular hyperbolas, invented a beautiful and original

---

[1] *Proceedings of the Cambridge Philosophical Society*, Vol 2 (Oct 1873) pp. 318–19.

machine for the purpose. It was shown at the Cambridge Philosophical Society in 1873; and, to explain its use, I read a paper (briefly reported in the *Proceedings*, Part XV, pp. 318–9), in which I described the theories of Multiple Positions of Equilibrium and of Monopoly values very nearly as they are given below (Book V, ch. v and viii).[2]

The *Proceedings* do indeed report a contribution by H. H. Cunynghame about 'A machine for constructing a series of rectangular hyperbolas with the same asymptotes' intended 'for the purpose indicated in the last paper',[3] but the details of the machine seem to have been forgotten.

Perhaps the most interesting feature of Marshall's brief note is the clear delineation in the last paragraph of the idea of 'compromise benefit'.[4]

Text   The price at which a given amount of any commodity can be disposed of in any market is determined by the circumstances of the buyers. If this amount be measured along Ox and this price along Oy, there is thus determined a value of y corresponding to each value of x; and the locus of the points so obtained may be called the demand curve: let its equation be $y = F(x)$. So if y be the price at which an amount x of the commodity can be produced for the market (x, y) is found, the locus of which may be called the supply curve: let its equation be $y = f(x)$. This method of expressing the problem of value has been known certainly for 35 years:[5] an intersection of the two curves has been explained as giving the 'average price' about which Adam Smith proved that the 'market price' will oscillate. But it has not been pointed out that, under some circumstances, there may be more than one point of intersection, and that Adam Smith's arguments apply only to the circumstances of every alternate point. Only at every alternate point of intersection can the exchange value remain in *stable* equilibrium: at the other points it is in *unstable* equilibrium.

If an individual has the monopoly of the supply of the commodity in the market, his immediate interest will, of

[2] *Principles II*, pp. 37–8.
[3] *Proceedings*, p. 319.
[4] *Principles I*, pp. 487–9.
[5] [Cournot's *Recherches* had been published thirty-five years before.]

course, lead him to determine x so that $x\{F(x)-f(x)\}$ shall be a maximum. Let the curve $y = F(x)-f(x)$ be traced, whether by direct inductions or otherwise, on a paper on which are already lithographed a series of rectangular hyperbolas having Ox and Oy for asymptotes. It will then be obvious by inspection for which of two amounts that the monopolist may throw upon the market – or, which is the same thing, for which of two prices that he may demand – he will obtain the greatest total net profit. Many striking results can thus be obtained in cases in which the curves cut one another more than once.

This mode of representation of the problem of monopolies is elastic, and lends itself to the treatment of some complex hypotheses. Specially important results will present themselves, if the assumption be introduced that the monopolist is willing to undergo some abatement of his claims, when, by so doing, he can confer great benefit on the consumers.

IV.4.2 '*Abstract Theory of a General Uniform Tax*'

Introduction The manuscript from which the present note is taken is a rather hasty draft, and so not easy to follow. Yet it is of considerable significance, as Marshall here anticipates rather fully the now-familiar 'excess-burden' argument on the advantage of direct over indirect taxation.[1] The entire manuscript runs to twenty-seven pages, and bears the much later superscription 'Unsuitable for the last volume'. The present version largely omits Marshall's rather disjointed treatment of the more practical aspects of taxation policy. He covered these more elaborately in the items reproduced in Section III.3, above, and Section V.3 below.

The reference to Jevons clearly dates the work as post 1871. The fact that the later paragraphs are essentially a leisurely preliminary version of Ch. II, § 4, of *The Pure Theory of Domestic Values*[2] makes it improbable that the manuscript was composed after 1875. Composition in 1873 or 1874 seems the most likely.

---

[1] This argument is usually attributed to Barone in 1912 (E. Barone, 'Studi di Economia Finanziaria', *Giornale degli Economisti*, Vol 44, pp. 309–53, 469–505, Vol 45, pp. 1–75). For such an attribution see A. T. Peacock and D. Berry, 'A Note on the Theory of Income Redistribution', *Economica*, Vol 18 (Feb 1951) pp. 83–90.

[2] See Section III.6, above.

Even without the evidence of the explicit reference to Jevons, the deference to his ideas and terminology is sufficiently marked to indicate his influence. Marshall's stance is much more explicitly 'hedonic' here than in the remainder of his early work, a fact which helps confirm the suspicion that Jevons's utilitarian calculus had more influence on Marshall's development than he was willing to admit.[3] Here we see him following Jevons in the explicit assumption of an additive utility function.

As Marshall makes clear in the opening paragraph, he is unable to employ the convenient assumption that the marginal utility of all goods but one remains constant, and is instead forced to look at an individual's expenditure on all commodities simultaneously. He takes the case of two commodities, and then of three, working on the assumption that the amount of labour supplied by the individual remains fixed.

Because Marshall's argument is rather obscure, the reader may find it convenient to read first the following exposition which includes somewhat fuller explanations.

A given set of indirect taxes is assumed to have been imposed in such a form that a proportion $1 - \alpha_i$ of the *gross* amount of labour allocated by a given individual to securing commodity i goes to paying the tax. Thus, $1/\alpha_i$ units of labour are needed to devote to the acquisition of commodity i one unit of labour *net* of tax. In the special case where the individual sells his labour at a fixed wage rate, and buys all the commodities at fixed market prices, this effect would be secured by the imposition of a given set of excise taxes (either specific or *ad valorem*) upon commodities. Let x_i denote the amount of labour *net* of tax devoted by the individual in question to acquiring commodity i, and let $f_i(x_i)$ denote the marginal or final rate of utility he obtains from a small increase in x_i. His total utility, in the general case with n commodities (so that $i = 1, 2, \ldots n$), is

$$(1) \qquad U = \sum_{i=1}^{n} \int_0^{x_i} f_i(x_i)\, dx_i$$

Given that l units of labour are to be utilised, the possible

---

[3] See the discussion of this point in Section I.2, above.

choices of $x_1, x_2 \ldots x_n$ must satisfy

(2)
$$\frac{x_1}{\alpha_1} + \frac{x_2}{\alpha_2} + \cdots + \frac{x_n}{\alpha_n} = l$$

Maximising (1) subject to (2) gives the marginal conditions

(3)
$$\alpha_1 f_1(x_1) = \alpha_2 f_2(x_2) = \ldots = \alpha_n f_n(x_n)$$

Equations (2) and (3) determine optimal values $x_1^0, x_2^0, \ldots x_n^0$ for $x_1, x_2, \ldots x_n$, given the tax structure $\alpha_1, \alpha_2, \ldots \alpha_n$.

The assumption of a given set of tax rates is now dropped. Instead, the individual is required to pay in a lump sum the same amount, t, of labour that he paid in taxes under the earlier scheme. The constraint (2) is now replaced by

(4)
$$x_1 + x_2 + \cdots + x_n = l - t = x_1^0 + x_2^0 + \cdots + x_n^0$$

Maximising (1) subject to (4) gives the marginal conditions

(5)
$$f_1(x_1) = f_2(x_2) = \ldots = f_n(x_n)$$

Comparing (3) and (5), and taking (4) into account, it is clear that $x_1^0, x_2^0 \ldots x_n^0$ will be the solution to the second problem if and only if $\alpha_1 = \alpha_2 = \ldots = \alpha_n$.[4] Otherwise, the solution for constraint (4) must yield more utility than the solution for constraint (2), yet the same amount of tax is paid in each case. Thus, to raise a given amount by indirect taxes from an individual, with least cost to him, the taxes should be set at the same proportional rate on all lines of expenditure, which is the essence of the excess-burden argument.

Marshall obviously intended to extend his analysis to the case with variable labour supply, and a rough note appended to his manuscript shows how he proposed to attempt this. Letting l be the total amount of labour and $F(l)$ the total disutility of labour, (1) is replaced by 'net pleasure'

(6)
$$\sum_{i=1}^{n} \int_0^{x_i} f_i(x_i) \, dx_i - F(l)$$

Constraints (2) and (4) continue to apply, and Marshall is able to show once more that the conditions $\alpha_1 = \alpha_2 = \ldots = \alpha_n$

---

[4] Assuming all marginal utilities are strictly diminishing.

are *necessary* for a correspondence between the two solutions. But he fails to recognise that these conditions are no longer *sufficient*, since a uniform expenditure tax has a different effect on labour supply than does a lump-sum tax: a point he in fact notes in the manuscript but fails to follow up here.[5]

Marshall's utilitarian analysis of optimal systems of direct taxes seems, unfortunately, to have had little impact on his thinking. Indeed, he appears to have rapidly forgotten his own warning about the inappropriateness of taking each commodity in turn and assuming constancy in the marginal utility of 'all other commodities' ('money'). This warning should have alerted him to the difficulty of analysing indirect-tax *systems* by cumulating the loss of consumers' surplus over all the separate commodities. For the consumers' surplus an individual gains for a given commodity is proportional to his utility surplus only if the marginal utility of 'money' is constant.[6] This forgetfulness led Marshall into distinct error in the *Principles* when – assuming supply prices constant – he argued:

> If therefore a given aggregate taxation has to be levied ruthlessly from any class it will cause less loss of consumers' surplus if levied on necessaries than if levied on comforts.[7]

Although the statement is factually correct, its implication – that such a tax system would be advantageous – is not. Replace 'class' by 'individual', and assume, as Marshall does in the *Principles*, that the individual has an additive utility function, and there is a direct violation of his early theorem on an optimal tax structure. It is ironic to find that, in this and related passages, some authors have discerned Marshall

---

[5] The essential difficulty is that a case with lump-sum tax has first-order conditions $f_1(x_1) = f_2(x_2) = \cdots = F'(l)$ whereas a case with a uniform proportional expenditure tax at rate α has first-order conditions

$$f_1(x_1) = f_2(x_2) = \cdots = F'(l)/\alpha$$

Here, $F'(l)$ is in the marginal, or final, disutility of labour.

[6] See *Principles I*, pp. 131–2, 842. The point is not clearly stated in the *Pure Theory of Domestic Values*.

[7] *Principles I*, p. 467n. The seeds of this argument already appear on p. 299 below.

'attempting to demonstrate by consumer surplus arguments the superiority of direct versus indirect taxation'.[8]

There are related difficulties with the partial-equilibrium method by which Marshall develops, first in the *Pure Theory of Domestic Values* and later in the *Principles*, the argument that

> ... it appears that account being taken of the interests of consumers and landlords together, it is not expedient that the revenue should be derived from taxes levied equally on all commodities; but that such revenue as is derived from taxes on commodities should be obtained almost exclusively from commodities the expenses of production of which increase, or at least do not diminish, as the amount produced increases.[9]

In contrast to the falsity of the argument that necessaries and luxuries should be taxed differentially, there is a distinct grain of truth in this argument for differential taxation of increasing-cost and decreasing-cost commodities. But Marshall's method of demonstration is defective for exactly the same reason in either case.

The following Text foreshadows clearly Marshall's argument for subsidising decreasing-cost industries. It also ends by abandoning the utility analysis adopted initially in favour of a simpler treatment in terms of consumers' surplus. It is tempting to speculate that this marked the reversion of Marshall's mind to its natural grooves, from which Jevons's ideas had temporarily jerked it.

Text   If we desire to compare the effects of an income tax with those of customs or excise duties, we cannot make the assumption which often gives a tolerably accurate approximation: viz. that the effect of the imposition of a tax on any commodity may be to this extent separately discussed – that

---

[8] D. Walker, 'The Direct-indirect Tax Problem: Fifteen Years of Controversy', *Public Finance*, Vol 10 (1955 no. 2) pp. 153–76. Walker gives references to the authors propounding the view indicated in the text. He also notices another intriguing fact: Pigou believed that Marshall did not attempt to prove the proposition on direct *v.* indirect taxes. Thus, Marshall's early theorem did *not* become part of the Cambridge oral tradition.

[9] *The Pure Theory of Domestic Values*, Ch. II § 8 (see Section III. 6, above, p. 233). Also see *Principles I*, Book V, Ch. XIII.

it shall not be necessary to investigate the effects on the demand for other commodities of a certain excess or deficit, as the case may be, in the amount spent on purchasing this [the taxed] one after the imposition of the tax. For this sum account has to be taken.

The final pain of the labour, which [a man performs] has to be equal to the final pleasure of the produce after paying the tax. Equilibrium will be found [after taxation] when the final net pleasure is less than before. If from any individual a definite sum be demanded, he will, at all events as far as economical considerations influence him, increase the total amount of the labour he performs. But if a certain percentage of the produce of his labour be demanded it will depend on the shapes of his pleasure and pain curves whether he exerts on the whole more labour than before or not.

As however when the amount of the tax to be levied is given it is obvious that an approximate result may be obtained by assuming the total amount of labour he does to be independent

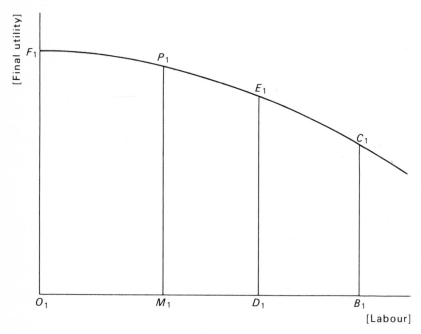

Fig. 1

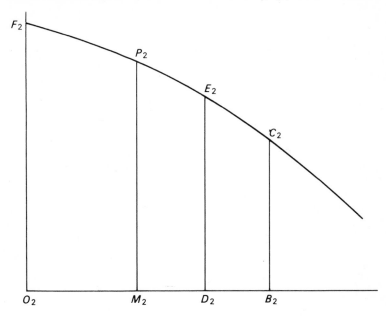

Fig. 2

of the way in which the tax is distributed, and as this case lends itself to a simple treatment without the aid of mathematical analysis, it will be advisable to discuss this first.

M_1P_1 [in Figure 1] denotes the pleasure to a consumer resulting from the produce of dose of labour OM_1 applied to one kind of production [class I]. Assume that all other kinds of labour can be classed together and represented similarly in class II. [Figure 2.] If there be no taxation, the amount of labour he will supply being assumed constant, we have the amount of each kind determined by the equations

$$O_1B_1 + O_2B_2 = \text{constant} = l$$

$$B_1C_1 = B_2C_2$$

Now let, on the same supposition, it be required to take from him in the form of a tax the produce of a given amount of labour (t). Let α_1 and α_2 be the proportions to the labour spent on the two classes respectively of that which the state allows him to retain in the corresponding amounts. Let O_1D_1, O_2D_2 be now the [net] amounts of labour spent on each of the two classes. [Let it be] required to find the values of α_1 and α_2 such as to make the total burden of the tax a minimum.

Equilibrium will be found when

$$(1) \qquad \frac{O_1D_1}{\alpha_1} + \frac{O_2D_2}{\alpha_2} = l$$

and since a unit of labour spent on class I has corresponding to it $(1-\alpha_1)/\alpha_1$ units due to the state, therefore the pleasure derived from the O_1D_1th unit is not D_1E_1 but $\alpha_1D_1E_1$.[10] Therefore:

$$(2) \qquad \alpha_1 D_1 E_1 = \alpha_2 D_2 E_2$$

When the sum of the two areas $F_1O_1D_1E_1$ and $F_2O_2D_2E_2$ [i.e. total utility] is a maximum, the net result of an infinitesimal variation must be zero.

That is

$$(3) \qquad 0 = D_1E_1 . \Delta O_1D_1 + D_2E_2 . \Delta O_2D_2$$

But the tax is of course assumed fixed in amount. That is

$$O_1D_1\left(\frac{1}{\alpha_1}-1\right) + O_2D_2\left(\frac{1}{\alpha_2}-1\right) = t$$

therefore from (1)

$$(4) \qquad O_1D_1 + O_2D_2 = l - t$$

Therefore (N.B. the following result can be established by general reasoning)

$$\Delta O_1D_1 + \Delta O_2D_2 = 0$$

Therefore from (3)

$$D_1E_1 = D_2E_2$$

---

[10] [One can only assume that this means to say that an extra unit of labour spent, net of tax, on class I involves the payment of $(1-\alpha_1)/\alpha_1$ units of labour as tax, so that the marginal utility of an extra unit of labour gross of tax, given that OD_1 units net of tax are already applied to class I, is $\alpha_1D_1E_1$, not D_1E_1.]

Therefore from (2)

$$\alpha_1 = \alpha_2$$

It has not been assumed that the cost of production obeys any given law. If this decrease rapidly while the amount produced increases, we may have a curve of this form [shown in Figure 3]. If however before the imposition of the tax the equilibrium position of B_1 be as here [Figures 3 and 4] (i.e. $O_1B_1 + O_2B_2 = l$ and $B_1C_1 = B_2C_2$) the equilibrium will be unstable if the curve at C_1 is inclined at a greater angle to the horizontal than the curve at C_2 is. And just the same remains true if we write throughout D, E for B, C respectively. This only means that the equation $\alpha_1 = \alpha_2$ combined with the others gives both the maximum and minimum.

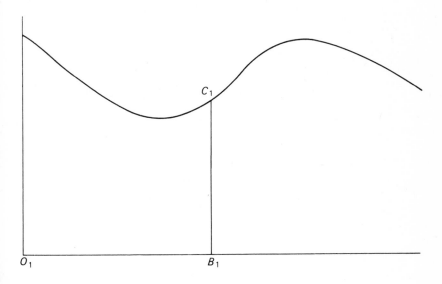

Fɪɢ. 3

It thus follows that if it be determined to raise a given amount in taxation from a given man who produces and consumes only two kinds of commodities, the burden of the taxation will be least when the taxes on the two commodities are of an equal *ad valorem* amount.

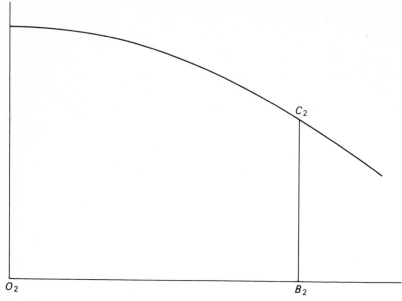

FIG. 4

And this of course may be extended to any number of commodities: taking three we have

$$O_1D_1 + O_2D_2 + O_3D_3 = l - t$$

$$\alpha_1 D_1 E_1 = \alpha_2 D_2 E_2 = \alpha_3 D_3 E_3$$

$$D_1 E_1 \Delta O_1 D_1 + D_2 E_2 \Delta O_2 D_2 + \cdots = 0$$

That is [since $D_1 E_1 = \lambda/\alpha_1$, $D_2 E_2 = \lambda/\alpha_2, \ldots$ for some value of λ]

$$\Delta O_1 D_1/\alpha_1 + \Delta O_2 D_2/\alpha_2 + \cdots = 0$$

Also

$$\Delta O_1 D_1 + \Delta O_2 D_2 + \cdots = 0$$

Therefore

$$\alpha_1 = \alpha_2 = \alpha_3$$

And the directest method of levying an *ad valorem* tax is of course an income tax.

Therefore this, as is otherwise obvious, is theoretically always the best tax on the supposition that the persons who produce commodities of any kind will always find it to their advantage to produce them in such quantities as to contribute most to the net happiness of mankind at large, themselves included. But this [supposition] is not so. Thus in the adjoining case [Figure 5] equilibrium is found at *A* and the net benefit of the production is *FGA*. But if the consumers and producers had the same interests, production might be carried to the amount *OD*. The net benefit is now *FKH* − *EKHC* and so long as *AGEL* is greater than *CLH* the community on the whole has been a gainer by the change.

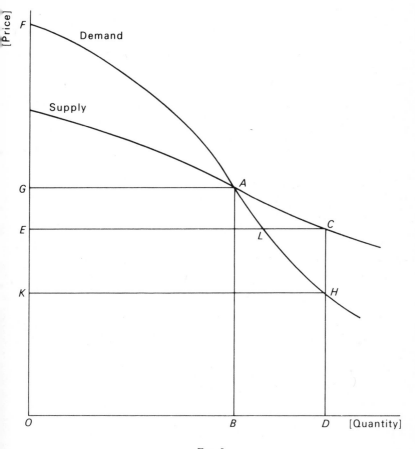

FIG. 5

In such cases it may be worth the while of the State to undertake losing business. It does this sometimes, as when it maintains national museums, or makes state roads in Skye. It is obvious that the result may be obtained, without the State's entering into the trade itself, by its offering a bounty to the trade. This has the disadvantages of being unlikely to be divided in fair proportions between producers and consumers; and of causing the support to be [retained], owing to the number of individuals who had a special interest in it, after the urgent need for it was passed. State guarantees to Indian Railways (though I do not see why it is not better still for the State itself to make the railways) are in every way better than bounties to Indian manufactures. The economical side of modern State-Socialistic theories is intimately bound up with the question to how great an extent this may with advantage be carried.

It is obvious that if the State may with advantage (considering only immediate economic effects) give a bounty in some cases, a complete exemption from taxation of some commodities may be right. It thus follows, that a uniform *ad valorem* system of taxation, i.e. an exclusive income-tax system, would be inferior in advantage to an excise system in some points. But if it were possible to adopt this system, its strong points would be so much more numerous and important than its weak ones that there can be but little doubt that it might with advantage be adopted, its weak points being covered by some form of state assistance, if necessary even of bounties to particular forms of production. On what might perhaps be called educational grounds a tax upon alcohol might be retained, even if economically the income tax were the sole basis of taxation.

Assuming that duties on particular commodities, whether levied by means of a State monopoly or otherwise, are to form an important feature in our financial system, it is important to consider the objections which are brought against the system and the extent to which they can be obviated.[11]

---

[11] It is hereafter assumed that cost of production is independent of amount produced.

In the front is the objection that those who in consequence of the tax are prevented from consuming the commodity lose while the state gains nothing. Thus, [Figure 6] besides the tax *EFGK* paid to the state there is a dead loss of pleasure represented by *EKD*. For it is assumed that in consequence of not buying *BC* the would-have-been purchasers expend their money on other commodities which do not in general (i.e. on the average) give them a greater return in pleasure than would be obtained by purchasing one of the commodities to which the figure refers at price *DC*.

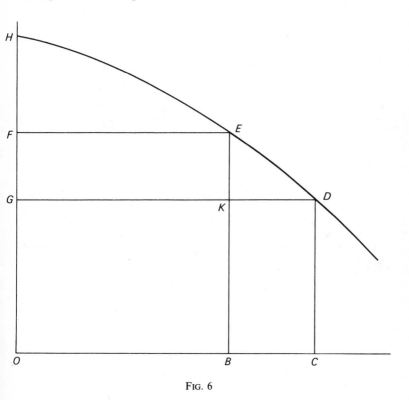

FIG. 6

It is then to be enquired under what conditions the ratio of *EKD* to *EFGK* is small. These are that the triangle formed by joining the three points *E*, *K* and *D* bear a small ratio to *EFGK*, and that the curve *ED* fall much inside the straight line *ED*

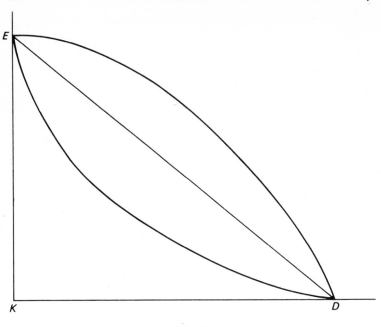

F<small>IG</small>. 7

[Figure 7]. The latter does not seem to have any important practical application. The former (i.e. $\frac{1}{2}KE^2 \tan KED$ must bear a small ratio to $EFGK$) reduces itself to two: (i) that the angle KED be small and (ii) that KE be small as compared with GK.[12] In other words, (i) for a tax of a given percentage the consumption must not fall off much and (ii) the percentage must not be great. The bearings of this latter consideration are sufficiently obvious. It will be seen that it is necessary to a great extent to neglect this consideration in order that the taxes may be concentrated on a few commodities. The most urgent objection to a high tax consists in the impracticability of collecting it well, and the consequent demoralisation of the people, and in the expense of collecting it at all.

The former consideration – that the imposition of a tax of a given percentage should not make the consumption fall off much – indicates that the commodities should not supply a

---

[12] The unit length for price and for quantity being supposed given.

want which can be easily supplied by anything else, or afford a pleasure for which some other is readily accepted as a substitute.

Thus, it might appear that necessaries should be taxed: and though on other grounds this is to be condemned, it appears that the fittest subjects for taxation are those luxuries which are almost necessaries. Whatever share of taxation the poor man is to bear is as well levied on his tobacco, alcohol and sugar as on anything else:[13] tea comes early on this count but is a preventative of drunkenness: house room again when too cramped leads to immorality. Houses and tea are as regards all other classes good subjects of taxation. One of the great

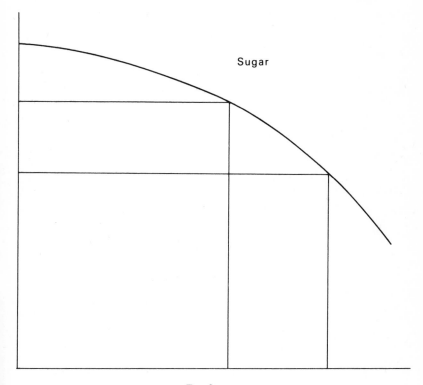

Sugar

Fɪɢ. 8

[13] [Marshall subsequently added the following comment.] No: experience has shown that a tax on sugar cannot be levied fairly: it leads to extensive uncertainties, frauds and other obstructions to trade.

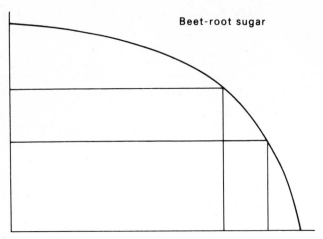

FIG. 9

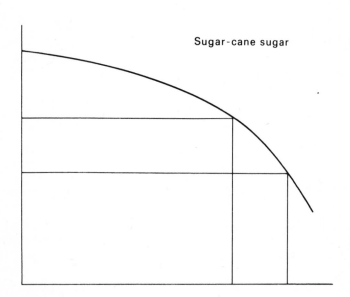

FIG. 10

advantages of tobacco is that nothing (unless it be opium, which ought indeed to be heavily taxed) is a substitute for it.

The attack which Mill directs against duties on one kind of a commodity, say on sugar-cane sugar, and not on another, as beet-root sugar, comes under this head. The curve for sugar may be of a form well adapted for taxation [as shown in Figure 8]: people using each kind for those purposes for which it was best adapted: and the demand curves for the two kinds might be of this form [shown in Figures 9 and 10] on the supposition that whatever tax might be imposed on the one kind, exactly the same would be imposed on the other. Whereas if the curve for sugar-cane sugar had to be drawn on the supposition that its price might be affected by a tax or some other cause not affecting the other, its curve would be somewhat of this shape [shown in Figure 11] and would be one of the worst possible subjects for taxation.

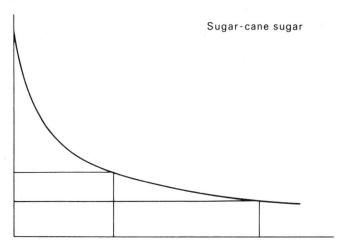

Sugar-cane sugar

Fig. 11

Thus, again, Mr Jevons[14] points out that for the purposes of most economical investigations beef and mutton should be regarded as one commodity, say butcher's meat. Writing this for sugar, beef for beet-root sugar and mutton for sugar-cane

[14] [W. S. Jevons, *The Theory of Political Economy* (Macmillan, London, 1871) pp. 127–8; Fourth edition, p. 135.]

sugar, we see the results of a tax on mutton and not on beef. Connected with this point is that which forbids taxing a commodity even though in one of its applications it is well adapted for taxation when in other and important uses it is not so suitable.

IV.4.3   On Competitive Equilibrium

Introduction   In a postscript to a letter to J. N. Keynes of 14 November 1888, Marshall remarked:

> I have been looking up my old notes on Cournot & find I have gone at some length into the question whether the marginal expense of production is to be regarded as $\phi(x)\,\Delta x$ or as $\Delta(x\phi(x))$ where $y = \phi(x)$ is [the equation] to supply curve, y being price & x amount of commodity. I will let you see the notes some time.[1]

The fragment referred to in this letter has survived, being identified by Marshall as 'part of a note on Cournot written probably in 1874'.[2] It deals only peripherally with Cournot, and is concerned primarily with the conditions of competitive equilibrium. Marshall is clearly groping, not wholly satisfactorily, with the problem of external effects in production, which can make marginal cost for the industry differ from the marginal cost perceived by the individual firm. It was difficulties of this kind which led to Marshall's 'Wander-jahre among factories, etc . . . to discover how Cournot's premises were wrong' and to the development of the representative-firm concept.[3]

---

[1] Marshall to J. N. Keynes, 14 Nov 1888. Marshall Library, Keynes 1 : 48.

[2] This corrects a previous attribution: 'Note relating to Cournot originally proposed as part of Note XIII of Appendix to Vol I (on unstable equilibrium)', which would suggest a date of about 1882. (Compare Vol 1, p. 85, above.) The 1874 attribution appears the more plausible, and in any case, the 1882 'proposal' could refer to the utilisation of an older manuscript rather than to actual composition.

[3] *Memorials*, p. 407. See the discussion above, Vol 1, p. 51. In a related manuscript fragment, possibly of somewhat later date, Marshall observes that 'A purely hedonic supply curve does not raise this difficulty . . . . And in the economic supply curve in which organization has to be taken account of xy (y being expenses of production on margin) is the only definition available of aggregate expenses of production; only the y to be taken note of now is the expenses of production of a business in general or of an extension of business in general.' The concept of the 'Representative Firm' is hinted at strongly in Book II, Ch. XII of the *Economics of Industry* (1879).

Marshall's strictures on Cournot in the present note are unjustified, given Cournot's implicit assumption of no external effects in production–though the assumption itself might be criticised. Surprisingly, Marshall fails to note that excess profits in Cournot's case would be absorbed in rent.

The notation needs to be introduced:

x = quantity produced by the whole industry
x_k = quantity produced by producer k
$f(x)$ = demand price for quantity x
$\psi(x)$ = average cost to the industry as a whole of producing quantity x.

Text   If the production were in the hands of a monopolist, his aim would be to make the excess of receipts over expenditure as great as possible. That is he would fix the production at that point at which

$$f(x) - \psi(x) + x\{f'(x) - \psi'(x)\} = 0$$

But under free competition, each person thinks only of the price that he will get for his own products. The gain to him of an extra production Δx is simply $f(x)\,\Delta x$; whereas if he had to consider the effect which his production had on the price which other producers receive, he would regard the extra receipts due to an extra production Δx as equal to $\Delta\{xf(x)\}$; that is $\{f(x) + xf'(x)\}\,\Delta x$. It requires but little consideration to see that not this, but $f(x)\,\Delta x$ is the attractive force which moves him onwards. There is perhaps more danger of mistaking the amount of deterrent force by which this is counterbalanced. It may seem plausible to say that the point at which he will stop his production is that at which the price which he gets for his goods is equal to the addition that the production will make to the total expenses of production; that is the point at which $f(x)\,\Delta x = \Delta\{x\psi(x)\}$; that is $f(x) = \psi(x) + x\psi'(x)$. But this is to suppose that he has to take into calculation the indirect results of his action on the expenses of producing the whole supply. For instance if by increasing the total production he facilitates the growth of subsidiary industries and thus causes $\psi(x)$ to tend to diminish, the part of the gain which he gets is of the second order of small quantities and may be neglected. Or again if an increase of the total production involves an extension of the margin of cultivation and thereby a rise of the supply price for the whole produce, a certain amount of income being transferred to the landlords from the producers as intermediaries for the consumers, then the gross rise in price so caused is not to be charged to the extra element produced; but only its share of this extra price; and this again is of the second order of small quantities and may be neglected. So that just as the impelling force is the actual price paid per unit; so the deterring force is the actual expenses of production per unit, that is the total expenses of production divided by the amount produced; that is $\psi(x)$.

The steps of this reasoning are doubtless somewhat difficult to follow; and it is perhaps well to add a *reductio ad absurdum* of the supposition that equilibrium is found when the demand price for an additional element is equal to the addition made to the total expenses of production by producing that element: i.e. that $f(x)\Delta x = \{\psi(x) + x\psi'(x)\}\Delta x$. If this were true then the total receipts of the trade, viz. $xf(x)$, would fall short of the total expenses of the trade, i.e. $x\psi(x)$, by the amount $x^2\psi'(x)$; and this may be a large sum either positive or negative: that is to say equilibrium is found at a point at which the capital and labour involved in it gets a remuneration different from its normal remuneration by $x^2\psi'(x)$: which is absurd.

Cournot finds equilibrium when $x_k f(x) - \phi(x_k)$ is a maximum, where x_k is the amount of the produce raised by an average producer and $\phi(x_k)$ is the total expenses which he incurs in raising it.[4] This gives him $x_k f'(x) + f(x) - \phi'(x_k) = 0$ (because since $x = \sum x_k$ therefore

$$\frac{df(x)}{dx_k} = \frac{df(x)}{dx} = f'(x))$$

He then throws away $x_k f'(x)$ as small in comparison with the other terms when the number of producers is indefinite. This gives him $f(x) = \phi'(x_k)$: and no interpretation can be given to $\phi'(x_k)$ which differs from $\psi(x)$ according to our notation.

---

[4] [This refers to § 50, Ch. VIII, of A. A. Cournot, *Recherches sur les Principes Mathématiques de la Théorie des Richesses* (L. Hachette, Paris, 1838). Cournot uses D_k instead of x_k, and ϕ_k instead of ϕ.]

He however says that $\phi''(x_k)$ must be positive; because if it were not $xf(x)$ would be less than $\sum \int \phi'(x_k)\,dx_k$ [i.e. $\sum \phi(x_k)$]. That is to say the trade would be carried on at a loss. He does not see that there is an equal objection to its being greater.[5] The fact is that the whole expense of production is equal to $x\psi(x)$: and as he does not see that, it is probable that he had not really considered what interpretation ought to be given to $\phi'(x_k)$: or rather that he has erred about it.

His whole plan of treating the producer as one of a very large number of monopolists leads to the right result only by a little violence being done it at a point at which he has given no interpretation; it is very cumbrous: and has no special advantage.

IV.4.4 *Notes on The Theory of Economic Growth*
Introduction This note and its two annexes are of great interest as they reveal Marshall attempting to set out formally a coherent macroeconomic model of economic growth. Indeed, for the first time we have really clear and explicit evidence of a neoclassical author actually working in terms of what has come to be known as 'the neoclassical aggregate growth model'.[1]

Marshall's equations develop naturally from the macroeconomic distribution theory of his *Economics of Industry* of 1879.[2] But the overt dynamisation goes much beyond the book's fragmentary treatment of issues of secular change. In

---

[5] [Marshall's copy of Cournot has an annotation, not reproduced in Item IV. 2.1 above, that is of some interest in the present context. It occurs on p. 102, referring to § 50 of Ch. VIII, and reads:

He has supposed that each ones production is independent of each other persons; and that is no doubt fair enough if we do not look forward beyond immediate results. But then $\phi'_k(D_k)$ depends entirely on the accidents of individual k, with wh. economics has nothing to do. Here he points out the terrible results wh. would arise if the total demand price fell short of the total supply price. But he seems to see no objection to its falling short. Yet from the point of view of normal theory, one plan is as bad as the other.]

[1] The modern discussion dates back essentially only to Solow's 1956 paper. (R. M. Solow, 'A Contribution to the Theory of Economic Growth', *Quarterly Journal of Economics*, Vol 70 (Feb 1956) pp. 65–94) though mention should possibly be made of Ramsey's 1928 paper (F. P. Ramsey, 'A Mathematical Theory of Saving', *Economic Journal*, Vol 38 (Dec 1928) pp. 543–59) which might almost conceivably reflect a Marshallian tradition.

[2] See Section I.5 above.

the following main note and its two annexes, Marshall outlines four different but related versions, each of which seems worth reproducing because it has certain distinctive features. The manuscript of the main note is a fragment of a more extensive manuscript and bears Marshall's superscription 'Date probably 1880.' It seems likely to have come from a sketch for a portion of the manuscript which grew into the *Principles*,[3] and a date of 1881 or 1882 might be more accurate. The first two annexes are rough working notes which appear to be contemporaneous with the main note, and also show firmly the imprint of the distribution theory of the *Economics of Industry*.

Although Marshall makes no explicit mention, it may be conjectured that long pondering on Book IV of Mill's *Principles* was one of the most important sources underlying the present notes. The treatment of accumulation and the growth of population and labour efficiency also appears to borrow heavily from Mill's Book I. It is worth noting that Marshall gave a lecture course 'Economic Progress' in the autumn of 1879 at Bristol, which was based on Mill's Book IV. There he planned 'to endeavour to show that all or almost all the piles of statistics which state how some things have fallen and others risen in value may be reduced under a few simple laws.'[4]

The main ideas present in Marshall's alternative versions are brought together in the following systematic outline statement, using a notation similar to that of Annexe 2.[5]

Variables

t = time
n = number of labourers

---

[3] There is 'Reference to passage in chapter on definitions where [the terms] are explained.' Such a chapter had been planned in 1882 (Vol 1, p. 85, above).
[4] For further details see J. K. Whitaker, 'Alfred Marshall: the Years 1877 to 1885', *History of Political Economy*, Vol 4 (Spring, 1972) pp. 18–20, 44–5. The quotation comes from the rough manuscript notes for the first lecture.
[5] A fuller account and interpretation of Marshall's thinking on these topics and of its relation to the *Economics of Industry* is given in J. K. Whitaker, 'The Marshallian System in 1881: Distribution and Growth', *Economic Journal*, Vol 84 (Mar 1974) pp. 1–17.

e = efficiency of labour

$n \cdot e$ = labour force in efficiency units

c = capital

s = standard of comfort (or conventional subsistence level of labourers)

a = arts of production

f = fertility of soil (constant)

w = task-wage rate (or wage rate for labour of fixed efficiency)[6]

$w' \equiv e \cdot w$ = time wages (or earnings per worker)

i = rate of interest

y = real net annual income (or net national income)[7]

r = rent

τ = taxes (constant)

$x \equiv y - r - \tau$ = 'earning and interest fund.'[8]

Relationships (all partial derivatives positive unless indicated)

(1) $y = F_1(n \cdot e, c, a, f)$ (aggregate production function)

(2) $r = F_2(n \cdot e, c, a, f)$ (share of rent in aggregate production)

(3) $x = F_1 - F_2 - \tau = F_3(n \cdot e, c, a, f)$ (earnings and interest fund)

(4) $w = F_4(n \cdot e, c, a, f)$ (determination of task wage by marginal-productivity considerations)[9]

with $\partial F_4 / \partial n.e < 0$ normally.

---

[6] On 'task wages' see *Economics of Industry*, Book II Ch. VII; *Principles II*, p. 616.

[7] The concept of real net annual income (or product) is used in the *Economics of Industry*, Book I Ch. VI, Book II Chs. VI, X. (The identification with the modern concept of net national income is made clear in Book II Ch. VI.) This concept is clearly what is intended by 'gross real income' in the main text below, where the term 'gross' is introduced for contrast with Mill's concept of 'net produce', or as Marshall terms it 'net income available for saving'. This is net annual income less necessary consumption. (See J. S. Mill, *Principles of Political Economy*, Book I Ch. XI.)

[8] On the 'earnings and interest fund' see *Economics of Industry*, Book II Chs. VI, X.

[9] See *Economics of Industry*, Book II Chs. XI, XII. Also see Section I.5 above.

(5) $x = w'n + ic = wne + ic$ (interest-rate determination by adding up)[10]

Alternatively,

(5′) $i = (F_3 - neF_4)/c \equiv F_5(n \cdot e, c, a, f)$

with $\partial F_5/\partial c < 0$ normally.

These five equations solve for a 'momentary equilibrium,' determining the values of y, x, r, w, i at a given date, conditionally upon the values of the parameters n, c, e, a, s, f and τ.

If it is supposed (in line with Marshall's only formal statement here) that

(6) $s = F_6(w', t) = F_6(w \cdot e, t)$ (level of standard of comfort)

then s ceases to be a parameter and must be added to the variables, t must be added to the parameters, and (6) must be added to the determining equations for the momentary equilibrium. But it seems more in keeping with the spirit, rather than the letter, of Marshall's approach to replace (6) by an assumption of *gradual* habituation of labourers to new living standards, so that

(6′) $\dfrac{ds}{dt} = F'_6(s, w', t)$

with $\partial F'_6/\partial s < 0$.[11] This allows s to be retained as a parameter at a point of time and supplies one equation for determining the evolution of the parameters over time: that is, for expressing all the parameters n, c, e, a, s, f and τ as functions of t alone. The remaining equations required for this purpose are supplied by

(7) $\dfrac{dn}{dt} = F_7(n, w', s)$ (population growth)[12]

with $\partial F_7/\partial s < 0$, representing a generalised Malthusianism.

---

[10] See *Economics of Industry*, Book II Chs. X, XII. On the question of 'adding up' see Section I.5 above.

[11] See *Economics of Industry*, Book I Ch. V, Book II Chs. VII, X.

[12] Compare *Economics of Industry*, Book I Ch. V, Book II Ch. X.

(8) $\quad \dfrac{dc}{dt} = F_8(y, i, c, e, n)$ (capital accumulation)[13]

(9) $\quad \dfrac{de}{dt} = F_9(n, e, c, a, w', t)$ (growth of labour efficiency)[14]

(10) $\quad \dfrac{da}{dt} = F_{10}(t)$ (change in the arts of production)

(11) $\quad \tau = $ constant

(12) $\quad f = $ constant.

There is no indication that Marshall enquired into the qualitative properties of solutions for secular growth paths: indeed the models as they stand are much too complex and unrestricted to lend themselves readily to such an analysis. His main interest in formulating the models appears rather to have been in the analysis of the rates of change of the variables at a point of time. Even here he appears to have not pushed very far and to have soon grown discouraged. Nevertheless, as a pioneering attempt at systematic formulation, and as a kind of mathematical appendix to some of the central ideas of the much-neglected *Economics of Industry*, the notes retain very considerable interest.

Text   The gross real income of a country depends on (i) the number and average efficiency of the workers in it, (ii) the amount of its accumulated wealth, (iii) the extent, richness and convenience of situation of its natural resources, (iv) the state of the arts of production, [and] (v) the state of public security and the assurance to industry and capital of the fruits of their labour and abstinence.

If *g* be the gross real income of the country, *n* the number and *e* the average efficiency of the workers in it, *w* the amount of

[13] Compare *Economics of Industry*, Book I Ch. VI.
[14] Labour efficiency depends partly upon investment by parents in the education of their offspring, and partly upon the beneficial aspects on both physique and morale of improved living standards. It thus has strong endogenous elements (*Economics of Industry*, Book II Chs. VII, VIII). Marshall gives no precise account of the reasoning leading to an equation like (9). Nevertheless, he was a strong proponent of the idea that in appropriate circumstances there could be an 'economy of high wages'.

wealth in it, F the fertility of its natural resources above and below the surface of the ground (this fertility being regarded as itself a product of the extent, the average richness and the convenience of situation of these resources), A the state of the arts of production, and S the state of public security, then we have:

(1) $$g = f_1(n, e, w, F, A, S)$$

The total net income available for saving is the excess of this gross income over what is required to provide the necessaries of life; that is those things which are required for sustaining the efficiency of the several grades of industry [i.e. labour]; and the price which has to be paid in taxes for the maintenance of public security. No separate allowance need be made for the taxes levied for maintaining public works, or education.

If s be the net incomes available for saving, $f_2(e)$ the average necessaries of a population whose average efficiency is e, [and] T the taxes that have to be paid for the maintenance of public security, [we have]:

(2) $$s = g - T - nf_2(e)$$

The extent to which the country makes use of the power of saving which this net income gives, or in other words the rate of growth of its wealth, depends on (i) the amount of this net income, (ii) the willingness of its inhabitants to sacrifice present enjoyment for future, (iii) the strength of family affections among them (since it is not a man's own future enjoyment but that of his family which is generally the chief motive of his saving) and (iv) the rate of interest on capital, which affords a premium to saving.

Since w is the wealth of the country therefore dw/dt is the rate of saving. [If] D is the rate of discount at which people on the average discount future enjoyments, A' the strength of the family affections, and i is the rate of interest, then:

(3) $$\frac{dw}{dt} = f_3(s, D, A', i)$$

The rates of increase of the number and efficiency of the working population of a country depend, broadly speaking, on (i) the number and efficiency of the population already existing, (ii) the gross real income that there is to be distributed among the different classes of the nation, (iii) the evenness of the distribution of that income (for an increase of income of a less wealthy class at the expense of an equal aggregate loss to a more wealthy class generally promotes the increase of the number and efficiency of the population, providing it is obtained without injury to public security), (iv) on the strength of the family affections in so far as they incline people to lead a domestic life and to incur trouble and expense on bringing up their children, and (v) their willingness to sacrifice present and immediate enjoyment for more distant enjoyment (this counting in two ways, leading them on the one hand to delay marriage so as to retain a high Standard of Comfort, and on the other to think highly of the advantages of a good education). In addition, the growth of the efficiency of the population depends on the magnitude of the reward that in the existing state of the arts of production can be obtained by industrial ability. But this itself depends on the elements that have just been enumerated: it therefore need not be reckoned separately here.

If E be the evenness of distribution of incomes, [then]:

$$(4) \qquad \frac{dn}{dt} = f_4(n, e, g, E, A', D)$$

$$(5) \qquad \frac{de}{dt} = f_5(n, e, g, E, A', D)$$

E may perhaps be regarded provisionally as measured by the ratio which the aggregate of the incomes bears to the sum of the differences between each individual income and the mean income: it depends so largely on causes which are not properly economic that in this stage at all events it must be accepted by the economist as an ultimate fact from the statistician or the historian.

The rate of interest depends on the labour which can be got in exchange for a given amount of the produce of past labour. This depends on (i) the amount of wealth already accumulated, (ii) the number and efficiency of the people, (iii) the scope that the arts of production offer for the use of machinery and other forms of capital, and (iv) the relative importance of present and future enjoyments as it appears on the one hand to spend-thrifts and others who borrow wealth for the purposes of immediate enjoyment, and on the other to their creditors.

If s' be the scope for employment of capital

(6) $$s' = f_6(n, e, w, A)$$

and

(7) $$i = f_7(n, e, w, A, s')$$

or if we prefer it

(8) $$i = F_7(n, e, w, A)$$

Annexe 1   General equations of growth of capital and labour generally, labour being all reduced to units of some one kind of labour. Assume l labourers [with] average efficiency e. a = arts of production. f = fertility of natural resources. A = area accessible. $Af \equiv F$ [is] fertility for our purposes (only note accessibility is a somewhat vague idea : and thus requires some analysis).

Then

(1) $$c' \equiv \frac{dc}{dt} = f(c, a, F, l, e)$$

[$c \equiv$ capital, $t \equiv$ time].[15] Of course it is a function also of the rate of interest, but as this is a function of just the same variables it need not be given separately.

(2) $$l' \equiv \frac{dl}{dt} = \theta(c, a, F, l, e, s)$$

(s = standard of comfort)[16]

(3) $$a' \equiv \frac{da}{dt} = \psi(c, l, e, t)$$

---

[15] [We have, with all derivatives partial]

$$\frac{dc'}{dc} = +, \qquad \frac{dc'}{da} = +, \qquad \frac{dc'}{dF} = +, \qquad \frac{dc'}{dl} = +, \qquad \frac{dc'}{de} = +$$

[16] [All partial derivatives for (2) are positive except that for s, which is not given but is presumably negative. All partial derivatives for (3) are positive, but $\partial a'/\partial t > 0$ is 'a separate induction'. All partial derivatives of (4) are positive but those with respect to e, a, t require 'separate inductions'.]

$$(4) \qquad\qquad e' \equiv \frac{de}{dt} = \chi(c, l, e, a, t)$$

F must be taken as given by the premisses of the problem. So we have four equations for four unknowns c, l, e, a. We have to add

$$i = \Phi(c, a, F, l, e)$$

and

$$w = X(c, a, F, l, e)$$

[$i \equiv$ interest rate, $w \equiv$ wage rate].[17] Of course these equations contain implicitly the equation of net produce of capital and labour after deducting rent and taxes. (Taxes are to be regarded as so much of the necessary expense of production of the rest of the income $= I$.) And

$$I = ci + lw$$

i.e. interest and earning fund.

Annexe 2 [Rough notes on the growth of labour and capital.]

$w = $ wages
$n = $ no. of labourers
$c = $ capital
$a = $ state of arts
$w = f(c, a, n)$

$\dfrac{dw}{dn}$ sometimes +, sometimes −

$\dfrac{dw}{dc} = +$

$\dfrac{dw}{da} = +$ insofar as progress is simple improvement in method but $= -$ve insofar as progress causes increased conversion of remuneratory capital into auxiliary or of circulating capital into fixed.

---

[17] [All partial derivatives are positive, except for $\partial i/\partial c$ are $\partial w/\partial l$, which are negative.]

$$\frac{dn}{dt} = \phi(w, s) \text{ where } s = \text{standard of comfort}$$

$$w = \text{task wages}$$

$$i = \psi(c, w, n, e, a)$$

$[e \equiv \text{efficiency of labour}, i \equiv \text{interest rate}]$

Partial $di/dc = -$ve nearly always: though in case in which great natural field for employment, waiting to be opened up by capital, it is conceivable that $di/dc = +$ve.

$di/dw = -$ve where w is task wages but may be $+$ when w is time wages i.e. if di/dw be total

$$\frac{di}{dw} = \frac{di}{dc}\frac{dc}{dw} + \frac{di}{dw} + \frac{di}{dn}\frac{dn}{dw} + \frac{di}{da}\frac{da}{dw}$$

[and]

$$\frac{di}{dc} = - ; \qquad \frac{dc}{dw} = - \quad \text{but small}$$

$$\frac{di}{dn} = + ; \qquad \frac{dn}{dw} = + \quad \text{and both } \textit{may} \text{ be large}$$

$$\frac{di}{da} \text{ and } \frac{da}{dw} \text{ are both } +\text{ve and may be considerable}$$

so that di/dw total may be $+$ve.

$$\frac{di}{dn} = + \text{ both for total and partial without exception.}$$

Take i, dc/dt, w, dn/dt and perhaps da/dt as functions then write down di/dc, di/dw, di/dn, di/da partial, then di/dc, di/dw, di/dn, di/da total.

There will be a difficulty because e.g.

$$\frac{di}{dc} = \left(\frac{di}{dw}\right)\frac{dw}{dc} \quad \text{etc.}$$

where $dw/dc = $ total and we don't yet know that. Again $dn/dw = +$ for time wages, but not necessarily for task, while

$di/dw = -$ for task wages but not necessarily for time. This rather points to taking e as efficiency, w as task wages, w' as w/e [correctly $w' = w.e$ where $w' = $ time wages: so that]

$$\frac{dn}{dw'} = +$$

$$\frac{dn}{dw} = \frac{dn}{dw'}\frac{dw'}{dw}\left[= \frac{dn}{dw'}\left(e + w\frac{de}{dw}\right) \text{ correctly}\right]$$

but we may assume that dw'/dw is $+$ve.

Try this:

    $w =$ task wages
    $i =$ interest
    $n =$ number of labourers
    $e =$ efficiency
    $c =$ capital
    $a =$ state of arts of production
    $f =$ fertility of soil, taking account of mines fisheries etc.; also of climate, fitness for hard work etc., also of extent so that f represents the return to a given amount of capital and labour in a given state of the arts of production: unit of measurement to be say [Scrope's]

Unknowns are w, i, n, e, c

(1) $w = F_1(n, e, c, a, f)$

(2) $i = F_2(n, e, c, a, f)$

$nw + ci$ [correctly $new + ci$] = earnings and interest fund

(3) $= \phi(n, e, c, a, f)$

because $r = \chi(n, e, c, a, f)$ ($r =$ rent) and rent + earnings and interest fund + taxes (note any taxes ought to be included) = $\psi(n, e, c, a, f)$

(4) $\dfrac{dc}{dt} = F_3(n, e, c, a, f)$ $[t \equiv \text{time}]$

(5) $\dfrac{dn}{dt} = F_4(n, w, s)$

when s = standard of comfort and may be taken as [a] known function of w and t, [correctly $w \cdot e$ and t] for we must take general improvements [in s] as a known function of t, or at least it and a may both be regarded as known functions of a, n, w and t.

IV.4.5 'On Utilitarianism: A Summum Bonum'

Introduction The present note represents the convergence of two lines of thought. The first, deriving from Bentham, is represented in the following fragment of a lecture note for 26 April 1884:[1]

Looking at happiness from [the] economic view as provisionally measured by income

$$x = \text{number of population}$$

$$y = \text{average income}.$$

Say that at present $x = 36\text{m}$ $y = £33$ would it be better to have

$$x = 72\text{m} \qquad y = £33$$

or

$$x = 36\text{m} \qquad y = £44$$

If you say the latter then I say that the former would be pretty sure to include 36m the average income of whom was over £44; or say that it was £44 and that there are another 30m whose income is £22. Is their existence a positive evil?

The second line of thought derives from Edgeworth's reformulation of the utilitarian calculus in his *Mathematical Psychics*, which Marshall reviewed in 1881.[2]

---

[1] The problem stated in this fragment had been very clearly posed by Sidgwick (H. Sidgwick, *The Methods of Ethics* (Macmillan, London, 1874) pp. 385–6).

[2] See Item IV.2.11, above. Edgeworth's work in this regard largely repeated arguments appearing in his *New and Old Methods of Ethics* (James Parker and Co., Oxford and London, 1877) and also in his 'The Hedonical Calculus', *Mind*, Vol 4 (July 1879) pp. 394–408.

The note deals in an intriguing way with the question of a utilitarian 'social welfare function', and looks forward to Ramsey's 1928 paper on 'A Mathematical Theory of Saving'.[3] It was probably written in the early 1880s[4] as part of the materials intended for the *Principles*, being headed 'Appendix'.[5] Little trace of the arguments remained in the *Principles*, when it appeared, but Marshall still proposed to use the ideas as late as 1912 – at age 69 – writing:

> This is to be the basis of a Note, the substance to be in the text, even if it be only for a single paragraph: the rest in footnote. Probably for the last chapter of IV, perhaps for the first. 13.1.12.

Text According to generally received doctrine [the] aim is to make hn = maximum, where n = number of individuals and h = average happiness: so that $hn = h_1 + h_2 + h_3 + \cdots + h_n$, where h_1, h_2, etc. are the happinesses of individuals. Or is it to make $h^2 n$ a maximum, or $h^3 n$ a maximum? On the other hand it may be argued that the aim is to develop the highest ideal of humanity, the number who enjoy it being of second rate importance.

The highest ideal may be taken to mean the highest capabilities of action, 'highest' being taken as defined according to the 'evolver' theory; and this may bring with it happiness so much more intense than can be got in any other way that the pursuit of the aim hn may really give the same results as the pursuit of this [i.e. the highest ideal]. But it is not probable.

Moreover there is this objection to this way of putting things: that we must suppose h to be the total amount of happiness enjoyed by any one at any time whatever, intensity and duration being taken into account. And as Bentham points out, propinquity of pleasures does as a matter of fact weigh with us. So that perhaps it would be better, following on

[3] *Economic Journal*, Vol 38 (Dec 1928) pp. 543–59.

[4] A closely-related discussion is found in the Lecture Notes on Taxation of 1881, reproduced in Section V.4 below, though the pages in question may have been added when the notes were re-used in 1884.

[5] Added to the heading is the characteristic warning 'N.B. Write as much as can be done without mathematics before beginning mathematics.'

Edgeworth's lines,[6] to say [maximise]

$$\int\!\!\int\!\!\int e^{-kt}\, dp\, dt\, dn$$

Also if we take account of the fact that the total happiness will be best promoted generally by each man's taking special account of the happiness of those around him, and not dissipating his attentions over space, we may introduce another factor $e^{-\lambda r}$, when r is the distance – measured perhaps partly in terms of geography and partly in terms of kindred – of a man from the several units. Thus we should get as the aim for any man [maximise]

$$\int\!\!\int\!\!\int e^{-(kt+\lambda r)}\, dp\, dt\, dn$$

But again looking away from the individual [and] enquiring simply what is the summum bonum we seem to waste ourselves if we look at the distant future: we can't act in the future, we can only act in the present. Therefore it is a question whether we should not regard the present values dh/dt and dn/dt, and higher differentials, rather than future values of dh/dt and dn/dt.

Let then $f(h, n)$ be that function – whether hn or h^2n or h^3n or whatnot – of h and n which [represents] the summum bonum with regard to the world at any particular time. Then what we have to aim at making the greatest now is
$f + \alpha_1 df/dt + \alpha_2 d^2f/dt^2 + \alpha_3 d^3f/dt^3 + \cdots$ etc. when α_1, α_2 etc. are factors (we might say constants perhaps for simplicity, but they need not be constant) which must be determined when we have decided how far the happiness of [the] present may give way to that of future.

---

[6] [The reference is to p. 57 of F. Y. Edgeworth, *Mathematical Psychics* (Kegan Paul, London, 1881). Edgeworth there introduces the assumption and notation that the greatest possible happiness is the 'greatest possible value of $\int\!\!\int\!\!\int dp\, dn\, dt$ (where dp corresponds to a just perceivable increment of pleasure, dn to a sentient individual, dt to an instant of time). The limits of the time integration are 0 and ∞, the present and the indefinite future. The other limits are variable, to be determined by the Calculus of Variations.']

Generally speaking we may be content to stop off with the third term: and the more enlightened will take α_2 very big. I would myself be contented with pursuing

$$f + \alpha_1 df/dt + \alpha_2 d^2f/dt^2 = F$$

where α_1 was equal to 1000 years and α_2 was equal to $(1000)^2/2$ years – so that really $F =$ first three terms of $f(h, n)$ 1000 years hence[7] – and with taking $f(h, n) = h^2n$. In this there is of course unlimited room for difference of opinion, but so there is [in] all such speculations, though the vagueness may be covered over.

There is this difficulty in coming to any conclusion about the most felicific distribution of wealth. How far is Bentham right in regarding the secondary influence of security to be so great that it may not be made to yield to equality at all: indeed what is security? But assuming this settled, how much are we to concede to Edgeworth's principle that most wealth is to be given to those most capable of pleasure? And again, how much to the principle that larger shares should be given to those most capable of so using it as to pioneer new ways? And again, how far do these two principles in reality cover the same ground?

IV.4.6 *A Mathematical Note on Rent*

Introduction This note comprises a rough sketch for part of a Ch. XIII on Rent, apparently proposed at an early stage of the composition of the *Principles*: quite possibly in 1881 or 1882.[1] The preamble to the argument reads

On the question of the influence of rent on expenses of production consider the difficulty about the margin of cultivation as between wheat and oats, compare Mill

---

[7] [That is to say, F is taken as the first three terms in the Taylor expansion

$$f(t + x) = f(t) + \frac{x\, df(t)}{dt} + \frac{x^2}{2!}\frac{d^2f(t)}{dt^2} + \cdots$$

with x taken as 1000 years and t the current date.]

[1] See Section I.6 above.

p. 346.[2] This point is referred to by Jevons p. liii,[3] who says that rent and wages enter into cost of production in the same way: investigate this argument.

While a postscript says: 'Study Thünen on Rent with the aid of Roscher and Kautz on Thünen.'[4]

The essential question being considered by Marshall is that of whether, and in what sense, rent is part of the cost of production for an individual commodity which competes for land with another crop. Marshall gives a very thorough and elegant statement of the conditions for equilibrium, showing that the demand for the two crops, and the technical properties of the various pieces of land, all combine to determine *simultaneously* the crop grown on each piece of land, the intensity of cultivation, and the prices of the outputs. It should be noted that Marshall expresses all values and prices in terms of doses of combined capital and labour, so that the price of such a dose is necessarily unity. As noted in the text, he also makes an important, but easily correctible, slip by working in terms of the value of production from a piece of land, rather than the surplus of this value over the cost of the labour and capital applied – a surplus which the process of competition absorbs into rent. It is clear from his earlier work that this must have been an oversight, rather than a basic misunderstanding.

The solution Marshall develops is hinted in the *Economics of Industry* and described fairly fully, but entirely non-mathematically, in the *Principles*.[5] The result is a nice example of Marshall's discarding of the formal analysis on which his

---

[2] The reference, which fits the People's Edition, is to the second of Mill's 'peculiar cases of value' which concerns 'values of the different kinds of agricultural produce' (see J. S. Mill, *Principles of Political Economy*, Book III, Ch. XVI, § 2). Marshall's discussion stands in marked contrast to Mill's rather vague and confusing treatment.

[3] W. S. Jevons, *The Theory of Political Economy* (Second edition, Macmillan, London, 1879). The reference is to the preface to the second edition, clearly dating the piece as post 1879.

[4] Possibly W. Roscher, *Geschichte der National-Ökonomik in Deutschland* (Munich, 1874); J. Kautz, *Theorie und Geschichte der National-Ökonomik etc.* (2 vols, Vienna, 1860).

[5] See *Economics of Industry*, Book II, Ch. IV; *Principles I*, Book V, Ch. X, § 5 (pp. 434–7).

argument rests, and also illustrates some of the costs of this practice.

Text If to capital and labour in amount x there be returned produce

$$z = \int y \, dx$$

then

$$\frac{dz}{dx} = y = \frac{1}{p}$$

where p = price of unit [of output]. In equilibrium

$$p = f(z)$$

where $f(z)$ is demand price for amount z, therefore in equilibrium

$$f(z) = \left(\frac{dz}{dx}\right)^{-1}$$

In this case the produce is from the whole land.

Now let there be a contest for the possession of a single field between two products wheat and oats: x, y, z [as above] all represent for wheat what X, Y, Z represent for oats. Then if it is just equally profitable to grow wheat and oats, then p being the price of a bushel of wheat and P of a bushel of oats, we have

$$\bar{z}p = \bar{Z}P \text{ [correctly } \bar{z}(p-\bar{x}) = \bar{Z}(P-\bar{X})]$$

when $\bar{z}$ and $\bar{Z}$ [and $\bar{x}, \bar{X}$] are determined by the equations

$$\frac{dz}{dx} = \frac{1}{p}, \qquad \frac{dZ}{dX} = \frac{1}{P}$$

Now suppose that fields $A_1, A_2, A_3 \cdots A_r$ are devoted to wheat [and] $A_{r+1} \cdots A_m$ to oats, A_r being a field which just gives equal returns to wheat or oats. Then the total crop of wheat equals

$$\sum_1^r (\bar{z}_n) \text{ (i.e. } \bar{z}_1 + \bar{z}_2 + \bar{z}_3 + \cdots + \bar{z}_r) \equiv W$$

$p = f(W)$ where f is the ordinary demand function.

So, the total crop of oats equals

$$\sum_{r+1}^{m} (\bar{Z}_n) \equiv O$$

and $P = F(O)$. Also

$$\bar{z}_1 p > \bar{Z}_1 P \quad [\text{correctly } \bar{z}_1(p - \bar{x}_1) >$$

$$\bar{z}_2 p > \bar{Z}_2 P \qquad \bar{Z}_1(P - \bar{X}_1) \text{ etc.}]$$

$$\bar{z}_3 p > \bar{Z}_3 P$$

$$\cdots$$

$$\bar{z}_r p = \bar{Z}_r P$$

$$\bar{z}_{r+1} p < \bar{Z}_{r+1} P$$

$$\bar{z}_{r+2} p < \bar{Z}_{r+2} P$$

$$\cdots$$

$$\bar{z}_m p < \bar{Z}_m P$$

IV.4.7   *Fragments on Marginal-Productivity Theory*

Introduction   The *Economics of Industry* of 1879 contains a clear outline of a marginal-productivity approach to distribution, but falls short of a precise statement,[1] and it appears to have been only in the early to mid-eighties that Marshall developed the details of his position. The following fragments seem to reflect a rather vital stage in the finalisation of his thought. They must date from the early 1880s, being clearly prior to the notes in IV.4.8 below, and being written on the reverse side of incompletely-contiguous sheets from a rough draft for 'Part IV Ch. II, III Distribution . . .', which can only refer to an early draft for the *Principles*.

The fragments give a clear formal account of marginal-productivity theory, expressed in terms of partial derivatives of the production function. Fragment II is particularly interesting in showing that Marshall perceived the 'adding up problem', though the solution he was groping for remains obscure.

---

[1] See Section I.5 above.

Text

I   [Let]
  $c \equiv$ capital, $l \equiv$ labour
  $p \equiv$ produce i.e. net after replacing capital $\equiv f(c, l)$
  $i \equiv$ interest, $w \equiv$ wages

We have:[2]

$$\Delta p = \frac{dp}{dc}\,\Delta c + \frac{dp}{dl}\,\Delta l$$

[By] hypothesis $dp/dc = i$; $dp/dl = w$, thus value of last produce $= i\,\Delta c + w\,\Delta l$. There are some cases where $(dp/dc)\,\Delta c$ is much greater than $(dp/dl)\,\Delta l$ when $\Delta c : \Delta l$ is such that $\Delta c . i = \Delta l . w$.
i.e.

$$\frac{dp}{dc}\Big/i > \frac{dp}{dl}\Big/w$$

and in such cases of course capital pushes out labour; and vice versa there are cases where labour easily pushes out capital. But when the two fractions are equal there is no pushing out, therefore in equilibrium

$$\frac{dp}{dl} : \frac{dp}{dc} = w : i$$

Taking units rightly $dp/dl = w$, $dp/dc = i$ and $\Delta p = w\,\Delta l + i\,\Delta c$, as it should.

To translate into curves, SS' is the supply curve of capital. The demand price for an amount OM of capital is such that OM capital with labour l would raise net produce in which the final utility [of] the addition to the produce due to a small increment of capital would be MP. This gives the demand curve. The two intersect at A [in Figure 1].

II   The remuneration for the last dose of capital and labour equals $i\,\Delta c + w\,\Delta l$. But the whole produce is p and is that $ic + wl$? Yes because the higher parts fall in value (except when they are applied in exploiting a monopoly, when the extra produce goes as rent or as monopolist profit). It will

---

[2] [The derivatives are clearly partial.]

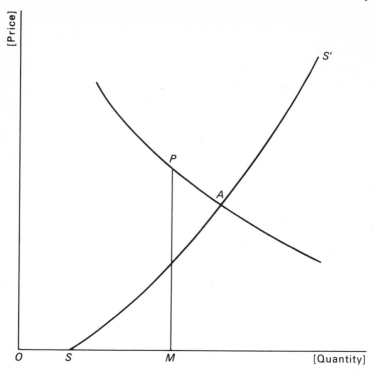

F<small>IG</small>. 1

be a job to make this clear and it should probably be done in an appendix.

III   Enquire: is the law of substitution equivalent to this? If P be the produce due to amounts $x_1, x_2, x_3 \ldots$ of the several factors of production and $p_1, p_2, p_3 \ldots$ their prices then

$$P = f(x_1, x_2, x_3 \ldots)$$

is a maximum subject to the condition that

$$x_1 p_1 + x_2 p_2 + x_3 p_3 + \cdots = 0 \quad \text{[correctly} = \text{constant]}$$

i.e.

$$\frac{dP}{dx_1}/p_1 = \left[\frac{dP}{dx_2}/p_2 = \cdots \right]$$

i.e. productiveness of x_1 in proportion as price of x_1. It seems that this though akin to Jevons's reasonings does not coincide with any of them. Although it is true that the law of indifference of two commodities (Jevons pp. 98–100)[3] is the same as the law of substitution as between two commodities.

IV.4.8 *Two Mathematical Notes on Distribution*

Introduction These two related notes seem to have been drafts for the Mathematical Appendix to the *Principles*. One of them (Note II) bears the inscription, probably applying to both:

> The question how much of these should be retained must be decided later. At present I incline to pretermit nearly all. Perhaps they will come into a later and independent treatise. Oct. 1 87.

The notes were probably written around 1885. Although rough in form, they are of great interest as they cover the ground in considerably greater detail than do the key Notes XIV and XXI eventually printed in the *Principles*. The hints set out in the preceding 'Fragments' (Item IV.4.7, above) are now developed into a systematic analysis, in terms of marginal productivity, of the determination of output, factor input, commodity prices and factor prices, first for the case of a single commodity (Note I), and then for several commodities (Note II). However, even Note II falls short of a full general-equilibrium analysis. For the commodity demand functions, and the factor supply functions, remain partial-equilibrium in conception, each admitting only an own-price effect and leaving an unbridged gap between commodity demands and factor earnings.

Marshall, writing in 1887 at the latest, thus anticipates the essential ideas stated by his younger colleagues A. Berry and W. E. Johnson in 1890 and 1891.[1] He also goes beyond

---

[3] [W. S. Jevons, *The Theory of Political Economy* (Macmillan, London). The page reference appears to fit both the 1871 and 1879 editions.]

[1] For the contributions of Berry and Johnson see W. J. Baumol and S. M. Goldfeld (eds.), *Precursors in Mathematical Economics: an Anthology*, Reprints of Scarce Works on Political Economy, No. 19 (London School of Economics, 1968) Selections 29, 30.

Edgeworth's 1889 analysis of 'commercial competition'.[2] Berry and Johnson treated the entrepreneur as residual legatee, but Marshall makes a distinct attempt to bring entrepreneurial earnings within the scope of marginal analysis. In this he is not really successful, failing to come to grips with the 'adding-up problem' whose resolution commenced only in 1894 with Wicksteed's *Coordination* . . . .[3]

Text

I   Let production be carried on by x homogeneous labourers, [with] no rent, no capital. [Let] w = earnings, P = amount of produce, p = its price. Then

$$P = f(x)$$

$$x = \phi(w) \quad \text{supply of labour equation}$$

$$p = \psi(P) \quad \text{demand equation}$$

and

$$xw = pP.$$

This assumes that there is no combination among labourers and that if an extra labourer Δx comes in, the inducement held out to him is[4]

$$\left(p + \frac{dp}{dP}\Delta P\right)\frac{P + \Delta P}{x + \Delta x} = \frac{pP}{x}$$

---

[2] In his Presidential Address to the British Association, 'On the Application of Mathematics to Political Economy', 1889 (*Journal of the Royal Statistical Society*, Vol 52 (Dec 1889) pp. 538–76, reprinted in F. Y. Edgeworth, *Papers Relating to Political Economy*, Vol II (Macmillan, London, 1925) pp. 273–312). The analysis of commercial competition is in note (f). Note (h), on 'industrial competition', deals essentially with occupational choice, a discrete decision involving comparisons of total, rather than marginal, utility.

[3] P. H. Wicksteed, *Coordination of the Laws of Distribution* (1894), reproduced as Reprints of Scarce Works in Political Economy, No. 12 (London School of Economics, 1932). Marshall in the third (1895) edition of the *Principles* appears to have accepted Wicksteed's arguments as justifying the statement that 'the national dividend is thus completely absorbed in remunerating the owner of each agent of production at its marginal rate' (Third edition, p. 605; *Principles I*, p. 830). On this, and the general 'adding-up' controversy, see G. J. Stigler, *Production and Distribution Theories: the Formative Period* (Macmillan, New York, 1941) Ch. XII.

[4] [The equation holds approximately for small increments.]

But suppose the rest of the labourers were to act in combination, and to consider how much [the extra labourer] should be allowed to work with them. They would have to consider the effect of increased production on (i) altering by diminishing returns or increasing returns the average cost of production and (ii) on lowering the demand price i.e. they would have to offer him $\Delta(Pp)$. It is only under these circumstances that the wages of a labourer are equal to what he adds to the value of the total product.[5]

Next suppose that each of the labourers is transformed into an undertaker. He then hires m other factors of production (capital and different kinds of labour). Let $x_a, x_b \ldots x_m$ be the amounts of the several factors which he employs and $p_a, p_b \ldots p_m$ the prices he pays them. Let θ be his product, p its price. Then in equilibrium $p(d\theta/dx_a) = p_a$, $p(d\theta/dx_b) = p_b, \ldots, p(d\theta/dx_m) = p_m$.

Let there be n such homogeneous undertakers; then

$$n\theta = \text{total product, so that}$$

$$p = \psi(n\theta) = \text{demand for product}$$

$$\theta = f(x_a, x_b, \ldots, x_m, X)$$

where X is the work of the undertaker

$$\left. \begin{array}{l} nx_a = \phi_a(p_a) \\ nx_b = \phi_b(p_b) \\ \quad \cdots \\ nx_m = \phi_m(p_m) \end{array} \right\} \text{supply of factors}$$

and if W be the earnings of the undertaker

$$\theta p = x_a p_a + x_b p_b + \cdots + x_m p_m + W$$

also the number of undertakers satisfies

$$n = \Phi(W)$$

[5] If l is the amount of labour that each puts forth and θ his [absolute] share of the produce then $p \, d\theta/dl = w$; an extra unknown with an extra equation. [Here, w is the wage per unit of labour: also, since $pP = px\theta = wxl$, it must be the case that $d\theta/dl = \theta/l$ i.e. $\theta = \lambda l$ for constant λ.] (Note the [supply of labour equation] becomes $x = \phi(w, l)$.) If the labourers are really homogeneous $\theta = P/x$: but there seems no harm in following the plan used later on and making them not homogeneous so that we have $\sum \theta [= P]$.

[There are thus] $2m+4$ equations for the $2m+4$ unknowns: $p_a, p_b, \ldots, p_m; x_a, x_b, \ldots x_m; n, p, \theta, W.$[6]

If we suppose X to be the [variable] amount of work the undertaker gives, we get an extra unknown. We have [instead of] $n = \Phi(W)$

$$n = \Phi(W, X)$$

and we [also] have

$$p\frac{d\theta}{dX} = W \quad [\text{correctly } W/X]$$

On the whole it seems best to adhere to this plan: it prepares the way better for the discussions on Rent. Of course, this might be extended, and for the labourer's x_a we might have the amount of exertion and the number: but this would be an unnecessary complication. For of course it is the product of the number of workers into the amount done by each that is a factor of production. There will always be something indeterminate here (I think: but this must be inquired into again at more leisure). On the other hand it seems best to allow the amount of work done by the employer to be variable; so as to get nearer life: but it is not theoretically necessary.

But now, in addition to the above factors of production let them have to hire each a piece of ground for which a rent R is paid. And in the first place assume that all the farms are of equal fertility etc. and that there are n of them. If n were not limited, of course there would be no rent. If n is limited, the number of unknowns remains as before $2m+4$, R, a new unknown, taking the place of n, which is now a constant; and the equations got before stand, except that now

$$\theta p = p_a x_a + p_b x_b + \cdots + p_m x_m + W + R$$

If the landlord is able to use the same discretion in choosing the farmer that the farmer is in choosing the other factors: if, in short, the farmer is the landlord's foreman or manager,

---

[6] If account be taken of the increased difficulty of managing an increased business we substitute for [the last] equation $n = \Phi(W, x_a, x_b \ldots x_m)$ and instead of these equations $[p\, d\theta/dx_a = p_a \text{ etc.}]$ we have $p_a = p\, d\theta/dx_a - dW/dx_a$ etc. [where presumably dW/dx_a etc. are defined for $\Phi(W, x_a, x_b \ldots x_m) = n = \text{constant}$].

we have[7]

$$n = \Phi(W, x_a, x_b, \ldots x_m)$$

and we have

$$p\frac{d\theta}{dX} = W \quad [\text{correctly } W/X]$$

thus leaving the size of the farms variable; i.e. the landlords having homogeneous land of N acres in aggregate extent choose n so that N/n = average farm.

We can now take the case of many different farms. On farm (i) we have equations exactly similar to those [above] except in this respect:—

If we assume for the present that all the farms supply one and the same market, and that p is the price of the produce in the market, and that $x_a, x_b \ldots$ include the factors of carriage to the market, there is no disturbance except that for $n\theta$ we have total produce $\Sigma\theta$ and for $nx_a = \phi_a(p_a)$ [etc.] we have $\sum x_a = \phi_a(p_a)$ [etc.].[8]

But if there are several markets we have a very complex set of equations since we must determine what farms will supply what markets.[9] It is very doubtful whether the problem will at present remunerate the great trouble of working it out: probably it should be left for a Ph[ilosophical] Society paper in the year 1895.[10]

II   Suppose all kinds of labour [are] expressed in terms of labour of one efficiency. Let

$$\left.\begin{array}{l} x_1, x_2, x_3 \ldots x_n \\ y_1, y_2, y_3 \ldots y_n \end{array}\right\} \text{ be the amounts of} \left\{\begin{array}{l} \text{labour} \\ \text{capital} \end{array}\right\} \begin{array}{l} \text{expended in} \\ \text{the production} \end{array}$$

---

[7] [It would seem appropriate to include X as an additional variable in the function Φ. Compare also footnote 6.]

[8] Flux points out we must here have a new supply equation for undertakers which makes the whole theory complex [Marshall added this note later. Flux's appended notes read on this point: 'Are the undertakers supposed to remain homogeneous? Apparently not since n is abolished. What then is the supply equation for undertakers.']

[9] The competition of different markets for the produce of a farm, is an analogous problem to that of the competition of different crops for the soil. Probably the two may be worked out together.

[10] N.B.   This seems to show that the paper was written in 1885. [Marshall added this note later.]

of commodities severally. [Let] $p_1, p_2, \ldots p_n$ [be] the prices of the commodities, $P_1, P_2, \ldots P_n$ their amounts. And firstly: let there be no case of rent.

$$w = \text{wages of unit of labour}$$

$$i = \text{interest of unit of capital}$$

There are then unknowns

$$x_1, x_2, \ldots x_n; \qquad y_1, y_2 \ldots y_n;$$

$$p_1 : p_2 : p_3 : \ldots : p_n; \qquad P_1, P_2 \ldots P_n; w, i$$

making $4n+1$ in all.[11]

These are determined by the equations[12]

$$\left. x_1 w + y_1 i = P_1 p_1; \qquad \frac{1}{w}\frac{dP_1}{dx_1} = \frac{1}{i}\frac{dP_1}{dy_1} \right\} \text{[etc.]}$$
$$P_1 = f_1(x_1, y_1) \quad \text{supply equation}$$

$$\frac{F_1(P_1)}{p_1} = \frac{F_2(P_2)}{p_2} = \cdots$$

when $p_1 = F_1(P_1)$ is the demand equation for commodity (1) [etc.].[13]

Lastly

$$x_1 + x_2 + \cdots = \phi(w)$$

$$y_1 + y_2 + \cdots = \Phi(i)$$

As factors of production we have taken only labour of one kind and capital but supposing we had had m separate

[11] [Note that there are only $n-1$ unknown ratios in $p_1 : p_2 : \ldots : p_n$.]

[12] [The derivatives are clearly partial ones or 'marginal products' so that $dP_1/dx_1 = \partial f_1(x_1, y_1)/\partial x_1$ etc.]

[13] [There are in fact n equations here, rather than $n-1$, since each of the $F_i(P_i)/p_i$ must equal unity if the demand conditions are to be satisfied. Marshall was apparently fumbling to exploit the zero-degree homogeneity of demand, without realising that his demand functions were written in a form precluding such homogeneity – a clear instance in which his partial-equilibrium preconceptions led him astray. On the other hand, the marginal-productivity conditions are only stated in their weaker form $(\partial P_1/\partial x_1)/(\partial P_1/\partial y_1) = w/i$, not in the more restrictive form $p_1 \, \partial P_1/\partial x_1 = w$ etc., and so the 'adding-up' problem is evaded. Note that what Marshall calls the supply function would now be termed a production function.]

factors, the amounts of which used in producing commodity (1) are

$$_1x_1, {}_2x_1, {}_3x_1, \cdots {}_mx_1$$

with prices (interest being a price) being

$$_1w, {}_2w, {}_3w, \cdots {}_mw$$

We should then have had precisely similar equations: the unknowns are

$$\left.\begin{array}{l} _1x_1, {}_2x_1, \cdots {}_mx_1 \\ \quad\cdots\cdots \\ _1x_n, {}_2x_n, \cdots {}_mx_n \end{array}\right\} \quad mn \text{ unknowns}$$

$$_1w, {}_2w, \cdots {}_mw = m \text{ unknowns}$$

$$P_1, P_2 \ldots P_n = n \text{ unknowns}$$

and

$$p_1 : p_2 : \ldots : p_n = n-1 \text{ unknowns}$$

making in all $mn + m + 2n - 1$ unknowns.

For equations we have

$$(_1x_1)(_1w) + (_2x_1)(_2w) + \cdots = P_1 p_1$$

$$\frac{1}{(_1w)}\frac{dP_1}{d(_1x_1)} = \frac{1}{(_2w)}\frac{dP_1}{d(_2x_1)} = \cdots$$

making m equations for commodity (1); in all mn equations. Also

$$P_1 = f_1(_1x_1, {}_2x_1, \cdots {}_mx_1) \quad \text{[etc.]}$$

making n supply equations,

$$\frac{F_1(P_1)}{p_1} = \frac{F_2(P_2)}{p_2} = \cdots$$

making $n-1$ demand equations

$$_1x_1 + {}_1x_2 \cdots + {}_1x_n = \phi_1(_1w) \quad \text{[etc.]}$$

m equations: in all $mn + m + 2n - 1$.   Q.E.D.

Next reverting to [the first] hypothesis (capital and one kind of labour being [the] only factors of production) take account of the fact that the sources of supply of one of the commodities is limited. Let this be commodity (1). Then instead of

$$x_1 w + y_1 i = P_1 p_1$$

we have in this case

$$x_1 w + y_1 i = P_1 p_1 - R$$

where R is rent. In this case[14]

$$w = p_1 \frac{dP_1}{dx_1}$$

and

$$i = p_1 \frac{dP_1}{dy_1}$$

In the next commodity there is supposed to be no rent

$$x_2 w + y_2 i = P_2 p_2 \qquad \text{and} \qquad w = p_2 \frac{dP_2}{dx_2}$$

(At least properly

$$w = (p_2 + \Delta p_2) \Delta P_2$$
$$= p_2 \Delta P_2$$

If this were $\gtrless p_3 \Delta P_3$ labour would flow from (2) to (3) or *vice versa*.)

IV.5   Fragments for the 'Principles'

IV.5.1   *Three Aides-Mémoire, 1881–86*

Introduction The main interest of these *aides-mémoire*, jotted down at various stages of the composition of the *Principles*, lies in the fact that they are dated. They thus give the only immediate glimpse available into the process of composition outlined in Section I.6 above. They cannot establish a great deal.

---

[14] [Marshall has slipped here into the stronger form of the marginal productivity condition. If we interpret commodity (1) as subject to decreasing returns to scale, and the remaining commodities as subject to constant returns to scale, his discussion creates no difficulty. But to import into the earlier discussion the stronger form of the marginal productivity condition without assuming constant returns to scale (homogeneity of degree one in the f_i) would clearly introduce overdeterminacy.]

I   is dated October 1881, and thus was probably written during the Sicilian sojourn. It shows Marshall facing up to questions of barter and the non-constancy of the marginal utility of income, both of which he saw as closely tied up with his 'foreign-trade' (or offer) curves.[1]

II   dated May 1884, and III dated November 1886, show Marshall still asking rather fundamental questions about the theory of distribution, tending to confirm his admission that 'There remained great lacunae in my theory till about 85; when ... I resolved to try to find out what I really did think about Distribution.'[2]

Text

I   In what was originally written as part of a chapter on market bargaining and is now probably to be taken over to a note at the end of the volume on some exceptional cases of value, there is a discussion of a case in which labourers increase their supply of labour in consequence of a fall in wages and vice versa. Using the 'domestic' curves we have a figure of this sort [Figure 1]. It will be seen that this curve violates our fundamental law of supply for Normal values.

It opens out a large field of inquiry: which had probably better not be entered on until this same problem has been worked out from the point of view of international trade. In fact the problem presented is this: – In the case in which money is supposed to have changing final utilities (for explanation see papers referred to).

We must really treat it as though it were barter, and in that case we must necessarily come very close to the problems of international trade. Of course it would be possible to treat

[1] For a subsequent discussion with Edgeworth about the theory of barter see *Principles II*, pp. 791–8. In particular 'It is now [1891] nearly twenty years since I decided that the plan which you ... follow would probably, if not necessarily, lead to hopeless unreality and unpracticality: and in consequence elected ..., the minor evil of making x = amount and y = ratio [i.e. price], though in consequence I had to sit upon changes in the marginal utility of money' (p. 797). Also: 'As to Barter. My MSS on the subject were of great length' (p. 796). However, little awareness of these topics can be found prior to this 1881 note (though see Item IV. 4.2 above) and it seems probable that Marshall's thought took on new sophistication and clarity when he returned to the basic questions of value theory in 1881–2.

[2] *Memorials*, p. 405.

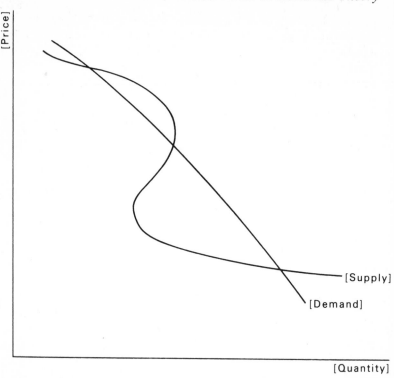

FIG. 1

the problem by domestic curves: but then we should have the old difficulty that whereas we have to deal with two curves that are fundamentally symmetrical we should have adopted a mode of expression that is fundamentally unsymmetrical.[3] Therefore conclusion [is] don't have curves on barter till it has been shown that the foreign trade curves won't do for them.   25.10.81

Further thoughts on the above.

The labour question is a little more worked out now in pp. $21\frac{7}{8}$, $21\frac{15}{16}$, $21\frac{31}{32}$ of the chapter referred to, the results

[3] See Ch. I of the *Pure Theory of Domestic Values* (Section III.6 above, p. 186) for such an argument.

being rather negative.[4] Perhaps what should be said about international curves is this. They are the best generally for expressing barter whether for temporary or permanent markets. The latter have generally no real existence except in the trade between industrial groups. The former if made to resemble real facts are too complex for theory.

Still the international curve method may be indicated as the right one for anybody who may care to work on these lines.   27.10.81

II   Problem to be solved in connection with [the] demand for factors of production.

Assuming that a tax on all profits (so far as and so long as it does not affect the supply of capital) falls entirely on the capitalists: How are we to explain the statement that a tax on profits in any one trade α falls chiefly on the consumers of the products A of that trade. Such a tax would of course raise the value of A; it would also push capital out of α; and possibly pull labour in. Anyhow it would render capital at a disadvantage in the production of other things as regards capital [labour?]. But if the tax is to fall entirely on capital, then – on the supposition that the consumers of [A] are capitalists and labourers in the same proportions as the consumers of things in general – the gain that labour gets as wage receiver in all trades put together must just equal its loss as a purchaser of [A].

Can this be proved mathematically? If so it may be stated dogmatically in the text and proved in an appendix.

18 May 84.

III   Demand for labour.

The form of capital is determined by the relative final utilities of different kinds of capital. When then we inquire how labour is interested in capital's taking a certain form we are in substance, and should be explicitly, raising the question whether there has been a change disadvantageous to labour in the final utilities of different kinds of labour [capital?] i.e. especially of auxiliary and remuneratory capital.   Nov. 86.

[4] [This method of numbering interpolated pages was frequently employed by Marshall.]

IV.5.2 *On Substitution in Joint Supply*

Introduction   Some rough manuscript notes, abstracted in the Text below, show Marshall's thoughts taking shape on the question of substitution in joint supply. The manuscript is described by Marshall as 'Part of a Note originally written for Book V Ch. IV § 4,'[1] an attribution which suggests composition sometime in the 1880s. If so, the tentative and half-formed conception suggests that his thinking on questions of input substitution can hardly have been developed in detail very early.

The original Note, of which this was a fragment, had been entitled 'Note D'. Marshall observed at the beginning of the fragment which survives: 'Unless some simpler method of treating this subject can be discovered it is best to omit from here to end of note.'[2] There is some indication that the final corrections and modifications were added over a period, rather than when the original Note D was written. Marshall's eventual solution, given in Mathematical Note XIX of the *Principles*, sidesteps the difficulties he poses here.

Abstract of Text   Next let it be possible, by altering the breed of cattle or otherwise, to alter the relative amounts of meat and hide produced. Let us suppose that the meat is all of one quality; or, that a pound of good quality being taken as equivalent to more than a pound of inferior quality, the whole amount can be regarded as equivalent to so many pounds of a certain average quality: and so with regard to hides. Let then $\psi(x_1, x_2)$ be the whole expenses of the process of production when x_1 pounds of meat and x_2 square feet of hide are produced. Let $f_1(x_1)$, $f_2(x_2)$ be the demand prices of x_1 pounds of meat and x_2 feet of hide. Then in equilibrium $x_1 f_1(x_1) + x_2 f_2(x_2) = \psi(x_1, x_2)$: but further the distribution of production between meat and hides must be such as to give the maximum gain; i.e. such that no gain would result from increasing one at the expense of the other; that is while

---

[1] This is surely meant to be Ch. VI § 4, which deals with joint supply in all editions of the *Principles*.

[2] If the earlier parts were eventually included in the *Principles*, it was most probably in Mathematical Note XVIII and the footnote on pp. 388–9 (ninth edition).

$\psi(x_1, x_2)$ is constant, $x_1 f_1(x_1) + x_2 f_2(x_2)$ is a maximum; that is

$$\{f_1(x_1) + x_1 f_1'(x_1)\} \frac{d\psi(x_1, x_2)}{dx_2}$$

$$- \{f_2 x_2 + x_2 f_2'(x_2)\} \frac{d\psi(x_1, x_2)}{dx_1} = 0$$

[This appears to mark the end of the original Note D. Marshall next observes that the foregoing 'would be true only in the case of a monopoly'. He concludes as follows.]

It would be much more reasonable to say $f_1(x_1) = d\psi(x_1, x_2)/dx_1$ and $f_2(x_2) = d\psi(x_1, x_2)/dx_2$: but even this involves the assumption that whatever anybody does in the way of increasing production exercises effects on cheapening or rendering dearer the production of others, which effects he takes into account.[3]

The solution seems to be: Let $\chi_1(x_1, x_2) \Delta x_1$ be the extra expense of producing Δx_1, no allowance being made for the effect of producing that Δx_1 on the expenses of producing the previous (x_1, x_2): then $\chi_1(x_1, x_2) = f_1(x_1)$; also $\chi_2(x_1, x_2) = f_2(x_2)$ and $x_1 \chi_1(x_1, x_2) + x_2 \chi_2(x_1, x_2) = \psi(x_1, x_2)$: that is to say the first equation [i.e. $x_1 f_1(x_1) + x_2 f_2(x_2) = \psi(x_1, x_2)$] is consistent with these two. The analysis is practically valueless because there is no means of ascertaining anything about $\chi_1(x_1, x_2)$.[4]

---

[3] [On this point, compare Item IV.4.3 above.]

[4] [In similar vein, a note appended to one of the Items IV.4.8 speaks of it having been written 'before the solution . . . as to the distinction between final production price for the individual firm and for the total production was made'.]

PART V

Wider Themes – Social Thought and Economic Policy

Wider Themes – Social Thought and Economic Policy

V.1 Introduction

Marshall's social philosophy and views on economic policy seem to have developed gradually without radical break from their earliest expression, still strongly under Mill's influence, to the mature form assumed by the time the *Principles* appeared.[1] The stage reached by 1885 is well epitomised in his declaration to the Industrial Remuneration Conference.

> In one sense indeed I am a socialist, for I believe that almost every existing institution must be changed. I hold that the ultimate good of all endeavour is a state of things in which there shall be no rights but only duties; where everyone shall work for the public weal with all his might, expecting no further reward than that he in common with his neighbours shall have whatever is necessary to enable him to work well, and to lead a refined and intellectual life, brightened by pleasures that have in them no taint of waste or extravagance. But I fear that socialists would refuse to admit me into their fold because I believe that change must be slow.
>
> I admit that even now every right-minded man must regard himself rather as the steward than the owner of what

[1] Their evolution up to 1884 can be traced from his 1873 paper on 'The Future of the Working Classes', through the *Economics of Industry* and various Bristol lectures – especially those on Progress and Poverty. In 1884 came his short essay 'Where to House the London Poor', then came his Inaugural Lecture and his paper to the Industrial Remuneration Conference, both in 1885, and his address on Co-operation in 1889. Finally, in 1890, came the *Principles* and the address on 'Some Aspects of Competition'. (For detailed references see Vol 1, pp. xxi–xxiii.)

the law calls his property. But there are very few directions in which I think it would be safe at present to curtail his legal rights. I admit that Utopian schemes for renovating society do good by raising our ideals, so long as they are only theories. But I think that they do harm when put prematurely into practice; for their failure causes reaction.

Economic institutions are the products of human nature, and cannot change much faster than human nature changes. Education, the raising of our moral and religious ideals, and the growth of the printing press and the telegraph have so changed English human nature that many things which economists rightly considered impossible thirty years ago are possible now. And the rate of change is increasing constantly and rapidly. But we have not now to speculate for the future; we have to act for the present, taking human nature not as it may be, but as it is.

Even as human nature is, an infinitely wise, virtuous, and powerful Government could, I will admit, rid us of many of our worst economic evils. But human nature is, unfortunately, to be found in Government as elsewhere; and in consequence Government management, even if perfectly virtuous, is very far from being infinitely wise. Where, as in the Post Office, centralisation is necessary, it does better than private enterprise; but when it has had no such advantage it has seldom or never done anything that private enterprise would not have done better and at less cost. The total remuneration that competition awards to men of business is probably less than would in most cases have been wasted without good to anybody if the same business had been done by Government. But wastefulness is the least evil of Government management. A greater evil is that it deadens the self-reliant and inventive faculties, and makes progress slow. But the greatest evil of all is that it tends to undermine political, and through political, social morality.[2]

[2] Sir Charles Dilke (editor), *Industrial Remuneration Conference: the Report of the Proceedings and Papers* (Cassell, London, 1885) pp. 173–4. Whatever its merits, Marshall's paper on 'How far do Remediable Causes Influence Prejudicially (a) the Continuity of Employment (b) the Rates of Wages?' was ill-judged for the occasion, and can only be described as a resounding failure. His main recommendations under heading (a) were less fashion, less gambling and more information.

Marshall's concern for the poor, especially those trapped in the insalubrious slums of the large cities, can hardly be doubted. However, he saw their best hope, not in violent interruption of property rights, or large-scale government intervention, but in improving the efficiency and morale of labour through education and wise charity.[3] The problem was to break out of the vicious circle of low wages, low efficiency, and reckless habits, which condemned the next generation to the same fate as their parents. The state had its part to play by encouraging education, and legislating away evil living and working conditions, while discriminating private charity and example could do much to initiate improvement. Even straightforwardly increasing wages might be sufficient, and could eventually lead to enough increase in labour efficiency to recoup the extra wage cost, except that no employer could act alone.

For the voluntary parts of the amelioration process to be forthcoming, and even for the collective parts to be politically feasible, a high sense of social duty on the part of the higher, and particularly the employing, classes would be necessary. Moreover, for the amelioration process to become *cumulative* it was necessary that economic improvement induce greater foresight and unselfishness among the lower classes, especially with regard to parents' willingness to bear the costs of educating and training their children to a higher level than they themselves had attained. Thus, Marshall saw 'ethical growth' as an integral and necessary component of the process of economic growth.

Undoubtedly the most important essay reproduced in the present Part is the lengthy discussion in Section V.3 of 'Some Features of American Industry'. This throws a flood of new light on Marshall's conception of the interrelations between ethical and economic factors, and helps show that his incessant harping on the effects of economic conditions on

---

[3] This is not meant to cast Marshall as a rigid or unthinking exponent of laissez-faire. Indeed, his arguments for subsidising increasing-return industries represent one of the earliest analytically-sound qualifications of laissez-faire policies. For a good account of Marshall's views on economic policy see D. Winch, *Economics and Policy: a Historical Study* (Hodder and Stoughton, London, 1969) Ch. 2. Also consult T. W. Hutchison, 'Economists and economic policy in Britain after 1870', *History of Political Economy*, Vol 1 (Fall 1969) pp 231–55.

'character' was not merely a deferential, or defensive, obeisance towards Comtean notions of unified social science,[4] but something much more integral to his thought.

The 'Fragments on Trades Unions', reproduced in Section V.2, take up the ethical questions connected with union action. Statesmanlike action on the part of unionists, like greater unselfishness of parents, appeared a necessary part of cumulative amelioration of poverty, and Marshall saw both unionism and the cooperative movement fulfilling important educational functions in training their members to take a less narrow and short-sighted view of their own interests, and more account of the interests of other groups. Thus, these institutions took on for Marshall a rather romantic role as civilising agents, on which much hope rested for the gradual movement towards an ideal form of society in which conceptions of duty would provide the over-riding stimulus to action.

The 'Lecture Notes on Taxation' of 1880, reproduced in Section V.4, reveal some of Marshall's views on property and taxation. He came to take a relatively relaxed view towards redistributive taxation – what he called the *financial* side of socialism – believing that it was incapable of effecting really significant improvement, but would cause little harm unless carried to extremes.[5] But all the force of his character came to be directed against the *administrative* side of socialism – that is, government control of industry – which he saw as threatening to choke up the well-springs of growth.[6] Even joint-stock companies were to be suspected of a certain lethargy and addiction to routine. Like the unions, the restless, pioneering (and usually Anglo-Saxon) 'undertaker' came to assume in Marshall's eyes a superhuman stature and played a crucial part in his conception of socio-economic evolution.

The final essay reproduced in the present Part is the treatment, in Section V.5, of 'The Pressure of Population on the Means of Subsistence'. This deals particularly with the

[4] Compare G. F. Shove, 'The Place of Marshall's *Principles* in the Development of Economic Theory', *Economic Journal*, Vol 52 (Dec 1942) pp. 294–329, especially pp. 309–10.
[5] See *Principles I*, pp. 712–14; *Memorials*, pp. 462–3.
[6] See, for example, *Memorials*, p. 334.

extent to which population growth is connected to the evils of 'close packing' of the residents of the industrial cities, and especially London. The essay appears to be the text of a lecture given at Toynbee Hall, London, in 1885.

V.2 'Fragments on Trades Unions'

V.2.1   *Introduction*

In these 'fragments' we find Marshall laying out the *pros* and *cons* of trades-union action, with a summing up, 'intended to be impartial'. There is little positive analysis, the chief concern being with ethical questions. It is observed that 'The province of the Economist is to separate the ethical and economical elements involved in the discussion of any rule; to point out the bearing of the latter, but to leave the former to individual judgement or to the analysis of the ethical philosopher.'[1] However, Marshall does not wholly forswear the philosophical role.

The ethical rule that 'it is unreasonable for any persons to adopt a line of action, the general adoption of which by all others in their position will be injurious to the whole number'[2] is referred to more than once. This rule, and the prospects for its increased application by unions, are further considered in the succeeding essay on 'Some Features of American Industry'.[3] Indeed, the 'fragments' take their main interest from their close connection with this profounder study. But there are also many small sidelights of interest on various aspects of Marshall's thought,[4] and the whole piece displays admirably the unique blend of moral earnestness and frequent acuteness, laced with occasional and endearing preposterousness, that pervades his early writings on social questions.

The manuscript, of twenty pages octavo, appears to have been written in 1874 or 1875, but is undated. The sub-headings were added after the text was written.

---

[1] See p. 349 below, and also compare Marshall's 1874 'Beehive' articles (reproduced in R. Harrison, 'Two Early Articles by Alfred Marshall', *Economic Journal*, Vol 73 (Sept 1963) pp. 422–30).

[2] See pp. 346–7 below.

[3] See Section V.3 below.

[4] Compare, in particular, Item II.4.1, above, and the chapters on trades unions in Book III of the *Economics of Industry*, especially Ch. VII.

V.2.2   *Text of 'Fragments on Trades Unions'*

I   *The conditions that a compact strong union (such as the Bricklayers) not restricted by foreign competition may raise wages much*

An enormous rise in the wages of bricklayers could be attained by a Union on the following conditions that
(i) The Union can prevent any bricks from being laid by persons who are not members of the Union.
(ii) Some houses will be built of bricks even though the total cost of such houses is largely increased: a doubling of the wages of bricklayers (other trades being unaffected) would not add a large percentage to the cost of houses.
(iii) The bricklayers, by means of the poor rates or otherwise, can and will hold out indefinitely.

II.   *Employers' side: considerations tending to dissuade them from attempting such a course*

If they are to be dissuaded from attempting this result it must be by its being shown that
(i) they cannot hope ever to control all persons who can lay bricks or can learn to lay them, or
(ii) that if other trades connected with building pursue a similar course, the cost of houses will be such as almost to stop building, so that the total wages paid to bricklayers will be diminished, or
(iii) that they have no right to adopt a course which thus injures the rest of the building trades, or
(iv) that they have no right to injure the masters whose profits will fall until some of them are driven from the trade, or
(v) that they have no right to injure the consumers, or
(vi) that inasmuch as demand for commodities consists simply of commodities, and inasmuch as only a small portion of the total produce of capital and labour will in any case fall to the share of capital, any line of conduct, the general adoption of which would cause a diminution in the efficiency of labour, would tend towards a falling off in the real wages of labour generally; and it is unreasonable

for any persons to adopt a line of action, the general adoption
of which by all others in their position will be injurious
to the whole number; that they cannot raise their wages
much above the natural wages without adopting such a
course.

(vii) that in the same way it is unreasonable to strive for a
rise in wages by a line of conduct the general adoption of
which by labourers generally would cause the rate of
profits to fall so as greatly to diminish the amount of
capital in the country, either in consequence of the migration of capital, or in consequence of capitalists being driven
to consume their capital, or

(viii) that having in view the well being of the next generation, they are bound above all things not to lay unnecessary
hindrances in the way of those who will learn a skilled trade :
that severe apprenticeship regulations may keep up the
rate of wages in skilled trades at the same time that they
diminish the total wages of labourers skilled and unskilled :
that it is far more to be desired that in the next generation
there should be 2,000,000 skilled labourers each earning
(the equivalent of) 40 quarters of corn a year, than that
there should be 1,000,000 each earning on the average
50 quarters of corn, the second million remaining in the
ranks of unskilled labourers and each earning on the
average 20 quarters of corn.

III   *Unionists' side, in answer [to the Employers]*

Bricklayers may answer in defence of action by which
they endeavour, without any very great pretensions, somewhat
to raise their wages : that

(i) As to the efficiency of their Union in controlling the
action of bricklayers, they are the best judges : that anyhow
it were un-English to despair of a movement on the ground
that its scope is somewhat narrow.

(ii) and (iii) The maxim of orthodox Political Economists
is that the world progresses on the whole best if each man
looks after his own interests : of course the Plasterers
Union might retaliate : but practically the various Unions
do get on tolerably well together : if the Unions found

themselves injuring one another palpably, their organisation would enable them to make efficient commercial treaties with one another.

(iv) and (v) That when their superiors in the commercial world set the example of refusing to increase their income by any means which inflict on others a loss greater than their gain, then they, the bricklayers, will think about following the example.

(vi) The Unions have few friends and many foes among newspapers: thus every injury that Unions inflict on the community is widely published and is exaggerated. Few people have at once the knowledge and candour requisite for giving, as Brassey has done, to Unions and notably to the leading officers of great Unions the credit that they deserve for facilitating production.[1]

(vii) Those who assert that an increase in that share of the national income which goes into the hands of the working classes must cause a diminution of the material prosperity of the country forget that the national prosperity of a country is as much promoted by a fine race of labourers as by a fine race of cart-horses.

(viii) Such bricklayers as have sons to be started in the world are not likely to take insufficient account of the evils which over-severe apprenticeship regulations are likely to inflict on the rising generation.

They allege further that

(a) if a few skilled labourers can rise they will soon pull the rest of the labourers after them

(b) if the present generation of labourers can better their condition, the next generation will be enabled to start well in life

(c) irregularities of trade cause to the well-to-do classes no important injury beyond pecuniary loss: but that they cause to the working classes physical suffering and grievous moral injury: that Unions are often accused of hindering production when they are but

---

[1] Wages for 1873 [T. Brassey, 'Wages in 1873', an Address to the Social Science Association, Norwich, 1873, reproduced in his *Lectures on the Labour Question* (Longmans Green, London, 1878). See especially p. 72.]

regulating trade: that in spite of occasional strikes, the net result of trades-union action is to steady trade.

IV *Summing up, intended to be impartial*

Action on the part of trades unions in limitation of trade is

(i) not likely to be carried on to such lengths, and as generally, as it must be thought to be by those whose information is mainly derived from journals and other writings intended to be read mainly by the well-to-do classes

(ii) is capable of being somewhat palliated if judged by ethical principles no more severe than those applied in judging the commerical morality of the well-to-do classes

(iii) is often excused in the minds of intelligent and upright workmen by the memory of cases in which they have done good service by checkmating the schemes of some un-scrupulous and grasping masters

(iv) is not of a virulent character excepting when it proceeds from ignorant good-for-nothing workmen who would have plagued society under any régime.

The best of workmen and the best of masters will admit that if there were none but upright industrious men, and none but upright and generous masters, on the one hand trades unions would scarcely be necessary, and on the other hand they would scarcely do any harm.

The grasping unscrupulous conduct of a few masters incites Unionists to justify their worst rules. The use made by the worst Unionists of the worst principles accepted in the trades-union rules goads masters into wholesale denunciation of the motives and the measures of trades unionists.

There is scarcely any trades-union rule or principle of action which may not in some cases be beneficial to the union in question and also to the community at large: scarcely any rule which may not be prejudicial to both. The province of the Economist is to separate the ethical and economical elements involved in the discussion of any rule; to point out the bearing of the latter, but to leave the former to individual judgement or to the analysis of the ethical philosopher.

There is an immensely strong *prima facie* case in support of the proposition that rules which hamper activity, and in particular rules which hinder a youth from learning a skilled trade, are economically injurious to Society; and therefore a strong *prima facie* case for condemning such rules as morally unjust. But nothing is likely to hinder Unionists from seeing the folly or wrongfulness of such portions of their conduct as are really to be condemned than the habit current in well-to-do society of condemning confidently, and without analysis, as foolish and wrong, every trades-union action which appears at first sight to be intended to benefit a particular union at the expense of a limitation of industry.

The only general conclusion at which we can arrive is the negative conclusion that as Mill says[2] 'The right and wrong of the proceedings of Trades' Unions becomes a common question of prudence and social duty, not one which is peremptorily decided by unbending necessities of political economy'.

Thornton, Mill in his two articles on Thornton, as well as in his *Political Economy*, and Cairnes[3] all say that a rise in wages in some particular trade may be obtained mainly at the expense of the consumer. Thornton and Mill say that a slight rise in all trades generally may *possibly* be effected at the expense of profits. But none of them call attention to the special cases in which a rise in wages might be obtained chiefly at the expense of rent.[4] A rise in agricultural wages now would probably much increase the efficiency of agricultural

---

[2] *Fortnightly Review*, May 1869, p. 517. [See J. S. Mill, *Collected Works*, Vol V, p. 646.].

[3] [See J. S. Mill, *Principles of Political Economy*, Book V, Ch. X, § 5; 'Thornton on Labour and its Claims', *Fortnightly Review*, Vol 5 (May, June 1869), reproduced in Mill's *Collected Works*, Vol V, pp. 633–68; J. E. Cairnes, *Some Leading Principles of Political Economy* ... (Macmillan, London, 1874) Part II, Ch. III; W. T. Thornton, *On Labour* ... (Macmillan, London, second edition 1870) Book III, Ch. IV, especially pp. 306–7. A copy of Thornton, preserved in the Marshall Library, bears Marshall's annotation on p. 306 'the consumers of course lose but the masons spend what would otherwise have been spent by them so that other laborers do not lose.']

[4] Of course on the supposition chiefly worked out in Mill's Book IV that the corn produced in a country is a fixed amount, a rise in agricultural labourers' wages would leave corn rents unaffected and raise real rents.

labour : but if it did not, rents would fall ; neither the consumer nor the capitalist (the farmer) would suffer much. Again, though the cases are not precisely parallel, one of the chief effects of a rise in the wages of miners would be to lower the rent of mines without raising the value of the produce of mines by the full amount of the increase of wages.

Putting aside the particular interests of particular trades, we may say that trades unions do or do not benefit working men as a whole according as they

(i) do or do not make the working classes more intelligent and more capable of governing themselves and of performing those functions which educated the citizens of small cities of Greece

(ii) do or do not cause unprofitable consumption on the part of the rich to be replaced by consumption on the part of the working classes of such kind as to increase the real welfare and the intelligence of the present and the coming generation of workers

(iii) do not or do cause capitalists to export or consume a large amount of capital.

Or, putting the question in another way, we may say that trades unionism as a whole is capable of being worked so as to confer an enormous benefit on England if their conduct is entrusted to their most upright and most far-seeing members : but that it will degenerate into a curse to England if narrow-minded men full of selfish notions as to their vested interests obtain the control. These questions history alone can decide. The economist and the moralist together are quite unable to break down trades unionism. A combination of capitalists could conquer trades unionism : but it is doubtful if it could do so without introducing social anarchy. The capitalist, the economist, and the moralist together may utilise trades unionism. But in order to do this they must give themselves very much more trouble in the matter than they have hitherto done : and they must be prepared to regard the notions not only of uprightness, but also of unselfishness as having a more important function in controlling the business transactions of the well-to-do classes than has hitherto been assigned to them. (If they will do this, they will do more perhaps than can be done in any other way towards promoting what appears to be the next process in the evolution of social life; *viz.* the integration of the various industrial classes.)

V.3 'Some Features of American Industry'

V.3.1 *Introduction*

On returning from America in 1875, Marshall 'read a paper to the Cambridge Moral Science Club on American Industry, Nov. 17, 1875'.[1] The essay reproduced below, entitled 'Some Features of American Industry', appears to be the text of that talk.[2] One of its themes is ethological, concerning the effect of economic conditions on human character, particularly 'the influence which the daily occupations of men exert on their character'. Since character is intimately related to ethical beliefs, this leads to Marshall's major theme: the mutual interdependence between economic conditions and ethical progress. He observes, 'I believe this mutual interdependence to be far closer than it is usually thought to be'. Eventually he distinguishes 'two principal factors of ethical growth'.[3] The first factor is 'the peaceful moulding of character into harmony with the conditions by which it is surrounded, so that a man... will without conscious moral effort be impelled in that course which is in union with the actions, the sympathies, and the interests of the society amid which he spends his life'.[4] The second factor is 'the education of a firm will by the overcoming of difficulties', a will which 'submits every particular action to the judgement of reason'.[5]

Contrasting the restless, mobile nature of American economic life with the more settled conditions of Europe, he finds that American conditions induce considerable ethical development of the second type. But Europe, where a worker

---

[1] *Memorials*, p. 14 (based on J. N. Keynes's diary).

[2] The quarto manuscript of forty-one pages bears no description beyond the title. but there was no other known occasion on which such a talk could have been given. Frequent slight alterations to the manuscript appear to be of later date and involve no substantive change. Here, the original version has been restored, wherever feasible, in the interest of stylistic uniformity.

[3] See p. 375, below.

[4] Ibid.

[5] Ibid.

has closer and more permanent ties to a particular locale and to a particular group of co-workers, exhibits far greater ethical development of the first type. This comes especially through the conduciveness of European economic conditions to the development of trades unionism and the cooperative movement. The ethical benefits of these forms of organisation are described in extravagant terms. Kant's categorical imperative[6] shows itself in Marshall's observation that 'Every ethical school admits that if not a source, yet at least a powerful aid, of the moral sentiment is the reflection by the individual that there must be something amiss with any course of action the general adoption of which by those around him would cause him injury greater than the direct benefit that he would derive by adopting it himself'.[7] Participation in trades unionism gives a man considerable exercise in such forms of reflection, so that unions or 'republics' are 'beginning to ask themselves whether any republic can be justified in adopting regulations, the general adoption of which by the surrounding republics would be injurious to all. In asking themselves this question they are giving themselves a great education'. From this, 'the American working man is almost debarred'.[8] Cooperation too, gives important moral education and also extends the personal influence of the best men in the movement.

Faint traces of the views expressed so forcefully by Marshall in this essay are to be found scattered among his other works, but a coherent statement can hardly be reconstructed from them. The essay thus has considerable value in clarifying, for the first time, Marshall's early views on the relations between economics and ethics. Its value is increased by the fact that these relations were obviously of pressing importance to Marshall himself. As late as 1907, in his paper on 'Social Possibilities of Economic Chivalry', he still looked forward to ethical progress, in the form of a growth of 'economic chivalry', as the chief hope 'to enlist wealth in the service of the

---

[6] See for example H. J. Paton, *The Categorical Imperative: a Study in Kant's Moral Philosophy* (Hutchinson, London, 1947).

[7] See p. 366, below.

[8] Ibid.

true glory of the world'.[9] His failure to make public a clearer statement of his theories of ethical change cannot have increased the plausibility of such pious aspirations.

After his return from America, probably in 1876 or 1877, Marshall included in his college lectures a discussion of economic conditions in America. The following passage from his rough lecture notes[10] is of some interest in the present connection.

It has been found that economic influences play a larger part in determining the higher life of men and women than was once considered. It has been found that activity and vigour of character cannot be obtained without a generous supply of food: that healthiness of character can scarcely exist in overcrowded cottages; that the time and the money which a generation of workers must sacrifice if the next generation is to be properly brought up can hardly be afforded by those who are in want of the necessaries of life. It is being found that the influences of association and habits of action to which a man is subject during most of his waking hours during at least six days in the week, are, generally speaking, so incomparably more powerful in the formation of his character than any other influences, that those who have attempted to guide man's destinies, but have neglected the influences which his daily work exerts on him, are like children who have tried to determine the course of a ship, not by controlling her rudder and properly trimming her sails; but by merely blowing on her sails with their breath.

At the same time, and in consequence in part of the same set of causes, Political Economy has to some extent changed its method. Instead of confining itself to a few simple premises and deducing conclusions from them, economists are getting to regard human nature as more complex, and the present condition of human life as more variable, than they once thought them. In Political Economy as in almost every other science the influence has been felt of the great notion that is forming the thought of the present generation:

[9] *Memorials*, pp. 323–46. The quotation is from p. 330.
[10] Now preserved in the Marshall Library. Some inessential passages are omitted.

namely that progress, or at least change, is continuous; that wherever exact experiment is impossible, recourse must [be had] to the Comparative Method. By the Comparative Method, I mean the method of comparing corresponding phenomena at different places and times, and under the operation of different disturbing causes. For the laws according to which changes are brought about cannot be discovered by merely observing the positions in which things are: it is necessary also to predict where they have been and how they have come into their present position. Thus economists have been led to investigate history; the history of the past, and the more accessible history of the present. Various observers have thrown light upon the fundamental laws of human nature with which Political Economy deals by studies of India, of Russia, of Belgium, of France and of Germany. They have thrown light directly on the phases through which England has passed, and indirectly on England's future. But it appears that many of the changes that are being worked out in England, America has with more rapid steps gone through before us, and that by a study of the present of America we may learn much directly about the future of England.

[I] wanted to see the history of the future in America. In particular [I] wanted to see what light American experience throws on the question to what extent we may hope for movement towards that state of things to which modern Utopians generally look forward.... I found the evils of American society to be in many respects far greater than I had expected: but I gradually got to see that the worst of these evils are extraneous to the American system, and that there are forces in America tending to remove these evils. I returned on the whole more sanguine with regard to the future of the world than I had set out.

V.3.2 *Text of 'Some Features of American Industry'*

After travelling in less than five months from Cambridge to San Francisco and back, I have been asked to give an account of my experiences. One of the chief of these consisted in the strange stories that were told by careless Englishmen about

America and by careless Americans about England. Englishmen told me that a working man in America could not buy more with two shillings than in England with one. They had fixed their attention on such things as house-rent (including local taxes), and woollen clothes, which cost twice as much there as here: they had overlooked the fact that bread, meat and dairy produce, on which the unskilled labourer in England spends more than half his wages, are cheaper there than here. On the other hand I had supposed that the half-starved 'pauper', who according to some American protectionist writers makes the manufactures that England exports, was a mere figure of political speech. I did not suppose that anybody believed that workers in English factories were paupers any more than anybody supposes that the modern Whig is conventicler, or the Tory a popish bandit. Yet several American manufacturers with whom I spoke about it replied 'But they *are* paupers: Americans who have travelled in England have told us so.' Such experiences made me a little careful. I made a rule not to accept any important statement as trustworthy until I had had it confirmed by several independent authorities. A foreigner may be easily misled, if in no other way yet in this, that his informant may take for granted, and omit to state, some element of the complete truth, an element which anyone but a foreigner would have supplied himself. By this rule I destroyed most of the piquant little notes that I should otherwise have brought home. My confidence in the results that remain is not very great; but on my return I was a little encouraged by reading Mr. Horace White's excellent account of his impressions of England.[1]

A minute statement of facts about a country is in general best written by a man who lives in the country. The rapid traveller should rather bring home with him, I think, accounts of the way in which facts grouped themselves together, the new combinations that he saw, the new points of view that he obtained for looking at problems of importance. I shall not therefore abstain from mentioning facts which I believed myself to have observed; but I shall endeavour to make the

---

[1] *Fortnightly Review*, September 1875 [H. White, 'An American's Impression of England', *Fortnightly Review*, Vol 24 (Sept 1875) pp. 291–305].

value of what I have to say as far as possible independent of the accuracy of my observations.

A foreigner is bound to some extent to estimate the value of his own impressions with regard to America by reference to the standard of de Tocqueville's conclusions.[2] For de Tocqueville's insight was stupendous. But many things have changed since his time. Population has moved westward, the habits and feelings which came down from the Puritan colonists of New England occupy a smaller area on the whole sphere of American life than they did in his time; railways have been developed: many things which were nearly stationary then are not stationary now. But again de Tocqueville professed to pay but little attention to those conditions of American life which were not directly connected either as cause or effect with political institutions. He spent little of his time, where I spent most of mine; in American workshops. France had passed through the spasms of revolutions and was yet throbbing with nerves and muscles over strung. Though one of the most effective of apologists of democracy, he considered it his special task to warn people against the imminent, if avertible, danger that democracy might entail over-centralisation, social despotism and even loss of energy.[3] If he overrated the extent of this danger in America in particular I think he may have done so in consequence of his not having regarded it as within his province to examine minutely the influence which the daily occupations of men exert on their character. This influence has I think in general been underrated. I think it is enormous, because people occupy the greater part of their time in their daily occupations. There are no thoughts, or actions, or feelings, which occupy a man, and which thus have the opportunity of forming the man, during so large a portion of his life as those thoughts and actions and feelings which make up his daily occupation. I do not wish to underrate the influence which is exercised on a man by his ideals of excellence – religious ideals, moral ideals, art ideals, ideals of action, ideals of power, ideals of affection. Though I believe the direct influence exerted on

[2] [A. de Tocqueville, *Democracy in America*. First published in French in 1835 and 1840. Many editions.]

[3] See in particular . . . [presumably Part II, Book IV of *Democracy in America*].

man by laws and dogmas to have been much overrated by historians, I believe that dogmas and laws can to some extent modify the dominant ideals of excellence: and that to whatever extent they may be able to do this their power is great. But the influence exerted by ideals of excellence does not come into competition with that exerted by a man's daily occupation: rather does this contribute much to the forming of those ideals. (With which, by way of precaution against being misinterpreted, let me dismiss the subject of ideals and proceed to my work.)

It appears to me that on the average an American has the habit of using his own individual judgement more consciously and deliberately, more freely and intrepidly, with regard to questions of Ethics than an Englishman uses his. This fact presented itself to me frequently grouped together with certain economic conditions, which appeared to me to be the chief causes of the fact. I shall explain those conditions as far as is necessary to make manifest the character of this grouping: and shall finally suggest for discussion certain remarks of general application.

The chief of the conditions of industry in America with which I have to do is its *mobility*: by which I mean the habit of passing readily from one occupation to another and from one district to another; either movement involving more or less a change of acquaintances.

Even de Tocqueville, who saw so much of staid New England, speaks with emphasis of American restlessness. Puritan traditions are still strong in rural New England: the tone of society there is quiet: but many a keen ambitious youth goes out from it and carries his impatience to the large towns or to the West. But with the exception of these and a few other rural districts there are probably not very many parts of the Northern States in which two-thirds of the inhabitants were born within a hundred miles of the place in which they are residing. There has been much movement since the census of 1870. Even then there were twelve States, chiefly Northern States, in each of which more than half of the resident population was born outside of that State. In each of six of these, more than half of the resident Americans was born in other States. In each of the important States of

Illinois, Missouri and Michigan nearly a half, and in each
of the States of Ohio, Indiana and Wisconsin about a third,
of the resident American population had been born in other
States: in Iowa more than a half. Each of a dozen States had
sent forth from a fourth to a third of all the citizens she had
reared to live in other States.

Next the mobility of the American shows itself in the
readiness with which he moves from one occupation to
another. Putting aside the farmers, I believe that it is not the
general rule for an American to spend the whole of his life
in one occupation. Many have at some time in their lives tried
their hands at farming for a few years. Many have taken to
shopkeeping once or twice. Those who adhere to shopkeeping
are perpetually trying new experiments. If a man starts in the
boot trade and does not make money so fast as he thinks
he ought to do, he tries, perhaps, grocery for a few years
and then he tries books, or watches, or dry goods. American
lads could learn their trades well in shorter apprenticeships
than the lads of other nations. But they abhor apprenticeships of all kinds on principle and in practice. The mere
fact of his being bound down to a particular occupation is
sufficient to create in the mind of an American youth a resolve
that he will do something else as soon as he has the power.
And the control over his actions comes to a lad at an early
age in America: by the time he is fifteen years old, parents
and masters, policemen and church ministers, have not much
power to keep him to an engagement. If, as is frequently the
case, he does as he is told till he is seventeen or nineteen,
the reason is in general that after carefully considering the
matter in many lights and with the aid of varied information,
he has come to the conclusion that that is the best course
open to him. Fathers do not in general contend that they have
a *right* to control the actions of their sons after they are
able to think for themselves. Even when the young American
has acquired highly specialised skill in one trade, and seems
to be settled down in it, there are many causes that may make
him leave it. The trade that he is engaged in may be dull:
he may just as well try some other trade that is not dull;
he is confident that he can pick it up tolerably well in a
few weeks; and if need be he can return to his old trade

when it has revived. Or he may try a new trade, not because his own is dull, but because he has heard that some new opening has been made for some other trade somewhere or other on the continent: after the fire of Chicago,[4] thousands of men dropped other occupations and took to carpentering. Or he may make a change simply because the monotony of one occupation has become burdensome to him. I have been told by good authorities that where improvements in machinery have increased the monotony in a particular trade Americans have shown a tendency to leave it to be done by immigrants, even before the increased simplicity of the work has had the effect of lowering wages in it.

But there is a still stronger motive which impels many Americans to a restless life: and this motive can be specially well understood by members of the commonwealth of letters: a commonwealth which in many particulars strikingly resembles the American republic. Many a bold student at the age of 20 or 25 is pretty confident that he has got hold of the right clue to *the* missing link in at least one important line of enquiry: that, if his life is not cut short, he will leave his mark in the world's history. As years go on, his confidence is shaken: but his hair is grey before he is quite reconciled to the notion that the utmost he can hope is that he may merit some slight gratitude at the hands of the next epoch-maker when he does come. The young American knows that in the ever-changing face of American trade and industry he will without difficulty find a field in which he may have a fair start: in which no monopoly of success can be secured by men starting with ready-made business connections. He dwells night and day on the stories that are told of men who with no other capital than a public school education and their own energy have accumulated wealth that has made them a place in history. Of course he desires wealth for its own sake; but his main motive is the ambition to prove himself superior in power to other men: this he can most readily do by beating them in the race for wealth, so he plays for a high stake. He continually remembers that his goal can be attained only by some brilliant achievement, that work

[4] [Presumably the Great Fire of Oct 8–10, 1871.]

various in kind and amid many varied conditions has proved the most efficient of all means for developing a man's natural powers. He bears in mind that a man who spends all his life in one workshop is found to be the most unlikely man of all even to make petty improvements in the machinery of that shop: that not only in America, but even in the old country, inventions of first rate importance have not very often been made by men educated only in one trade. His heroes, the money kings, have hated monotony; and he hates it. Yet I do not believe that the American is less capable of thorough work than the Englishman or the German. When he thinks it worth his while to do thorough work he does it: but he seldom does think it worth his while. During that period of life, at all events, in which his habits are being formed, he is loth to regard himself as a man not having sufficient brains or 'smartness' to rise before long to a higher condition of life. He will not expend his energies in acquiring a minute technical proficiency that he may soon cease to require. Hence it arises that there are many classes of work, even of work to which Americans are not specially averse, in which, though the controlling mind may be American and much of the manual labour may be done by Americans, the foremen of the workshops are as a rule not Americans but Teutons who have been educated in patience on this side of the Atlantic. Where a brisk intelligence is the chief faculty demanded of a foreman, the American rises naturally to the top; but he leaves to others those posts the duties of which cannot be discharged without a skill and knowledge that can be acquired only by persistent work from youth up in one line.

Of course the agriculturist in America as elsewhere has more, if not of monotony yet at least of uniformity, than most other workers. But even he is specially provoked to restlessness. The growth of population and the extension of railways are continually enabling fresh land to return high profits to the farmer. But shiftiness, the power of doing anything and everything tolerably well, fertility in expedients for overcoming new difficulties, and bold self reliance, are of more service beyond the limits of civilisation than elsewhere; and in these qualities the American excels the immigrant. But further, a farmer who has lived but just within the limits of civilisation is likely to have these qualities more highly developed, to have more experience in the class of work that the pioneer has to do, and to be more inured to hardship, than one whose habits have been formed in more settled districts. Hence results a chief cause of the movements from one State to another of which I have already spoken. The expansion outwards from the old centres is not chiefly effected by the passing of new comers over the heads of those who are already cultivating land. But Eastern men sell their farms to Irish and other immigrants and buy larger and more fertile farms somewhere between the Alleghenies and the Pacific; while those who have just seen a settlement grow up around them are those who are most prone to take up land where there is yet no settlement; they readily sell the comforts of the home they have just made to new arrivals.

The causes which have just been described as tending to increase the mobility of American industry seem likely to operate more or less in every new country which is being rapidly developed. Another such cause is to be found in the fact that emigrants are more likely to be of a restless disposition than their neighbours whom they leave behind them. But Canada and other British colonies attract a large share of those emigrants from this country who are retentive of old habits and traditions. And together with many steady-going Germans and Scandinavians, the United States receive a large portion of the most restless energy, the most impatient ambition, that Europe sends forth.

Again the influences due to the climate of each new country must be allowed for separately. It is probable that the influence of the climate of the United States in developing a restless temperament by its direct action on the constitution has been overrated: partly, perhaps, because it forces itself upon the notice of the careless observer. But the climate exercises an important influence, which is much overlooked, indirectly, by causing interruptions of industry. There is a great slackening of many kinds of business in most towns east of the Rocky Mountains during the 'heated term'. And with the exception of the Pacific Slope there is in America north of the latitude of Gibraltar a cold so intense during a great part of the winter as partially, or wholly, to suspend many kinds of outdoor labour.

These causes increase the unsteadiness that even without them would be characteristic of American industry. The total work done by an American in the course of a year is greater on the average than that done by an Englishman at home; but it is concentrated into a smaller number of days. Every time a man is thrown out of work he is as it were directly prompted to ask himself the question 'Is it worth my while to stay in this place or in this employment?'

These then appear to me to be the chief causes of the extreme mobility of American industry. Let us look at its effects. The American is seldom secure from finding himself impelled to deliberate whether he will not change fundamentally his mode of life: he is often deprived of those connecting links by which in more stationary societies a man's life is bound up with those of his neighbours and of his fellow craftsmen. There occur in the life of the ordinary Englishman several occasions on which he has to look far forwards, to weigh a multitude of various considerations, and ultimately to decide a practical question of vital moment to himself with but little direct aid from others. But even then he is not very likely to contemplate the abandonment of the trade to which his parents have brought him up. He has probably become accustomed to a certain tone of local or trade society and this supplies him with certain guiding lines, *axiomata media* of practice, which exert an influence on him that is none the less because he has become so accustomed to their presence as to be scarcely conscious of their action. The American may not be wholly devoid of such guiding lines: but on the average he is less under their influence. In the ordering of his industrial career, the motives that weigh with him present themselves to him in more distinct form and are more deliberately analysed by his reason; fewer data with regard to his future course are assumed consciously or unconsciously as beyond question by him than by the Englishman. If such be the habit of mind in which the American deals with questions that concern his industrial interests and material well-being, can a similar habit fail to be induced in relation to questions that concern his moral well-being? Is it not probable that the American is wont to decide questions of right and wrong by the deliberate exercise of his own powers of analysis and judgement, with less conscious or unconscious subservience to custom than the Englishman is? Is it not clear that the influences by which the moral character of the American is formed, and the influences which he in turn exerts on the ethical doctrines and the ethical tone of society, differ in important respects from the influences that operate in England?

The instability of the conditions of industrial life in America affects the development of moral character in some ways not only indirectly but also directly. Money is a more portable commodity than a high moral reputation. The doctrine that honesty is the best policy is at a disadvantage when it submits itself to the judgement of a man whose associates would continually be changing even were he stationary; who knows that if he makes money but loses his reputation, he can pack up his money and make it help him to earn a new reputation amid new surroundings; but that if he starts by building up a good reputation it is not unlikely that he may want to migrate into a new career to which but little of his reputation will follow him. It cannot, I think, be denied that a short-sighted man is thus exposed to great temptations in America.

The process by which a man earns the approbation and the confidence of his associates, though it does not always elevate his own character, yet in general it does. The happiness and the general well-being of the English working man and in particular of the English trade unionist depend largely upon the esteem and the trust of a particular set of his fellow men. Probably no institutions have ever surpassed some of the old gilds and modern English unions in their efficiency in rendering it difficult for a man to shake himself loose from his reputation. We are continually reminded that in the villages – the 'townships' as distinguished from the 'cities' – of New England, local government imposes on every citizen direct responsibility; that it gives him, in the ordering of public matters and the discharge of public functions, scope for the same judgement, resource, self-control and knowledge of his fellow-men as did the small republics of ancient Greece or mediaeval Europe. But the same may be said of that admirably organised republic a first class English trades union. There are in general no public affairs of as vital, or I should rather say of as palpable, importance to the American working man as is to the English

trades unionist the government of the little republic to which
he has attached himself. His connection with it on the one
hand diminishes his freedom and his responsibility with regard
to the conduct of his own life, and on the other hand gives
him a responsibility in the ordering of the affairs of others. It
educates him in the virtues and in the vices of patriotism. His
behaviour to those against whom the republic may have
declared war, just or unjust, is governed rather by 'patriotic'
sentiment than by a calm judgement formed under the sense
of his individual responsibility as a moral being. When the
interests of his republic appear to clash with his own, his
'patriotism' teaches him to bear and forbear: in adversity
he will suffer hunger, in prosperity he will decline his own
advancement. It is his part to secure that his leaders have the
high qualities of statesmanship: it is their part to control the
passions and to correct the short sightedness of the less
intelligent masses: heavy is the penalty that the republic must
pay if it puts its trust in men who are willing to manoeuvre the
republic into a war in order to cover their own incapacity.
Trades unions are gradually being educated by organised
experience and systematic discussion to analyse and to anticipate the more remote consequences of their actions. An
isolated working man may consider that trade ought to be
artificially 'regulated', with the aim of diminishing extreme
fluctuations. But questions concerning it have for him a
purely speculative interest. They have a practical meaning for
the member of a union who has to vote on the adoption of
some measure which has at least a *prima facie* claim to be
effective in the regulation of trade. Doubtless much, though by
no means all, of what trades unions say about their power to
regulate trade is distinct nonsense. But to minds untrained to
the severe processes of science, the surest mode of acquiring
knowledge on complex questions is to apply false principles
to practice and to spend a long time in contemplating the
result. Trades unions are doing this: they are purchasing
experience; but they get what they pay for. They are slowly
being taught that every loss which employers undergo reflects
injury on the employed; that it is a suicidal policy to adopt
any course that involves detriment to their employers unless
for a weighty and certain purpose. And what is far more

important they are, though very slowly, being led up to an exercise of a far-reaching wisdom which verges on morality. Every ethical school admits that if not a source, yet at least a powerful aid, of the moral sentiment is the reflection by the individual that there must be something amiss with any course of action the general adoption of which by those around him would cause him injury greater than the direct benefit that he would derive from adopting it himself. When the parallel reflection with regard to the relation of his own republic to other republics is forced upon a man, when he discusses it with others and prepares for joint action with them upon it, he is receiving a training of the highest order. For instance by extreme laws with regard to apprentices, a trades union secure from foreign rivalry, can in some cases obtain a considerable immediate gain for its own members at the expense of a vastly greater loss to the whole body of consumers. The deliberations of the union as to whether it is right for them to adopt such a course are assisted by a contemplation of the loss that they would suffer if similar regulations diminished the number of efficient labourers in all other trades; and thus diminished the supply of the things which they themselves may want to purchase. They know that there are not many trades in which such regulations can be sustained. But unions generally are showing signs of beginning to ask themselves whether any republic can be justified in adopting regulations, the general adoption of which by the surrounding republics would be injurious to all. In asking themselves this question they are giving themselves a great education. From this particular education the American working man is almost debarred. His mobility and his aversion to being controlled by others have hindered him from entering into the elaborate organisation of English trades unionism. Americans will organise a union as they will any other company to meet a particular emergency. But such rude associations are not to be compared to English unions. The Miners' Union at Virginia City is powerful; but its resources consist of little more than a quiet terror: it is an accident; it has no ambition to earn for itself a history. Some unions with complex machinery have sprung up in America but they were planted by foreigners; and they do not in general flourish. The American gains scope for his energy, through his freedom from those obstructive rules from which no union can wholly escape. The mental and moral injury that he would suffer from the presence of unionism is sufficiently obvious: but in polite society, at least, there is but slight recognition of the mental and moral gain that he might derive from it.

I proceed to another of the direct influences which the instability of industrial conditions exerts on the development of moral character in America. Cooperation does not flourish in America. The difficulties which beset cooperative production are so various that I may not speak of them here. But the conditions required for the success of cooperative distribution are few. By cooperative distribution I do not mean the sale by a joint stock company of heterogeneous wares on the strict cash principle. Such an undertaking, whatever praise it may merit, is not cooperative unless the purchasers as a body contribute not only the capital which is risked in it, but also the supreme control of the business. Those who deal with the Halifax Cooperative store do, in large part, consist of men who retain the supreme control of the store in their hands: at least to this extent, that they not only decide directly on questions of general principle, but, what is of even more vital importance, they control matters of detail by means of their personal knowledge of the character of those into whose hands they commit the administration of detail. A chief factor of the success of a man who controls business on a large scale is the power of reading the character of his subordinates. Generally speaking in the early and more difficult days of cooperative stores, properly so called, a most important portion of the capital which its proprietors have thrown into the common stock has consisted of the knowledge, which the contact of daily life has given them, of those in whom they put their trust. This element must dwindle as the store increases: but it need not ever vanish. I can then perceive several reasons why co-operative stores should not flourish in America: probably I do not know all. (1) Knots of working men who have got to know and trust one another are, comparatively speaking, rare: (2) a man will not trouble himself about a local movement if he does not expect to remain where he is: (3) an American will not willingly admit that he cannot defend himself against the impositions of a shopkeeper, or any body else : (4) although an American working man is in general better provided against a day of adversity than an English working man who trusts to his own resources he is more likely to be in need of credit than the English working man, who when sick or otherwise out of work is supported by the funds of a strong and temperate union : the necessity of the purchaser is the opportunity of the private dealer who can relax at his own discretion his rules about prompt payment. The mobility of the American store – or shop – keeper has already been spoken of : this together with the just confidence which the purchaser of limited means has in his, or her, own knowledge of the quality and value of commodities have produced a strange result. Large classes of store-keepers have no fixed price, but get from each customer just what they can – a practice which I had imagined was confined to barbarous or at least to un-business-like nations. On the whole the retailer's profit is said to be much larger in America than in England ; and the pecuniary loss which consumers suffer from the want of cooperative stores is probably large. But the pecuniary loss is exceeded by the moral loss. The simple practical problems with which cooperation had to do in its earlier stages have been developed in England until they involve many of the subtlest economic principles which have yet been worked out, and subtler principles still. The daring genius of Lassalle has familiarised the German people with the question whether trade risk may not be abolished by means of a state-controlled federation of industry.[5] The leading English cooperators are working for such a federation of groups of producers and consumers as may diminish risk. The plans which they discuss lead them to analyse economic forces, and to appreciate and gauge the supply among their fellow men of the intelligence, and of the upright and brotherly instincts, which are the material on which these forces are to work. Their thought runs before their practice, and their practice directs their thought. The education that they thus obtain does not end with themselves. Cooperation extends the influence of the best men. The leaders of local movements, themselves able men, cause

[5] [On Lassalle's scheme see pp. 37–8, above.]

to circulate the notions propounded by the ablest men in the movement. I did not know the full power of the Cooperative spirit until at an annual national congress of delegates I heard terse, pointed, business-like arguments mingled with utterances of high aspiration, and saw in the rough shrewd face of the speaker the bright eye sparkle with enthusiasm as he spoke of 'the grand Cooperative Faith'. Special causes have enabled communistic societies to spring up in America. Associations of citizens to meet particular emergencies can be improvised with more strength and rapidity in America than in any other country. But the present phase of American industry is not well adapted for the slow organic development of cooperation.

It is even more difficult in a rapid travel to discern the emotional character of a nation than their mental habits. But I would venture one or two remarks which have a direct bearing on my main point. It struck me that, with the exception of a few immigrants, I met no one, man or woman, in America whose appearance indicated an utterly dull or insipid life. Every one seemed to possess enough knowledge, energy and conscious power to be lifted above the fog of a glum sensuality : to have interests in life sufficiently active and varied to develop emotions that were not simply animal. I did not see a single American face full of that gross deathly coarseness which is to be seen in the lowest and most stagnant classes not only of England, but even of Germany. The absence of such faces gives America a strong claim to be the first country in the world. I know no other single fact which gives so strong a claim.[6]

It is certain that sentiment, other than political sentiment, is less strong in America than in Europe. It is certain also that the affections there are more under the control of cool reason : but it is not certain that they are weaker. The American working man spends more of his resources on the comforts of his household, less in selfish enjoyments, from which they are

---

[6] I did not see the 'mean whites' of the Southern States. But America is free from slavery; and she may claim to be judged without reference to the products of slavery. The immigrants are, I hold, the main cause of whatever political corruption exists in the Republic. The evil work is no doubt often, though by no means always, engineered by Americans, but it could not in general have been executed had not cheap hands for it been supplied by voters born in Europe – born under aristocratic rule to a meaner birthright than the public-school education and the self-respect of the American citizen.

excluded, than the immigrant in America or than men in his position in Western Europe. The American woman, whose cool self-command and self-indulgent habits during her girlhood have provoked the comment of the censor, enters with marriage upon a new life. She does not indeed impulsively seek hard work or self-sacrifice, but to whatever work or sacrifice her reason points the way she moves with intrepid step. If it be necessary, but only if it be necessary, she will harden her hands with unceasing drudgery in order that her daughters may be nurtured in delicacy. I think that the affections of the Americans are strong: my impressions on the subject are formed from slight data; but I express them partly because the character of the American lends itself on this side easily to a harsh interpretation.[7]

I am compelled also to say a word of the religious beliefs of the Americans.[8] The march of population westwards, the immigration of Germans and Irish, together with the general progress of critical thought and feeling, have loosened the Puritan traditions by which de Tocqueville was so much impressed. It struck me that now, as in his time, Americans are in general averse from troubling themselves with inquiries or doubts as to the historical basis of Christianity: but it struck me also that they did not in general care to settle by Scriptural authority practical questions on which their own reason could pronounce a decision. They seemed to me to base their judgements on data supplied by the instincts within their own breasts, and by the experience of their lives: and to take for granted that the decision at which they had thus arrived could be found to be consistent with Scripture providing it were rightly interpreted. I am treading on firmer ground when I say that not only spiritualism but each of the three most solid of the innovating religious movements of modern America, that of the Mormons, that of the Shakers and

[7] Even de Tocqueville's judgement on the matter seems to me a little hard in tone. (Part II, Bk III, Ch. X). [de Tocqueville's judgement was quoted *in extenso* 'as it partly confirms and partly supplements mine.']

[8] Again I would willingly shield myself, if it were possible, behind the judgement of de Tocqueville. But I suspect that there are few chapters into which, if he were to go over the ground again, he would introduce more important modifications than those in which he speaks of religion. [Compare *Democracy in America*, Part I Ch. XVII; Part II, Book I Ch. V–VII, Book II Ch. IX, XV.]

that of the Oneida Perfectionists (and I believe the scope of the remark might be extended) accept the Bible, but interpret it for themselves, and incorporate it in the body of Inspiration which they claim to be still active. I will select for quotation a passage from the preface to the fourth edition of *Christ's First and Second Appearing.*[9] This, a thick octavo volume, was given to me by one of the leading Elders of the Shakers, as an exposition of their doctrine. The preface asserts the claim of the book to be inspired and continues:

3. The idea which so extensively prevails that all inspired revelation ceased with the canon of Scripture, is inconsistent with both reason and *Scripture.* Is it not unreasonable to suppose, that the spiritual work of God should alone remain

---

[9] 1st Edition 1808, 4th Edition 1854 [The correct reference is: *The Testimony of Christ's Second Appearing*... (Fourth edition rewritten by Benjamin S. Youngs and Calvin Green and published by the United Society Called Shakers. Van Benthuysen, printer, Albany, 1856. First edition by Benjamin S. Youngs, Lebanon Ohio, 1808). See p. iii of the preface, dated 1854. Marshall described his visit to the Shakers in a letter to his mother of 10 July 1875, written from Niagara. Marshall Library, Marshall 3:71.] On Wednesday [July 6] I travelled to New Lebanon the chief settlement of the Shakers. I slept at the settlement & came on the next day to Oneida, near which is the most important communistic settlement outside of the body of the Shakers. I spent five or six hours at the Community & came on to Rochester on Friday.... Although I had read largely about them before, the contact with communists, having thought out theories of life widely different from those in common vogue was highly instructive. I send you a paper of the Shakers. I have many of their publications. They go against the Art of 'the world'. The Spiritual Kingdom is gradually evolving music for itself; the supply of Shaker tunes is very large, a new one in almost every number of their journals, & many others besides: & gradually doubtless they will evolve a Spiritual Architecture. This was said in answer to my question why they did not spend some of the energies on adorning their buildings: these approach nearly to cubes. Yet I must confess there is a sort of picturesqueness about them when taken together with the scenery.

The brother who was told off to wait upon me, & with whom I spoke more than with anyone except Elder Evans (the leader of the whole movement) was a young Swede: an angelic character. A student at a Swedish University, he had been dissatisfied with the customary views of life, & becoming interested in some account of the Shakers, he visited America in order to see them, & became convinced that here alone in the world was the spirit of early Christianity worked out in life.... He is cheerful though always quiet, utterly devoid of self assertion, which is more than I can say for Elder Evans. Agriculture & horticulture are the occupations that the Shakers most affect; & if you saw only the cotton frock which he wears, the brown cotton trousers clay-stained towards the feet & the rough uncouth shoes below you would think he was an ordinary agricultural laborer. But in his face you would perceive the refinement of the true gentleman. There are few men with whom I would so readily change lots as with him: but I would rathest stay where I am.

stationary, whilst all the natural arts and sciences among men, are continually improving and increasing, by newly manifested principles of natural light, and are constantly progressing more and more, by the knowledge and further application of the original principles from whence all these are derived?

4. It may be seen by every attentive observer, that these natural revealments and improvements are now more frequent and rapidly developing and increasing, in the present age and time, than in any preceding age of the world. Therefore we may consistently conclude, that the spiritual work of God must be increasing and improving in a corresponding progression, or the things of by far the greatest importance will be left behind; for, in comparison with the spiritual work of redemption and salvation, all earthly knowledge, and all natural improvements, sink into insignificance.

The testimony here supplied to the influence exercised by improvements in the arts and sciences in giving elasticity to religious and ethical feeling is specially striking because it proceeds from a quarter from which it might have been least expected. I hold then that however firmly rooted in the past American ethics may be, they develop themselves freely under the influence of present conditions; that their growth is not subject to any considerable disturbing influence due to the authority of a rigid code.

I wish next to say something of the industrial equality which to a greater or less extent manifests itself in various parts of the country. De Tocqueville pays this tribute to economic forces that he regards political equality, rather as an inevitable consequence, than as the cause of 'equality of conditions'. In consequence partly of the fact that the most shiftless of the immigrants remain as a rule in the neighbourhood of the Atlantic, equality of conditions manifests itself with increasing force as the traveller moves westwards, until, on the Pacific slope, it becomes well nigh absolute. It is not only, or chiefly, that in the west there are not many who are very rich and scarcely any who are very poor. It is rather that the circumstances of the industry of the country educate in every man, whatever his occupation be, the power of taking care of himself. A state of society in which it is known that a man in a certain occupation is not likely to have as much general intelligence, as much power of comprehending the present, as much insight into the future, as much delicacy of feeling, as men in other occupations – such a state of society cannot be free from ranks and grades, it cannot be democratic. But where all receive nearly the same school education, where the incomparably more important education which is derived from the business of life, however various in form it be, yet is for every one nearly equally thorough, nearly equally effective in developing the faculties of men, there cannot but be true democracy. There will of course be great inequalities of wealth, at least there will be some very wealthy men. But there will be no clearly marked gradations of classes. There will be nothing like what Mill calls 'A so strongly marked line of demarcation between the different grades of labourers as to be almost equivalent to a hereditary distinction of caste.'[10] This is then what I mean by the equality of conditions when I speak of it as the true kernel of democracy.[11]

Here then I terminate my account of some of the conditions of American life which so grouped themselves together before me as to enforce in me the belief that insufficient account had been taken of the industrial factors of ethical progress. I proceed to disentangle, as far as may be, the problems thus suggested to me, from the particular opinions with regard to matters of fact to which I have given expression: and to state the problems in such a general form that they may be discussed without any dependence on the accuracy of opinions based on the slight experiences that came to me in the course of a few months' travel.

It is conceded by all schools of theologians and of ethical philosophers that during historical times unreasoning obedience to the letter of particular laws or moral precepts has gradually yielded in importance to a devotion to the spirit

[10] [J. S. Mill, *Principles of Political Economy*, Book II, Ch. XIV, § 2, p. 387 (not an exact quotation).]

[11] A chief reason why whatever religious belief there is in America is more genuine [than] in England, I find in the fact that there are not many Americans who feel themselves under an obligation to believe in the Bible in order to set a good example to their neighbours.

which underlies them. In the earlier stages of society the provinces of law, morals and social etiquette are not distinguished: in stationary societies, rules which have been adopted for sanitary, economical, military or other purposes, have been imbedded among the rules of duty and of law that have been handed down from one generation to another, and have continued in force after the purposes for which they were required have ceased to exist. Ethical progress has, on one of its sides, consisted in analysing and relegating to their proper sphere rules of etiquette and customs which have had their origin in temporary exigencies of society. It is universally conceded that the ethical progress in this direction which has been made in any country at any time has been closely connected with the condition of industry then and there. I believe this mutual interdependence to be far more close than it is usually thought to be; and hold that ethical science cannot be on a proper basis until much fuller account is taken of it. I hold that the ethical situation in any society, in so far as it depends upon the extent to which particular rules are subordinated in importance to the principles from which they proceed, is controlled not by the philosophic insight of the few, but by the range of the understanding of the masses – by their power of analysing practical questions. I hold that this depends, partly of course upon their school education, but mainly on the nature of the work in which their days are spent. In a society in which there is any considerable inequality of conditions, the majority of thinking men, when called upon to give an opinion upon any problem of practical ethics, instinctively consider the problem as it affects the conduct of the masses: they consider not how any proposed modification of a particular ethical doctrine would work in their own hands, but how it would work in the hands of the masses. They oppose an effective resistance to any movement of ethical theory for which the masses are not ready. They prevent the movement from working to any considerable extent in any class of society; from having any fair trial. Whereas in other sciences progress depends mainly upon the capacity of a few specialists, the progress of one of the chief factors of ethical science – the knowledge of the capabilities of human nature – is limited by the average capacity of the lowest classes. If this be so, ethical philosophers are bound to pay special attention to the phenomena of a society in which there is no considerable body of people who have not sufficient analytical power to be safely trusted with elastic principles as a substitute for the rigid rules of morality: a state of society in which a thinking man would naturally consider how a particular ethical doctrine would work in his own hands, and not chiefly how it would work in the hands of people inferior to him in discernment.

Again let us look at the character which is likely to emerge from such habits of movement on the part of large numbers of a people as will prevent a man's life from being, as a rule, bound up and interwoven with the lives of any particular set of men. Let us call before us the times of the old village communities of which we have recently heard so much. Let us contrast modern life in England with life then. May we not expect a similar, if less extensive, contrast between the general character, and in particular the ethical phenomena, of a country where industry is as ever-shifting as that of America and those which accompany the more settled industries of Europe? I would say, generally speaking, that there are two principal factors of ethical growth. I would describe one as the peaceful moulding of character into harmony with the conditions by which it is surrounded; so that a man acting with free genial temper according to his own idiosyncracy will without conscious moral effort be impelled in that course which is in union with the actions, the sympathies, and the interests of the society amid which he spends his life. In such a society the abstract or outcome of the experience of a few generations become 'conserved' in maxims or proverbs, and in customs which proverb-like mean more than they seem to say. Such a society may degenerate into insipidity, and thence into meanness: but in its higher forms it is the home of sympathetic fancy, of graceful enthusiasm, of beautiful ideals. What I take Hegel to mean by 'objective freedom', will flourish in it. The other factor I would describe as the education of a firm will through the overcoming of difficulties. This will does not glide carelessly into conformity with the conditions by which it is surrounded, but submits every particular action to the judgement of reason: this sits, as it were, enthroned as a judge, disentangling the problem, simplifying it for the comprehension of the jury; the jury consisting of his instincts – those which he has acquired during life, and those which were born with him, transmitted into his life as I believe from the experience of his ancestors. The reason receives the verdict from the instincts and orders action accordingly. This is a habit which makes a man solitary in the midst of a crowd, and this is a habit which a man whose occupation forces him to be solitary in the midst of a crowd naturally obtains. Under such conditions, a generation may differ widely from that which went before it; but it will show marvellous instances of what biologists call atavism, an outcrop of that human nature which contains, if nothing else, at all events the outcome of the experiences of humanity. Such a society may degenerate into licentiousness and thence into depravity. But in its higher forms it will develop a mighty system of law: and it will obey law. It will deal boldly and consciously with moral difficulties; it will be prompt to meet every moral emergency. The free arbitrament of man's will, will be unshackled by outward restraints. Such a society will be the empire of energy, of strong but subdued enthusiasm, of grand ideals. What I take Hegel to mean by 'subjective freedom', will flourish in it. Without wishing too much importance to be attached to it, I would throw out the suggestion that when one race conquered and ruled a large territory the daily business of its life would resemble on many sides the daily business of America now; the arts of war and dominion being substituted for those of industry. I am not then surprised that Hegel should contrast India and ancient Greece with ancient Persia and Rome, much in the same way as I contrast Western Europe with America now. However this may be, I hold that ethical progress consists in the main of these two factors: that these two factors have not in general advanced together but that one of them has frequently made huge progress at a place and a time at which the other was stationary or even retrograding. I hold that one of the chief, if not the chief, of the causes which affect the absolute and relative progress of these two factors is to be found in the habits and relations engendered in the daily business of life, or in other words in the character and conditions of the industry of the country: while of course the ethical conditions react on the industrial conditions of the country. I hold that in spite of some superficial indications to the contrary, there is much ethical advance in America at the present : but it is an advance almost exclusively as regards one factor. A loosening of social ties may have prevented any considerable advance on the side of moral habits : but there has been, I believe, an advance which, if less attractive to the foreign observer, is of certainly not less vital importance for the well-being of the world, a development of conscious responsibility and ethical will.

I have then to invite a discussion of the relations in which the industrial phenomena of a country stand to its ethical, firstly with reference to the closeness of the bonds which his daily work weaves between each man and some particular group of other men ; and secondly with reference to the amount of intelligence, discernment and power of analysis of practical problems which the business of life educates in the mass of the people.

Such a discussion may bring forth some casuistical difficulties which may divert the *a priori* philosopher, suggestions of deeper interest for the Utilitarian, and considerations of fundamental importance and vital concern to those who are working their way, as I am, towards that ethical creed which is according to the Doctrine of Evolution.

V.4 Lecture Notes on Taxation, 1880

V.4.1 *Introduction*

Marshall published little in the way of a systematic discussion of tax policy, his chief contributions being expressed only in evidence to the Royal Commission on Local Taxation, in 1897, and in an essay on 'National Taxation After the War', written near the end of his life, in 1917.[1] Part I, Ch. VI of the abandoned international-trade volume deals in detail with certain aspects of the question, but its treatment is far from comprehensive.[2] Some interest attaches, therefore, to the notes for a series of nine lectures on 'The Economic Influence

---

[1] This essay appeared in W. H. Dawson, editor, *After War Problems* (George Allen and Unwin, London, 1917). The official evidence is to be found in *Official Papers*, pp. 329–64.

[2] See Section III.3, above, and also Item IV.4.2.

of Government', given by Marshall at Bristol in the Spring term of 1880.

The Calendar of University College, Bristol, for the session 1879–80, announced the syllabus as

> the general principles of taxation. The law which determines whether a tax is really paid by the persons on whom it is levied in the first instance. How the various taxes that are levied in England affect the different classes of the community. Income tax. Local rates. Discriminating duties. Influence of customs duties on foreign trade. The proper meaning of the term 'Free Trade'. Why the policy of Protection would be especially injurious to England. Protection on the Continent and in new countries. Government as an administrator of railways and other commercial enterprises. The grounds and limits of the *laissez-faire*, or non-interference principle.[3]

The text was Book V of J. S. Mill's, *Principles of Political Economy*. The lecture notes, which are dated for each of the nine meetings of the class, and appear to have been written just before the day, indicate that the later parts of the syllabus were dealt with hurriedly, and that its plan was not followed with any exactitude. The forty octavo pages which survive appear to be incomplete and are frequently crude and sketchy. But they give a sufficiently clear indication of Marshall's views to justify the reproduction of the pruned version which follows.[4]

The greatest interest attaches to the first three lectures, which outline Marshall's general approach to property and redistribution. But the fifth and sixth lectures are also of interest in disclosing his views on detailed questions of tax policy. These appear broadly consistent with the ones made public in later years.

---

[3] For details see J. K. Whitaker, 'Alfred Marshall: the Years 1877 to 1885', *History of Political Economy*, Vol 4 (Springer 1972) pp. 1–61. The syllabus is given on pp. 44–5.

[4] Marshall seems to have written few systematic lecture notes after the early 1870s, but his lectures prior to 1890 do not seem to have attained the extreme of informality, even inconsequentiality, reported of later years. These 1881 notes were used on at least one other occasion (in Oxford during the session 1883–4) and a few additions may have been made then.

V.4.2 *Text of Lecture Notes on Taxation*[1]

(1) The question what are the proper functions of government is at once very broad and very compact. It is difficult to inquire what are its functions with reference to property without inquiring what are its functions generally: we must however confine ourselves as far as possible to our special subject.

But it will be necessary to enter upon several broad inquiries, applied especially to the condition of England now: but the method of inquiry will be applicable to any conditions.

We have to inquire I, what share of the property of an individual the community acting through its government has a right to take for common purposes. Also II, given that a certain revenue has to be levied from any person, *how* that revenue should be raised. Also III, what part government should take in controlling or aiding or itself undertaking different forms of business.

I resolves itself at starting into 3 preliminary and closely connected inquiries. (a) What is meant by the phrase 'the community acting through its government'? (b) What is meant by justice? (c) What is meant by property?

[There followed a brief sketch, or parable, of the development of government. This development led, around the time of the French Revolution, to] the popularisation of the notions : –

 (i) the state exists for the people
(ii) all people are equally important

Now here everything was arranged for a deliberate investigation on this basis.... What was wanted was a man of clear head, resolute determination and unlimited power of analysis. The time was come, and the man. Bentham was born.

(2) [There followed some discussion of Bentham's ideas, leading to the conclusion that] while distinctions of quality are of exceptional importance to the moralist, the legislator can take but slight account of them: partly because, though he can make [individuals] more prosperous by levying taxes well

---

[1] The numbered paragraphs correspond to the successive lectures. Portions in square brackets paraphrase Marshall's words.

rather than badly, he can't make them more virtuous ... and outside of ethics, and perhaps of all questions directly bearing on the development of man, it is a great gain to have clear quantitative notions, though we can't have exact quantitative statements. That, Bentham – as Jevons has pointed out – helped us to by his analysis.

Now when we come to taxation the first notion that strikes us is that it is a question of the relation in which the state's right of property stands to the individual's. Thus really the fundamental notion is that of property.

[There followed a discussion of the concept of property which included critical consideration of Adam Smith's dictum that every man has a natural right to the produce of his own hands.] So that we are brought down to this : – the test by which we must decide whether a man should have rights in property, and what he should have; depends on this : is it expedient for the public good?

Well firstly straight off history vociferates that some sort of clearly defined rights in property are always present when there has been prosperity. But to go further *what* rights? It is of no use to say that we must have justice for the difficulty is to find what is just. So there seems to be no way out save that of analysing by Bentham's Method.

[There followed some discussion of Bentham's views on property, especially as to his aims of Equality and Security.]

(3) [As to security] we may say any interference with property is *prima facie* unjust which will disappoint just expectations i.e. expectations which must be satisfied at the penalty of causing a feeling of insecurity of greater evil effects than the good that can arise.

We must always bear in mind that security rests on general rules, and that a breaking of general rules, the effects of which in the first order would be good, will often – indeed generally – be bad in the second and third order.

Thus the position with regard to community of goods is not that it is in itself wrong; but that it is inexpedient and therefore wrong for people as frail and faulty as we are. Therefore the problem is : – given that men are what they are, that they will not work energetically and accumulate [property] unless they have some privileges with regard to it: how great should those privileges be? Bentham's answer is absolute subject only to [a few] limitations. But he was timid: but he lived in times when revolution was the great dread of all. And now we may reopen the question with more fortitude.

And at all events security [of property] must [be] endangered when [the] country goes to war. Therefore if security is [the] chief aim, going to war should be surrounded by special difficulties: e.g. a two-thirds vote.

If we accept for the present the position that security is the chief aim, we have two methods proposed for attaining that fairness or justice or equality which consists in securing to every one just those rights of property which he would have if the state had no taxes to levy.

One is to tax him in proportion to his stake, on the principle that any call raised by a Joint Stock Company should be the same percentage on all shares. The other is one which might be levied in a place where blackmail had to be paid: those who were furthest from the frontier, and those who lived in the strongest holds, and had the most armed retainers, paying least. This latter [is] unworkable, the former not to be defended by strict argument. We must go more to the roots.

What amount of insecurity is occasioned

(i) by the notion that taxes on large properties might become very large
(ii) by the notion that they might be voted by people who escaped them – and so recklessly and perhaps corruptly?

Since for general purposes it is expedient the people should vote: therefore special taxes on large properties are specially likely to cause secondary evils of alarm that other heavy taxes will be levied. Still, this evil is only of finite dimension. So that if we had not to look at distant results we should have no hesitation in saying 'So levy taxes as to tend to equalise wealth so far as possible without creating great alarm.' And if we took this basis we might certainly go *very* much further in the direction of relieving the poorer classes than, as we shall presently see, has actually been done in England.

But it may be argued that taking taxes off the poor would lead to an increase of population, but no increase of happiness, and a diminution of (i) capital saved by the rich (ii) the means of pioneering on the part of the rich. There is force in this. To begin with, nh = max is no doubt right (where n = number and h = average happiness) if n is fixed, but if not perhaps nh^2 = maximum or nh^3 = maximum, or better still[2]

$$n(h + \alpha \, dh/dt) = \text{maximum}$$

or

$$n(h + \alpha \, dh/dt + \beta \, d^2h/dt^2 + \cdots) = \text{maximum}$$

and though there may be some doubt as to whether a comparatively wealthy republic in which almost all men were nearly equal might not be able to pioneer for itself and accumulate capital for itself; and though the claims of the aristocratic party to be necessary to society may be exaggerated. Yet, equal division would not make people very rich : it would but give £35 per head per annum . . . . Therefore there is something like a balance of arguments in favour of and against most plans for shifting taxation from rich on to poor, unless it can be shown that they will increase $n \, dh/dt$ or $n \, d^2h/dt^2$ etc. and in particular will lead to investment of human capital. Moral : don't take all taxes off working man but

(i) spend state money on raising him, and
(ii) be careful how far state money is spent [on] luxuries of the rich, the most extravagant of which is war.

(4) [There followed a consideration of Adam Smith's four maxims.]

(5) [After this, differential duties and the principle of free trade were considered. As to the former :] Differential duties fall not only on those who pay them, but on those who evade paying them . . . [every tax] involves some destruction of consumers' rent, but those most which involve most disturbance of ordinary action. This [is] a special case of Smith's rule about cost to the consumer. [As to the latter] Is it contrary to [the] principles of free trade to charge for using roads? Yes, tolls are contrary, but if special expense [is] involved for each separate transit then so far [a] toll system is just and economical.

[Next, the mode of collection of taxes was considered.] Tendency of the age [is] against farming [of taxes]. Govern-

---

[2] [See Item IV.4.5, above, for an explanation of these formulae.]

ment used to rule the land : now the Press rules the land through the Government.

(6) [The discussion next turned to various forms of direct taxation.] Taxes on expenditure [are] preferable to taxes on income, because things saved go to promote public well being generally and it is in the interest of [the] public to put a premium on saving.

Moreover, things saved are taxed again: at least if any income is derived from them or even, in [the] case of houses, if not. But a piano is not taxed when in the hands of the owner, though income derived from letting out pianos is taxed. (This brings us to [a] question for Advanced Students: If a tax on expenditure is to be levied how would you define expenditure? e.g. is purchase of a house expenditure, or of a piano? Answer: Theoretically, for purposes of taxation, expenditure equals depreciation plus interest on the piano, and should be charged year by year till it is worn out.)

A tax on property has this objection: that it is a tax which can only be paid by those who save. A man who spends all his income as fast as he gets it, escapes this tax nearly altogether. On the other hand there is this to be said for it: that if a man owns his own 'sources of enjoyment' instead of hiring them and owning some other property (as e.g. shares in coal mines) he [otherwise] escapes taxes on their usufruct.

A tax on income may depart from the principle of uniform percentage on two grounds. First, that the poor should be taxed less than the rich, either generally or in this particular case because they are so heavily taxed already by indirect taxes. This leads either to exemptions of the kind now made in England or to a graduated tax of say[3]

$$c \sqrt[3]{\frac{n-a}{100}} \times \frac{n}{100}$$

when a is 'necessary income'. The chief objection to this is that it could be evaded if the rich man would split up his income between relations and himself. It might be said that incomes of husband, wife, and children who were minors, should be treated as one.

[3] [Here, c is an appropriate constant and n is income. Marshall gave a numerical illustration for $a = £100$ and $c = 1$.]

The second principle [or ground] is that permanent incomes should be taxed more heavily than temporary on the ground that a man ought to and generally does save out of a [temporary] income for his children. This is on the supposition that property *qua* property is not taxed. If on other grounds we decided to have a property tax this might drop out.

[The] best plan on the whole [is to] keep [income] tax as it is for a peace tax to complement others which press specially on the poor. For a war tax impose extra income tax reaching down as low as it will go, increase malt tax, or do something of the kind.

[There followed a brief discussion of legacy duty which pointed out that probate duty, while small, was actually regressive.]

(7) [The next topics were the taxation of land, capital invested in land, and houses. The latter, as a source for tax revenue was regarded as] first rate, because (i) universal, (ii) approximately proportional to income or rather, what is more important, to expenditures, (iii) can be raised or lowered without disturbing trade, (iv) can be raised [that is, collected] without much expense and without hampering trade.... On the whole the house tax ought perhaps to be used to a larger extent than it is for imperial purposes, the local authorities being allowed to tax incomes if they like; or if it should be felt that the house tax should go no higher.

As to their incidence, if [house taxes] are a part of a regular system economic conclusions are right enough. But if the tax were used – say to make those below the income-tax level pay part of the expense of a war, or generally – as a tax that could be quickly raised or lowered, it would become very important to inquire how far the tenant could put it on the landlord at once. Probably ... it would fall much as it is meant to.

(8) [The next topic was customs duties, leading to the final question.]

(9) Next should government look forward in selecting its taxes, so as to prefer one tax to another on account of distant results? Yes: other things being equal a tax on a commodity which obeys the law of diminishing return is good; for the tax

raises price, therefore diminishes consumption, therefore diminishes cost of production of that produced under the [least] favourable circumstances, [and] therefore raises price by less than [the] tax. Also [it] can be proved [to inflict] small injury to consumers' rent. On the other hand, tax on [a] commodity which obeys the law of increasing return raises price by more than [the] amount of a tax : or at all events prevents a fall.

[As a] parallel case : by taxing importation of raw commodities you keep up their real price for ever, or rather check population. But it may be that by taxing importation of manufactures you do not. That, then, is a special reason against taxes on England's imports, which are chiefly raw. England imports scarcely any manufactures [while] the raw commodities are either not produced at home – protectionists don't want tax on those – or produced at home. Tax on [the latter] causes cost of production under [the] most unfavourable circumstances to increase.

V.5 'The Pressure of Population on the Means of Subsistence'

V.5.1 *Introduction*

In the autumn of 1885, Marshall gave a public lecture on 'The Pressure of Population on the Means of Subsistence' at the newly-established Toynbee Hall in the East End of London. The manuscript reproduced below appears to be the text prepared for that lecture, or, at least, a draft for it.[1] The *Malthusian*, the journal of the Malthusian League, carried the following brief report of the lecture.[2]

Malthus at Toynbee Hall

Professor Marshall lectured at the above admirable Institution, on the 10th ult., on 'The Pressure of Population on the Means of Subsistence'.

[1] The first page of the twenty-two page octavo manuscript bears a note by Mrs Marshall : 'I think this was a lecture given at Toynbee Hall Sep 10 1885.'

[2] The report, initialled J.K.P., appeared in the *Malthusian* for November, 1885, pp. 653–4. (This is wrongly cited as October 1885 in *Memorials*, p. 501, reflecting an error in the Marshall Scrapbook, compiled by Mrs Marshall and now preserved in the Marshall Library, which seems to have been the basis for J. M. Keynes's bibliographic list.) The lecture must have been given on 10 Oct, rather than 10 Sept, as the Marshalls were in the North of England in September (see Vol 1, pp. 55–7, above).

After saying that he believed no one had been able to shake the principles of Malthus, and that – except in the matter of his unfortunate statement that while food increased in an arithmetical ratio, animal life tended to increase in a geometrical ratio, which he himself withdrew – those who had claimed to refute him had simply failed to understand him, the lecturer proceeded to state and explain the law of diminishing returns to agriculture. This he did in a very lucid manner, showing how, through the operation of this law, when once agriculture has attained to a certain stage, any additional application of capital and labour to the soil does not give a return in proportion. Supposing that one 'dose' (as he called it) of capital and labour will yield a given return, two 'doses' will not yield double that return. This was particularly true of the production of animal food. Some of the richest pastures in this country were almost as Nature had made them, and no human effort could greatly increase their fertility. He then explained that improvements in production generally tended to counteract the prejudicial effects of the law of diminishing returns; but he pointed out that unfortunately most of the things consumed by the working classes were articles of raw produce, just the things which are least affected by improvements in production.

Altogether, the lecture seemed to me the most clearly stated exposition of the Malthusian position I had heard for a long time, and a most powerful argument in favour of a low birth-rate; but, strange to say, when the lecturer himself came to give his conclusions from the evidence submitted, he had not a word to say in favour of limitation of births. I understood him to say that it would be a calamity if we English, by limiting our numbers, allowed foreigners to have a larger share than ourselves in peopling the world; and there was no need to fear the effects of our prospective increase at home. We had a clergyman in the chair, and Toynbee Hall is next door to the church, which may possibly have had something to do with the lame conclusion arrived at. At any rate, it seemed a grievous pity that anyone should speak on the subject in question, and shrink from the logical conclusion.

The correspondence between the manuscript and the report is close, though not exact, but the differences could easily be accounted for by Marshall's propensity to use his notes only as a basis for extemporisation.[3] And the manuscript certainly appears to have been aimed at a London audience.

Marshall finds the most serious evil for England resulting from population pressure to be 'close packing' in large cities, especially London. This deprives the rising generation of needful pure air and recreational space, and he urges parents to consider abandoning for their childrens' sake the dubious advantages of city life. The evils of London must have been impressed on Marshall during his boyhood there, and their alleviation always remained for him a question of great moment.[4]

The report in the *Malthusian* correctly observes Marshall's reluctance to espouse a policy of birth limitation. This reflected more than the inhibition of the moment. Explanation seems to lie in his belief that the emigration of Anglo-Saxon stock to new countries represented one of the chief hopes for the future progress of the world.

> There can be no doubt that this extension of the English race has been a benefit to the world. A check to the growth of population would do great harm if it affected only the more intelligent races, and particularly the more intelligent classes of these races.... if Englishmen multiply less rapidly than the Chinese, this spiritless race will overrun portions of the earth that otherwise would have been peopled by English vigour.[5]

V.5.2 Text of 'The Pressure of Population on the Means of Subsistence'

It is often said that one of the most hopeful signs of the age is the prevalence of discontent. In earlier stages of civilisation people suffer, and are yet contented: they don't set themselves to

---

[3] He is reputed to have given his Inaugural Lecture of 1885 without notes.
[4] For relevant passages in Marshall's writings see: *Economics of Industry*, p. 26; *Principles I*, pp. 166, 199–200, 321, 718, 803; *Principles II*, pp. 280, 301–3; *Memorials*, pp. 142–51, 409, 445, 460; etc.
[5] *Economics of Industry*, p. 31.

make things better. We are now discontented with so many things which our ancestors patiently endured, and are improving them away. And one reason why the discontent has grown and flourished and not been choked off is that it has on the whole been founded on knowledge; often on imperfect knowledge, but nearly always on better knowledge than that of our forefathers. We therefore who most want to keep alive the noble spirit of discontent, must be most anxious to stop off any of it which is based on error.

I have noticed that there is much misunderstanding as to the way in which the growth of population acts on the means of subsistence. There are indeed some who think that the economic doctrine on this subject has recently been overthrown. But I believe its assailants have not accomplished this task: they have achieved the very different and very much easier one of misunderstanding it. It is indeed one singularly easy to misunderstand because it is really rather a complex doctrine: and it has been often stated for popular purposes carelessly and loosely.

I propose tonight to try to make clear what it really does mean so that we may not expect the growth of knowledge [and] of total wealth to do more for man than they can do. No doubt they might do much more than they do. But if our discontent with their shortcomings is to have good fruit, it must be a discontent based on knowledge; it must not ignore the material difficulties that lie in the way of progress and that have to be overcome.

[The] law of diminishing returns [has] never [been] denied, but only corollaries from it. It [states] that one additional man's labour plus a given amount of capital will, after cultivation on any plot has gone a good way, not raise a proportionately increased amount of agricultural produce from that plot; unless there has been some external change such as an improvement in the arts of production or in the intelligence of the cultivators.

The law says nothing as to value. A railway may have opened up the district and the value of the produce may have risen in consequence. Or there may have grown up beside the agriculturists a body of townspeople who make a good market for their produce. That is not in question in the proposition:

only in its corollaries. The law as it stands is incontrovertible. If not there would be a short way for each farmer to save nine-tenths of his rent by applying all his capital and labour to one-tenth of his farm. The law acts with different force as to different things; in descending order are

> wood
> cattle
> corn
> fruit, vegetables and fancy flowers
> (mines have a law to themselves).

But it does not follow from this law that an increase of population would increase the pressure on the means of subsistence.[1]

For man wants not only raw but also manufactured commodities: and in producing these the organisation that is rendered possible by numbers cheapens production, so that it would be possible for the growth of population (the capital per head being constant) to increase the means of supporting life in some directions as much as it diminishes it in others.

I don't deny that that may possibly be the result in some places where the cost of raw material is a small part of the whole cost of living. But in such a country as England where sufficient raw produce can be got only by importing from a distance; where the cost of the raw produce consumed by the working classes is a very large part of their whole cost of living: there I think it is certainly not so. No doubt this is a matter of opinion: but I never knew any one who examined the question, clearly understanding what it is, and with a full knowledge of the facts, who denied it. It is true that many people have said they deny it: but on examination it will be found that what they deny is something else.

What they assert in opposition to it is this:

'Taking for granted that capital increases at the rate at which it is increasing in England now (i.e. at least twice as fast as population: population about 1·4% per annum and capital about 3% per annum) and taking for granted

---

[1] [An added note indicates that importation should be mentioned here.]

also the improvements in production and transport, then the produce per head is not diminishing.'

Certainly they are right in this supposition. But they do not contradict the law of diminishing returns in saying this.

The doctrine of the tendency of an increasing population to press on the means of subsistence asserts that: whereas if population did not increase fast the average wealth of all classes and particularly of the working classes would be very much increased by these two causes

(i) growth of capital per head,
(ii) growth of knowledge,

the result of a very rapid growth of population is to cause these benefits to be less than they otherwise would be. (But for all that, in the interest of the world, I do not want the increase of English population to be slower than it is.) The paradox thus disappears when it is clearly stated. They assert that whereas power of production increases enormously the incomes of the working classes increase but little. But (i) the greatly increased power relates only to manufactured goods, and the working classes spend the greater part of their wages on food and the cheaper kinds of clothing, (ii) the increased production is due to a great increase of capital and comparatively small increase of labour. There would have been very little increase in the production per head, probably even a decrease, if capital per head had not increased.

So long as property exists it is natural that while capital per head is increasing capital should get an increasing share of the whole. As a fact, so great is the fall of interest that the share of capital increases far less in proportion to the increase of capital than does the share of labour in proportion to the increase of labour.

I will just guard against a fallacy. It may be said that though there is an increased difficulty in raising raw produce, yet there is an increased facility in producing manufactures, and with these we buy raw produce. Of course we do: and if other nations were unable to manufacture and had their choice between making their goods by the old method and buying them from us at a monopoly price we could get all our needs satisfied with very little labour. But as it is the manufactures due to one man's labour (without extra capital) buy abroad only the raw produce due to one man's labour abroad (without extra capital): and after paying the expenses of transport, this comes to what a man of equal general ability would raise in England.[2]

But I want to go now to a more subtle, and yet for Londoners more important source of confusion. As yet I have spoken as though all man's physical wants were met by raw and manufactured commodities. But there is a third set of physical needs – pure air and pure water and space for recreation. Pure water is impossible for a large population without a great deal of capital, but with it can generally be got pretty cheaply. Pure air and free space: they are the difficulties.

In thinking over the ways in which manufacture is facilitated by increase of numbers, thus so far counteracting the pressure of population on subsistence, we tacitly assume that people will be more or less packed close together. But when we come to [grapple] with facts as they are, some of our chief charges against them are really founded on the evils that are caused by close packing.

No doubt the Londoner gets on the average higher wages than he would in the country: no doubt he gets most things cheap, including even animal food (except milk), the only great exception being rent: no doubt he gets the great advantages of streets where there is always light, and easy access to many forms of amusement and excitement.

But he can't get fresh air except on an occasional holiday at very great expense, he can't get decent houseroom except at very great expense, he gets scarcely any recreation properly so called: his digestion is weak and he can't get along on the simple food that would suffice for him in the country: and worst of all his children get no wholesome play: they will be weaker than he and their children, if they stay on in London, weaker than they.

This is I think the most important side of the pressure of population growth. It is a chief cause of progress being slower

[2] [This appears to hold that the marginal physical product of the labour raising raw produce is the same both at home and abroad, and similarly in manufacturing. It seems doubtful if this was intended by Marshall as more than a rough approximation, perhaps to be supported by his doctrine of the tendency towards an international equalisation of task wages (on which see *Economics of Industry*, Book III, Ch. III).]

than at first sight we should expect. Much of what is best, of what would make England prosper, and especially raise the working classes of England goes to London and other large towns and dies out simply because of the law of diminishing returns with reference to fresh air, and pure and free recreation.[3]

An aggravation of this evil is that the enjoyments of London life come to the parents and the chief ill results of it to the children. If there is any case for government interference it is when the interests of the coming generation are in danger of being sacrificed by the mistakes of this. If there is any expenditure of national money on behalf of the working classes of large towns that is justifiable it is in the direction of diminishing the evils which life there is bringing on the rising generation. It is in preparing recreation grounds for all, but above all playgrounds for the young. This should be the use to which [the] government should put any of the money it can spare from the sale of the prisons. It should make with that or equivalent ground playgrounds where noisy, healthy play, even with a little energy, is allowed: where cricket may be played with hard balls, and where the joyous young creatures need not keep one eye always on the policeman.

To build cheap houses would give no more than a temporary respite even to the evils against which it is aimed. Scarcely any of the benefit would go to the working classes, nearly all to the employers of labour and owners of ground rents. After a while all would be as before, except that there would be a larger population, suffering from want of healthy recreation and fresh air, which are on the whole the deadliest evils that are caused by the pressure of population on the means of subsistence.

Not only in this but in every way should we try to diminish these evils. Let anyone who is living in London ask himself: Am I right to stay here? Have I the power to go away: even if I lose some money earnings, even if I miss some of the

---

[3] [In his brief note 'Is London Healthy?' in the *Pall Mall Gazette* for 13 Apr 1887, Marshall argues that the morbidity and mortality figures for London tend to be understated because there is a continual influx of the young and healthy in search of fortune, while the old and infirm return to the country to die. See also *Principles I*, p. 200.]

attractions of London life, would not my children gain more than I lose? Is there any joy in London as pure and as healthy for them as that of the free sky and the open air? Are not they worth more than all the luxuries that can be bought by the money even of the very rich: and cannot I get them for myself and my children very cheaply? If there is in my own life a murk here cannot I give the cloud a silver lining by taking my children where they can grow up in health and vigour to lead a happier life than I?

The conclusion then is:

A The growth of knowledge and of capital are increasing the real income per capita in England.

B Owing to the greater rapidity of growth of capital than of labour the share got by a dose of capital and a dose of labour is divided more and more in favour of labour.

C In consequence real wages are rising: but not so fast as might otherwise have been expected because (i) the earnings of the working classes are spent chiefly on raw commodities or on space, and (ii) town life is counteracting the other tendencies which are raising the quality of labour and (iii) town life requires more expensive food than country life.

D A check to the growth of population would raise average wages provided (i) it did not considerably check the growth of capital and knowledge (ii) the average quality of the children was high, but:

E Since the whole English people, except the residuum, is a long way above the average of the world, it is scarcely possible to suppose any curtailment of English population which would not lower the average quality of the inhabitants of the world, their average wealth and average well being.

F By checking the growth of population it is possible while raising average well being to lower total well being. If there might be in England 25 millions with an average income of £60 and 25 millions with an average income of £30, that is 50 millions with an average income of £45, and instead you have as a total 25 millions with an income of £50, or even £60, you have lowered total utility unless the existence of the second 25 million was a positive evil.[4]

---

[4] [Compare Item IV.4.5, above.]

Appendix
The Marshall Papers and Their Editing

The Marshall papers have passed into the keeping of the Marshall Library, Cambridge, through A. C. Pigou, who was Marshall's literary executor, through Mrs Marshall, and through C. W. Guillebaud, Marshall's nephew and editor. Besides a large number of letters to or from Marshall (amalgamated with the Library's extensive collection of letters) and the books (some annotated) which originally belonged to Marshall, there are[1]

9 boxes of miscellaneous notes, manuscripts, examination questions, etc.
1 box of manuscripts, including the international-trade ones
1 large box of miscellaneous items
1 scrapbook.

The contents of the 9 boxes are too miscellaneous and jumbled to make any catalogue useful, the items being only roughly grouped by subject. Many pages are missing, and many sheets are simply the relics of old working notes, whose meaning is now elusive. To illustrate the confusion in which Marshall left the material, the case of Part I, Ch. VII of the abandoned international-trade manuscript may be cited. A portion of this was included with the rest of the surviving manuscript of the volume. But several pages had been removed, cut in half, renumbered, and incorporated with notes on a different subject. Fortunately, there was no difficulty in recognising

[1] A comprehensive list is given by Rita McWilliams, 'The Papers of Alfred Marshall', *History of Economic Thought Newsletter*, No. 3 (Nov 1969) pp. 9–19.

the lost pages, but the manuscript, as it survives, still remains incomplete.[2] In other cases too, manuscripts had to be pieced together from scattered fragments. In some cases not all fragments could be found: in others, the surviving portion appeared to end prematurely. The truth seems to be that Marshall retained these early manuscripts partly out of sentiment, but partly because he felt that he might still be able to use them. In such an eventuality he seems to have had little compunction about cannibalisation.

Despite these difficulties and limitations, sufficient material seems to have survived, in a sufficiently intact state, to make the collection a valuable further source of information about Marshall's views and writings. There still remains, however, the difficult question of exactly how such material, often rough and unpolished, should be edited for the reader. To change Marshall's words without warning would be indefensible, yet to attempt to reproduce the materials exactly as in the manuscripts, or to indicate every change no matter how slight, would be both typographically difficult and extremely burdensome for the reader. After considerable experiment, the following working rules seemed to offer the most satisfactory compromise, and they have been followed as consistently as possible.

(i) All substitutions or additions of words are indicated by the usual editorial square brackets, with footnote explanation given only in exceptional cases.[3]

(ii) Spellings are standardised (e.g. labor to labour), and abbreviations written out in full, without explicit notice. Among the abbreviations are Marshall's own private shorthand expressions, such as $=^m$ for equilibrium, XoP for expenses of production, D and S for demand and supply, and so on.

(iii) Marshall's sparse punctuation is augmented sparingly whenever it is an obstacle to easy reading, but is otherwise left unchanged. (Since any notation for editorial punctuation would be cumbersome, it was decided, reluctantly, to add this without explicit notification.)

[2] See Section III.4, above.
[3] A few cases in which editorial substitutions or additions are neither self explanatory, nor accounted for in footnotes, are covered in the list which follows this Appendix.

An exception to these rules is made in the case of letters, which were written for other eyes, and are reproduced exactly as written, unless indication to the contrary is given.

In applying such rules there are many marginal cases and it would be impossible to resolve them to the satisfaction of everyone. There are other difficulties too. One is the existence of frequent later emendations on the manuscripts, usually quite trivial rewordings. Other things equal, the earlier reading has been preferred for stylistic uniformity and authenticity of period unless the revised reading was much clearer. In cases where a revision involved changes of substance, both the original and the variant readings are given. A final difficulty is that of the elucidation of sometimes obscure arguments. I have not hesitated to add an editorial footnote when this promised to be of real help to the reader, but have tried so far as possible to concentrate editorial discussion in the Introductions.

Explanatory List of Editorial Additions and Substitutions

At certain points in both Volumes, square brackets indicate the presence of editorial changes. A few of these changes are explained in the relevant introductions or footnotes, but many are left unaccounted for. The purpose of the present appendix is to allow the reader to infer the nature of the changes made. To that end, there follows a list of all substitutions. Changes not included in this list, and not explained in the text or otherwise obvious, may be assumed to be additions inserted either for clarity or because of a lacuna in the manuscript. Changes in capitalisation required by such insertions have been made silently.

Volume 1

p. 193 The ending of 'Malthusians' replaces an illegible one.

p. 194 'Between' replaces a colon. The subsequent period also replaces a colon.

p. 195 'Sacrifice' replaces 'preparation', correcting an obvious slip of the pen.

p. 222 Brackets enclose condensations and paraphrasings.

p. 234 'Figures 4, 5 and 6' replaces 'the adjacent figures (i), (ii) and (iii)'.

p. 236 'Figure 4' replaces '(i)', etc. Similarly, 'in Figure 6 the land' replaces '(iii)' and '7' replaces '(iv)'.

p. 238 'Figure 4' and 'Figure 7' replace '(i)' and '(iv)', respectively.

p. 241 'in Figure 2' replaces 'below'.

p. 243 'Figures 4 and 5' replaces 'the two adjoined figures', and 'Figure 3' replaces 'the last figure'. 'Fgure 4' replaces 'the upper case', and 'the case' replaces 'that'.

p. 244 '6 and 7' replaces '5 and 6' etc., Figure 2 having been unnumbered. (Similar changes occur on pp. 246–7.)

p. 252 'line *DC*' replaces 'black line'; 'line *dc*' replaces 'red line'.

p. 259 'I and I'' replaces 'black and red positions of I' and 'black and red I curves'.

p. 260 'international-trade' replaces a schematic sketch of a pair of offer curves.

p. 265 'the next paragraph' replaces 'p. 12'; 3, 4 and 5 replace 5, 3 and 4, respectively (and similarly on p. 267).

p. 279 'I'' replaces 'the dotted line'.

p. 280 'the origin' replaces *O*.

(*Note:* The editorial insertions 'and the value of each unit' on p. 246 and 'lies' on p. 279 appear to be required for sense and a slip of the pen may be suspected.)

Volume 2

p. 34 'his stated' replaces 'this', as required by the elision.

p. 56 'nascent' fills a blank left for a word the copyist apparently could not decipher.

p. 61 'history' fills another blank left by the copyist.

p. 79 'to' replaces a comma.

p. 83 'is' replaces 'are'.

p. 88 'is' replaces a comma.

p. 103 'producer' replaces 'purchaser', a transcription error?

p. 104 'in' replaces 'for'.

p. 107 'monopoly' replaces a blank left by the copyist.

p. 109 The insertion of 'manufacturers' in the quotation is actually Marshall's.

p. 121 'Mill' replaces 'he'.

p. 137 'ex' replaces 'im'.

p. 139 '*p*' replaces '*P*'.

p. 148 'cloth' replaces 'linen'.

p. 150 '*OG*' replaces '*Oy*'.

p. 151 'is' replaces 'are'.

p. 178 '*S*' replaces '*V*', correcting an obvious slip.

p. 191 'neither . . . nor' replaces 'either . . . or'.

p. 200 'XIX' replaces 'XIV'.

p. 203 '*DD*' replaces '*OG*'.

p. 220 '*Cc*' replaces '*C*'.

p. 230   '*ss*' replaces '*SS*'.

p. 260   'In these cases' replaces 'their'.

p. 270   'although the diminution' replaces 'and this'.

p. 271   'Figure 2' replaces 'figure nearly at other end of book'.

p. 277   'want' replaces 'wanted'.

p. 283   'the locus of P'''' replaces 'this curve'.

p. 296   'retained' replaces 'obtained'.

p. 302   'the equation' replaces ' $= {}^n$'.

p. 306   'the terms' replaces 'these'.

p. 315   In the second equation set off, the derivation shown replaces an incorrect one resting on the slip previously noted. Scrope's, which would presumably refer to G. Poulett Scrope, is not a confident reading.

p. 318   'represents' replaces 'regards'.

p. 323   'of' replaces 'in'.

p. 327   'the extra labourer' replaces 'he'; 'supply of labour equation' replaces an asterisk corresponding to one marked against the equation.

p. 328   'instead of' replaces 'for'; 'the last' replaces 'this', accompanied by an asterisk.

p. 329   'above' replaces 'on p. 2 modified by p. 3'.

p. 335   'A' replaces 'α'.

p. 379   'individuals' replaces 'them'.

p. 381   'a few' is a paraphrase.

p. 382   'every tax' replaces 'everything'.

p. 384   'temporary' replaces 'permanent', correcting an obvious slip. (Compare J. S. Mill, *Principles of Political Economy*, p. 814.) 'House taxes' replaces 'they'.

p. 385   'least' replaces 'most', as sense requires; 'the latter' replaces 'those'.

p. 388   'states' replaces 'is'.

p. 391   'grapple' replaces an illegible word—possibly 'fumble'.

(*Note:* The editorial additions 'enjoyed' on p. 29, 'be' on p. 65, 'engaged' on p. 70, 'the arguments against' on p. 81, 'have' on p. 111, 'amount he' on p. 275, 'a man performs' on p. 290, 'than' on p. 373, 'be' on p. 381, and 'on' on p. 382, all fill inexplicable lacunae in the manuscripts.)

Index of Names for Volume 2

Index of Subjects for Volume 2